UNIX®

Database

Management

Systems

Selected titles from the YOURDON PRESS COMPUTING SERIES
Ed Yourdon, *Advisor*

UNIX®
Database
Management
Systems

Ulka Rodgers

YOURDON PRESS
Prentice Hall Building
Englewood Cliffs, New Jersey 07632

Library of Congress Cataloging-in-Publication Data

RODGERS, ULKA (date)
    UNIX database management systems / Ulka Rodgers.
        p.   cm.
    Bibliography: p.
    Includes index.
    ISBN 0-13-945593-0
    1. Data base management.   2. UNIX (Computer operating system)
    1. Title.   II. Title: UNIX data base management systems.
    QA76.9.D3R65   1990
    005.75′6—dc 19   89-30740
                                                           CIP

Cover design: *Lundgren Graphics, Ltd.*
Cover photo credit: *Slide Graphics of New England, Inc.*
Manufacturing buyer: *Mary Ann Gloriande*

© 1990 by Prentice-Hall, Inc.
A Division of Simon & Schuster
Englewood Cliffs, New Jersey 07632

This book can be made available to businesses
and organizations at a special discount when
ordered in large quantities. For more information
contact:

Prentice-Hall, Inc.
Special Sales and Markets
College Division
Englewood Cliffs, N.J. 07632

Printed in the United States of America

10 9 8 7 6 5 4 3

ISBN   0-13-945593-0

For information about our audio products, write us at:
Newbridge Book Clubs, 3000 Cindel Drive, Delran, NJ   08370

PRENTICE-HALL INTERNATIONAL (UK) LIMITED, *London*
PRENTICE-HALL OF AUSTRALIA PTY. LIMITED, *Sydney*
PRENTICE-HALL CANADA INC., *Toronto*
PRENTICE-HALL HISPANOAMERICANA, S.A., *Mexico*
PRENTICE-HALL OF INDIA PRIVATE LIMITED, *New Delhi*
PRENTICE-HALL OF JAPAN, INC., *Tokyo*
SIMON & SCHUSTER ASIA PTE. LTD., *Singapore*
EDITORA PRENTICE-HALL DO BRASIL, LTDA., *Rio de Janeiro*

Contents

Part 3: Four UNIX DBMS   **147**

Part 5: Future Directions   **303**

Preface

UNIX has made its debut into the Data Processing world in recent years; its impact is noticeable with the growing number of applications and software packages now available in the marketplace. Custom applications and packaged systems can now be developed using a wide variety of tools, in particular Database Management Systems (DBMS).

The users of any UNIX DBMS need to understand the influence of the operating system on their applications. We also need to know which limitations the implementation of the selected DBMS imposes. Application designers and developers need to understand the tradeoffs involved in selecting one DBMS over another. There is little literature to date that clarifies these issues. This book is an attempt to fulfill this need.

I assume the reader is already interested or involved in the UNIX world, either as a user or developer of applications. This book does not contain introductory material on the UNIX operating system. It assumes you already have some knowledge of data processing and UNIX concepts. It should be useful reading material for

- Users of an application based on a UNIX DBMS who have a technical interest.
- Designers and developers of an application who are either already using or planning to use a UNIX DBMS.
- Data processing managers who wish to gain some background in the subject.
- Readers who wish to increase their knowledge in this area and who may have some knowledge of other environments such as MS-DOS.

This book is a practical guide to the UNIX DBMS world. It is based largely on my experience in selecting DBMSs, implementing and supporting applications based on DBMSs under UNIX. It does not, therefore, reiterate the well-known theories of databases, nor is it a substitute for the reference manuals available with each product.

It covers the necessary foundation for a discussion of tradeoffs in implementing an application. It also discusses the issues faced by the DBMS user community in the UNIX environment. Where a comparison is possible, the differences between MS-DOS, OS/2, and UNIX environments are distinguished, so that the reader can see why DBMSs in each environment are different.

The book is divided into five major parts. Each part consists of several chapters which expand on a common theme.

Part 1: The Theoretical Foundation

This part is a historical perspective on the theories of database management systems. The emphasis is on the relational approach, since the majority of UNIX DBMSs are based on the relational model. We lay the groundwork in this part with the buzzwords common in this industry so you can follow later, more technical discussions.

Part 2: UNIX and DBMS Applications

Chapters in this part examine how database management systems interact with the underlying operating system. UNIX has an influence on what facilities a DBMS can provide and how they are implemented. It also affects the way a developer builds an application. These chapters should be of great interest to application designers, developers, and end-users. Development managers should like some of the project planning tips included in these chapters.

Part 3: Four UNIX DBMSs

All readers should find interesting material in this part. We review the facilities provided by four of the major DBMS products: INFORMIX, INGRES, ORACLE, and UNIFY. We review these products on the basis of the ground rules established in Part 1 and the application needs described in Part 2.

Part 4: Selecting a UNIX DBMS

This part examines the nebulous area of requirements analysis. It contains a lot of practical hints on how to go about choosing a product that best meets your application's needs in its three chapters. A large number of features does not mean that a DBMS will fulfill the needs of every application. This part focuses on how to determine which of the DBMS facilities are important to specific applications.

Part 5: Future Directions

A look at the future developments in the DBMS front. These developments will have a significant impact on the way future applications will operate.

My intention is not to cover all of the theoretical aspects of DBMS. There are already several publications covering this subject well. I simply survey the necessary theoretical concepts to discuss the four DBMS packages described in this book.

Some aspects of the UNIX environment are important in order to understand the options for implementing an application based on a UNIX DBMS. These aspects are discussed in this book. However, I do not intend to describe all aspects of the operating system and its utilities in detail. I only discuss those aspects that interact with DBMSs and applications using them.

There are, of course, many packages available under UNIX at present. The concepts described in Parts 1, 2, and 4 apply equally to these products. I chose four of the most popular products: INFORMIX, INGRES, ORACLE, and ACCELL (UNIFY) for detailed review in the book for several reasons.

Invariably, all four products support the industry standard SQL language. But, some are better suited for small to medium database sizes while others are better for large databases.

Informix has been a widely used product on small UNIX systems: its PC-like user interface techniques show great promise in improving the traditional UNIX methods. INGRES has good productivity improvement tools: it certainly has the widest selection of tools for developers; some of which could almost be used by nontechnical users. ORACLE and ACCELL both use the unusual *raw disk* mechanism of UNIX: necessary for producing good performance with multivolume databases. The difference is that ACCELL is native to UNIX, while ORACLE originated elsewhere and was ported to UNIX.

You may question how useful this review of specific versions of products might be. Don't worry, the book discusses the fundamental facilities of these products, not their specifics. Changing these underlying philosophies is more difficult for DBMS vendors than converting your application from one product to another. So vendors are unlikely to make major changes to their base facilities over the next several years. However, a few specific features we discuss might change: So we list the version of the product to which they apply. This book provides sufficient grounding in the basics to enable you to make your own comparisons.

It is almost impossible to discuss every aspect of every system in a single book. This book attempts to cover most of the important features. I encourage you to refer to the manuals for each product for details not covered in this book.

My heartfelt thanks to all of the people who have helped me write this book. My particular thanks to my husband, Paul, who spent countless evenings discussing the ideas and criticizing the contents of this book. Also, thanks to Martin Heneck, Gerry Boyd, and Dennis Pierson whose practical suggestions have helped to make this book useful. Thanks also to R.S. Tare for encouraging me to start this project. My special thanks to the vendors of the products described in this book, for permission to discuss their respective products, for supplying me with the information needed, and clarifying many questions. Finally, thanks to my editor, Ed Moura, and everyone at Prentice Hall who made the production of this book possible.

Ulka Rodgers
Annandale, New Jersey

Trademarks

---

dBASE is a trademark of Ashton-Tate Corporation.

FOCUS is a trademark of Information Builders Inc.

FourGen is a trademark of Fourgen Software Inc.

IBM, VM/CMS, DB2, IMS, SQL, SNA, LU6.2, APPC, OS/2 are registered trademarks of International Business Machines Corporation.

IDMS is a trademark of Cullinet Software, Inc.

INFOEXEC is a trademark of UNISYS Corporation.

INFORMIX is a registered trademark of Informix Software Inc.
File-it!, REPORT/DB2, Informix Datasheet Add-In, C-ISAM, INFORMIX-SQL, RDSQL, INFORMIX-TURBO, INFORMIX-ESQL/C, INFORMIX-ESQL/COBOL, INFORMIX-4GL are trademarks of Informix Software, Inc.

INGRES is a registered trademark of Relational Technology.
Applications-By-Form, INGRES/APPLICATIONS, INGRES/EQUEL, INGRES/ESQL, INGRES/FORMS, INGRES/GRAPHICS, INGRES/MENU, INGRES/NET, INGRES/PCLINK, INGRES/QUERY, INGRES/STAR, INGRES/REPORTS, Query-By-Forms, Report-By-Forms, Visual-Forms-Editor (VIFRED), Visual-Graphics-Editor (VIGRAPH) and Visual Programming are trademarks of Relational Technology.

Lotus 1-2-3 is a trademark of Lotus Development Corporation.

MS-DOS, Microsoft OS/2 is a trademark of Microsoft Corporation.

ORACLE is a registered trademark of Oracle Corporation.
Easy*SQL, SQL*Forms, SQL*Plus, SQL*QMX, SQL*Report, SQL*Report Writer, PRO*C, SQL*Menu, SQL*Net, SQL*Connect, SQL*Star, SQL*Calc, SQL*Loader are trademarks of Oracle Corporation.

PROGRESS is a trademark of Progress Software Inc.

SYBASE is a trademark of Sybase, Inc.

TUXEDO is a trademark of AT&T.

UNIBATCH is a trademark of Unisystems Software Ltd.

UNIFY is a registered trademark of Unify Corporation.
ACCELL, Direct HLI, ENTER, PAINT, RPT are trademarks of Unify Corporation.

UNIX is a trademark of AT&T Bell Laboratories.

UQUEUE is a trademark of Unitech Software Inc.

Part 1

The Theoretical Foundation

Despite the title, this part is actually only an overview of the theories underlying DBMS technology. It aims to introduce you to the terminology prevalent in this industry, rather than to provide a rigorous discourse on the technicalities. For this reason, we merely skim the surface of the theories in an informal manner.

One of the primary objectives of the following chapters is to provide sufficient background so you can follow the later, more technical parts of the book. We do, however, cover some very important ground on what DBMS products do for your development methods and why you would want to use them. Chapter 1 discusses some of the problems developers face when using non-DBMS data storage methods.

Chapter 2 covers the basic terminology used in the relational database management systems and some of the useful data design techniques. The remaining two chapters concentrate on describing the types of facilities found in commercial products. The purpose is to establish some ground rules on how UNIX affects these facilities, which facilities are offered by the products discussed in this book, and probable directions for future developments.

1

What Is a DBMS?

Everyone *knows* what a database management system is, right? But what is the difference between a ***database*** and a ***database management system*** (DBMS)? We have all heard these buzzwords for quite some time; some of us even use them every day. We don't always know what differentiates them from each other. That is what this chapter is all about.

We hear that we must use these DBMS products, that they are the way of the future. But it is rather difficult to judge what they really do for you. Over the next few sections, we will take a look at where these ideas came from and some of the buzzwords common in the industry. We will also discuss what these products mean to your company no matter which business you are in.

Although the book itself is primarily aimed at the UNIX environment, most of the discussions in this chapter do not relate to any specific operating system. After all, UNIX was not commercially available until after these principles had matured.

1.1 A Historical Perspective

We have had databases ever since man started keeping written records. Whether carved into stone slabs, written on paper and stored in a file cabinet, or stored electronically in a computer, a database is simply a store of data. Of course, in the early days of computing and even today, we used the term *files.* Because of the limitations of the early computer hardware, most of these files were stored on cards and paper tapes. With the advent of magnetic storage media, we started using magnetic tapes, and finally keeping these files on-line on disks.

The buzzword database appeared at about the time we started keeping more and more of our files on-line. It refers to a collection of files that are related in some way. For example, we speak of the accounting database, the marketing database, or a personnel database. Each database might consist of several files such as general ledger, vendor, and customer files in an accounting database.

So, if we have had databases for such a long time and managed to use them to our advantage, why do we need a DBMS? The answer lies in how changes in our methods of software development over the years have improved our development productivity. We need to examine how systems are built without a DBMS and why it helps to improve such systems development.

The earliest software was written in machine code using the basic computer terms of 1's and 0's. Then, we developed *assembler* languages to make it easier to write this software. We call the era of machine code programs as *first generation* languages, and assembler as *second generation* languages. With assembler languages we could write software and make it work much more quickly than we could when writing in machine code. In other words, we increased productivity of the software developers.

Then came high level languages such as COBOL, FORTRAN, and later many others. We call these the *third generation* of programming languages. Again, we increased development productivity by an order of magnitude because these languages were even easier to program in than assembler. Besides, many more people could learn and effectively use these languages than those who could make sense out of assembler languages. A DBMS improves the development productivity yet again by taking these developments to the next logical step. Its *fourth generation* languages provide a higher level of development interface than the third generation programming languages like COBOL.

A DBMS provides many tools to speedily develop screen interfaces such as menus and interactive forms which require several pages of third generation programming language code. By providing standard tools, they not only reduce repetitive code in programs but also enforce consistency in the user interface. A DBMS offers you an easier and faster way of developing typical forms-based interactive programs. Similarly, it offers report generators, so you can produce a typical report with a few commands, not pages and pages of code in a language like COBOL. These tools improve productivity in the same way as languages like COBOL improved it over assembler languages: by giving you a higher level of development interface.

A DBMS changes your views on accessing data with its end-user query tools. Non-technical people could use such ad hoc query tools with a little training. You still need programmers to write programs for prettily laid out reports or those that are used frequently. But, if you need the data *now*, and are not fussy about the layout, ad hoc query tools let you do the job yourself!

While there were improvements in development languages, operating systems also improved to relieve us from developing code to access storage and peripheral devices. Operating systems manage hardware devices and the running of programs. In the context of data management, what these improvements meant was that we no longer had to worry about which disk block a particular file started and ended. We could refer to files by a meaningful name, and specify a record in the file as being a specific size. The file management portion of the operating system translates these file names and record specifications into blocks on disks.

The file management parts of operating systems developed further to provide different types of files: sequential access, indexed access, and random access files. With these types of files, specifying fast access to records in a file became a lot easier because we could use key values for searching in an index rather than sequentially searching through the whole file. So again, we improved the productivity of programmers. (*Unfortunately, UNIX only developed one type of file: a stream of bytes. The only type of record it supports is an arbitrary convention of using the ASCII NL [newline] character as a record terminator in files containing printable characters. For files containing binary data, no such convention exists.*)

Even with all of these developments, programmers face many time consuming tasks. For example, the file management facilities of an operating system really do not know what kind of data a record contains. They simply treat a record as a set of bytes. It is up to the accessing program to interpret where each data item (field) starts and ends within a record.

A DBMS can identify individual data items (fields), thus providing a higher level of abstraction than file management parts of an operating system. So we no longer need to access a record made up of bytes and interpret them into meaningful fields. The order and positioning of fields within a record become less important and in most DBMS products quite irrelevant.

When using ordinary operating system files, programs must read the entire record even if they only need a few fields from it. Each program must know the exact position of each field within this record. Suppose that we decide to add another field to records in a file (a frequent occurrence in any application). This additional field might possibly increase the size of the record. So, we have to modify all programs which access this record to account for the new field, even if they do not use it. Thus, we are forced to modify more programs than absolutely necessary, and of course, test each one. All of these activities consume a significant portion of our programming resources.

A DBMS provides us with a way around such unnecessary modifications. Its interface lets us deal directly with fields, rather than an entire record, and *only* those fields that are needed in each program. Thus, adding a new field to a record does not affect all programs which access this record, but only those which need to use the new field.

There are other problems faced by developers using ordinary operating system files. For example, consider the common types of data stored in business applications such as a date. We frequently store dates, such as order date, hire date, invoice date, and so on in our application databases. We develop routines to decipher dates, manipulate them, and use them in reports: say to restrict the report to a period of time. The unfortunate part is that we develop such routines repeatedly, sometimes even within one application.

A DBMS provides standard facilities to deal with such commonly used data. It associates a data type with each field, so that it can manipulate data such as dates and money in a reasonable way. This set of common tools allows you to specify data search conditions such as **today** and **this week**. We no longer have to develop (and maintain!) custom routines for these common functions.

The principle of providing a set of tools to perform commonly used functions is really similar to the way operating systems developed. An operating system provides a set of tools to access commonly used peripheral devices, and the common concept of using files. A DBMS provides tools at the next higher level: tools to access data logically rather than by byte position within a record, and tools to manipulate data using forms and reports. In Chapter 3, we will discuss in detail the types of functions these tools provide.

1.2 Objectives of a DBMS

In Section 1.1, we saw how a DBMS is a natural progression in the way development methods have changed since the early days of computing. In this section, we concentrate on the aims it expects to achieve.

The DBMS technology has three objectives which form the cornerstone of its foundation. These are all based around the idea of *independence* from hardware specific issues. The overall aim is to bring the development of information systems closer to the way people work, rather than making people conform to the way a computer works.

- *Physical independence:* One of the aims is removing our dependence on physical configurations. To some extent, operating systems relieve us from specifying low level storage mechanisms such as disk blocks and cylinders. UNIX provides a higher level interface to storage in its filesystem organization. However, if we are to use UNIX raw disks, we still have to manage start and end of a file within the disk in terms of blocks or characters. This type of development is quite complex and therefore prone to error. It is difficult for a programmer to perceive the relationship between a logical file and some blocks on a disk.

  Another type of physical dependence inherent in the use of ordinary files is the breakdown of a record into data fields. Fields must always be stored in some particular sequence. For example, field A occupies 10 bytes from the beginning of the record, field B occupies bytes 11 and 12, and so on. Developers have to carefully match such positioning sequences to obtain correct data: A mismatch of even a single byte can be fatal. Achieving independence from such tedious details clearly would reduce the amount of midnight oil burned by programmers.

  Other types of physical dependence might include handling specific terminal types or printers. While developing an application, programmers have to be aware of which physical devices to support in order to embed appropriate handling routines in their programs. With DBMS forms and report development facilities, these issues are already taken care of.

- *Access independence:* When using each of the different types of files, such as sequential, indexed, and random, the accessing program must specify how to reach the record it needs in each file. For example, suppose a user wants to display customer information and an order placed by a specific customer. The program to do this has to open the customer file, read each index record in turn to locate the customer number, read in the record, and interpret the data. Similarly, it has to contain code to find and access the customer order records for that customer.

The key point is that each program must contain the access path for searching and accessing the required files with the necessary conditions. A program catering to a user accessing the same data using some other field, say customer name, must specify a different access path. The objective of a DBMS is to remove such concerns with the access path. For example, the query language facilities do not require you to specify *how* to access a specific record. They merely require you to specify *what* data you wish displayed.

An analogy to the impact of this objective is in a typical office environment. A manager merely asks a secretary to find the March 12th memo to J. Smith. There is no need to specify detailed instructions such as: go to the file cabinets, locate the drawer marked "S—W", examine the name on each folder, and so on. A DBMS aims to achieve the level of instruction a manager provides a secretary.

- *Data independence:* A DBMS aims to reduce the upheaval caused by a necessary change to our database structure, a frequent occurrence in any application. In paper databases (in file cabinets), the manager is not aware of changes to the filing method, and so the instructions to the secretary do not change. When you add a "date received" data item to a form for your own use, you do not need to inform every person who uses the form. In fact, those people who have no interest in this data item can simply ignore it.

So why should computer based databases be so inflexible that every program that accesses the form should require modification in similar circumstances? Such inflexibility is, unfortunately, the case when your database is stored in ordinary files.

Thus, one of the aims of a DBMS is to hide changes to the application database from users, or programs, except those that need the new data items. It aims to remove our dependence on particular methods of access to data. A DBMS aims to behave rather like the secretary who can translate a manager's request for a memo as appropriate to the new filing method. Users, or programs, refer to only required data items, ignoring any additional data that might also exist in the databases.

There are many other effects a DBMS has on your development methods and effort expended. One of the benefits attributed to database management systems is removal of data redundancy. They certainly provide you with the means to remove such redundancy, although actually reducing data redundancy is up to you. A DBMS does not have the intelligence to detect and resolve data duplicated in several places.

To design a database shared by many different applications, you need to employ a database *guru,* alias a DBA (Database Administrator). A DBA is responsible for organizing your data such that all applications can share it. These responsibilities include understanding the needs of the entire company, not just an individual application. This position is a very senior one as database administration has to cross all boundaries between applications.

Since a DBMS purports to increase productivity, you might be tempted to think that you could manage with fewer programmers. In practice, what it actually means is that your application development suffers fewer technical difficulties during system test, and modifications require less effort. The emphasis in your company might shift from short design and lengthy coding periods to longer design/prototyping and shorter coding cycles. The real benefit is not fewer personnel, but more completed applications with the same number of personnel. In fact, you will probably get requests for development which no one would have thought of requesting when development of the simplest facility took a long time.

So how can you justify the cost of a DBMS? The benefits are really in the indirect effects of timely delivery of information systems. Suppose, for example, a particular small application takes 12 man-months to develop and the fastest delivery could be six months from the start of project. Also suppose you could deliver the same system in three months using a DBMS. The benefit to your company is the availability of information three months earlier than before. In some cases, this might mean increased competitiveness, say by launching a new campaign ahead of other competitors.

1.3 DBMS Models

Each commercial DBMS is based on some data model which determines its basic facilities. Most recent systems, especially those on UNIX, are based on the *relational* model. Older systems used data models such as *hierarchical* and *network* models, which are now offering a relational-like interface to their products. Systems in the near future might well use *semantic* models, or some other form. We are not going to conduct a lengthy discussion of the theories of each data model. These theories are quite adequately covered in many other books listed in the bibliography. Instead, the remainder of this chapter introduces the basic terminology associated with these data models.

It is important to realize that data models are simply ways of describing the relationships between data items. They are merely the view presented to a user or a programmer. They are not necessarily the method used to store data internally by a product, though there is often a relationship between internal storage and the logical view presented to users. Our discussions will illustrate how an application database could be molded into any of the data models, albeit with varying degrees of flexibility. The purpose of this chapter is only to make you aware of the differences without going into a thorough comparison.

We limit our discussion to the four data models previously mentioned. We omit the *inverted list* data model in this chapter for several reasons. Firstly, it is quite an old data model, used by mature mainframe DBMS products such as ADABAS, DATACOM/DB, and MODEL 204. Secondly, none of the commercial UNIX DBMS products implements this model, though these mainframe database management systems might be ported in the future. The interface provided by these products is fairly low level. For example, indexes in many cases are visible to the programmers. Finally, there is some similarity between the inverted list data model and the internal implementation of many relational DBMS products. So a discussion of this model does not add significantly to our higher level views of data.

In the following sections, we use the example customer orders system shown in Figure 1-1. A few notes about this database will clarify some of the assumptions in this system. A customer can place many orders, each of which contains a number of order items. For each order, we send an invoice. The customer may not pay the entire amount of the invoice, so we might send multiple invoices. Therefore, there can be multiple invoices per order, and multiple payments per invoice. We shall represent the database required for this system in each of the data models discussed in order to illustrate the differences between them.

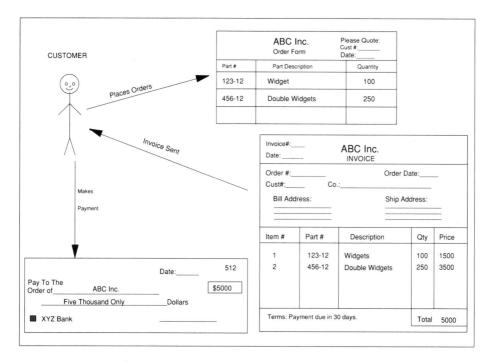

Figure 1-1 Customer Orders System for ABC Inc.

It is important to note that the data model of a particular DBMS is quite irrelevant while you are analyzing the data for your application or for the entire corporation. Analysis involves examining the data to determine how it relates to other data items — that is, understanding the data. Analysis performed with a particular DBMS in mind is likely to ignore issues which do not fit into the mold of its data model. You might possibly miss such issues altogether, blinded by the peculiarities of the DBMS. Identifying these issues and finding workarounds for them is best done in the database and application design stage. In the database design stage, you probably will need extensive knowledge of a particular DBMS. The data normalization concepts introduced in Chapter 2 are useful during both analysis and design stages. These concepts therefore apply not only to relational database models but also to all other data models.

There are many tools to help you with data analysis and design. These are generally grouped under the umbrella of Computer Aided Software Engineering (CASE) tools. Many of these will work with your favorite symbols and provide a pictorial representation of your understanding of data. Realize that you still need considerable analysis skills to collect the information in the first place. However, diagrams can be a good communication vehicle to clear up misunderstanding between the analyst and the subject expert. A feature of these tools that you might find useful is the database schemas they can generate from your data models. Some tools can generate appropriately worded schema generation statements for several different DBMS products.

Other aspects of these CASE tools have similar uses in application design, especially when using the fourth generation development facilities of a DBMS. Be warned, however, that most of the code generation components of CASE tools generate only third generation programming language code, for example, COBOL. Their prototyping facilities do not yet interface to forms drivers, report generators, or fourth generation languages. Since many DBMS vendors themselves are entering the CASE arena, we will probably see better prototyping facilities in the near future.

1.4 The Hierarchical Model

This model was the first to be implemented and is probably the most limited. Its most well-known implementation is the IBM IMS database management system. Under UNIX, this model is only used by DBMS products which were ported from their original mainframe environments. A prime example is FOCUS from Information Builders Inc. Such products, of course, provide some form of a relational interface, usually via their query language.

As the name implies, this model requires that data be arranged hierarchically, such as in a tree structure or an organization chart. Figure 1-2 illustrates one way of arranging our example application database in a hierarchical manner. A database can consist of many separate tree structures. A record is commonly called a *segment.* Customer, order, and invoice are all examples of records in Figure 1-2.

Segments are linked in a *parent-child* relationship denoted by the lines connecting segments in Figure 1-2. Thus, *customer* segment is the parent of the child segment, *order*, in our example. These *links* commonly represent a *one-to-many* link; that is, for each customer there can be many orders but for any one order there can be one and only one customer. Clearly, you can easily represent a *one-to-one* link as well. All instances of a segment are stored as an *ordered* set; they can only be accessed in a specific order. Links and the order of segment occurrences play an important role in the methods of access in a hierarchical DBMS.

It should be clear from this example that a *many-to-many* relationship is difficult to express in this model. Suppose in our example, a customer sent one payment check for a number of invoices. We cannot accept such a payment in our current data structure since it changes the relationship between *payment* and *invoice* to a many-to-many relationship. Obviously we would not want to return the check just because our database was not designed to handle such a case! Some products, such as IMS, allow a child to have *two* parents in order to deal with such cases. But this feature merely defers the problem. For example, what happens if we also needed to include payments in our accounts receivable application: An account can have many payments!

Notice the lack of an identifying *ord_no* field in the *order items* segment. The identification is actually the link itself, so you do not need to keep the identifying value. Thus, the only way you can relate a particular order item to an order is via this link. The link information is generated by the DBMS when you add an instance of an order item. You must, therefore, have the appropriate parent instance as your *current* parent when you add instances of the child segment. Since instances of child segments are ordered, you must also select the appropriate point amongst the child instances at which a new instance is inserted.

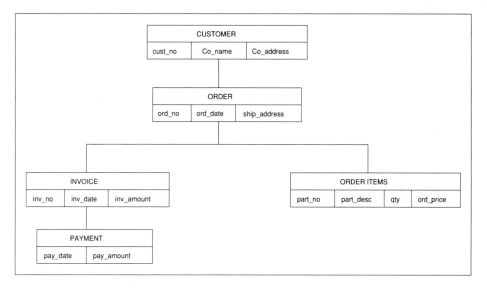

Figure 1-2 A Hierarchical Representation of Customer Orders System

Access in hierarchical products is record oriented; that is, you start by finding the first record and then step through each subsequent record. End-user tools, such as the ***modify*** component of FOCUS, hide this record at a time processing, but the programming interface remains obviously record oriented. You can access records in a hierarchical database in three ways: directly, sequentially, or sequentially under current parent.

The ***direct*** access method involves using a selection condition on the record key. For example, you might search for a particular invoice number in the invoice segment. The ***sequential*** access method might simply start at the first record and step through subsequent records using a next record command. The ***sequentially under current parent*** access method utilizes the ordering of child records within one parent. This method is common for accessing all children of a particular instance of a parent segment; for example, all order items within a particular order.

The concept of the sequentially under current parent access method also extends to an ***ancestor*** – that is, the parent of a parent segment ad infinitum. For example, we could access all instances where a particular customer ordered a particular part by using sequential under the current parent method even though the customer segment is a grandparent of the order items segment.

1.5 The Network Model

This model could be thought of as a variation on the hierarchical model. The main improvement in this model over the hierarchical one is that the structure need not be a tree. An example of a UNIX implementation of this model is the AT&T TUXEDO product. Although none of the four UNIX DBMS products discussed in this book use a network model, UNIFY provides similar concepts in its ***explicit reference*** mechanism. A better known mainframe example of a network implementation is Cullinet's IDMS product.

Figure 1-3 illustrates one representation of our example database as a network model. Connections, called *sets* in network terminology, can exist between any two records provided conditions discussed below are met. The connections between records, in this case, represent an ***owner-member*** relationship, which is essentially the same as a parent-child relationship in the hierarchical model. Some of the restrictions in defining sets on two records are:

- An instance of the ***member*** record in a set can only occur zero or one times in an occurrence of that set.

- An instance of the ***owner*** record in a set occurs exactly once in an occurrence of that set.

What these restrictions mean in practice is that a single instance of a record cannot participate as a member to more than one instance of an owner. Thus, we have to add distinct instances of an order item record for two orders containing the same part number, just like in the hierarchical model. We can represent a one-to-one and a one-to-many relationship by defining sets. Representing a many-to-many relationship between two records requires you to create a third record and define a set between this record type and each of the first two records.

There are three basic ways of accessing records: ***direct, sequential access using a set definition***, and ***simple sequential*** access. Direct access depends on a ***calc*** key definition in your database schema. This key often translates to a hashed access method (discussed in Chapter 3). Sequential access using a set definition is called ***via,*** and is basically a navigational access method. It depends on using a connection between two records together with the order implied in instances of the member record belonging to the current instance of the owner. In our example database, we might use the calc key, cust_no, to make current the desired customer record, then use the customer-order set to step through the orders (via) for that customer, and for each order use the order-items set to step though the order items in sequence.

When you add a new instance to a record, the DBMS usually takes care of updating the sets involving the record. Of course, it is important to maintain the ordering of member instances. The ordering might be based on sorting a field value, first-in-last-out, last-in-first-out, or simply left up to the application program. In this last method, the application program must procedurally define the point at which the new instance should be connected.

Determining which sets are necessary and the access method for each record type is a complex process. Conflicts between needs of varying applications occur frequently and reconfiguring the database is anything but straightforward. The hairy task of resolving conflicts, of course, falls on the Database Administrator — application programmers are, hopefully, shielded from it.

Unlike the hierarchical model, the network model was proposed by the CODASYL Database Task Group (DBTG) in 1971. Network model products were developed through the 1970s based on these proposed definitions.

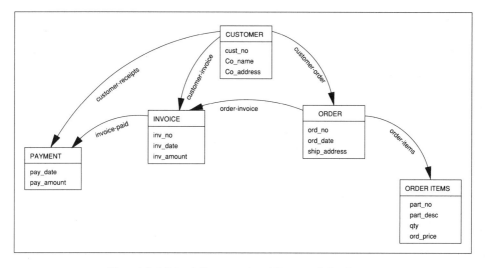

Figure 1-3 A Network Representation of Customer Orders System

1.6 The Relational Model

This model is one of the simplest to comprehend and certainly the most popular in the 1980s. All of the products discussed in this book profess this model as their basis, albeit with varying degrees of completeness. The theoretical model arises from the work of Dr. E. F. Codd in the 1970s and early 1980s. The commercial implementations of DBMS products certainly fit well in the UNIX environment.

There is a great deal of literature expounding the details of this model, the most well known being *An Introduction to Database Systems*, by C.J. Date. Chapter 2 provides much more detail on the specific terminology used in the relational environment. This section is only intended to stimulate your appetite. For the sake of completeness in this chapter, we illustrate the relational representation of our example database in Figure 1-4.

Academic terminology for relational models is rather different from that used by commercial products. Record types in relational terminology are called *relations*, records are called *tuples,* and fields within a record are *attributes.* Commercial products use more obvious terms: record types are *tables,* records are *rows* in a table, and fields are *columns*. We will use these terms interchangeably throughout this book.

There are no predefined connections in a relational database as in the hierarchical and network models discussed earlier. Instead, we duplicate the fields we would use to base the connections on. For example, the order table contains a cust_no field whose values allow us to connect to the customer table. Such duplicated fields actually perform the same functions as links in hierarchical systems, and sets in network systems. The additional capability of the relational approach is that there are no physical links built into the database itself. Actual connections are done dynamically. Fields duplicated for the purposes of connecting are sometimes called *foreign* keys. *Primary* keys are the fields which identify a row in a table.

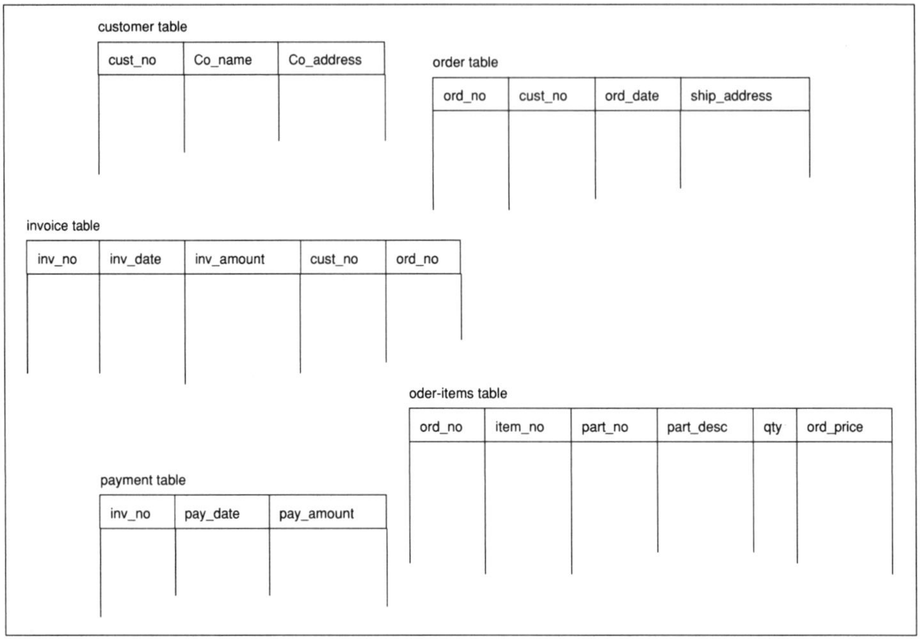

customer table

cust_no	Co_name	Co_address

order table

ord_no	cust_no	ord_date	ship_address

invoice table

inv_no	inv_date	inv_amount	cust_no	ord_no

oder-items table

ord_no	item_no	part_no	part_desc	qty	ord_price

payment table

inv_no	pay_date	pay_amount

Figure 1-4 A Relational Representation of Customer Orders System

This dynamic connection capability means that we can modify the structure of any individual table without affecting the remainder of the system. In practice, you might have to unload and reload the database with some products; with others such a long-winded procedure is not necessary.

Relational access is quite unlike the other two models we discussed earlier. Data is accessed a *set* of records at a time, rather than one record at a time. Note that this use of the word set simply means several records rather than its rather specialized use in the network model. No navigational methods exist in this method, that is, even when connecting (*joining*) two tables together you simply specify the condition for the connection. For example, to connect the order and order-items tables, you would simply specify

```
where order.ord_no = order-items.ord_no
```

In a navigational system, you would have to say

```
Find the first order record,
Get the first order items record within this order record,
Get the next order items record ....
```

This flexibility of the relational model has made it very popular. Because it is easy to learn and allows easy restructuring of the application database, application enhancements are easier to implement than with the hierarchical or network models. So, it is very suitable for implementing applications in a modular fashion. You can develop a minimal system and put it into production quickly. Then, you can improve its functionality as users accept the benefits of the new system.

There are UNIX commands that mimic relational functions such as join, project, and so on, which work on only flat text files. They do not supply other features of a DBMS, particularly productivity improvement tools, concurrency control, and access security management.

1.7 Entity-Relationship and Other Models

You can think of these models as attempts at improving the relational model. Because of the simple representation inherent in a relational model, we lost some of the constraints imposed by the hierarchical and network models. The connections (links and sets) of these earlier models enforced certain logical restrictions between record types. For example, a link in a hierarchical system enforces a one-to-many relationship. A relational model has no mechanisms to define and enforce such relationships. Each relation is a stand-alone entity with no direct relationship with other relations – only implied relationships via the duplicated fields.

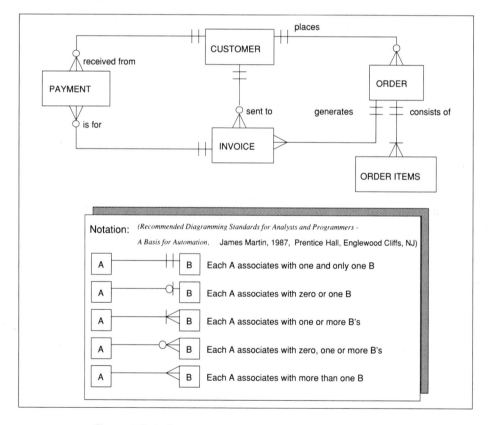

Figure 1-5 Entity-Relationship Representation of Customer Orders System

The entity-relationship modeling technique is widely used during the data analysis activity because it clearly illustrates the ***relationships*** that exist between ***entities***. An entity in this context is some thing that we want to store information about. Thus, customers, invoices, and payments in our example are all entities. Figure 1-5 shows the entities in our example application and relationships we have defined for them.

This diagram illustrates with almost no ambiguity the constraints on the relationships. It would be nice indeed to have a DBMS enforce these restrictions. A very few products are trying to implement facilities to achieve this objective; unfortunately, none in the UNIX environment (as far as the author is aware).

There is, of course, much more semantic information not represented in this diagram. There is no information on how the relationships affect the usual database operations of adding, deleting, and updating. For example, if we delete a customer from the customer record type, what should happen to records in the orders record type for this deleted customer? Logic tells us that data in all other record types relating to this customer must be deleted. At present, there are no formal techniques for defining such rules in a DBMS product. Early attempts include the INFOEXEC Series from UNISYS Corporation. So, for the present, we must continue to code such logic into our application programs.

1.8 Conclusions

This chapter provided an overview of how and why DBMSs were developed. One of the important points of the discussion was an informal review of the problems encountered in developing systems without using a DBMS. The aim is not to exhaustively qualify the pros and cons of the DBMS technology, but to provide a flavor of its capabilities. The key points included: productivity improvement, reduction in application maintenance effort, and a change in development methods.

The remainder of the chapter concentrated on explaining some of the buzz words you hear from vendors. Again, our intention is to familiarize you with these terms in the context of the DBMS technology. We discussed some of the important data models which form the basis of current commercial DBMS products. In particular, we illustrated the hierarchical, network, relational, and entity-relationship models. For a more academic and detailed discussion of this subject, please refer to the texts listed in the bibliography.

2

Relational Concepts

Having introduced the major models underlying DBMS products in the marketplace, we turn our attention solely to the relational model. The other models are less significant in the context of this book because all of the four products which we examine use the relational model.

Do not be put off by the title of this chapter; this is not a theoretical discussion. Our purpose is simply to introduce the concepts of this model so that you can relate to later discussions in this book. Formal mathematical definitions are covered very well, in any case, in the literature published by experts such as E. F. Codd and C. J. Date listed in the bibliography. This chapter will, instead, concentrate on providing examples of the concepts in terms of our customer orders system.

This chapter also covers the topic of data normalization. Although these techniques were initiated under the auspices of relational theories, they apply to database design in general regardless of the model. They are used widely by practitioners of the database technology. The topics covered in this chapter are

- Relational terminology as defined in academic texts and its loose correspondence to that used by commercial products.

- A discussion of data normalization techniques and why they are useful for data analysis and database design. We also discuss their use in conjunction with the popular entity-relationship diagrams provided by most CASE tools.

- An informal description of the normal forms with examples based on the customer orders system illustrated in Chapter 1.

- An explanation of relational operators with particular reference to their implementation in SQL.

2.1 Relational Terminology

We start with the basic terms used in this technology. Table 2-1 lists some the important formal terms and corresponding informal terms used in commercial products. Note that this list is by no means exhaustive but covers the four products discussed in this book. Throughout this book, we will use these terms interchangeably.

Formal Terms	Corresponding Commercial Product Terms
Relation	Table, Record Type, File
Tuple	Row, Record
Attribute	Column, Field
Domain of an Attribute	Possible Valid Values for a Column

Table 2-1 Basic Relational Terms

A relation is different from the traditional concept of a file. For example, a traditional file can contain more than one *type* of records; that is, the collection of fields can be different from one record to another. (*Remember the common construction of a file with a header record followed by several associated detail records? We used to have a record type field in each to identify how to interpret the remaining fields in the record.*) A relation, or a table, has only one type of record; that is, the collection of fields in each row of a relation table is always the same.

Another difference is that rows in a relation have no implied order unlike traditional files whose structure dictated some order. For example, in a traditional file, detail records always follow their associated header in physical storage sequence. The order of rows in a relation table is usually determined by an index on selected fields. In practice, you might choose to impose a physical order on the storage of rows, for example by *clustering,* for performance gains. The important point is that whether or not rows are physically stored in some order is irrelevant to the user or programmer. The operation of the product does not fail just because of a lack of row ordering.

Tuples in a relation are essentially the same as rows in a table — namely, a collection of fields. One of the formal properties of a relation states that duplicate tuples do not exist. What this property implies is that every row must have a unique key; that is, an identifier composed of one or more fields that uniquely distinguishes each row from all others. In many commercial products, you might think that this condition is missing since these products allow you to define duplicate keys. Actually what happens is the product assigns a hidden unique value to each row in such cases. This unique value is sometimes called a *rowid*.

In formal theory, the order of attributes within a relation is irrelevant. Of course, our knowledge of the lower level storage mechanisms suggests that they have to be stored in some order. The point is that order of columns is not apparent to the user, or programmer, in any way. When we refer to column names, say in a query statement, we can list them in any order.

An attribute is just a *simple* field which can take individual values from its domain. By simple, we mean that it is the smallest logical unit of data such as a customer number or customer name. Packed fields containing more than one data item, which we sometimes used in traditional files, are not permitted as one attribute. This restriction does not necessarily mean that a great deal of space is wasted as we would expect if we stored all fields individually in a traditional file. The DBMS product might internally pack fields together before storing them. However, its internal packing is of no concern to us.

The concept of a *domain* in really not implemented at present by most commercial products. In relational theory it does play a part. In simplistic terms, a domain of an attribute is all of the possible values the attribute might assume. For example, if you had an attribute *days-in-month*, its domain might consist of the values *28, 29, 30, 31*. One might implement this simple case by defining a domain listing these values. But, what should the domain for an attribute like *customer name* be?

There are other complications relating to domains. Consider an attribute day-of-month whose domain also includes the values 28, 29, 30, 31. These particular values in the domain for day-of-month do not *mean* the same thing as in the domain for days-in-month. It would not make any sense to compare day-of-month to days-in-month. So the concept of a domain involves much more than just a set of values; it involves meaning of the data as well.

DBMS products do implement a very simple form of domains when they require you to specify a *data type* for a field. Some products, such as UNIFY, also allow you to specify a set of valid values. With these mechanisms, they can impose some restrictions which logically do not make sense; for example, comparing customer name with order number. They cannot, however, make the semantic distinction between two attributes of the same data type, such as customer name and customer address.

2.2 What Is Normalization?

In a paper database, we often duplicate data. For example, consider a paper version of our customer orders system: We would keep forms containing customer information, order forms, and a copy of the corresponding invoice forms. Between these forms, we duplicate customer information three times, and parts information twice. If we simply build our computer database to mirror this paper system, we also get duplicated data.

Now, consider what happens when some duplicated data item, say the customer address, changes. We would have to change the address in several different places: in the customer record, and in all of the order records and invoice records for that customer. We might cut corners and keep the old address in the older order and invoice records, and suffer the consequences when we had to send a duplicate copy of an unmodified invoice.

Wouldn't life be a great deal easier, though, if we could consolidate all this redundancy and only keep the customer address in one record only? In a paper database, we do not have such a choice, but in a computer database we do! For example, we could keep the customer address once in the customer record. Then when generating invoices, we could simply read it from the customer record, instead of the order record. In fact, the order record does not need to contain the customer address at all.

Rearranging data to remove redundancy is a vital part of designing a database. Normalization is just a formal method for putting into practice this otherwise intuitive process. Of course, there is a lot more to designing a database, such as estimating volumes, choosing a data type for each field, and so on. We will discuss these other issues later in the book.

The basic principle in normalization is the concept of *functional dependency*. This concept, in informal terms, means that we group data items into one relation such that there is a one-to-one relationship between the values of the data items. For example, the attributes customer name and customer address in our customer orders system are functionally dependent on the attribute customer number. In other words, for a given customer number we have one, and only one, value of customer name and also of customer address.

The process of normalization consists of composing relations by applying this concept. There are further rules governing the process of normalization, each of which might progressively decompose a relation into smaller relations. At each stage, a relation is said to be in a higher level *normal form*. Section 2.3 covers the different normal forms defined to date with particular reference to our example customer orders system.

Note that deciding whether or not a functional dependency exists between two data items depends on the nature of the data and the application requirements. It is a human decision rather than some rule cast in concrete by predefined computer science laws. Different business circumstances can dictate different choices and end results. As an example, consider changing our assumption in the customer orders example (Chapter 1) that a customer might make more than one payment for a given invoice. Suppose, instead, we assumed that each invoice is paid in full with one and only one payment. We no longer need to keep a *pay_amount* field separate from *inv_amount.* We would not therefore need to keep a *payment* record separate from the *invoice* record; marking the payment date in the invoice record itself is sufficient.

An important point is that normalizing data constitutes a good practice, rather than a necessity. It encourages us to keep one piece of data in one place, resulting in obvious benefits. There are some practical circumstances when you might choose to deliberately store unnormalized data. For example, to reduce the extra disk I/O of accessing two tables rather than one, in the interests of improved performance. Denormalization strategies, however, do have a price in making updates more complex. They probably will have an impact on the ease of maintaining database consistency. Such choices must be made with extreme caution after considering all possible effects of the decision in a shared database. Making decisions such as these are where DBAs earn their salary.

There are tools that aid a designer in the database design process. These Computer Aided Software Engineering (CASE) tools usually allow you to draw an entity-relationship diagram together with a *dictionary* containing descriptions of data items. Some CASE tools generate dictionary entries as you specify application data flow diagrams.

There is a close correspondence between entity-relationship diagrams and normalized relations. Entities correspond to relation tables in a relational database. As an exercise, compare the entity-relationship diagram and the relational representation of our customer orders system in Chapter 1. Some relationships, for example many-to-many relationships, also correspond to tables in the relational database.

You might wonder whether you need both normalization and entity-relationship diagrams when designing a database. Realize that you use the relationship information in the normalization process, whether or not a formal entity-relationship diagram is constructed. In a small database consisting of only a few relations, you might not need a formal diagram or a CASE tool. In larger databases keeping track of hundreds of data items and relationships becomes tricky and CASE tools become invaluable.

2.3 The Normal Forms

There are five normal forms formally defined at present, although only the first three are most commonly applicable in database design. These normal forms, called first normal form, second normal form and so on, form a layered onion. The first normal form is the outermost layer of the onion and the fifth normal form is the innermost. The inner layers of the onion automatically pass the test of any layer outside it. Thus a relation in the second normal form is automatically in the first normal form. The converse does not, however, apply; that is, a first normal form is only in the second normal form if it passes the test for the second normal form. The normalization process aims to decompose data up to the most sensible inner layer. More discussion on this in Section 2.3.6.

2.3.1 First Normal Form (1NF)

The test for first normal form is whether each attribute in the relation takes only *atomic* values. By atomic values, we mean individual values such as taken by attributes like customer number and customer name. A first normal form relation cannot have any attribute which takes multiple values packed into a single attribute. Note that a date could be treated as an atomic value whether as a combination of day, month, year; or as three separate attributes of day, month, and year. Whether to separate or not depends on your business needs. By this definition, any table in a relational DBMS is in first normal form; for example,

Order Table:

ord_no	cust_no	ord_date	ship_address	part_no	part_desc	qty	ord_price
1234	1111	12/1/88	Newcity	123-12	Widgets	100	1500
1234	1111	12/1/88	Newcity	456-12	Double Widgets	250	3500

A first normal form relation frequently has redundant duplicated data.

2.3.2 Second Normal Form (2NF)

The test for whether a first normal form relation is also in the second normal form depends on identifying the key attribute of the relation. Each value of the key must uniquely identify a row in the table. In the *order* relation just shown, the key is obviously *ord_no*. The test for second normal form is whether every non-key attribute depends on the key. In the preceding order relation this is clearly not true; for example, *qty* and ***ord_price*** depend on the combination of ord_no and part_no. In fact, working from instinct to remove redundancy we would group as follows:

Order Table:

ord_no	cust_no	ord_date	ship_address
1234	1111	12/1/88	Newcity

Order-detail Table:

ord_no	part_no	part_desc	qty	ord_price
1234	123-12	widgets	100	1500
1234	456-12	Double Widgets	250	3500

The key for the order table is still the ord_no field, but the key for order-detail table is the combination of ord_no and part_no. The order-detail table is still not in second normal form. Consider, in this example, if we had another order containing part number 123-12. We would have two rows containing the same value in part description. The *part_desc* attribute, in fact, depends entirely on part_no which is only a portion of the key. Thus, according to the rules for second normal form, we should decompose it into

Order-items Table:

ord_no	part_no	qty	ord_price
1234	123-12	100	1500
1234	456-12	250	3500

Parts Table:

part_no	part_desc
123-12	Widgets
456-12	Double Widgets

Note that we did not use this fully normalized set of relations in our examples of data models in Chapter 1. This was deliberate: The relationship of the parts table to order-items table is a many-to-many relationship. Such a relationship cannot be expressed in hierarchical and network models without increasing the complexity of the example.

An interesting question: Is the ord_price attribute functionally dependent on part_no or on the combination ord_no & part_no? In the first case, the attribute actually belongs in the parts table. The determining factor is the way the business works: If the price for a part is always fixed — that is, no quantity or volume discounts — then price should be stated once in the parts table. It is then a property of a part, unrelated to the order. In our case, the model assumes that the actual price charged to a customer might be different on each order, so price is a property of the combination ord_no and part_no. This example is a fairly good illustration of how business needs can change the design of a database.

2.3.3 Third Normal Form (3NF)

The test for whether a second normal form relation is also in third normal form checks for any dependencies between non-key attributes. Our examples of second normal form relations actually do pass this test; that is, none of the non-key attributes depend on other non-key attributes. Consider, though, the case of the order table. Suppose that the shipping address depended on the customer number, as would happen if each customer number was assigned to a single geographic business location. In this case, knowing the customer number would imply the shipping address and we would have to break up the table into the order and customer tables shown next.

Order Table:

ord_no	cust_no	ord_date
1234	1111	12/1/88

Customer Table:

cust_no	ship_address
1111	Newcity

Deciding whether it is sensible to assign a different customer number for each branch of a customer company illustrates the types of issues a database designer, or a DBA, must resolve. In addition to the business impact of such decisions, the designer must consider technical issues such as potential wastage of disk space, and impact on the amount of disk I/O required in an application due to a particular design choice. It is important to note that no decision is right or wrong in a universal sense, only in the context of the requirements of a particular business. Even in a particular company business needs change often. Decisions that were right for last year's needs may not be totally right this year.

The Boyce/Codd normal form is actually a stricter definition of a third normal form, but applies rather rarely in a business application. For details on the difference between this form and the third normal form, please refer to the book, *An Introduction to Database Systems*, by C.J. Date.

2.3.4 Fourth Normal Form (4NF)

In most everyday databases, third normal form is a sufficient level of decomposition. We really could not decompose our example tables further than the third normal form. Occasionally, though, you might notice update problems in an unnormalized form such as the following seminar-instructor-text table.

Seminar-Instructor-Text Table:

Seminar	Instructor	Text
DB-1	Smith	Database Principles
DB-2	Smith	Advanced Techniques
DB-1	Smith	Data Modeling Techniques
DB-1	Jones	Database Principles
DB-1	Jones	Data Modeling Techniques
DB-2	White	Advanced Techniques

The assumptions in this table are that a seminar uses a set of texts, and a seminar is taught by one or more instructors. It passes the test for second normal form because each non-key attribute (instructor, text) depends entirely on the key (seminar). It also passes the test for third normal form since non-key attributes instructor and text are independent of each other. Yet the redundancy of data is obvious. The reason for this is that each of the instructor and text attributes have multiple values for each value of the seminar attribute. For example, for the DB-1 seminar there are two instructors, Smith and Jones; and two texts, Database Principles and Data Modeling Techniques. In jargon, this is an example of a *multi valued dependency*.

The fourth normal form in such cases decomposes the tables until no more than one multi valued dependency exists in any one resulting table. So, our resulting tables are seminar-instructor and seminar-texts tables shown next.

Seminar-Instructor Table:

Seminar	Instructor
DB-1	Smith
DB-2	Smith
DB-1	Jones
DB-2	White

Seminar-Texts Table:

Seminar	Texts
DB-1	Database Principles
DB-1	Data Modeling Techniques
DB-2	Advanced Techniques

2.3.5 Fifth Normal Form (5NF)

The fifth normal form is also rare in everyday databases. We include an example here for the sake of completeness. Consider the table shown below. The assumption is that an instructor can teach any seminar and will work in specified locations. Seminars can be taught by several instructors and take place in advertised locations. The table actually holds only those combinations of information that have occurred to date.

Instructor-Seminar-Location Table:

Instructor	Seminar	Location
Smith	DB-1	New York
Smith	DB-2	Chicago
Jones	DB-1	Chicago

Suppose, that we now wanted to offer the DB-2 seminar in New York; how can we update this table to reflect this without specifying a row for each instructor? Or, if we wanted to reflect the fact that Jones can teach DB-2; do we have to add two rows one for each city, or do we use a null location?

The problem with the instructor-seminar-locations table is that we are trying to represent a complex relationship in the table. The only combination of attributes that could be called a key is all three attributes; no other combination uniquely identifies a row. Yet there is obvious redundancy in the data. We could decompose this table into the following three tables which are in fifth normal form:

Instructor-Seminar Table:

Instructor	Seminar
Smith	DB-1
Smith	DB-2
Jones	DB-1

Seminar-Location Table:

Seminar	Location
DB-1	New York
DB-1	Chicago
DB-2	Chicago

Instructor-Location Table:

Instructor	Location
Smith	New York
Smith	Chicago
Jones	Chicago

Note that we need three tables such that the joining of all three tables is necessary to obtain the original table data. As an exercise, try joining any two tables to see whether you get the data exactly as in the original table.

The updates we wanted to apply are now obvious. Note that the formal definition of a fifth normal form is rather involved, so refer to the references in the bibliography if you are interested. We content ourselves with our very informal way of detecting relations that need further decomposition.

2.3.6 How Far to Normalize?

A good rule of thumb is to normalize at least up to the third normal form. This practice will usually remove most of the redundancy in your database. Cases requiring fourth and fifth normal form decomposition occur only occasionally, and so are not that critical. When they do occur, you will probably find yourself puzzling over rules for updating them.

In a few cases, full normalization does not make sense — that is, you do not achieve any benefits due to the decomposition. These cases usually involve some common sense fact such as the values of an attribute do not change frequently. A prime example is a U.S. address: If you know the zip code, you also know the city and state. However, is it really worth decomposing an address into two tables? After all, zip codes do not change often. But we almost always require city, state, and zip code together as part of the address.

Realize that normalization is only one part of the database design process. It depends heavily on understanding the data and business needs. Analysts must not only follow the techniques but apply them appropriately to the business problems to be solved. This is one of the reasons why it is better to analyze the data used by the entire company rather than piecemeal by application. There is almost always an overlap between data used by applications. Also, business needs change, implying changes to the database design. So, a database is rarely static. Designing for flexibility means normalization is important.

There can be good and bad decompositions. Bad decompositions simply lead to complications in maintaining data integrity. One of the ways to distinguish *bad* decompositions from *good* decompositions is to ask yourself whether a decomposition causes dependencies between separate tables. A rule of thumb is to choose the decomposition that keeps dependencies within one table. This choice is really a matter of judgment as you cannot always avoid dependencies between tables. However, an entity-relationship diagram can help in making good decompositions.

2.4 Relational Operations

In this section, we cover the basic operations defined in a relational system, although they may not all be available in every relational DBMS products. Consistent with our strategy of informal discussion, we avoid any formal definition of relational algebra and relational calculus. If you are interested in such information, please refer to some of the classic literature listed in the bibliography. To make it easy for you to identify the operations, we will also use SQL examples where possible.

Relational operations can be visualized very easily as cutting and pasting tables, rows, and columns in tables. This simplicity is one of the attractive features of the relational model: You can ignore the jargon and simply concentrate on understanding the concepts in terms of a table.

A common feature of many relational operations, such as *join* and *project*, is that the result is always a relation. This property arises from the similarities between mathematical set theory and relational theory. What it means in practice is that you can apply an operation to the result of another operation, since an operation always yields a table as a result. Of course, the table might be as simple as a single column or contain only a single row, depending on the operation performed. It might be, on the other hand, more complex than any other table in the database.

Selection:

This operation results in a set of rows from a table which satisfy a selection condition such as *"A = 1."* It is equivalent to cutting out rows from a table and discarding those rows you do not want. Do not confuse it with the *select* clause of SQL; it actually relates to the *where* clause only. You can use standard comparison operators including =, <, <=, >, >=. Since it restricts the rows which appear in the result, it is sometimes called a ***restriction*** operation. It is the simplest form of the SQL where clause is a statement. For example, the following statement will result in all rows of the order-items table which contain the value 123-12 in the part_no column.

```
SELECT *
FROM order-items
WHERE part_no = '123-12'
```

Projection:

This operation causes only the specified set of columns to appear in the result. Think of it as cutting a table vertically along column seams. In SQL, projection is achieved by specifying names of columns in the select clause of the statement. For example, the following statement will list all values of part_no in the order-items table.

```
SELECT part_no
FROM order-items
```

Cartesian Product:

This operation allows us to combine two tables. The result includes each row from the first table concatenated with each row from the second table; that is, all possible pairs of one row from each table. For example, we obtain a cartesian product of order-items and parts tables with the following statement:

```
SELECT *
FROM order-items, parts
```

Join:

This operation lets us combine two or more tables based on matching values from corresponding columns in each table. It is analogous to pasting two tables side by side such that corresponding column values in adjoining rows match. It is basically the reverse of decomposing a table. You can also think of it as a cartesian product with the result restricted to only those rows which satisfy the match condition; that is, a combination of cartesian product and selection operations. For example, we can join order-items and parts tables to obtain part descriptions for each part in the order-items table with the following statement:

```
SELECT ord_no, part_no, part_desc
FROM order-items, parts
WHERE order-items.part_no = parts.part_no
```

Note that to specify this operation in SQL we used the where clause with an equality operator. Do not confuse this use of the comparison operator with the selection operation described earlier. In this case, the comparison is between an attribute from one table against an attribute from the second table. Each attribute is qualified by the table name. Other languages implement a different clause, for example *joining,* to differentiate between selection and join operations.

Equality is not the only comparison operator permitted; you can also use other available operators including <, <=, >, >=. In practice, equality is the most common condition used when joining tables and is called *equijoin.* Other types of joins also have names but are infrequently used in ordinary data processing applications.

Union:

This operation lets us concatenate two tables one after another. It applies only to tables containing identical columns. It is analogous to pasting two tables one above the other. For example, to obtain all order numbers which contained orders for part number 123-12 and part number 456-12, we would use the following statement.

```
(SELECT ord_no
FROM order-items
WHERE part_no = '123-12'
UNION
SELECT ord_no
FROM order-items
WHERE part_no = '456-12')
```

Intersection:

The result of this operation is the set of rows common to two tables. It obviously applies only to tables containing identical columns. You can think of this operation as performing two separate selection operations, each resulting in a table, and then choosing the rows which appear in both. Rows which appear in only one of the two tables are not in the result. For example, the following statement results in rows from the order-items table which contain part number 123-12 and a order quantity of greater than 100:

```
SELECT *
FROM order-items
WHERE part_no = '123-12'
AND    qty > 100
```

Difference:

This operation also operates on two tables containing identical columns. It results in all rows in the first table which do not appear in the second table. A trivial example is to find all order-items rows which do not contain the part_no 123-12, written in SQL as:

```
SELECT *
FROM order-items
WHERE part_no != '123-12'
```

A more complex example involving two tables from our example database uses the SQL *not exists* comparison operation. For example, to obtain order numbers of all orders which do not contain a part with the part description of widgets, we use the statement:

```
SELECT ord_no
FROM order-items
WHERE NOT EXISTS
     ( SELECT *
       FROM parts
       WHERE parts.part_no = order-items.part_no
       AND    part_desc = 'widgets*' )
```

The first conceptual table is the entire order-items table, and the second table is one containing only those order-items which contain a part with the part description of 'widgets'. What the operation does is take the difference between the first and the second in that order. Note that the order of the tables is vital; the difference between the second and first table does not yield the same result. The not exists comparison operator is discussed in more detail in Chapter 4.

Division:

This operation is best illustrated by an example. Consider the list of all order numbers for orders which contain at least all of those parts contained in order number 1234. We need to examine the problem in three steps.

1. Get a table of all parts in order number 1234.

2. Arrange the order-items table into several smaller tables, each containing the rows for one order number.

3. The ***division*** then consists of comparing the set of part numbers from the table in step 1 with the set of part numbers in each table in step 2. The quotient contains the order number from those tables from step 2 which contain at least the part numbers from the table from step 1.

Many products do not support this operation directly in their implementation of SQL. A close SQL equivalent to perform this operation looks rather involved. It is shown next for interested readers.

```
SELECT DISTINCT ord_no
FROM order-items o1                      {for each order number
WHERE NOT EXISTS
   (SELECT *
   FROM order-items o2
   WHERE ord_no = 1234                   {select all records for 1234
   AND NOT EXISTS
      (SELECT *
      FROM order-items o3
      WHERE o3.ord_no = o1.ord_no        {restrict to current order number
      AND    o3.part_no = o2.part_no ))  {part # as in above selection
```

2.5 Conclusions

In this chapter we introduced in an informal manner the basic concepts underlying relational database management systems. One of the most important discussions in this chapter was the data normalization concepts. These concepts are useful whether or not you use a relational DBMS. They deal with decomposing data to remove redundancy, a desirable objective of any database design. Using normalization techniques requires a good under-standing of the data and business requirements and may appear to be a tedious process. It does, however, pay for itself in achieving a flexible database design requiring minimum application coding to maintain its consistency.

An understanding of the relational concepts can be very helpful when selecting a DBMS product for your application. It provides you with a product-independent way of expressing the types of operations your application might need. If you depend on the features supported by only the product you already know, you might simply miss some application requirement which cannot be easily expressed in the product you know.

Of course, if you are only dealing with a private database which is not shared by any other users, you could simply ignore all this theoretical jargon and build your application any way you choose. Keep in mind though that you might be painting yourself into a corner if you completely ignore the flexibility achieved by normalizing your data. Unnormalized data needs rather more work to update than is really necessary.

3

Why Use a DBMS?

This chapter concentrates on the advantages of using a DBMS over a normal file storage mechanism. With non-DBMS storage mechanisms, you choose the physical format of fields in a record. You must then develop your own access methods, which means that your programs change every time the physical storage format changes. DBMSs hide such physical details from programmers and users.

While managing data storage and access is its major function, a DBMS provides many more facilities useful for developing an application. These integrated facilities are a major reason for the productivity gains claimed by users of these products. They provide mechanisms for you to develop consistent user interfaces which make your applications easy to learn and use. The common UNIX facilities cannot provide the consistency as they do not use common data storage or user interface principles.

This chapter discusses two major facets of database management systems:

- Data Control facilities, which provide independence from physical storage mechanisms. They also include tools for access security management, concurrency control, and maintaining data integrity. These facilities help you to define and maintain the logical consistency of data and avoid corruption. They also provide recovery mechanisms to overcome hardware failures which are beyond software control.

- Utility packages, which are application building blocks based on the data control mechanisms. They speed the development of forms based data entry and retrieval functions as well as report generation. Additional development facilities include fourth generation languages and interfaces for third generation programming languages such as C and COBOL.

3.1 Data Control

Data control facilities are one of the major reasons for using a DBMS. Without a DBMS, you have to incorporate the functions discussed next into each individual program. In this section, we examine the components needed to provide central data description and their effect on data management. We establish generic terms to describe the types and scope of these facilities as a common ground for discussions of specific products later in this book. The first time these terms appear in this chapter, they are printed in ***bold italics***.

3.1.1 Data Dictionary

The data dictionary, also called a ***database schema***, is a central description of the structure of the data you store in the database. All utilities use this dictionary to determine where and how data is stored. A data dictionary therefore contains a description of each table and each field comprising the record.

For each table, it might contain information such as the number of records expected, descriptions of who can access data in the table, and the types of operations allowed. It also contains information on the size of a record and which operating system files or disks contain the data. For large databases, it will describe the disk volumes used. It can also contain descriptions of which fields are key fields — that is, have indexes.

For each field, the data dictionary contains description of the data type of the field, who has access to the field, and the type of access allowed. In some case, it also defines restrictions on the field data such as a value cannot be null or that value must be unique.

The main purpose of the information in a data dictionary is to hide details of physical storage from developers and end-users. It also enforces storage format consistency, so that you cannot write an incorrectly formatted record and thus corrupt the database. A data dictionary is more than just documentation of file formats as most facilities offered by a DBMS depend on this information for their operation.

3.1.2 Data Types

Data types describe the contents of a field in a database. Data types supported by a DBMS let you avoid specifying trivial processing details and validation rules common to the type of data. For example, on fields of type ***date,*** you need not check for the correct number of days in a given month. Most products support a range of machine-independent data types which aid portability of your application. There are two major reasons why the supported range is important in a database management system:

- It limits the types of information you can store easily. For example, if a data type of ***money*** does not exist, you have to use an alternative data type, say an integer. In this case, you have to explicitly provide the decimal point every time you display or print this field.

- It limits how you can manipulate the data. For example, if a data type of date is not supported, you cannot search for customer orders in the last five days in a straight-forward manner.

Let us look at the data types needed to make development simpler by letting the database management system do more work. We classify them into two groups: essential and useful. The data types in the second group are variations of the basic types included in the first group. So, you can construct them with some work in your application programs using the essential data types.

Integer:

This type is similar to those provided in most programming languages and is useful for any data where you keep a number, for example employee age, part quantity and so on. You may want to control the disk storage space it requires if you can specify either a *small integer* or a *large integer*.

Floating Point:

This type corresponds to its namesake provided in most programming languages. It is generally a binary fraction in two parts: the mantissa holds the significant digits and the exponent holds the multiplier value for the mantissa. It is useful for data items which cover a very wide range of values, for example dimensional values in an engineering database. You should be careful in using this type since the least significant digits are rounded during mathematical operations on values close to the limit of its range. It is not suitable for describing money values where accurate mathematical results are important. Its value range can be limited if you have *small floating point* and *large floating point* definitions, which also determine its disk space usage.

Decimal:

This type is provided only by some programming languages such as COBOL. It differs from floating point data types in that its value is always correct to the least significant digit after mathematical operations. On machines which do not provide decimal mathematical operations in its instruction set, this type uses integer data types with an implied decimal point according to your specification. The DBMS performs the necessary operations to display the decimal point at its correct position. This type is suitable for storing money values.

Money:

This data type is a variation of the decimal type. Its additional features include display of an appropriate currency symbol. The DBMS should provide the means for you to define the symbol appropriate to the currency you use. Some products limit you to either the U.S. "$" or the U.K. "£" symbols, or the accuracy to two decimal places.

Date:

This data type usually uses the Gregorian calendar used in the west. These are three part dates with components of day, month, and year. All DBMSs store it in Julian date format in an integer field. Three common display formats of date components are North American (month/day/year), European (day/month/year), and international (year/month/day). You can specify mathematical operations such as subtracting two dates to get number of days, or adding a number of days to a date on fields of this type. There may be limitations on the range of dates you can specify; for example, the product may not support a date beyond the year 2000. Such limitations are only important if your application deals with dates that far in the future, for example a system supporting trading of futures markets.

Some applications deal only with months in a year or years only, which would require support of a two part (month/year) or one part (year) date. A few products, such as INGRES, support such formats. With other products, your programs must perform the necessary conversions.

Time:

Time can be three parts, hour, minutes, and seconds, or two parts, hour and minutes only. Either of these formats are usually sufficient for an application data type. You may be able to present time as a 24-hour clock or 12-hour AM and PM format. Other forms of time specification such as morning, afternoon, or time units such as quarter-hour are rarely supported. Of course, you can program your own conversions.

String:

This data type is suitable for describing alphanumeric text — for example, company name and address fields. They may be stored in *fixed length* format on disk, or *variable length* format. Fixed length descriptions always occupy the same amount of space whether or not the field contains that much data. This data type is frequently the culprit for wasted disk space in a database if used for fields such as comments where the actual amount of data varies widely between field occurrences. Variable length formats economize disk space usage by only storing the amount of data actually contained in the field, or if no data exists, using a minimum amount of space.

Note that the C language character data type is inherently fixed length. When you declare a variable as char[100], it occupies 100 bytes even if the actual data is two characters. When you write such a variable to a file as a field, your program has to decide whether to write all 100 characters, or only its current length. If you write the current length, you have to figure out a way to read back from the file the same number of characters. In a DBMS variable length string, such processing is done for you.

Autoincrement Numeric:

This type is useful for generating sequential numbers – for example, invoice numbers. The amount of increment may be customizable.

Bit Map:

You might use this type to store graphical information, such as an image digitized using a scanner. Without this data type, you would have to store such information as a nondatabase file. Note that if the DBMS does not provide a utility for graphical editing of such data, you have to supply your own editing utility. Most commercially available graphics editing tools probably operate on separate operating system files. Such information must be stored in a variable length format as its size may vary widely.

Telephone Numbers:

Very few products support this data type directly as no mathematical operations apply to it. The number of digits in this type would also differ in geographical areas. You have to implement it using the format enforcement rules provided by DBMS utilities.

Postal Area Identification:

This is another data type useful in limited contexts. Its size and contents differ between countries; for example, U.S. format is five digits but Canadian format is six alphanumeric characters.

Personal Identification:

This type might define items meaningful within a country, for example social security numbers in the U.S. or National Health numbers in the U.K. They would be used typically in applications involving personnel information, banking, and insurance.

Constructed Data Types:

Secondary data types can be constructed from the essential data types by applying format and validation criteria. This means that you have to define the basic data type, format, and validation restrictions on every occurrence of the field. DBMS products do not provide a facility to construct your own data types. In some products, you can define restrictions only in a standard utility such as a forms driver, which means that data added by other means is not checked for validity. Ideally, all values written to field data types should be checked regardless of the method used to write the value.

With all of these trivialities taken care of, you might wonder why a DBMS does not simply build your application! Perhaps future tools will. In the mean time, DBMS tools are just a first step towards future applications.

3.1.3 Management of Data Storage

An important feature of a database management system is that it hides machine-dependent restrictions from you. You need not concern yourself with machine characteristics such as whether an integer is a two byte (16 bit) value or a one word (32 bit) value. You simply use the machine-independent data types supported by the DBMS. You need not worry about alignment of consecutive data fields in a record, such as filler space to align an integer to a word boundary. The DBMS aligns data as appropriate to your machine and maintains it. You need to worry about such issues only when accessing data with a third generation programming language such as C.

Another advantage of a DBMS is that it can store data internally in a different format from that presented to users. For example, a date might be stored internally as Julian date, to allow mathematical operations on it, but presented to users as day, month, and year. Similarly, the order of fields within a record need not be the order in which you retrieve them from the database. You need not read an entire record, if you only want some of the fields from the record. If new fields are added to a table, in most cases, your existing programs need not change. Thus, a DBMS provides data independence.

When adding or deleting records, you no longer worry about whether to add at the end of the file or reuse space created by a deleted record. The DBMS manages record storage, reuse of free space created by deletions, and sequencing of records within a file. It also provides methods for accessing records faster than by sequentially examining each record. We discuss the access methods in use in Section 3.1.4.

It also hides from you access to a physical disk needed for accessing operating system files and records within the file. Whether each table is a separate file or several tables stored in one file is only of concern to database administrators. Other users, even programmers, need not know the correspondence between their view of tables and fields and operating system storage entities. With a relational DBMS, you see data as stored in fields, fields grouped into records, and records of the same type grouped into a table. You simply specify the fields you require from a database table. Thus, a database management system provides physical independence. In Part 2 of this book, we discuss how the UNIX operating system helps in some of these facilities.

Although the DBMS stores records in no particular order, you can direct it to sort them into a particular order through *clustering*. You might cluster data in a table to improve the speed in sequential access, since more than one record is retrieved with one disk access. *Intrafile* clustering arranges records in a table sorted in the order specified. Clearly data can be clustered in only one sequence at any time: If you cluster on the employee's last name, it cannot be stored in zip code order as well.

Interfile clustering stores related records from more than one table close to each other. It is most useful where data from these tables is frequently accessed together, for example customer order and order items tables are most often accessed together. Note that inserting new records, except at the end of clustered data, requires significant shuffling of data in the table. Therefore, it should be used on data which is static and does not change frequently.

Simultaneous access to a database by several users is inherently tricky. For example, an order entry clerk might think that an item is in stock while another clerk is in the process of updating it for a different order. To prevent mishaps due to such *concurrent access,* a DBMS uses *locks* on data being updated. Locks can be applied to simple transactions, which involve changes to a single record; or to complex transactions, which involve changes to several records in one or more tables. We detail the problems of controlling concurrent access in Section 3.1.7. Realize that such problems do not occur at all on single user systems such as MS-DOS or even OS/2 which is multitasking but designed for single user operation. Multiuser operating systems like UNIX have to provide services to support DBMS locking facilities. We will examine such UNIX services in Chapter 5.

Some older products avoided the concurrency control problems by using a single *server* program to manage all accesses to the database. When you specify access via a program or a DBMS utility, your request is communicated to this server. The server manages a queue of requests from all concurrent users but processes only one user's request at a time. This method is called *single threading* of database transactions. Its main advantage is that two users cannot interfere with each other's data partway through an update.

A product implementing *multithreading* method of processing transactions allows several programs to access the database simultaneously. Products implementing this method use concurrency control mechanisms detailed in Section 3.1.7.

Don't confuse this terminology with a single process server or multiple servers. Products such as SYBASE have a single process server which implements the multithreading method. Other products such as INGRES implement multithreading by using several server processes. The net effect of either architecture is the same: a multithreaded DBMS. We will discuss process architectures in more detail in Chapter 5.

3.1.4 Access Methods

Sequential access — that is, reading every record — is a common way of accessing data. But this method requires you to read many records to find the ones you want. It is quite fast when your file only contains a few records, say less than 300. To reduce the number of records you have to read before selecting the one you need, you might sort the data based on some field. You must then sort every time you add new records, which is a time consuming process. When your database contains more than this small number of records, you need methods which are faster than the sequential method for accessing data.

Database management systems provide several methods for selecting specific records based on *key* fields. Unlike the *key attributes* we discussed in the last chapter, a key field, in this context, is any field or group of fields on which you might base your search. For example, you might choose an employee based on the last name field, or a group of employees based on a salary range. Key attributes are *primary* keys since they are the most frequent basis for access. Primary keys must uniquely identify each record in a table, a restriction also applied to key attributes in relational theory. Other key fields are called *secondary* keys: these need not be unique in a table.

Indexing methods are applied to key fields for fast access using a search condition. The common indexing methods in use are hashing and B-tree indexes. We look at the peculiarities of each of these that make them suitable in different contexts in an informal manner. Realize, though, that a user or a programmer is rarely aware of the internal workings of indexing schemes. The higher level DBMS interfaces hide such details.

Hash Index:

The technique of hashing involves applying an algorithm to the required key value yielding a number called the hash key. This hash key is used as an index into a table (the hash table) which contains the address of the matching record. Figure 3-1 shows an example of a hash table. Clearly, hash table entries do not maintain keys in any particular sequence.

The hash key is not always unique since the hash table is smaller than the possible number of values of a key. When two keys yield the same hash key, there is a conflict for the hash table slot. Realize that conflicts can occur with disparate key values. Such conflict is resolved with an alternative placement method, such as simply using the next empty entry in the table with the original slot indicating the new position (chaining), or using a secondary hash table or an overflow area. Chaining is the most common conflict resolution method used.

As more items are entered into the hash table, conflicts occur more frequently and chains get longer. Clearly, longer chains degrade access speed since the access routine must follow each chain rather than immediately finding the record address. Increasing the size of the hash table causes the hash algorithm to spread the index values to fit the new size, thus reducing the number of conflicts. A good hash algorithm will achieve approximately 50% occupancy of the hash table before the conflict level gets severe enough to affect performance.

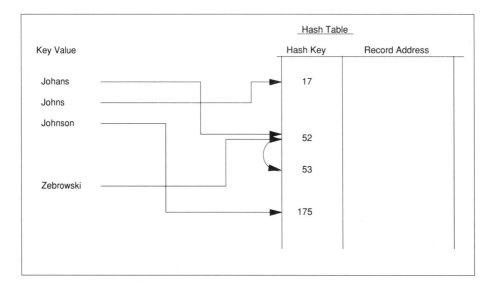

Figure 3-1 Example of a Hash Table

This technique allows very fast access to a record, but you must specify the exact key value. Without an exact key value, the hash algorithm calculations cannot yield the appropriate hash table index. You could not use this access method to find partial matches, for example, all employees whose name start with an "S." It is best suited to types of data where you would know the entire key value, such as order numbers and employee numbers. You could use a hash method on string fields such as employee names, but you must then specify the name exactly matching the spelling and punctuation as entered into the database. Even a slight spelling change will alter the value yielded by the hash algorithm.

B-Tree Index:

B-tree access method uses a **binary-chop** search technique and therefore sorts the key values into either ascending or descending order. In its simplest form, it chops the sorted range of key values into two halves and compares the required key to determine which half to search further. Successive divisions continue until it finds the required key.

Obviously the access routine cannot read all key values into a memory table, especially for a large number of records. Keys are therefore organized into a tree structure with root and branch nodes, as illustrated in Figure 3-2. The root node has exactly two branch nodes and each branch node may in turn have two branches; hence it is called a **binary tree**.

Notice that only a leaf contains the address of the matching record. The root and each branch node contains a key value which divides the range of actual key values into two equal halves. Search for a given key then consists of following appropriate branches starting from the root node, which is equivalent to dividing the range of keys into two halves. The search is complete when a leaf is reached. If this leaf value matches the required key, the record is found; otherwise, the search is considered unsuccessful.

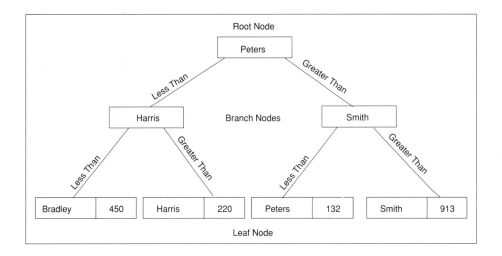

Figure 3-2 B-Tree Structure

The construction of nodes and the conditions for their creation differ between products. However, for disk access efficiency, a node usually contains several keys rather than one key per node as shown in our example. For maximum search efficiency, the tree is organized such that the distance between the root and any leaf is the same; that is, the tree is **balanced**. Balanced trees ensure that the search time for any key is predictable. Search time using an unbalanced tree is unpredictable, as some leaf nodes may be farther from the root than others.

This method is significantly faster than a sequential search as it does not examine every record. Since it maintains keys in a sorted order, you can use it to select records based on a partial key value or a range of values. In case of a partial key value, such as names starting with "S," the index allows you to select the first value which matches the specified portion of the key. Other matching records are simply the keys following the matched value in the index. Keep in mind that the index maintains only the keys in sorted order. Unless data in the file is clustered in the same order, records themselves are in no particular order.

Sometimes you need to access a particular set of records in sequence — for example, to send mail to all customers in a particular city. You want to select the first customer in the required city, then sequentially access other customers in that city. Such **indexed sequential** access is possible with a B-tree index on the city field of the table, but not with a hash index. Although access using a B-tree is not as fast as using hash indexes, its versatility has made it a popular access method.

3.1.5 User Views

You can consider user views to be windows into the database. They allow you to define **virtual** tables based on the data items in the database. They are commonly used to restrict the data a particular group of users are allowed to see. For example, a department manager's view of personnel data contains records for employees only in that department. This view is actually based on a database table containing data on all employees of the company, but the *view* restricts what each manager sees to a single department.

A view can span more than one database table or other views. For example, a view might combine address information from the customer table with the customer orders table, so that the user is not aware of two separate tables. Views can also contain virtual fields, whose values are calculated from other fields. For example, a view of customer orders might contain a total order value field which is the sum of values of individual items ordered. Such a view would not include the order items table records directly.

If a view excludes key attributes from a table, the DBMS may restrict add, update, and delete operations based on the view. In other cases, it might enforce restrictions specified in the view definition. For example, suppose a view restricted sales representatives to their assigned customer accounts. A sales representative could not alter data on another's accounts. If a view defined access only to customers with a specified credit line, you could only alter a customer's credit line within this restriction. You would have to give new customers a credit line within the limit.

Views mainly present data in a group meaningful to its target users, even if all the data items in the view do not reside in a single table. You can use views to exclude sensitive information, such as salaries in a personnel application. However, it is not intended as an access security control mechanism.

3.1.6 Access Security Control

Database management systems provide mechanisms for you to control who can access which data and which operations they are allowed to perform. These controls can be specified and altered without affecting application programs. In non-DBMS applications, you would build such controls into each application program.

Most DBMSs use some method of user identification as the basis of access security controls. They may require you to identify yourself at the start of a session possibly together with a password or they may use operating system mechanisms to obtain user identification. This type of control is the first level of access control. Other levels from which you might access application data and facilities are application menus and query language for ad hoc access. Some products allow you to control access from these levels as well. At menu level, you might specify which menu items are permitted to a user. If access to a menu item is denied, the user will not be able to execute that operation.

A common implementation is to control access to data. Such controls involve specifying which operations (add, update, read, or delete) a user is permitted on which data. For example, a user might be allowed read access to all data but denied delete access to the entire database. A DBMS might provide access controls on individual fields, tables, or the entire database.

Access controls on data items cannot depend on their contents. For example, you cannot specify controls such that a department manager can access salary data for employees in that department. You have to use views to impose such a restriction, with no access controls on the salary field.

Access controls are obeyed regardless of which DBMS utility you use. The restrictions might confuse users who have different access permissions but use a common program. For example, if user A has update access, program P allows updates to this data by user A. If user B does not have update access, program P will reject updates by user B.

Some DBMS products use passwords to control access instead of *user ids*. In this method, anyone supplying the appropriate password gains access to the data. You would then distribute the password only to those users who need access to controlled data. This method is useful in situations where you only need to control access to very few data items. You have to watch out for proliferating passwords which would be a nightmare to control. Realize that once a password is distributed to users, you have no control over any leaks.

3.1.7 Concurrency Control

Concurrency in a database environment means more than one user can access and manipulate data at the same time. Concurrent processing only occurs on multiuser operating systems such as UNIX; it cannot occur on single user operating systems such as MS-DOS or OS/2. To understand the potential havoc which needs to be prevented, let us consider the stock control application example illustrated in Figure 3-3.

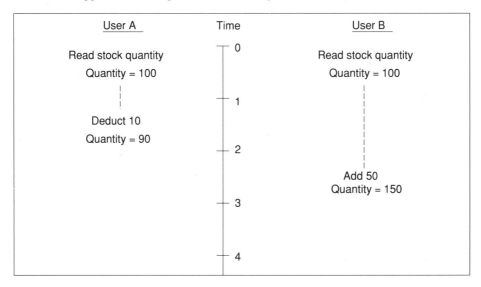

Figure 3-3 Example of a Concurrency Problem

Suppose, users A and B both read the current quantity in stock, say a value of 100, for some item. User A decides to subtract 10 from stock for shipment, and updates the quantity in stock (now 90). User B receives a delivery from the supplier for 50 units and thus adds 50 to the previously read value of 100; result: 150 items. We have mysteriously gained 10 items in stock which really don't exist! The quantity in stock is now 150 instead of the correct value of 140. This problem could be eliminated if one of these users had completed the update before the next was allowed to read. The order of the individual update is irrelevant as long as the result is correct.

Controlling concurrent access while making each user appear to be the only one accessing the database is the challenge faced by concurrency control mechanisms. In traditional application environments, concurrency issues were controlled by simply restricting concurrent updates, or by locking entire files during an update. Thus, only one update could take place at any time, even if two users wanted to update unrelated records.

Most commercial products implement locks for concurrency control at one or more of the following levels:

- *Database level:* that is, the entire database is locked and becomes unavailable to other users. Although the database would only be locked for the small period of time taken by an update, it causes unnecessary annoyance for other users. It thus has limited application such as during a backup of the entire database.

- *Table level:* that is, the table containing the particular record is locked. All records in this table become unavailable. This type of a lock is useful for performing bulk updates, such as increase price of all parts by 5%.

- *Block level or page level:* that is, the block containing the particular record is locked. Any other records in the same block become unavailable. Since records in a table are not in any particular order, such a lock can prevent access to disparate records. The disruptive effect of this type of lock is negligible if a record occupies the entire block.

- *Record level:* that is, only the particular record is locked. Other records are available to other users. A record level lock is the most commonly implemented type. It does impose an overhead at runtime if several records are involved in an update.

- *Field level:* that is, only the particular field in the record is locked. Other fields in that record are available as are other records in the database. A field level lock is useful when most updates affect only one or two fields in a record, the remainder of the record is static. For example, in a stock control application, the quantity of items in stock changes very frequently, but item descriptions are rarely updated.

Some products practice *lock promotion* when the number of locks reaches a certain threshold. Lock promotion simply increases the lock level to the next higher level lock to reduce the number of locks it must track; for example, record level locks might be promoted to a single table level lock. Since large number of record locks consume resources and can degrade performance, this strategy is reasonable. However, you would do better to delay the processing of transactions that cause lock promotion to off-peak hours.

So far we have only discussed locks preventing all access to locked items. There is no reason, however, to prevent a user from reading a record if the user who locked it does not intend to update. Thus we can have two types of locks: *shared* and *exclusive*. Do not be confused by products which use the term exclusive even though they do not prevent other users from reading an exclusively locked record.

In theoretical terms, the different types of locks implement *levels of isolation* between separate transactions on the database. Levels of isolation define the amount of interference one transaction can tolerate from other transactions. We discuss four levels of isolation: *dirty read*, *committed read*, *cursor stability*, and *repeatable read*. Some products have explicit statements for levels of isolation control, others require you to specify the type of lock to apply which in turn defines the level of isolation.

A dirty read is reading a record when an update may be in progress. The data is not guaranteed consistent. In its worst form, the data in the record is changing but the data you read does not show all of the changes. A typical use for this level of isolation is for producing reports, where you take a snapshot of the data and changes applied after you read are irrelevant as far as the report is concerned. A dirty read occurs when some user has a shared lock on the record you accessed. This level of isolation is the default in products which implement only shared locks but have no concept of exclusive locks.

A committed read guarantees that no updates are in progress at the time of reading; that is, no other user has a shared lock on the data. This level of isolation is the default with many products. This level is necessary for you to be sure that data you read does not change. Obtaining a shared lock prevents other users from updating until you release the lock, but it does not prevent them from reading. An exclusive lock cannot be used, as it would prevent others from reading the locked data.

The cursor stability level of isolation guarantees that when you have selected a set of records, the record you are currently accessing does not change. This type is particularly suited to cases where you can only view one record from the selected set at a time. For example, you select all employees from department A, but your screen form can only display information on one employee at a time. You can achieve this level using an exclusive lock on the current record. Note that records other than your current record in the selected set may change at any time. Thus, if you update a record and later view it again, another user might have changed the data.

The repeatable read level of isolation guarantees that other users cannot change any record in the selected set until you complete your updates on all records. In this case, you can read a record as many times as you wish within the transaction; the data will be identical. You achieve this level of isolation with a combination of shared and exclusive locks. All records in the selected set are locked with a shared lock, so other users can read them but cannot update. You apply an exclusive lock only to the record currently being updated, to prevent others from reading partially updated data.

Level of Isolation	Locks Needed
Dirty Read	No locks
Committed Read	Shared lock
Cursor Stability	Exclusive lock only on current record.
Repeatable Read	Shared lock on selected set of records and Exclusive lock on current record.

Table 3-1 Locks to Achieve Each Level of Isolation

In most products, your interface to concurrency control mechanisms is at a higher level than described here. For simple transactions involving one record you may have to request locks explicitly and then release them. In complex transactions, you would use transaction level controls discussed next. In some products you simply set the required level of isolation and reset it at the end of your transaction.

3.1.8 Transaction Control and Recovery

A transaction is a logical group of tasks which you think of as a single unit of work. If all tasks are not completed together, the different data items involved would not be consistent with each other. For example, consider an education database consisting of information about instructors who teach courses. Changing an instructor from one course to another involves two tasks: one to add a new record for the new course-instructor pair and another to remove the instructor as teaching the old course. If you successfully added the new record but failed to remove the old course-instructor pair, the database would be inconsistent. Worse yet, another user may access the instructor information before the second task is done and find the instructor teaching two courses! The update must be completed as a single transaction.

Most products provide transaction control mechanisms with *start transaction* and *end transaction* statements to mark the transaction boundary. Within these delimiters you can perform several tasks using appropriate concurrency control mechanisms. If all tasks in the transaction are successful, the end transaction statement commits the updates to the database. Data in the database is not changed until the transaction is complete, thus preventing other users viewing partially updated data. If any of the tasks fails, you have the option to *roll back* tasks already completed in the transaction without affecting the consistency of the database.

If you lock several items in a transaction, beware of potential *deadlocks.* To understand deadlock situations, let us consider another simple case. Suppose two concurrent transactions (1 and 2) both require access to records A and B. Transaction 1 locks record A, performs some processing, and then tries to lock record B. In the meantime, transaction 2 has already locked record B and now tries to lock record A. Both transactions cannot proceed further; that is, a deadlock has occurred. In practice, the deadlock condition can be very complex as you will find discussed in theoretical texts listed in the bibliography.

Many products attempt to detect possible deadlocks and try to resolve them by temporarily rolling back one of the transactions. You can help avoid deadlocks by developing transactions which all access common records in a particular order. In our example, if transaction 2 had tried locking record A first, it would not have proceeded further and deadlock would have been avoided. Alternatively, you can roll back transactions and release all locks whenever a lock request fails rather than wait for the lock.

Transaction based operations in some products depend on a *journal* or a *transaction log* facility. This facility logs every task within a transaction to a designated file. You must enable this facility if you wish to use transaction operations such as rollback. The log might also serve as an incremental backup of updates to the database, so you can recover the database up to the last committed transaction. Recovering from a log is sometimes called transaction *rollforward*.

A transaction log might contain any two of the following types of information about the data updated: a *before* image, an *after* image and an *update* description. Any two of these items provide sufficient information to roll back from a transaction, or to roll forward.

In addition to these items, there may also be *checkpoint* facilities which provide a synchronization point. They are useful for recovering from a system failure which did not affect the database storage. Checkpoint records contain status information on all transactions in progress at the time of failure, so recovery mechanisms know which transaction to undo and which ones to redo.

Keep in mind that transaction logging means every update is written twice: once to the log file and then to the database itself. Thus, the facility exacts considerable performance penalties, although its advantage of up-to-the-minute data recovery usually makes it worthwhile.

3.1.9 Data Integrity Controls

Data integrity controls are rules for maintaining consistency of data which are logically obvious to us. For example, in the parts supplier database, a supplier cannot supply a part that does not exist in the parts table. There may be other constraints on the values that data items can take. DBMSs provide many facilities to enforce such consistency rules, in some instances independent of application programs.

The simplest integrity rule is that primary key fields cannot take null values, also known as the *entity integrity* rule. This restriction is obvious when you consider the basic tenet of relational theory that a key attribute must uniquely identify the record. If key attributes take null values, the DBMS cannot satisfy this requirement. You can generalize this requirement to other fields based on the requirements of your application. Fields needing such a restriction should be obvious; for example, a customer order must have a non-null customer number even though this is not the key attribute.

The *referential integrity* rule involves pairs of relations where the value of a field in one table (*foreign* key) depends on the primary key values of the other. An example of its use is you cannot create an order for a customer not listed in the customer table. The foreign key, customer number, in the orders table depends on the primary key customer number in the customer table. In most products, you have to enforce this rule through *lookup* facilities in the standard utilities, although a few products enforce it at the database level.

You can also specify more complex integrity rules for fields including valid value ranges, and format restrictions peculiar to the data. For example, a part number rule might be that it must have the first three characters alpha followed by six numeric digits. These rules are sometimes specified as attributes of a field, or defined in standard utilities as data validation rules. Ideally, they would be enforced at the database level for consistent use throughout the application rather than at the individual utility level. The following are some of the commonly supported validation criteria.

Range Check:

On numeric fields this check allows you to define absolute value ranges, such as > 100, or between 100 and 1000. On string fields, it is of dubious benefit, as the range comparisons are based on ASCII sequences. For example, suppose we wanted to restrict a string field of customer numbers to two alpha characters followed by four numeric digits with a range check of between "AA0000" and "ZZ9999." An invalid customer number of "AAA001" will be accepted as valid.

List of Valid Values:

You should be able to specify a list of valid values together with a range check. This type of check is most useful for string fields where you can enumerate all the valid values. For example, a color field can take values "Red," "Green," "Blue." All other values are invalid. If you are allowed to combine this check with a range check, you can specify comprehensive checks on numeric fields.

Required Entry:

This check actually enforces the entity integrity rule at the data entry level. Its purpose is to force a value to be entered so that the field will not be null.

Lookup in Other Table:

This check allows you to enforce the referential integrity rule by checking a given value for existence in another table. When you specify this in a data entry utility, you may also be able to extract data from fields in the other table if a match is found. Such a facility is useful to save typing in data entry programs; for example, given a customer number in order entry, you can extract the customer name and address from the customer table.

Double Entry Verification:

This type of check is sometimes used to prevent errors due to transposing characters. It requires the same data to be entered twice, the two entries compared, and if they match exactly, data is considered valid. For rapid data entry applications, this check is really only useful if performed by two separate people. If one person has to enter data twice, possibly on one field at a time, data entry speed suffers significantly.

Field Format Enforcement:

On many fields, you cannot specify any of the preceding checks, but you can define format rules peculiar to your application. For example, a part must have two digits in the range 11-99, then a "-", followed by four alpha characters excluding punctuation and space characters. A format for a numeric field could specify leading zeros or some other characters. You can specify such format rules in most products.

3.2 Utility Packages

Most DBMS products provide an integrated set of application development tools. Using these tools has two major benefits:

- They speed development of the bulk of your application; that is, they are productivity improvement aids.

- They allow you to build consistent user interfaces which help users to understand and learn your application quickly.

In fact, many small applications can be developed without any third generation language programming. You could develop prototypes during the analysis and design phases using these tools.

The main purpose of this section is to establish terms which describe the generic features of each utility. These terms are used as a common base for discussions of specific products later in the book. We also discuss how these tools use the Data Control mechanisms described in Section 3.1 for providing interactive forms-based interfaces, ad hoc data access, and report generation capabilities. This section examines how these tools allow you to maintain your applications with minimum effort.

3.2.1 Menu Generation Utilities

A DBMS includes a utility to generate a menu interface for your application. This utility consists of a menu definition and a menu driver program. The *menu definition program* is a form-based data entry and inquiry program which allows you to define menu titles, selection items, and associate programs to execute when a selection item is chosen. A menu is a tree structure with a root menu and branches which may be program selection or other menus. Each menu in turn consists of further branches. Your menu definitions are stored into a menu database, sometimes in the same structure as an application database.

The *menu driver* reads the definition database and displays menus and selections to the user. The user can then choose a selection item, which causes a new menu to be displayed, or causes execution of the associated program. You can change the definition or restructure the menu tree at any time without any effect on application programs. There are two types of menu displays in common use: a full-screen menu and a ring menu.

A sample full-screen menu is illustrated in Figure 3-4. Selections in this type of a menu may be arranged in a single column, if there are only a few items, or in two columns. You choose a selection either by using the highlight or by typing the selection number associated. Some utilities also associate a short mnemonic, such as the program or menu name, with each selection for use in an expert mode. Expert users can directly execute a selection even

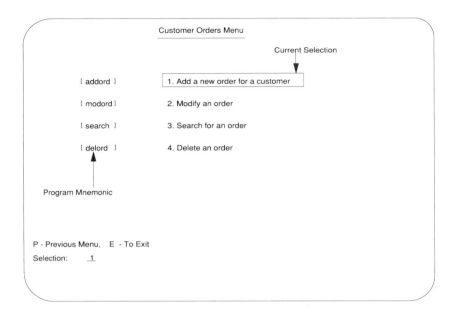

Figure 3-4 A Sample Full-Screen Menu

if the selection is not on the current menu display. The utility may allow you to define help messages or screens with menus and each selection items, which you access with some keyword. Special commands, such as help, refresh, previous menu, and exit, may be activated by either function keys, control sequences, or keywords. The menu driver usually has a system display indicating these commands.

A ring menu, as shown in Figure 3-5, occupies only the top portion of the screen, usually only the top two lines. One line displays short mnemonics indicating selection items, the second line giving a longer explanation of the currently highlighted selection. This metaphor was popularized by the PC based LOTUS 1-2-3 spreadsheet program. You choose a selection using either the highlight or typing the first character of a unique mnemonic. The highlight moves from item to item, until it circles from the last menu item back to the first item, hence its name "ring menu."

The advantage of a ring menu is that the remainder of the screen is free for use by the selected program, rather than the menu disappearing when the program starts as in the full-screen menu. If the program also uses a similar menu for its commands, the screen redisplay is a smooth process. In this type of menu, special commands such as help and exit are normally included as selection items. Otherwise, a separate display line indicates the function keys or control sequences to activate these commands.

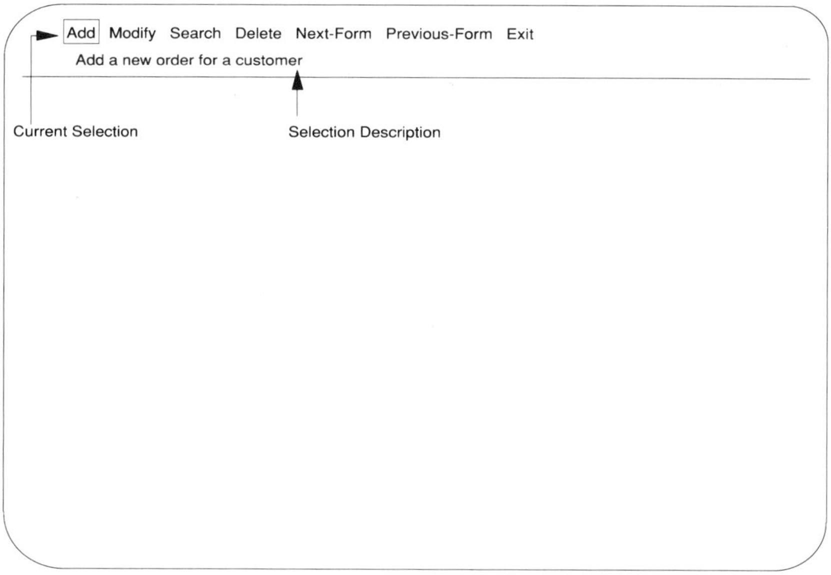

Figure 3-5 A Sample Ring Menu

3.2.2 Screen Form Utilities

Screen form utilities supplied with the DBMS allow you to generate and use forms for data entry and query of data in the database. Thus, you can avoid writing third generation language programs for straightforward data entry and maintenance tasks. You define data validation criteria and associate form fields with database fields with these utilities.

There are two parts to these utilities: a *forms definition* component and a *forms driver* component. Forms can be generated in default format from one or more tables from the database. Default layout varies between products but you can customize the layout and add validation criteria using the forms definition component. Custom form definition utilities can work in two ways: compiled from a text file or a screen-based special purpose editor.

Compilation-type utilities require you to create the form description using a standard operating system text editor, preferably a screen-based editor. They usually use a special purpose language for describing the layout of the screen, associating form fields with database fields, specifying display formats of each field including video attributes and data validation criteria. You can define the sequence of the cursor movement between fields through special commands. You compile the completed definition file before using it with the forms driver. Errors flagged by the compiler must be corrected.

Special purpose editors allow you paint the layout of the form. They might use windows to display forms for defining display formats, specifying data validation criteria, and associating form fields with database fields. You can also define the cursor movement sequence between fields on the painted form. The advantage of this type is that you see the

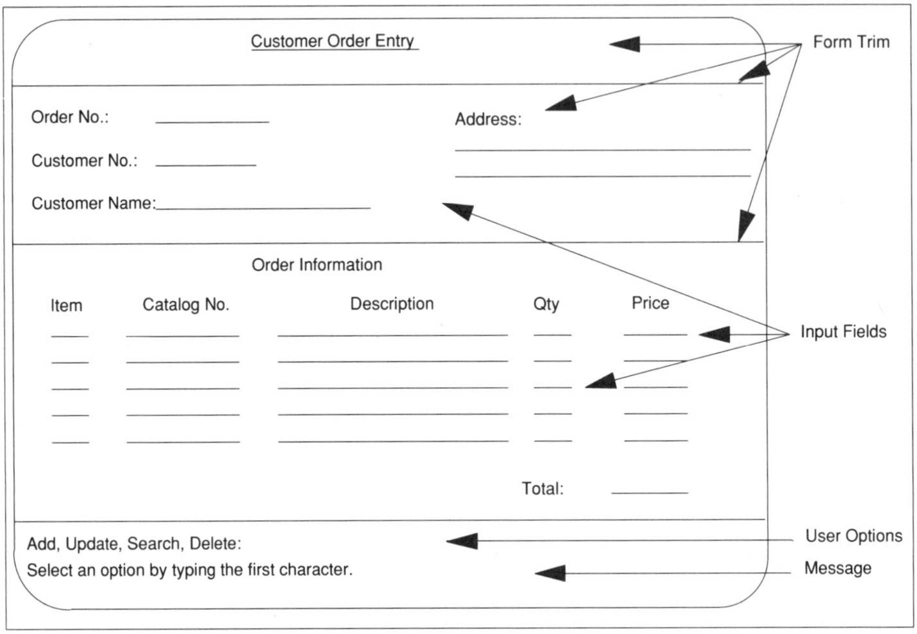

Figure 3-6 Components of a Screen Form

form as it would appear in the final application. The editors access the data dictionary to verify your field definitions as you paint fields on screen. The basic features offered by forms definition utilities are

- Layout and description of the form components as illustrated in Figure 3-6.
- Field display characteristics, including video attributes, size, and special characters such as currency symbols.
- Association between form fields and database fields.
- Data validation criteria discussed in Section 3.1.9.
- Sequence of cursor movement among fields, for data entry.
- Comments, error, and help messages associated with form fields.

A forms driver uses forms definitions to present the form to users and control their actions during data entry and inquiry operations. The basic commands offered by a forms driver are:

- *Add:* This is the basic data entry mode; all data is checked according to the validation criteria specified in the form definition.

- *Inquire:* Simple queries — that is, involving only fields contained in the form — can be performed with this mode. You can type selection criteria such as value ranges for numeric fields, and wildcard characters in character fields. A logical AND relationship is assumed between each selection criteria, so the results will match all criteria.

- *Browse:* This operation allows you to step through the results of an inquiry forward and backward.

- *Update:* In this operation, you first display the required record using the inquire and browse operations. Then, you can change the displayed data. As in the add operation, all data validation criteria are enforced.

- *Delete:* This operation allows you to delete records, usually in only one table at a time.

Some products provide additional facilities and hence additional commands. Multiple screen definitions need commands to flip between forms. Multiple table forms need commands to allow you to select the table to work with. They may provide control points for customization, where you can attach your own functions to perform tasks not available in the standard forms driver.

Forms drivers provide facilities to aid data entry which we call *field editing criteria*.

Case Control:

These facilities causes alphabetic data to be changed into a specified upper or lower case. They are useful to defeat problems caused by case-sensitive text data.

Default Value:

This is sometimes specified as a data integrity criterion. It is very useful to reduce operator keystrokes in data entry. If a field cannot be null, you might want to specify a default value; for example, order date field default could be the keyword "today."

Field Format:

This facility reformats field data in a specified format on behalf of the user. For example, you might type a date as a string of six digits (say 111188), and it might be redisplayed with day, month, and four-digit year separated by dashes (11-11-1988).

Field Display Attributes:

Some products require you to define a video attribute, such as reverse video or underline, as a separate command rather than when you paint the form.

Justification:

You might want trimming of leading spaces to left justify a string or numeric field, or remove trailing spaces to right justify. The user does not have to type data properly justified if this facility is available.

Field Padding:

You may specify pad characters to put leading zeros (or some other character) in a numeric field.

3.2.3 Report Generation Utilities

An important part of any application is the reports it must produce. For this purpose, DBMSs provide report generation utilities suitable for quickly developing many types of reports. These utilities use a fixed execution cycle, similar to languages such as RPGII, consisting of three basic components: page layout specification, data extraction, and data formatting. Most products use their query language to extract the data for the report.

Figure 3-7 illustrates the typical report components including report title, page headers and footers, column titles, data rows containing field values, and totals at various levels. Report generators can easily format such reports, as well as some unusual ones such as form letters.

Reports scripts are a text file containing commands for each component. You may need to compile these scripts in some products. The report generator executes these commands to produce the report. Consider the fixed execution cycle as a loop which processes one record at a time as illustrated in Figure 3-8. Processed before the beginning of the loop are page layout specification and data extraction commands. There are exception points in the cycle triggered by page size controls and also any data grouping that you specify. You can define and use variables with a report script as well as mathematical functions for performing calculations. We discuss the types of facilities available in report generators, although you can add new facilities through the hooks provided to attach functions written with the host language interface.

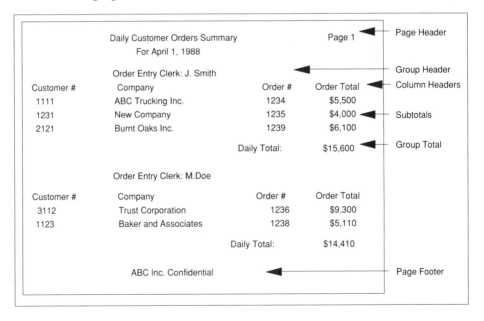

Figure 3-7 Components of a Report

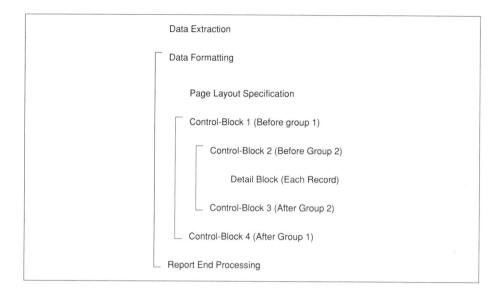

Figure 3-8 Typical Execution Cycle of a Report Generator

Page Size Control:

These facilities allow to you specify the width and length of the report page, so you can size the page to fit either an 80 column, 24 line screen or a 132 column, 60 line printer paper. You can also define left, right, top, and bottom margins for the page.

Page Layout:

These facilities include formatting specifications for page header and footer blocks to print page titles and footnote text, which will be repeated on every page. You can print report distribution and requestor information using an exception control block before start of the report, sometimes called first page header. Commands to start a new page unconditionally or based on number of lines remaining in the current page are also available.

Line Format Control:

Within each report line, you can specify the start column position for each item, or the number of spaces from the end of the last item. You can leave blank lines using skip commands. Some products provide default formatting which prints every data item on a new line. A few products provide facilities for formatting columnar data.

Field Format Control:

These facilities allow you to print field data in a specific format. You can trim trailing spaces in string fields and concatenate these fields with others or with literals. Numeric fields can be aligned left, right or on decimal point and you can specify their print format, often using specifications similar to the ***printf*** function in the C language.

Data Control:

Defining which data to extract from the database is often done using statements in the query language supported by the DBMS. The most common language is SQL, which also allows you to extract from multiple tables with a join and sort the data into a specified order. With other query languages, the report generator provides a sort mechanism. Sorting the data is important to allow you to use control blocks described next.

Control Blocks:

You specify special processing at group level in these control blocks. You associate a block with each field value group; for example, department and project groups. Consider each group as nested loops, with the outermost being the entire report, and each group nested within each other in order of their sorting. An innermost group processes each record. These are useful for printing group title, signaling the start of a new page, say for every project, or performing group totals at the end of every group. Control blocks are available before the start of a group and after the end of a group. Note that groups, and hence control blocks, depend on the fields used as keys in the sort option. The execution sequence follows the sort sequence. Thus, if you sort by department number and project numbers within it, the department group processing is the outer loop, the project group processing the inner loop.

Conditional Branch:

You have facilities to test and conditionally perform some actions, usually with an if-then-else statement.

Loop Control:

Within a processing block, you can construct your own loops using FORTRAN-like for-do loops to loop a fixed number of times, or using a while condition. Note that data used within a loop can only come from a single data record. Loops usually cannot span processing blocks.

Internal Variables:

These variables are declared for each report script. They usually follow the data types supported by the DBMS product. You may have to declare their type explicitly or imply it by initializing them. You can use these variables for any operations within the report.

Date and Time Functions:

Special functions allow you to format dates into any common layout composed of numeric day, month, and year values. You can also print alphabetic names or abbreviations for day of the week, and month name. Special keywords, such as today, help to make the report script readable.

Group Calculations:

Several supplied functions operate on groups of data. Typical functions are: count (number of records), total, average, minimum, and maximum calculations. Some products depend on query language facilities for obtaining such results.

Runtime Interaction:

Some products allow you to pass parameters to the script at run time, which may be used for data selection criteria or other purposes. Others provide an interface to a forms driver utility to obtain runtime parameters. They may also provide commands to prompt the user for parameters, and scrolling control for reports displayed on screen.

Output Control:

Using these facilities, you can redirect report output to the print spooler, or an operating system file, or into another program for further processing.

3.2.4 Ad Hoc Query Facilities

This facility is the main source of improved productivity in application development as well as in a production environment. It allows you to extract data from the database without writing a program. It consists of a simple nonprocedural command language, a *query language*, that you use to specify the fields to extract together with any selection conditions. The language is usually based on the relational operators we discussed in Chapter 2. SQL is the commonly implemented query language in many products. It deserves a detailed discussion which we cover in the next chapter.

Relational query languages always work on *sets* of data rather than one record at a time. For example, you can give all employees a 5% raise with a single statement. This set oriented operation makes their operation very powerful while keeping the syntax simpler than a programming language. The nonprocedural nature of relational languages means that you need not specify a navigation path through the database. For example, you need not define which access method to use when reading a table, and how to match field values from multiple tables. You simply list the fields you require, the tables (or views) they belong to, and conditions for their selection such as "salary > 10000." The query execution system will determine the best access path and method to use in extracting the results.

They often provide facilities to sort and group the data before presenting you with the results, and perform group calculation functions such as count records in the result, total or average on a field. Other functions to calculate minimum and maximum values are also provided. Some products provide an optimizing tool which lets you view the selected path for resolving the query and reword your statements for improved execution.

Although most products provide interactive query language facilities, you can save a script of statements for repeated use. Typically, you use a text editor to create and edit a query script in an ordinary text file. You can run saved scripts in a batch mode or execute them interactively. Most implementations of query languages operate only on one statement at a time without carrying over the results for a further query. Some products allow you to save results in a temporary table, or a set, which can then be used as part of the subsequent query. Temporary tables disappear when you end the interactive session.

3.2.5 Host Language Interface

Many early database systems had only programming languages and query languages as interfaces to the data. They did not have facilities such as form generation and report generation which are an integral part of a modern DBMS. These modern facilities allow you to quickly develop application components such as data entry, update, retrieval, and report generation which form the bulk of a typical application. However, they do not cater to any unusual tasks specific to an application. For example, consider a form where you want to display several records from one table. Most forms drivers limit you to displaying one record at a time in a form. To develop such a complex form, you might need to write a program using a host language interface.

Host language interfaces provide a high level interface to the data, so you do not need detailed knowledge of the database storage structures. You can also use this interface to customize the standard utilities supplied in a product with your own functions. There are two types of interface in common use: function call based, and embedded query language.

A *function call based* interface consists of a library of functions which you call directly from a third generation programming language. Variables are passed as arguments to these functions to receive data and to write information to the database. Modern interfaces also provide functions for screen form handling and report generation. Data access functions include all facilities we discussed in the data control section, such as access security control, concurrency control with locks, and transaction processing. High level data selection and extraction routines reduce the need for directly specifying access paths and indexes. This type of interface is more difficult to use well than the embedded query language interface. Since it provides greater control over program execution, you can tune your programs for high performance systems.

An **embedded query language** interface lets you use the familiar query language statements directly in the program. You can associate program variables with field names used in the statements to exchange data between the program and the database. Looping mechanisms allow you to process data one record at a time even though the query language is set oriented. A preprocessor, supplied with the product, converts the embedded query language statements into appropriate function calls prior to compilation. This type of interface makes program maintenance easier because data access code is much easier to read and understand. Productivity improvements are gained because less training is needed for using the query language than for the function call based interface.

There are three classes of facilities provided by a host language interface: data access and control, user interaction control, and utility functions. **Data access** functions allow you to exchange data items with the database independent of the storage order. Access methods may be totally transparent as in embedded query language interfaces, or you can choose the level of transparency as in function call-based interfaces.

You have to use the data types of the programming language which correspond to the database data types for program variables. For this reason, you need to understand the internal storage format for the database data types, such as, date values are stored in Julian date format. **Data control** functions might also include transaction level operations such as start and end transaction facilities, data locking facilities for concurrency control, and in some products, data definition facilities to manipulate the database structure.

User interaction control includes form manipulation facilities such as exchanging data between form fields and program buffers or database fields. You can display and clear forms on a user screen, control the movement of the cursor between fields, and provide commands for user actions. You can control the display of prompts, help, and error messages to users with custom programming of data validation or use facilities supplied by the product. Report formatting functions are also included, either in the form of interfaces to the report generator or for custom programming.

Utility functions allow you to manipulate data formats used internally by the database; for example, functions to perform mathematical operations on date data types, conversion between data types such as date to ASCII text, and in some products, validation checking on data. If the interface does not provide forms handling functions, it may include other lower level screen manipulation functions.

3.2.6 Fourth Generation Languages

The term *language* is a misnomer for fourth generation facilities, as it implies procedural definition in the data processing context. Unfortunately, fourth generation systems are not as clearly defined as their third generation language counterparts. However, the aims of fourth generation systems are clear: improved development productivity and improved ease of use for application users. Commercial products use widely varying techniques and syntax to achieve these goals.

First of all, understand that fourth generation systems are targeted at commercial data processing applications. They are not suitable for systems programming work such as operating system or compiler development. At least in the UNIX environment, they are unsuitable for applications requiring time-critical operation, such as process control in manufacturing, or performance critical systems which need subsecond processing in a heavy transaction volume environment. We discuss the reasons for this restriction in connection with the UNIX operating system in Part 2 of this book.

Fourth generation systems aim to reduce the effort required to develop day-to-day information storage and retrieval applications. They generally cater to typical tasks in such applications, rather than providing a comprehensive range of development facilities. Their facilities reflect tasks which are the bulk of the development effort, such as forms based data entry and inquiry, and report production. Although their eventual goal is to be so easy to use that nontechnical users can use them with minimum training, they currently require technical background as a prerequisite in their use.

Fourth generation languages consist of two major components: procedural and nonprocedural. Procedural components are basically a sequence of instructions which you write in a high level language, each of which corresponds to several statements in a third generation programming language. These components are associated with appropriate nonprocedural components in an application.

Consider nonprocedural components to be *events* which trigger procedural code sections. Events might be caused by user actions or database access mechanisms. The typical events supported are: forms display, initial cursor entry into a field, cursor exit from a field, during data entry in a field, user request to start inquiry, add, update, or delete operations, retrieval of data records, and writing of records to the database. Ideally, you could also define events that relate to data items, such as a field reaching a threshold value. SYBASE is the only product which currently allows such user defined events.

Additional facilities allow you to link forms together in some sequence for a multiform program, and develop forms for help and error messages. Note that forms need not occupy the entire screen, and so can be overlapped for a windowing effect. Whenever you do not attach procedural code with an event, default actions are executed. Data validation criteria are defined separately in a fourth generation definition utility. Thus, you can easily get a mismatch of validation criteria between this utility and other data manipulation utilities. Avoiding such mismatches is the reason why database level definition of these criteria is vital.

The development environment of fourth generation systems may itself work in a similar manner to the applications you develop. Thus, it may consist of nonprocedural components to develop forms and report layouts and to develop code for each event and compile it. It should let you test an incomplete program, say consisting only of a form and some event processing code. Many of the products allow you to do so.

Fourth generation programs which associate procedural code to a specific form can be considered *frame-based* systems, where a frame consists of one form definition and all of its associated procedural code. Other products use the conceptual layout of a third generation program for their fourth generation programs. Such a program then has a *main* function, subsidiary functions as needed, and possibly special purpose functions for *reports* and individual event processing. However, the breakdown of functions is up to individual programmers, and thus you have to set coding standards for program maintainability. Frame based systems also use a function per form but the development environment enforces the correlation between forms and procedures making maintenance simpler.

In some products, the fourth generation system might be simply a combination of the individual forms facilities and report generation facilities we discussed in earlier sections. The method of linking all of these together is generally a high level language which allows you freedom from the concerns typical in a third generation program development. Data manipulation is typically done using the set oriented query language, form layout with a special purpose forms editor. Report layout should be done with a report editor, and report format definition with a similar language to the report generator.

Many products achieve this effect by linking forms driver facilities with separate programs running the report generation portion. The difference between fourth generation systems and combined stand-alone utilities is the way data is passed between them. In fourth generation systems, sets of data pass directly between the components, whereas stand-alone utilities must use the database as the medium.

3.3 Conclusions

Modern DBMS systems offer facilities which can significantly reduce the effort involved in developing information processing applications. They provide extensive data storage and management facilities which help to make application programs independent of the physical structures and location of data items. The security control mechanisms are no longer built individually into programs, but are applied in a consistent manner independent of programs. Most important of all, their concurrency control mechanisms allow several users to share data at the same time without worrying about problems such as lost or erroneous updates which corrupt the database.

Typical data entry and retrieval operations necessary for maintenance of data can be developed very quickly using the utilities provided. However, these utilities cannot cater to every need of applications; they focus on typical tasks only. Host language interfaces and fourth generation systems step in where the standard utilities cannot perform a task. You can customize standard utilities, including forms drivers and report generators, with additional functions using the host language interface.

One of the most important benefits of using the facilities of a DBMS is the reduction in the effort of maintaining and enhancing the application. Since applications change and evolve at a rapid pace in commercial operations, you can be more responsive to the needs of users. Applications built with a DBMS also offer portability across hardware systems in the UNIX environment, and in many cases across operating systems as well. However, portability does not extend between the DBMS products; thus changing from one product to another requires almost as much effort as developing the application from the start. These products provide independence from hardware and in some cases from operating systems, which is certainly a step in the right direction for the future.

4

The SQL Query Language

In this chapter, we discuss a popular query language, SQL. It deserves a detailed discussion as all products described in this book support this query language. It has become a de facto standard which is an essential first step towards future data sharing amongst disparate products. This trend is reinforced by the American National Standards Institute's (ANSI) activities to define an SQL standard in the U.S.

The implementation of SQL in most products differs slightly from each other. So, there are many *dialects* of the language, though the differences between the dialects are trivial compared to those between proprietary query languages. Hopefully, these trivial differences will disappear as more vendors of UNIX DBMS products abandon their isolationist policies and interface to their competitors' products. Then applications developed with disparate products can live in one environment just like one big happy family!

This chapter concentrates on the basic principles of the language without going into an academic discussion of its structure. We lay the groundwork for later chapters which discuss how specific implementations in commercial products differ from the features described here. The features discussed are

- The data definition statements of SQL, which allow you to define the structure and the data in your application database.

- The data manipulation statements, which you use to add, update, delete, and extract data. We devote a separate section to a discussion of the flexibility and power of the data extraction statement.

- Vendor specific extensions to the basic language, why they are needed, and the types of tasks supported by such extensions.

- Embedded SQL in third generation programming languages for data access, and how its implementations can differ between vendors.

4.1 Why Is SQL Important?

SQL has become important because many disparate relational database products support it under different operating system environments. Its popular acceptance leads to benefits similar to those gained from third generation programming languages such as COBOL and FORTRAN in the early days of computing. These benefits include

- Availability of skills that are transferable from one product to another.

- Reduced effort for retraining staff when changing from one product to another.

- Increased portability of your application programs between products.

- Increased possibility of shared data between applications implemented with disparate DBMS products.

Like many relational query languages, SQL is a *set oriented* language rather than *record oriented* like the early nonrelational query languages. You specify operations on a set of records which can encompass an entire table, or any number of records that satisfy a specified condition. For example, you can increase, by 5%, the credit line of all customers with a current credit line of under $1,000 in a single statement. You do not need to specify how to navigate between records which satisfy the selection condition, as required by record oriented languages.

```
UPDATE customer
SET    cust-credit = cust-credit * 1.05
WHERE  cust-credit < 1000;
```

This set oriented approach means that you do not specify the data manipulation operations with step-by-step, or procedural, instructions. Instead, your instructions are a nonprocedural description of the required task. You thus concentrate on *what* the task should do rather than *how* it should be performed.

Customer Table

cust-num	cust-name	cust-credit
1234	ABC Inc.	5000
1453	All Hardware	900
1675	Supplies Unlimited	800

cust-order Table

order-num	cust-num	order-date
1001	1234	12-5-87
1050	1453	1- 1-88
1006	1675	11- 5-87

order-item table

order-num	item-num	catalog-num	qty	price
1001	3	123-11	10	1210.00
1001	1	123-23	50	2512.50
1001	2	145-34	5	11.25
1006	1	167-11	10	100.00
1050	1	176-55	10	100.00

Figure 4-1 Sample Customer Orders Database

The query language processor determines the best access method for selecting the required records and applying the required change to the fields specified. It uses available indexes to speed the search, or in some cases, it may build indexes on intermediate data. You do not need to specify which index should be used; in fact you need not be aware of the existence of any indexes.

There are two basic classes of the SQL query language statements: data definition and data manipulation. We discuss these statements in the sections that follow. Figure 4-1 shows a sample customer orders database. Examples in this chapter will illustrate how you can manipulate this database using SQL statements.

4.2 The SQL Data Definition Language

The data definition statements allow you to define the structure of the application database. It allows you to create, modify, and delete data dictionary entities: attributes that apply to the database such as its name, tables in the database, fields in each table, indexes on fields, and user views.

4.2.1 Database Definition

The statements relating to the database itself are usually very specific to a particular product and operating system. The common facilities provided by the *create database* statement include naming the application database and defining its ownership. Other facilities such as defining the operating system files available for its use, or the directories where the files reside, vary amongst products and operating systems. The *drop database* statement deletes the entire database including its contents and frees the operating system disk resources for other uses.

4.2.2 Table Definition

Create Table:

The *create table* statement allows you to create a new table in an existing database at any time. The basic format of this statement is

```
CREATE TABLE table-name
    (field-1-definition (, field-2-definition, ...) );
```

The *table-name* must be unique within the database. The specific syntax of a field definition varies between products depending on the naming conventions of data types supported. A typical field definition contains:

```
field-name  data-type [NOT NULL]
```

Field-name must be unique within a single table, but you can repeat it in a different table in the same database. Repeating field-names is a good idea if the data in these fields has exactly the same meaning. However, using the same name to represent different data in more than one table only confuses users. For example, it is confusing to use a field-name of date in more than one table referring to two different types of dates, such as order date and shipping date.

The *not null* option allows you to differentiate between a field value of no data — that is, an empty field, and a field containing zeros or blanks. This facility is necessary for defining *entity integrity* restrictions which we discussed in the previous chapter. Fields with *null* values are ignored in arithmetic operations. For example, a *total* operation on such a field includes only the *non-null* data, *even if the data is zeros*. In a match operation on a field which can take *null* values, such fields may be excluded from the result.

Alter Table:

The *alter table* statement allows you to add or drop fields from a specified table, and to change the data type of a field. A typical syntax of this statement is

```
ALTER TABLE table-name
    ADD field-name data-type ;
```

In some products, the change affects only the table description in the data dictionary at the time of executing this statement. The next operation involving this field causes its creation. Other products implement this facility with a combination of create, copy, delete, and rename operations. Such products perform these operations at the time of executing the alter table statement. Watch out for potential database corruption if you neglect to provide sufficient spare disk space for such products!

Drop Table:

The *drop table* statement deletes the table definition and all data contained in it. In addition, it might automatically delete any indexes and user views associated with this table.

```
DROP TABLE table-name ;
```

4.2.3 Index Definition

Create Index:

The typical syntax for creating indexes is

```
CREATE [ UNIQUE ] INDEX index-name ON table-name
    (field-1 [Ascending [ or Descending ] order ]
    [, field-2 [Ascending [ or Descending ] order ] ...
    [ CLUSTER ];
```

Indexes can encompass either individual fields or a combination of fields. Fields combined in an index need not be consecutively placed within the record. They can be different data types and fixed length or variable length. However, you cannot combine fields from more than one table in one index. In our customer orders database, we may create an index on the customer name (variable length field) and credit line (money field) as follows:

```
CREATE INDEX custcred ON customer
    (cust-name ASC,
     cust-credit ASC) ;
```

You can build as many indexes on fields in a single table as you need, but think about their effect on performance. The DBMS has to update each index every time you add, delete, or update a record. You can include one field in more than one index where its order could be different from that in another index.

For example, we might have a second index on customer number and customer name fields as follows:

```
CREATE INDEX cust ON customer
   (cust-num ASC,
    cust-name DESC) ;
```

The *cluster* option indicates that data in the table should be clustered to obtain *intrafile* clustering discussed in Chapter 3. Not all products support this facility and those that do support it may have a slightly different manner of defining it.

The option *unique* defines that the field or combination of fields always have unique values within a table. Thus, if we use this option in our *custcred* index definition, we specify that each combination of cust-name and cust-credit values will exist at most once in the table. This option is useful mainly for an index on the primary key of a table.

Drop Index:

You can delete an index at any time using the *drop index* command:

```
DROP INDEX index-name ;
```

In SQL, create and drop index commands are your only way to reference indexes. Other commands do not refer to them directly. The query processor determines which indexes are relevant for a particular query. In products which precompile SQL commands, creating or dropping indexes causes a command to be recompiled. Interpretive products always determine which indexes to use each time they execute a command.

4.2.4 View Definition

Create View:

A *view* looks just like a table to the user; however, the process of creating it is different from that of a table. You create a view using a data retrieval statement:

```
CREATE VIEW view-name AS
   SELECT  statement ;
```

The *select* statement can be as complex as you need to describe each field in the view. Fields in the view can be fields taken directly from one or more tables. They can also be *virtual* fields which are calculated from table fields using the available arithmetic functions. Virtual fields could also define a portion of the values possible in an underlying table field. In our customer orders database, we might define a view which includes only customers who have a credit line of under $1,000 as follows:

```
CREATE VIEW new-cust AS
   SELECT  cust-num, cust-name
   FROM    customer
   WHERE   cust-credit < 1000 ;
```

When you use this view, the only customers you could access are those with a credit line of under $1000. You use the view name in place of the table name to access data through the view. We discuss the select statement in more detail in Section 4.3. Note that a view need not include every field from the underlying table. You can thus restrict what data a user sees using a view. You can also define a view in terms of other views.

Drop View:

You can create and *drop views* at any time. The syntax for dropping a view is similar to that of dropping a table.

```
DROP VIEW view-name ;
```

When you drop an underlying table, all views which use the table are automatically dropped. Note that if you alter the underlying table by adding new fields or changing the data type of fields on which the view is based, the view may not be affected. It is affected if the change in data type invalidates a condition specified in the *where* clause, or if you deleted a field which was part of the view definition.

4.3 The SQL Retrieval Statement

The SQL select statement provides powerful data retrieval facilities. You can retrieve data from one or more tables and specify selection conditions using comparative operators. You can join tables and then project fields from them.

```
SELECT [ DISTINCT ] field-1 [, field-2 ...]
FROM    table-1 [, table-2 ...]
[ WHERE clause ]
[ GROUP BY field-1 [, field-2 ...] [ HAVING clause ] ]
[ ORDER BY field-1 [, field-2 ...] ;
```

4.3.1 Single Table Queries

A simple example of a query in our customer orders database might be to retrieve customer numbers of all customers who have placed an order:

```
SELECT cust-num
FROM   cust-order ;
```

Result:

```
cust-num
1234
1234
1453
1675
```

The *distinct* option in the select statement suppresses duplicate rows in the result. In this example, it would suppress duplicate customer numbers. You can use a wildcard *asterisk* character if you wish to retrieve all fields in the specified tables. To retrieve specific fields, you must list the name of each field required. You can include expressions instead of a field. For example, we list catalog numbers from the order-item table together with their actual unit price with the following statement:

```
SELECT catalog-num, price / qty
FROM   order-item ;
```

Result:

```
catalog-num    --------
     123-11       12.10
     123-23       50.25
     145-34        2.25
     167-11       10.00
     176-55       10.00
```

Expressions can involve any field in the table referenced, or can be simply literal strings. Literal strings will simply be printed on every line in the result. You can use the normal arithmetic operators, such as * (multiplication), / (division), - (subtraction), and + (addition), with parenthesis to define the order of evaluation if required.

The Where Clause:

The where clause in a simple query specifies any conditions which the resulting data must satisfy. For example, to list customers who have a credit line of less than $1,000, we use

```
SELECT  cust-num
FROM    customer
WHERE   cust-credit < 1000 ;
```

Some simple comparison operators available are < (less than), > (greater than), = (equal to), <= (less than or equal), >= (greater than or equal). Boolean operators such as AND, OR, and NOT can be combined with the comparison operators. You can include parenthesis to define the order of evaluation. More operators for use in a where clause are described in Section 4.3.3.

The Group By Clause:

The *group by* clause allows the results to be grouped on the basis of values in a field. For example, to list order totals for each order in our customer orders database, we use the statement:

```
SELECT    order-num, SUM(price)
FROM      order-item
GROUP BY order-num ;
```

Note that specifying the group by clause does not affect the data in the table; the grouping applies only to the results. We also used a built-in function of the SQL language, *sum*, to obtain total of the price field. Without the group by clause, the sum function would have totalled prices for all orders.

Using the group by clause, our results are

```
order-num   --------
     1001   3733.75
     1050    100.00
     1006    100.00
```

The Order By Clause:

Did you notice the sequence of order numbers in the result? You must use the *order by* clause if you want *any* specific ordering. In the preceding example, you would sort the order numbers into ascending order as follows:

```
SELECT    order-num, SUM(price)
FROM      order-item
GROUP BY order-num
ORDER BY order-num ASC ;
```

You can use the order by clause in any statement whether or not it includes the group by clause.

Group Calculations:

You can perform some calculation on grouped values by combining the group by clause with a built-in function. Built-in functions usually exclude null values in fields in their calculations. You can use the distinct option to eliminate redundant duplicate rows. Other built-in functions, in addition to the sum function just used, are

- COUNT: To count number of values of a field. Specifying count(*) counts all records including duplicate rows and null values.

- AVG: To calculate the average value of a field.

- MAX: To calculate the maximum value of a field.

- MIN: To calculate the minimum value of a field.

4.3.2 Multitable Queries

Joining Tables:

Retrieval of data from more than one table involves the relational join operation discussed in Chapter 2. You specify a join on equivalent fields in separate tables. These fields should logically contain the same data, although products insist only on equivalent data types. You use the where clause to specify the fields to join. For example, to retrieve order information for a given customer by joining the cust-order and order-item tables, we use

```
SELECT cust-num, order-date, item-num, qty
FROM   cust-order, order-item
WHERE  cust-order.order-num = order-item.order-num
AND    cust-num = 1234 ;
```

The where clause, in this example, specifies the join condition that values in the order-num field of the cust-order table should match those of the order-num field of the order-item table. Note that we had to define which table the order-num field belongs in since we used the same field name in both the cust-order and order-item tables. The where clause also specifies a selection condition to restrict the results for a single customer.

Result:

```
cust-num     order-date   item-num      qty
    1234       12-5-87          3         10
    1234       12-5-87          1         50
    1234       12-5-87          2          5
```

Note that the items in the order are in no particular sequence, which you may remedy by using the order by clause. You can join any number of tables, theoretically, although most products have a limit for technical reasons. The where clause must specify each join condition. For example, to retrieve customer names in addition to the order information retrieved by the preceding query, we write

```
SELECT cust-order.cust-num, cust-name, order-date,
       item-num, qty
FROM   cust-order, customer, order-item
WHERE  cust-order.order-num = order-item.order-num
AND    cust-order.cust-num = 1234
AND    cust-order.cust-num = customer.cust-num ;
```

Note that we have to add table name qualification to the ***cust-num*** field since its name is ambiguous between the cust-order and customer table. The result of this query is

```
cust-num      cust-name     order-date    item-num    qty
    1234      ABC Inc.      12-5-87              3      10
    1234      ABC Inc.      12-5-87              1      50
    1234      ABC Inc.      12-5-87              2       5
```

An equivalence join condition between separate tables is the most common type of join. You can specify other comparison operators in a join, although their use is uncommon.

Self-Join and Aliases:

Another common type is joining a table to itself, sometimes called a ***self-join***. For example, we might list all catalog numbers which appear in more than one order as follows:

```
SELECT DISTINCT one.catalog-num
FROM    order-item one, order-item two
WHERE   one.catalog-num = two.catalog-num
AND     one.order-num ~= two.order-num ;
```

The second condition in the where clause ensures that we do not select a catalog number which only appears in one order. A more practical example of a self-join would count the number of orders in which each catalog number appears, to report the popularity of each catalog item. You could produce such a report using the count built-in function together with the group by clause.

Note that in this example we could not use the table name to qualify ambiguous field names, since the ambiguous fields belong in the same actual table. Instead, we assign two distinct ***aliases: one*** and ***two***, to the table to disambiguate the field names. Aliases are named in the ***from*** clause as shown in the example. They provide temporary table names for the duration of the query with no effect on the underlying table. You can use aliases in any query, although they are not essential in most.

4.3.3 Additional Conditional Operators

We used simple comparison operators useful for numeric comparisons in the previous example queries. There are several other special purpose operators available in a where clause for comparing character fields for partial matches, and fields containing null values.

Partial Matches:

For partial matches on character fields, you use the ***like*** operator. For example, to list all customers whose name starts with an "A," we write

```
SELECT cust-name
FROM    customer
WHERE   cust-name LIKE 'A%' ;
```

The metacharacter % (percent) in this example matches zero or more characters. So, the constant string specifies that the first character must be an *A,* followed by any number of any characters. The result of this query is

```
cust-name
ABC Inc.
All Hardware
```

You could select an exact number of characters using the _ (underscore) meta-character. For example, you might select a customer name which starts with an *A* and has exactly seven more characters with the constant string `'A_____'`. You can combine literal characters with metacharacters anywhere in the constant string. For example, to list all customers whose name contains the characters *Hardware,* the constant string `'%Hardwa-re%'`. The logical negation operator, NOT, provides the converse of a match.

Selecting Null Fields:

Fields with null values are normally excluded from the results when you specify any selection condition. You may wish to list records containing such fields, perhaps with the intention of modifying them. A special comparison operator *is null* allows you to select null value fields. For example, we list all customers with no credit line as follows

```
SELECT cust-num
FROM    customer
WHERE   cust-credit IS NULL ;
```

You can specify the converse using the phrase *is not null.* You cannot use the equality operator for finding *null* values as no value is ever *equal* to null.

Using a List of Search Values:

You can compare a field value being within a range by combining the less than and greater than operators with a Boolean AND operator. However, sometimes you need to compare with a list of values rather than a range. The *in* operator allows you to specify such a list. For example, to list customer numbers who placed an order on 12-5-87 or 11-5-87, we use the statement

```
SELECT cust-num
FROM    cust-order
WHERE   order-date IN ( 12-5-87, 11-5-87 ) ;
```

The list of values need not be fixed, as in this example. In Section 4.3.4, we see how the list of values might be retrieved from another table.

4.3.4 Nested SQL Statements

Some queries involving multiple tables do not involve a join — for example, to list customer numbers of all customers who ordered catalog number "123-11." In this query we are not interested in any fields from the order-items table in the result. We could join the two tables to obtain the result, but the following nested query is easier to understand

```
SELECT cust-num
FROM    cust-order
WHERE   order-num =
    ( SELECT order-num
      FROM    order-item
      WHERE   catalog-num = '123-11' ) ;
```

In this query, the nested part (subquery) is evaluated to provide exactly one value for the main query. Thus, the order number which includes catalog number 123-11 is found, then the customer number of the customer who ordered it. You can use the equality operator only when you know that the subquery results in exactly one value.

You can use the in operand to specify a list of comparison values. Thus, to list all customer numbers of customers who ordered more than quantity 5 of any item, we use

```
SELECT  cust-num
FROM    cust-order
WHERE   order-num IN
    ( SELECT order-num
      FROM    order-item
      WHERE   qty > 5 ) ;
```

Group calculation functions also work in a subquery. For example, to list all customers whose order quantity is more than the average order quantity, we say

```
SELECT  cust-num
FROM    cust-order
WHERE   order-num IN
    ( SELECT order-num
      FROM    order-item
      WHERE   qty >
        ( SELECT AVG(qty)
          FROM    order-item )  ) ;
```

This example illustrates how you can nest several levels of subqueries. Clearly, this nesting can accommodate very complex queries. A more readable way would simply perform each query one at a time using temporary tables to store intermediate results. However, nesting is essential with products which do not provide a temporary table facility.

The Union Operator:

The *union* operator allows you to append the results of a subquery to the main query provided the results contain the same fields. We could send back-order notices, for example, to all customers who ordered catalog number 123-11 or catalog number 123-23:

```
SELECT  cust-num
FROM    cust-order
WHERE   order-num IN
    ( SELECT order-num
      FROM    order-item
      WHERE   catalog-num = '123-11'
    UNION
      SELECT order-num
      FROM    order-item
      WHERE   catalog-num = '123-23' ) ;
```

The Exists Operator:

A where clause condition using the existential operator, EXISTS, is satisfied *if and only if* the subquery result contains at least one record. The subquery involves some field from a table referenced in the from clause of the main query. We could, for example, list those customers who have a current order:

```
SELECT  cust-name
FROM    customer c
WHERE EXISTS
    ( SELECT *
      FROM    cust-order
      WHERE   cust-num = c.cust-num );
```

The Not Exists Operator:

The converse of the *exists* operator is often useful for queries on tables where one table will not contain matching records to the other — that is, a join is not possible. For example, to list customer names of all customers who do not have an order, we write

```
SELECT cust-name
FROM    customer c
WHERE NOT EXISTS
     ( SELECT *
       FROM    cust-order
       WHERE   cust-num = c.cust-num );
```

In this example, the customer name is listed only for those customer numbers where the subquery results in an empty set. Note that we use the customer number from the main query (c.cust-num) in the where clause of the subquery.

Subquery Execution:

You can consider subqueries to be similar to a nested loop, where each record in the subquery is compared with the current record of the main query. You can, of course, nest queries several levels deep, rather than the two or three level nesting illustrated in our examples. It should be abundantly clear that each subquery is executed once for each record in the higher level query. Little imagination is needed to understand the speed implications of several levels of nesting especially when large tables are involved.

Note that some of the examples could be written using the in operator, or its negative form. In such cases, your preferences, and the readability of query, dictate the best way to write it. Depending on the implementation of the query language, one way of wording a query may perform better than other ways. A way that performs well in one product may not perform as well in other products.

4.4 The SQL Data Manipulation Language

There are four data manipulation functions provided in SQL: insert, update, delete, and retrieve. We have discussed the powerful retrieval function in Section 4.3. The three statements discussed here, *insert, update*, and *delete*, can all work on a single record or multiple records in one table. They also share the where clause and its operators described in Section 4.3.3.

Since these three statements can operate on only one table at a time, you must use other controls to maintain referential integrity between tables. We discussed some of the methods for doing this in the last chapter under "Transaction Control and Recovery." Section 4.5 illustrates how some vendors implement such mechanisms in their SQL products.

4.4.1 Data Insertion

You can insert constant values into a table using the following syntax:

```
INSERT INTO table-name [ ( field-1 [, field-2 ...] ) ]
VALUES        ( value-1 [, value-2 ...] ) ;
```

This is clearly useful only for inserting one record at a time. Some products may require you to always provide the key value first, although most do not place any restrictions on the order of the fields. Products also have minor differences such as the presentation of string constants using either single or double quotes.

A multirecord insertion requires you to use a select statement. The insertion then consists of retrieving values from one or more tables to generate the records to insert. The syntax of the statement is

```
INSERT INTO table-name [ ( field-1 [, field-2 ...] ) ]
    SELECT  statement ;
```

In our customer order database, we might have a historical summary of orders where we do not wish to keep the details of an order. Suppose we add summaries to this table periodically using the following statement:

```
INSERT INTO  hist-order  ( order-num, cust-num, order-date,
                           order-value )
    SELECT   order-item.order-num, cust-num, order-date,
                           SUM(price)
    FROM     cust-order, order-item
    WHERE    cust-order.order-num = order-item.order-num
    GROUP BY order-item.order-num ;
```

Any field in the table for which you do not specify a value, defaults to a null value. If any such field cannot take a null value — that is, defined using the not null clause of the *create table* statement — the insert operation fails.

4.4.2 Data Update

The update statement syntax is

```
UPDATE   table-name
    SET  field-1 = expression
       [, field-2 = expression ...]
[ WHERE clause ] ;
```

The *set* clause defines the fields to update and their respective values. You can use any arithmetic expression to calculate the value of a field. For example, if we wished to increase the credit line of all customers by 20%, we use the statement

```
UPDATE   customer
    SET  cust-credit = cust-credit * 1.20 ;
```

The where clause allows you to select subsets of records from a table for updating. In this clause, you can specify any selection condition including subqueries containing select statements. For example, if you only wanted to increase the credit line for customers who placed at least one order in the last 30 days, the statement is

```
UPDATE   customer
    SET  cust-credit = cust-credit * 1.20
    WHERE cust-num =
       ( SELECT DISTINCT cust-num
         FROM  cust-order
         WHERE order-date <= TODAY
         AND   order-date >= ( TODAY-30 ) );
```

You can update individual records with an appropriate where clause; for example,

```
UPDATE    customer
   SET    cust-credit = cust-credit * 1.20
   WHERE cust-num = 1234 ;
```

Note that since you update only one table at a time, you need to use transaction level concurrency control mechanisms to group logical tasks into a single update unit. You may also have to perform your own referential integrity checks if the DBMS does not provide built-in facilities to do so.

4.4.3 Data Deletion

The *delete* statement, like the other data manipulation statements, also selects records to delete using the where clause. Its syntax is

```
DELETE FROM table-name
   [ WHERE clause ] ;
```

The where clause can cause selection of individual records or a group of records. Without a where clause, this statement is at least as dangerous as the UNIX "*rm -rf* *" command, especially in products that do not prompt for confirmation! Referential integrity checks are your own problem with DBMSs that do not provide automatic facilities.

```
DELETE FROM customer
   WHERE   cust-num = 1234 ;
```

4.5 Extensions to SQL

In this section, we discuss some of the important extensions made to *standard* SQL by some of the vendors. An important point is that some of these extensions are essential in a practical application development environment. Their implementation differs from vendor to vendor in the absence of standards, and so their use could lead to extra effort in porting applications. We discuss only the concepts implemented by these extensions in this section, rather than each specific implementation. Information on specific implementation, where appropriate, is contained in chapters on products later in this book.

Transaction Controls:

Data manipulation operations, such as insert, update, and delete, are dangerous to the integrity of the database since they work on only one table at a time. You have to write multiple statements to perform a logical unit of work; that is, a complex transaction. This restriction puts the burden of maintaining referential integrity on the developer. Think about the disastrous consequences of a system crash when adding an order for a brand new customer: A crash occurring anytime between adding a customer record and the several rows of order items table leaves the database inconsistent! Although some products such as UNIFY implement their own measures for referential integrity, no product provides any explicit facilities in the query language.

You have to write SQL data manipulation statements in an appropriate order. For example, you had better delete order items and order table rows before deleting the customer row; else you might end up with orders for a *ghost* customer! Most products provide transaction level lock control mechanisms to allow treatment of multiple statements as a single unit of work.

Transaction level control mechanisms consist of a ***start transaction***, a ***commit***, and a ***rollback*** statement. Actual syntax of these statements differs in each product. The commit statement causes all operations performed since the start transaction to be applied to the database. The rollback statement allows you to abort the transaction and release any resources locked up to that point. A ***rollforward*** statement is sometimes provided to allow you to recover the database by applying the journal log to a backup.

Lock and ***unlock*** statements may be available for explicit locking of records or tables. Alternatively, the start transaction statement may require parameters to define the level of concurrency control desired. Additional statements, such as ***set isolation***, may be available to set the desired levels of isolation.

Access Security Control:

Statements to set access privileges, such as ***grant*** and ***revoke*** are provided with products that allow you to change privileges at any time. These statements require parameters to specify read, write, update, and delete privileges for each user or for groups of users. Privileges can be set at field level, table level, and at the entire database level. The exact syntax depends on the product.

Outer Join:

Another important extension, called an ***outer join***, allows the result of a join to contain records even if no match was found. The results of a normal join contain only those records which have a matching record in each of the joined tables. This facility is currently offered only by the INFORMIX-SQL and ORACLE products amongst those discussed in this book. So the details of this facility are described in Chapter 8.

Temporary Tables:

Some products allow you to implicitly create temporary tables for storage of inter-mediate data in a multistatement retrieval. Others require you to explicitly create such tables just like any permanent table with the create statement. Most products provide facilities to save the results of a query in an operating system file.

Loading and Unloading Data:

Most products provide facilities to ***unload*** (***export***) and ***load*** (***import***) data between the database and operating system files. These facilities usually operate on one table at a time. The level of validation checking, when loading data from operating system files, ranges from simple data type checking to referential integrity checking.

Interactive Help:

You need to know the names of fields and tables in the database in order to use SQL statements. So, some products provide a ***help*** statement which lists table and field names. This statement may require a table name parameter before it lists the fields in the table.

4.6 Embedded SQL Interface

Most products support SQL not only as a common interactive query language but also embedded into third generation programming languages. This embedded SQL interface is another important step towards data exchange between products in the future. At the time of writing this book, there are some minor differences among the implementations of this interface in the various products. The emerging consensus, however, appears to be compatibility with the mainframe DB2 product. Future application developers will probably be grateful for the unifying influence this IBM product appears to have on UNIX DBMS.

In this section, we briefly review the facilities that are common in the embedded SQL interfaces. We also note some of the important differences of interest to developers who are planning to port from one product to another based on the fact that both products support the *standard* (!) SQL. The ORACLE PRO*SQL and INGRES ESQL products appear to come closest to the DB2 method, although you still need to be wary of the extensions each product implements. In any embedded query language, the important areas of programming are

- *Identification of SQL statements:* The product's preprocessor needs to differentiate the embedded statements from other program statements. The common method, used by INGRES ESQL and ORACLE PRO*SQL, is to use the keywords *EXEC SQL* as a prefix to each embedded statement. INFORMIX ESQL products use a $ (dollar sign) prefix and INGRES EQUEL interfaces use ## (two hash symbols).

- *Identification of host variables:* First of all, you have to indicate which program variables you use in an SQL statement. The common method is to enclose variable declaration statements between the statements:

  ```
  EXEC SQL BEGIN DECLARE SECTION
  ....
  EXEC SQL END DECLARE SECTION
  ```
  In interfaces following other conventions, the appropriate symbol ($ or ##) is a required prefix for the declaration statements.

- *Host variables in embedded statements:* The rule of thumb is that you can use a host variable wherever you can use a constant or a literal in the SQL. For example, you could pass values for inserting a row by listing variables in the values clause of the insert statement. The SQL select statement is extended with a new clause, *into,* which allows you to list the variables receiving the result of a query.

  The common identifying prefix for variable names in an embedded statement is the : (colon symbol). Its main purpose is to distinguish between variables and database field names in the statement which might have identical spelling.

- *Common data areas:* There are two important data structures commonly used: SQLCA and SQLDA. These are provided as *include* header files such as *sqlca.h* for C. The SQLCA contains important return codes and errors from the runtime processor which are valuable for error detection. SQLDA is used internally by the runtime processor to store information such as the statement being processed.

- *Conversion from set orientation to record orientation:* SQL is a set oriented language — that is, a statement operates on sets of records. Third generation programming languages are record oriented and have no facilities to deal with multiple records at once. So, a *cursor* facility is implemented in the embedded SQL interface to convert between these two orientations.

You start by associating a select statement with a named cursor. You must *open* the cursor before any data retrieval. Then, you can define your own loop including the *fetch* statement to obtain data for further processing. *Closing* the cursor terminates the query statement.

This sequence is quite similar to the traditional file manipulation scheme, but has some important differences. The sequence in which records are presented by the fetch statement depends on the order by clause of the associated SQL statement. If no order is specified, records will be presented in a random order. You can use the full power of the select statement, including joins and projections, so that the record being retrieved might bear little resemblance to the stored information. Field order is relevant only in that it must match the order of the receiving host variables. Database field order is quite irrelevant.

Specific products might implement extensions, or have some limitations. For example, the ORACLE interface includes a very useful facility for using *arrays* to contain a set of records. So, you could retrieve several rows with a select statement into an array and process them at your program's leisure. INGRES extends the embedded interface to include forms handling commands which are prefixed by EXEC FRS keywords.

Limitations are usually temporary until the release of the product, so we won't dwell on them. The two most frustrating limitations include a lack of dynamic SQL statement composition, and limitations on backing out of a transaction. Dynamic SQL statements allow you to compose a statement as a string in a program variable, *prepare* it, and then execute it. This facility is essential if you need to dynamically choose field and table names in the statement. Transaction limitations might not undo certain operations such as table creation when you roll the transaction back. In this case, you have to remember to remove temporary tables explicitly if a transaction is aborted.

4.7 Conclusions

An important reason for SQL becoming a de facto standard is the trend for providing compatibility with mainframe products such as DB2. Such compatibility is desirable for ease of porting between DBMS products. However, many implementations under UNIX are interpretive, unlike the mainframe products which precompile query language statements. As the market pressure for higher performance increases, the interpretive implementations will offer improvements by compiling query statements.

In this chapter we have discussed the basic features of the SQL language. The language provides simple, yet powerful, nonprocedural constructs for easily performing complex searches on single tables. Multiple table searches are also easy if joins are possible between these tables. The language provides many facilities for retrieving data from tables which do not join, but these facilities are somewhat difficult to use.

The basic language supports many of the relational operators advocated by the theorists. However, there are some practical needs which are supported only by some vendors as extensions to the language. These facilities include data validation when inserting and updating data, entity and referential integrity constraints, and transaction level control mechanisms. To use SQL successfully for all development in an application, you also need the outer join facility. This facility is essential in many reporting tasks.

Keep in mind that our description of the syntax is based on the proposed standard by ANSI. There are minor differences between vendor products leading to dialects of the language. Such differences will persist amongst the vendor specific extensions, although they will disappear in other cases when standards are published. Be warned that you may not be able to distinguish the standard constructs from vendor extensions, unless the technical documentation differentiates between them.

You can teach nontechnical users to use SQL successfully for many straightforward searches on the database. Users have to know the names of fields and tables to perform any queries. They also need knowledge of data structures, such as which fields belong in which table. Further technical understanding of the language is necessary when you perform relatively complex queries. However, complex queries are infrequent; most data retrieval needs can be satisfied with straightforward queries.

Part 2

UNIX and DBMS Applications

DBMS products have to interact with the underlying operating system, in our case UNIX. They depend on the facilities provided by the operating system in their operation. The operating system influences the facilities they can offer, and the behavior of these facilities. In this part of the book, we examine those facilities of UNIX which affect the operation and behavior of a DBMS.

UNIX is a general purpose, time-sharing operating system. It tries to divide CPU time as equally as possible among the tasks in progress. It provides facilities for users to share resources and data with as few restrictions as possible. Its philosophy is based on building blocks which allow you to build your application. So, a DBMS fits easily in this philosophy as a tool to build applications. However, A DBMS is a higher level tool, which in turn uses the basic utilities provided by UNIX. Its functionality is limited by the operation of the underlying facilities.

UNIX is attractive because of its machine independence. It is not dependent on a particular manufacturer's hardware architecture. The recent trend for DBMSs has also followed this approach. DBMS products running under UNIX not only run on different hardware, they have attempted to achieve independence from operating systems as well. Such products need particular UNIX facilities in order to connect to other operating systems. The following chapters also attempt to clarify such facilities.

5

UNIX Facilities and Constraints

In this chapter, we take a brief look at the UNIX features used by DBMSs. We discuss how they may use these features rather than describe how UNIX implements them. Details of their implementation are beyond the scope of this book. Readers familiar with the issues may wish to skip to the next chapter. The topics covered are

- The process based architecture of UNIX which DBMSs use for providing multiuser capabilities such as sharing data between several users simultaneously. We also examine the implications of products offering a single process multithreading server and those offering multiple server processes.

- The choice of data storage options that determine whether the database can span more than one physical disk. This choice also affects the speed of access to the data.

- The UNIX terminal driver controls all interaction to a user. Each DBMS utility uses different facilities of this driver. We examine these facilities and their effect on what the user sees.

- The UNIX security control system may allow a user to bypass the facilities of a DBMS. You should be aware of these facilities.

- Each product's concurrency control subsystem uses UNIX facilities to implement locking mechanisms. The efficiency and the level of these mechanisms depend on the limitations of these facilities.

- Networking facilities are an essential basis for distributed databases. We look at those facilities which help in the implementation of databases distributed between UNIX machines and also to other operating systems.

- The size of the UNIX kernel buffers can affect the performance of your application. Tuning the configuration parameters that define these sizes can improve performance. However, you should consider the tradeoffs involved in tuning the kernel.

- Many tools, such as SDB and MAKE, are available for application developers. We look at which of these tools you can use in a DBMS environment.

5.1 The Process Based Architecture of UNIX

This section describes how the scheduling and swapping activities of the kernel allow multiple processes to run at the same time. Without these activities, only one user could access a database at a time. UNIX DBMSs use this capability to provide shared access to a database. However, running multiple processes divides available processor resources and is thus costly. We look at where these costs are incurred and if they affect the performance of the application.

5.1.1 Scheduling and Swapping

UNIX runs several processes concurrently by scheduling the CPU time equally between those that are ready to run. A process is simply a program during its execution. A process that is waiting for some I/O activity, such as input from the terminal, is not ready to run. The kernel may swap such a process to the swap area on disk, so it can use the freed memory for another process that is ready to run. This feature is very different from MS-DOS. MS-DOS only allows one process at a time, so it does not need scheduling or swapping facilities. OS/2 has a process based architecture similar to UNIX and hence provides similar facilities.

Swapping is essential to support more processes than the physical memory available. However, it increases the disk I/O activity as the number of processes increases, resulting in a performance degradation. Earlier versions of SYSTEM V UNIX swap the entire process to disk. BSD and SYSTEM V Release 3 support demand paging which swaps only parts (pages) of a process. Demand paging requires less disk I/O and hence is more efficient. Swapping the entire process is a strategy developed when memory was expensive.

DBMS products use several processes *per user* in their architecture. Each DBMS process can be quite large; runtime sizes of up to one megabyte are fairly common. So, you need lots of *real* memory on your machine or suffer the overheads of swapping or paging. For high performance applications, a good rule of thumb is to keep adding memory until swapping or paging activities stop.

5.1.2 User Processes

Each user logged in to the system has a command interpreter process, called SHELL, which maintains a separate runtime environment from other users. This process executes all programs run by the user. Although users have independent runtime environments, they can access the same files simultaneously or share a database. Note that UNIX does not automatically lock a file to prevent access by other users.

One of the performance bottlenecks is the number of system calls a processor can execute. System calls are requests by user processes for a kernel service consisting of privileged operations such as disk or terminal access. A **context switch** occurs at both the start and end of a system call. It involves saving and restoring the current state of the process and hence carries a small overhead. This can be a bottleneck since a processor can only perform a certain number of context switches per second and system performance degrades when requests exceed this capacity. The limit varies for different processors – a few hundred switches per second for smaller machines and a few thousand for large machines.

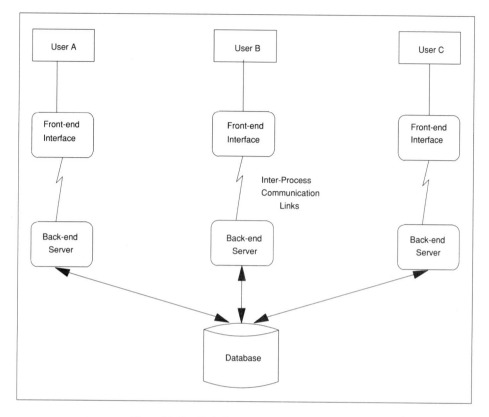

Figure 5-1 One Back-End Server per User Architecture

A process can create other processes called its ***children***. Some DBMSs use this approach to divide their processing into two parts: the front-end interface and the back-end server. A common approach is to have one back-end server process per user as shown in Figure 5-1. In this case, the back-end server is a child of the front-end interface process. It is possible to have one back-end server for each database in use, as shown in Figure 5-2. In this case, the two processes do not have a parent-child relationship.

Using two processes per user allows each one to be smaller than using a single process. This approach results in lower disk activity due to swapping, important in systems which swap an entire process. However, it has the drawback of increasing the number of processes running concurrently; that is, increasing the scheduler load.

On the other hand, the single back-end server architecture must implement its own scheduling mechanism to allow it to serve multiple front-end processes concurrently. It has to duplicate a great deal of the facilities provided by a typical multiuser system. Realize that this server is just like any other process on the machine, and hence shares the available CPU time with other processes running on the same machine. In turn, it divides its time between

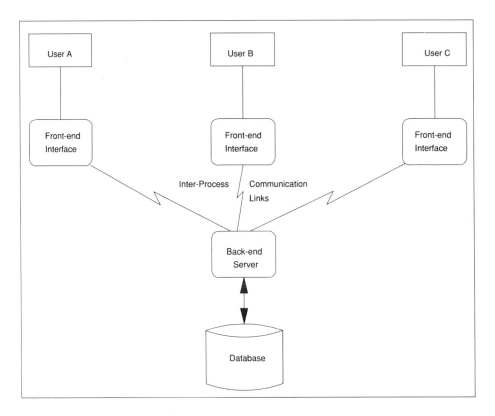

Figure 5-2 One Back-End Server per Database Architecture

its client front-end processes to provide multithreading. In order to divide its time between several front-end processes, the server must itself implement a ***process switch*** with similar overheads to a context switch.

In addition to the front-end and back-end processes, there might be other processes for each user. For example, the user's login Shell process probably exists all the time. There might be another process for the menu driver providing the application interface to the user. The DBMS might create other child processes for particular tasks, such as report formatting and print spooling, which add to the total number of processes per user. The point is that there can easily be four or more processes for each user on the system. The potential for swapping and paging for several users on a single machine should be abundantly clear.

5.1.3 Interprocess Communication

The front-end interface and the back-end server are independent processes regardless of their relationship. They need to communicate with each other to pass user commands and data. We examine some interprocess communication methods on a single machine to understand their effect on system performance, and the architectures to which they apply. Section 5.6 describes methods used for communication between separate machines.

Pipes:

The simplest communication method is a *pipe*, which provides a one way flow of bytes. The front-end and back-end processes can use two pipes, one for each flow direction. Processes with a parent-child relationship can use unnamed pipes. Processes without a common ancestor must use named pipes.

Note that the behavior of pipes in a UNIX system is very different from those in an MS-DOS system. Under UNIX, the receiving process can read data from the pipe while the sending process is writing to the pipe. Under MS-DOS the sending process must complete processing before the receiving process can read data from the pipe.

The information passed via pipes has no implicit messages or information on the size of the messages. Communicating processes must set up their own protocol for message type, size, and structure. Pipes are a fixed size structure and you cannot increase their size. Thus, the maximum size of an atomic message is limited. Read and write operations on a pipe are system calls — that is, a context switch. Since each context switch is expensive, frequent system calls necessary in this method affect the overall system performance.

SYSTEM V Shared Memory:

This widely used method consists of unrelated processes using a common memory area called a shared memory segment. This segment does not have any structure and the communicating processes must agree to its organization. DBMSs based on this facility might use one shared memory segment for each back-end server. Thus, if there is one back-end server per active user, there will be one shared segment per user. Alternatively, one back-end server per database means there will be one segment per database regardless of the number of users.

The advantage of this method is that after attaching a shared memory segment, accessing data does not cost system calls. Thus, it does not incur the context switch overheads as is the case in the pipes method. Many products do not use this method because of its dependence on SYSTEM V UNIX. However, several BSD implementations now offer compatible functions. So its use will probably increase in the near future.

SYSTEM V Message Queues:

Only ORACLE, among the products discussed in this book, can use this facility. It allows unrelated processes to exchange structured messages consisting of message text, type, and size. Processes can also find out the number of messages currently on a queue.

The disadvantage of this method is that the overhead of using message queues is similar to using pipes. Send and receive message operations involve system calls with associated context switches. Similar to the shared memory facility, you need to raise the kernel parameters which define the maximum size and number of message queues permitted. Thus, the kernel size increases reducing the memory available to user processes.

BSD Sockets:

BSD UNIX provides a method called *sockets,* which is similar to message queues discussed earlier. This facility is useful for communication on a single machine as well as a networked environment of distributed DBMS. We discuss its details in Section 5.6.

Note that since BSD provides demand paging memory management, the process size does not affect disk activity due to swapping. Thus, systems running under it frequently use a single larger process rather than the two processes per user architecture. The only other important point is that message send and receive operations in this method are system calls.

Semaphores:

Semaphores, available on both versions of UNIX, are another means of interprocess communication. They allow unrelated processes to exchange the value of a semaphore or to reset it. Processes cannot pass data using this mechanism which is necessary between the front-end interface and the back-end server. Therefore, in our context, they do not provide a useful interprocess communication facility. They are useful to the DBMS concurrency control subsystem and are detailed in Section 5.5.

5.2 Data Storage under UNIX

There are two types of data storage schemes available, the UNIX filesystem or a "raw" disk. Many commercial products allow you to use either one or both of these schemes. Before we discuss each scheme individually, let us see how they relate to the physical disk.

A physical disk consists of one or more partitions. Each partition has two interfaces, as a block device and a character device. The filesystem uses the block device interface while the raw disk is simply the character device interface. The kernel treats the raw disk as a single file, and hence without any structure. It buffers only accesses via the block interface — that is, the filesystem; raw disk access is unbuffered.

A DBMS may store the database as one file per relation. In this case, it uses the filesystem for flexible growth of each file. However, this alternative results in the limitations and overheads discussed in Section 5.2.1. Alternatively, it may store all relations in one file. This alternative allows it to offer a raw disk option with no changes to its strategy.

5.2.1 The Filesystem

The UNIX filesystem consists of hierarchical directories, each containing a number of files. Each file is simply a stream of bytes; there are no record based files, either sequential or indexed. Since a filesystem occupies one partition, it cannot span more than one physical disk. However, one physical disk can contain one or more filesystems.

UNIX uses a flexible and elegant storage strategy for files under its filesystem. This strategy allows fast access to small files, and can store very large files without changing the structure. Figure 5-3 shows this storage structure. As you can see, it is very flexible for storing files which change size frequently. However, it affects the database environment, which typically uses large files, in several ways.

1. Sequential data blocks in a file may not be adjacent on the physical disk. This causes a disk seek before reading each sequential data block. As you create and remove files, the fragmentation of the disk increases. Thus, disk seeks will occur more frequently. Since a disk seek involves a mechanical movement of the disk read/write heads, it can reduce system performance significantly.

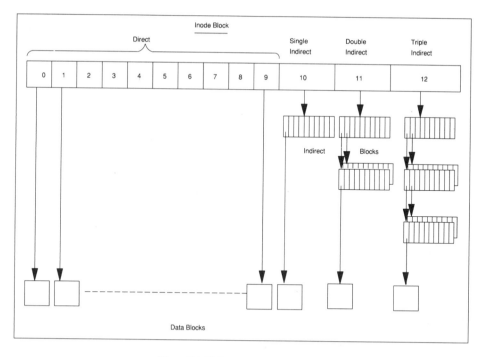

Figure 5-3 UNIX File Storage Structure

2. Access to data blocks beyond the first 10K[1] requires several read operations on the disk. The kernel first reads the indirect blocks to determine the address of the data block before reading it. If the file requires double indirect blocks (size is greater than 266K[2]) the kernel performs up to three read operations for each data block. The kernel buffers indirect blocks and data, so some read operations may simply result in copying data from its buffers. This buffering is worthwhile for sequential access, but of little use for random access typical in a database environment.

3. The block device interface underlying a filesystem restricts the size of each read to one logical block. Thus, the kernel will loop internally to satisfy a read request for larger data blocks.

4. A UNIX configuration parameter (ULIMIT) defines the maximum size for a file. For larger files typical in a database, you must change this parameter appropriately. Since a file cannot span more than one filesystem, the size of the physical disk is the limit.

---

[1] Assume logical blocks of 1K.

[2] Assume logical blocks of 1K and indirect blocks of 256 entries.

5. A process can open only a certain number of files, normally 20, depending on the UNIX implementation. Although it can be a tunable parameter, versions of SYSTEM V UNIX older than Release 3 had this limit hard-coded. Each process has three open files when it starts: stdin, stdout, and stderr. Thus, a process can open up to 17 additional files, an important consideration for relational systems storing each relation as one file.

5.2.2 The Raw Disk

Some DBMSs use the raw disk facility to overcome the limitations of the UNIX file-system. They can implement a strategy for contiguous storage of data blocks. This strategy can remove the need for indirect blocks, thus improving disk access speed. Such systems still use the filesystem for storing files such as the data dictionary and secondary indexes. These files are small and typically read sequentially, taking advantage of the filesystem buffering methods.

DBMSs must apply their own structure for storing more than one file or relation on a raw disk, since it is a single file. They frequently require the programmer to provide estimates of database size for this reason. They also provide a facility to store data on more than one raw disk. Thus, they support databases which can span more than one physical disk.

Since raw disk access is unbuffered, each read or write operation results in a physical disk access. An access for small sections of data adds to the overheads of the system calls. Some DBMSs provide a buffering scheme to reduce the number of accesses to the physical disk.

5.3 The UNIX Terminal Interface

UNIX provides facilities for supporting asynchronous, full duplex terminals from several vendors. These facilities allow development of software which is independent of the terminals used at runtime. They are a major reason why you need not buy all your hardware from a single manufacturer and can use terminals from one machine on another. The penalty for this flexible handling is, as usual, performance degradation. Many application developers have noticed a mysterious degradation in system throughput after adding interactive components to their application.

In this section, we look at two aspects of terminal handling: terminal independence and the use of the terminal driver facilities. DBMS utilities must use both aspects for providing their user interface. Since there are no UNIX facilities supporting block mode operation, they do not take advantage of such operation.

5.3.1 Terminal Independent User Interface

UNIX provides terminal independence with TERMCAP and TERMINFO utilities. These utilities consist of a set of library functions which use terminal command descriptions defined in a file. Programs can use the appropriate function library to send a terminal command without knowing the command syntax for the particular terminal. Users can add new terminals by simply developing a terminal description for it.

Some systems provide only the TERMCAP library which depends on a TERMCAP file. The TERMCAP file contains many terminal descriptions stored as ASCII text. This results in inefficient access due to long searches for appropriate terminal description. SYSTEM V UNIX provides the more efficient TERMINFO library which uses compiled descriptions for individual terminals, each stored in a separate file.

Each program determines the terminal type at runtime using the library functions. Therefore, you may find many packages which still use TERMCAP under SYSTEM V. The kernel or the SHELL process has no concept of a terminal type.

The CURSES library provides a higher level programming interface for screen handling than the TERMCAP and TERMINFO libraries. CURSES functions themselves use these lower level libraries. In addition, they optimize the output, reducing the number of characters transmitted to the terminal. This optimization improves the perceived display speed on slow terminals such as those running at 1200 baud. Most DBMS screen based utilities use CURSES functions or their own libraries that provide similar features.

Note that only programs providing screen based interface need to use CURSES functions. The gains from optimizing the output comes at some expense in CPU processing time. Faster terminals and communication channels reduce the need to perform such optimization.

Interfaces such as X-WINDOWS are a higher level of abstraction than CURSES. They provide a very attractive user interface effective on intelligent workstations. On dumb terminals, the same interface requires quite a lot of CPU time to provide the high level of interaction.

5.3.2 Terminal Driver Facilities

The terminal driver controls all interaction between a terminal and a process. To understand the comprehensive facilities it provides, let us see the behavior it expects from the terminals.

Full duplex terminals send each character typed on the keyboard to the host. The host program interprets this input according to its parameters and sends the character back to the terminal. The terminal then displays the character. The host program does not expect terminals to interpret any keys locally.

The terminal driver relieves the host program from tasks such as buffering the input and interpreting key codes like erase. It can also echo input characters back to the terminal. Such processing is called *canonical processing.*

Most interaction such as SHELL command input requires canonical processing. Since SHELL interprets the entire command line, input buffering of characters up to a carriage return character is practical. Buffering is also practical when typing query language statements. Programs using the driver for such interaction use the *cooked mode* — that is, with the canonical processing on.

However, forms based interaction needs the use of keys such as the arrow keys for movement within a form. The forms program must act immediately when the user presses a single key, without waiting for a carriage return. In this case, buffering is not practical. Another difference between command based input and forms based interaction is the control sequences used to activate field editing commands. Since these sequences may be terminal commands, echoing them to the terminal would result in unexpected display. Thus, the forms program must examine each input character and either echo it or perform some other action.

A program can control processing of input by setting the terminal driver into *raw mode*. Programs can set terminal parameters such as echo and canonical processing facilities individually. The different combinations possible are various flavors of raw mode. All DBMS utilities change some of these terminal settings.

Using raw mode results in considerable processing overhead. The program must process each input character as soon as the user types it. They must, therefore, read input from the terminal one character at a time and write the characters back to the terminal so the user sees the response. A lot of system calls incurring context switch overhead!

To reduce the overhead, the driver provides another facility. Even in raw mode, it captures all characters arriving from the terminal. Programs can read several characters with one system call, with a timeout provision if fewer characters arrived. They can then use their own buffers to reduce the number of read operations. This scheme is essential for handling fast bursts of input efficiently.

5.4 Security Control Facilities

We discussed, in Chapter 3, the access control facilities available in DBMSs. Whether or not you use these controls, you should consider how users could accidentally damage application data via their UNIX access. For example, the deleted file might be a database file resulting in time consuming recovery! The application is unavailable, of course, during recovery. Such an accident happens easily since most UNIX commands do not give you a second chance. For example, the command *rm -rf* * for deleting files does not confirm your intention, unlike the MS-DOS command *erase *.*.*

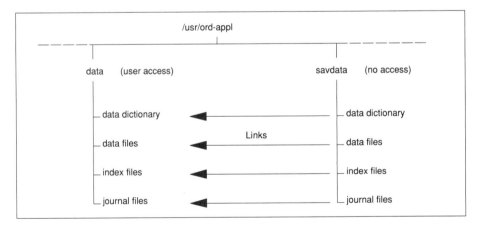

Figure 5-4 Links to Prevent File Deletion

UNIX provides two types of access security: user access and file access. Login procedures, together with a password, control a user's access to UNIX. The system administrator can set a login id to start a restricted shell which prevents the use of certain commands. If required, you can set up the application to bypass the login procedure and its SHELL process. We will discuss the pros and cons of such a set-up in Chapter 7.

Access to a file depends on three categories of permissions: owner, group, and public. These categories are based on the user and group ids corresponding to a user's login id, assigned when you create the login id. Permissions for each category define a combination of read, write, and execute access. Read and write permissions define whether you can change a data file. However, you must have both read and execute permission for a program file to run it.

Directories are a special case. Read and write permissions define permission to change directory entries for files. Execute permission is necessary to search or list directory contents. For example, suppose you have no permission to access a file, but you have read and write access to the directory in which the file resides. You can delete the file even though you have no permission to the file itself. However, you cannot list the files in this directory without execute permission. This can cause embarrassing downtime, since you cannot simply restore a single database file: You must recover the entire database.

One standard trick for quick recovery in such circumstances is to link all database files to another directory. Only the superuser should have permission to access this directory. These links will prevent the file contents from being deleted when a database file is deleted from the data directory. This method is illustrated in Figure 5-4. Recovery of a data file then only requires you to relink the file from the protected link directory into the data directory.

The drawback of this method is that every database file must be linked individually when it is created, a process not performed by the DBMS create facility. This link must be created each time the database structure is changed, or re-created as in a complete recovery process. A complete recovery is still necessary when the contents of the database are corrupted. In this case, the old links must be removed to free any data blocks associated with the old contents.

There are many UNIX utilities for data encryption and decryption. Most of these are useless for encrypting DBMS data files. This unfortunate circumstance is because a DBMS not only determines the layout of data in the file, but also controls all means of access. In a few instances, you can connect these encryption and decryption utilities — for example, as a subroutine call from a host language interface program or a fourth generation language program. This solution, however, merely adds to the problem of database access.

You cannot alter the index access routines internal to the DBMS. So at best, you could encrypt data which is not part of any index. This might be fine once your application settles down to a static structure. But how could you handle the periodic tuning activities which might create new indexes on encrypted fields? Only by the tedious process of unloading and reloading your database. Ad hoc access via a query language is completely beyond your reach if you encrypt the data — there are no hooks to connect your subroutines in this component of a DBMS.

5.5 Concurrency Control Tools

In Chapter 3, we discussed the types and levels of concurrency control mechanisms. Such mechanisms are essential in a multiuser environment where many processes can access files simultaneously. Since UNIX does not enforce any locks, separate processes can overwrite each others' changes. These changes could be intermixed in any order because UNIX can only guarantee completion of individual write operations (atomic writes). Since a transaction can affect many separate parts of the database, it cannot write an entire transaction as an atomic write. Therefore, concurrency control techniques are essential to ensure consistent states of the database.

The most common method for concurrency control applies locks on the database. Other methods include processing all transactions serially so that an entire transaction must be complete before the next one starts. In this section, we discuss the tools used for both strategies. The concurrency level provided depends on the limitations of the tools chosen.

Any lock based strategy depends on locking data items as the transaction executes. As we discussed in Chapter 3, deadlock situations can easily occur in multistatement transactions. The strategy must then include a deadlock detection or avoidance method. The tools described next do not provide any facilities to help in this area.

The serial processing strategy is simpler since deadlock conditions cannot exist. However, it must implement a single threaded back-end server, and suffer the bottlenecks we discussed in Chapter 3. Such a strategy degrades system performance as the transaction load increases.

5.5.1 Lock Files

The simplest lock is an ordinary file. Utilities such as UUCP, CU, and LP SPOOLER use the presence of a special file to mean that another process is using the required resource. This method is useful for locking devices, such as dial lines and printers, to prevent sharing them. However, if the process which created the file aborts without removing it, the resource remains locked.

Note that existence of the file locks the entire resource, which could be a relation or the entire database. DBMS programs need to lock only parts of data files. Locking the entire database or relation defeats the purpose of sharing the database. Creating one lock file for each record is obviously inefficient since it leads to creating and removing thousands of files. Therefore, they must store additional information in the lock file to indicate the part of the data locked. The lock file could also contain information on whether the lock is for reading or writing.

This method causes several processing overheads. Each process accessing the database must first examine this file for access conflicts before adding the lock information. Each time it changes the lock file, it must make sure that UNIX completes the operation. It must also read the entire file every time it needs to access the database, since another process may have changed the contents.

If a lock exists on the required portion of the database, the process should wait. However, the process does not know when the lock is free. The only solution to this problem is for the process to loop, retrying periodically, which consumes CPU time.

All of these operations are expensive because they take place frequently in a DBMS environment. The structure of the lock information is crucial, since poor organization results in further performance degradation. All writes to the lock file must be atomic to prevent inconsistent data.

5.5.2 Semaphores for Locking

We mentioned semaphores as an interprocess communication method in Section 5.1. They allow unrelated processes to exchange a "yes or no" message which is ideal for a lock. Many DBMSs used this method before SYSTEM V file and record locking facilities became available.

Suppose a semaphore implies a lock when its value is 0 and no lock when its value is 1. A process decreases the value of a semaphore to imply a lock, and the value increases when the lock is released. If a semaphore value is 0 and a process requests its value to be decreased, the kernel puts the process to sleep. When its value becomes 1, the kernel wakes up all waiting processes. The first process to run will lock it and the kernel will put the remaining processes to sleep.

Semaphores are a very efficient way of handling locks. This is because the kernel puts the waiting process to sleep and wakes all such processes when the semaphore is free. Thus, the waiting process need not loop on a retry as in the lock files method and does not use CPU time while it waits. A process can choose whether the kernel should put it to sleep in a wait condition, or return unsuccessfully. Thus, DBMSs can provide options that inform users of a lock condition.

Another advantage is the cleanup service provided by the kernel. In this service, the kernel will undo all semaphore operations carried out by a process up to the time when the process crashes. Thus, locks would not be left behind by accident.

Each DBMS applies its own interpretation of the data block a semaphore represents. Those systems implementing field level locks may use a semaphore to represent a single field. For those allowing record level locking, it could represent a tuple. The systems must use some algorithm to generate unique semaphore keys to represent each item of data.

Note that you need to change kernel parameters relating to semaphores at install time. The values you should set depend on what you estimate as the number of concurrent locks needed for your application.

5.5.3 SYSTEM V File and Record Locking

Earlier versions of UNIX did not provide internal locking mechanisms. In these systems semaphores or lock files are still the common method. SYSTEM V now provides file and record locking system calls on its filesystem. A record, in this context, is simply data bytes between two offsets in a file. This mechanism is advisory only and does not prevent access by a process. Each process must inquire the status of the lock before accessing a data area.

File level locking is useful in very few cases, such as database backup. Some systems use this facility to support locks explicitly requested by a user using — for example — an SQL statement. You may use such locks for batch transaction processing when other users cannot use the database.

In most cases, DBMS utilities need to lock either records or fields in the database. Note that this facility is available only on files within the filesystem — it does not apply to raw disk databases. Some systems use a file under the filesystem which represents the database stored on a raw disk. They lock a portion of this file to represent a locked area of the database. This method is as efficient as semaphores, but is significantly easier to code and maintain.

5.5.4 Tools for Serial Handling of Transactions

The previous tools all provide different ways of implementing a locking mechanism. The methods for serial processing of transactions use the principle of first-start, first-completed. These methods are mainly useful with a single back-end server process per database; that is, in single threaded architectures.

One method of determining which transaction started first uses time stamps on each transaction. The transaction which started earliest will complete entirely before starting the next transaction. UNIX provides a clock from which processes can retrieve time (time(2)), with a granularity of one second, to stamp a transaction. Since DBMSs execute several transactions in a second, this tool is impractical.

Processes can use the process time system call (times(2)) to obtain a finer granularity. This granularity depends on the underlying hardware, but frequently is a hundredth of a second. The hardware clock usually allows a finer granularity than provided by the system call. So another way is to develop a clock device driver which takes advantage of the hardware.

Another method of serializing transactions could use FIFO pipes from multiple front-end processes to a single back-end server process. Processes would need to write the transaction information with a single write statement. The database server process could simply start the first transaction to arrive on the pipe. It could stack all others until the current transaction completes.

In this method, bottlenecks would occur under heavy transaction loads at the server process because of its one-transaction-at-a-time processing. Another reason for a bottleneck would be the size limit on a pipe. Some early noncommercial databases tried this method and suffered consequent performance penalties.

5.6 Networking Facilities

Networking facilities are essential for DBMSs to provide three types of features:

- Network databases, which allow transfer of data between individual databases residing on separate machines. The user must know that separate databases exist and must specify their location.

- Distributed databases, which present the user with the view of a single database, even though the data resides on several machines.

- Heterogeneous databases, which are distributed databases consisting of databases created by different packages on different machines.

In this section, we look at what facilities these features would need from UNIX. Note that the implementation of these features is complex and we highlight its problems in Part 4 of this book. Few DBMSs provide these features at present, but most promise them in the near future. We divide the following discussion into UNIX-to-UNIX communication and that to other operating systems.

5.6.1 Communication between UNIX Systems

The most basic networking utilities, such as UUCP and CU, use a dial-up telephone network. UUCP is primarily a batch file transfer utility and CU enables a remote terminal connection. Designed for operation with other UNIX systems, they do not work well with other operating systems. Some network database environments use UUCP, when queued batch transfer is sufficient. In most cases, network environments need immediate data upload and download capability where these basic services are slow and impractical. They are still a popular method of communication between different manufacturers' UNIX machines, particularly as the basis for electronic mail.

Both network databases and distributed databases can use Ethernet networks. Most manufacturers provide a network connection within their family of UNIX machines. Some implementations allow connection between different manufacturers' machines. These networks provide a practical throughput of about 600Kbytes per second, allowing for the overhead of the protocol. This throughput is sufficient under the conditions described in Chapter 15, for both of the network and distributed databases.

Earlier releases of network utilities depended on knowing the protocol used. They were therefore of limited use. SYSTEM V Release 3 provides STREAMS facilities which allow very flexible network support. However, DBMS vendors need significant development to use these facilities, which are only available on SYSTEM V, and therefore not portable.

BSD UNIX provides the SOCKETS mechanism which allows process-to-process communication across machines. SOCKETS is an elegant method of interprocess communication both on a single machine and across a network interface.

The most common use of networking facilities at present is the concept of Remote File Systems (RFS). The concept is that a filesystem residing on a remote machine can be mounted on a local machine. Access to this filesystem via the network is then transparent to the user. The concept was first developed by Sun Microsystems, Inc. and called Network File System (NFS). SYSTEM V Release 3 RFS is a conceptually similar implementation. Only DBMSs storing a database as separate files under multiple directories can use this method to provide distributed databases.

Using RFS (or NFS) leads to several problems, mainly in the area of concurrency control. The difficulty lies in determining which machine should perform the locking functions. Another problem is the volume of traffic could flood the network, causing performance degradation. For example, suppose a user starts a database search on the local machine.

Unknown to the user, some (or all) of the database files reside on a remote filesystem. In this instance, RFS transfers all data from these "remote" files over the network for processing by the local machine.

A more efficient way to perform the search operation would have transported only the results of the search. This is possible only if DBMSs themselves determine which machine should perform the search operation. Their strategy can take advantage of the location information in their data dictionary. They do not need the transparent access facility of RFS (or NFS).

To be able to execute an intelligent processing strategy, DBMSs need the process-to-process communication facilities. At present, only BSD SOCKETS and SYSTEM V Release 3 networking utilities provide the needed facilities. Earlier versions of UNIX provide facilities sufficient only for network databases.

5.6.2 Communication to Other Operating Systems

An important development for departmental UNIX machines is the connectivity to IBM machines. Most manufacturers supply software for SNA emulation with 3270 or LU6.2 support. Since 3270 emulation is a terminal interface, only a system implementing network databases can use it. As we discussed in the previous section, process-to-process communication facilities are essential for distributed database. Hence, LU6.2 with Advanced Program-to-Program Communication (APPC) is necessary before distributed databases can be built.

Products which run on UNIX as well as IBM operating systems could provide distributed databases. They could also use SNA connectivity for providing access to other DBMSs, notably DB2. Such heterogeneous access will initially support only SQL based systems and may expand later.

This is a major advance in the UNIX world where interproduct database support does not exist. Products on IBM systems allow access to databases created by many different vendors' systems.

Most DBMS products run on many operating systems other than UNIX. If a network connection to these exists, the distributed database concept is possible. Few products have attempted an implementation at present, mainly due to the lack of network connectivity. Another reason may be the differences in the way these ported versions operate.

5.7 Real-Time Features

Many manufacturers have enhanced their implementation of UNIX to allow its use in real-time environments. Some of these enhancements affect the way a DBMS performs by providing you with a greater control of process priorities.

Note that the term *real-time* is sometimes used to describe high performance transaction oriented systems. In this case, real-time can mean up to a few seconds response times per transaction, as perceived by a human. Such requirements are really features of *on-line* systems. Real-time in this section refers to a system requiring guaranteed responses within a predictable amount of time ranging from milliseconds through micro-seconds depending on the application. Typical use of such real-time facilities are in process control applications rather than data processing applications.

Typical enhancements for real-time UNIX implementations are

- Priority based interrupt handling available to programs, in order to respond to external events within the time required. These are not normally available as a generic features.

- Stacking of concurrent signals, not available at least in standard SYSTEM V. Without this feature, a process sees only one signal out of several occurring simultaneously; other signals are irretrievably lost. Some hardware vendors, such as Hewlett-Packard, have extended their implementation of UNIX to do such signal stacking.

- Priority based scheduling, so that tasks defined as most important are serviced within the required time. Without this feature, all tasks are treated fairly. This feature should also allow higher priority processes to preempt those with lower priority, even in the middle of a system call. In a single server architecture, the server also needs to provide priority based scheduling.

- Response time constraints which can be defined with subsecond time granularity. Normal utilities provide a granularity of one second which is not fine enough in many real-time environments.

- Facilities to lock a program, or parts of a program, in real memory to reduce disk accesses due to swapping. The normal facilities ensure only that the program does not have to be loaded from the filesystem, they do not guarantee that it will not be swapped.

Many of these features do not affect a DBMS application directly, since the code to take advantage of them must be written in a third generation language. DBMS products can aid performance by improving disk access speeds using a raw disk, and coordinating the sharing of data between multiple processes.

Products which use a back-end server approach might perform better, if these back-end server processes run at a higher priority than their front-end counterparts. However, you must specify these priorities for your application; the products do not automatically take advantage of them.

Note that real-time features are not standard between UNIX implementations. Until such standards are established and implemented, using these features will make your application difficult to port.

5.8 UNIX Tuning

The kernel has several parameters which determine the size of its internal tables. They contain default values when you first install UNIX. You can improve system performance by tuning some of these parameters. Which parameters to tune depends on the chosen product and which facilities it uses. We discuss only those applicable to a database environment, covering three aspects of the environment: data access, terminal activity, and user load.

Note that most systems can operate without any tuning. When kernel tables overflow, you will see error messages on the system console. However, the user may not know why a program failed to run. Such episodes make system administrators' work interesting.

There are no exact algorithms to decide the new value of a parameter for a specific installation. Some determining factors are the selected DBMS, capabilities of the hardware, number of application users, and types of user activity. On SYSTEM V, you may use the System Activity Reporter (SAR) information to detect bottlenecks and tune to reduce their effects. On BSD, VMSTAT and IOSTAT utilities are available for such investigation.

Note that increasing the size of kernel tables makes the kernel bigger and hence processes have less memory available. Then, the kernel may swap (or page) processes frequently, causing performance degradation. You should consider these tradeoffs when reconfiguring the UNIX kernel. These considerations are the reason why most UNIX systems benefit from more physical memory than would appear necessary.

5.8.1 Data Access

There are two parameters that affect the filesystem access performance: the buffer cache and the hash queues. They only help databases stored under the filesystem rather than the raw disk.

The buffer cache is the space used by the kernel for disk access buffers. Increasing the size of these buffers improves the cache hit rate, which reduces the number of physical read operations. On the other hand, a write operation may only affect the buffer. The kernel may not update the disk from the buffers for long periods, leading to lost transactions in a system crash. Note that this disk update period is another parameter in SYSTEM V (NAUTOUP) which can be reduced to get frequent buffer flushes. But consider the gains against the overheads of flushing large buffers to disk for your application.

The kernel uses hash queues for fast access to blocks in the buffer cache. The hash queue size, therefore, depends on the buffer cache size. You should change the hash queue size to match the new buffer cache size.

Another important parameter is the size of the kernel file table, where it holds information on all open files. If a DBMS uses one file per relation, you need to increase this size as the number of simultaneous users increases. This is important if each user is likely to access several files at once. If the file table is too small, overflow may occur as the number of open files throughout the system increases.

5.8.2 Terminal Activity

Clists are buffers used by the terminal driver. You should increase their size if your application involves heavy data input at a fast pace. Users performing database searches and browsing through results slowly may not benefit from the tuning. If available clists are not enough for the user activity, some input may be lost under heavy loads.

5.8.3 User Load

Most of the parameters listed next need to increase as the number of users increases. They are essential for your application to operate properly, but do not improve system performance. The values of some parameters already discussed depend to some extent on the number of users on the system.

If your product uses shared memory segments, tune the parameters governing the maximum segment size and number of segments allowed. The product installation guide will recommend values based on its architecture. Note that the product may not operate at all with incorrect configuration.

The semaphore parameters affect the number of locks allowed simultaneously in the system. You have to estimate these based on the typical number and complexity of update transactions executed concurrently. Estimates should include lockable data items between transaction start and commit operations.

When you use a product which needs at least two processes per user — that is, a front-end interface and a back-end server — you probably need to increase the kernel's process table size parameter. This parameter setting represents the total number of processes that can run at any given time. Thus, as the number of active users increases, the kernel can run out space in its process table. Bear in mind that some DBMS products have several background processes running which are transparent to a user.

5.9 Application Development Tools

UNIX provides several tools for development and control of applications. Some of these tools such as the C language and MAKE compilation utility are available on other operating systems. You can use these to varying degrees when developing a database application. This section contains an overview so you can understand the extent to which they are useful.

5.9.1 Programming Languages

The primary programming language under UNIX is C. Since most DBMSs are developed in this language, they provide an interface to it. The interface may be either function calls or an embedded SQL form. Many fourth generation languages convert into C after the preprocessor phase and then are compiled into executable modules.

There are other languages such as FORTRAN, COBOL, and BASIC provided by third party vendors. Note, however, that many DBMSs support only one of the many COBOL compilers available. Another important point is that not all languages compile into the *a.out* standard executable format. They are instead interpreted from an intermediate format. Programs in such languages are significantly slower than their equivalents in C.

5.9.2 Program Development Tools

Make is a rule based processor which allows easy control of program compilation. It has built-in rules for handling compilations and Source Code Control System (SCCS) files. You can define dependencies between source files which it uses to compile only the changed files and their dependents. It accepts new rules for conditions not covered by those built in.

UNIX also provides an object library archiving tool, ***ar***, which enables gathering of several object files into a library. The link loader (***ld***) only takes the objects referenced from the library for inclusion in an executable module. This tool is useful in a 4GL or embedded SQL based application, since these convert their programs into C for compilation. You could use it to build project specific utility libraries for commonly used code.

Most DBMSs provide a development environment based on menus or forms which make development and programmer training easy. However, few provide built-in hooks for using MAKE or application specific object libraries. Some provide functions similar to MAKE built in their environment, and compile only changed functions.

The symbolic debugger, ***sdb***, is an important development tool which you cannot use in a DBMS environment. It applies only to C programs and frequently has trouble handling function calls where the source is not available. Most host language interface programs in this environment include such calls. The tool is also of limited use with an embedded query language or a 4GL program since the code generated by the product's precompiler is difficult to follow at best. A few of the products discussed in this book do provide a substitute especially desirable for 4GL and other host language programs.

5.9.3 Project Control Utilities

When developing an application you need to track who is doing what, especially with medium to large teams. The tracking may be easier on paper with very small teams. However, it is best to automate the change tracking for source code and control versions of software released into production. UNIX itself has no provisions for keeping multiple versions of a file, so you cannot easily recover from accidental changes.

The Source Code Control System (SCCS) allows version and access control of files. It tracks changes between file versions and lets you control concurrent access for changing files. Project leaders can use it to ensure only one person changes a file at any one time. Tracking who changed the file, when, and what changed becomes easy.

Most definitions, such as forms, reports or SQL, produced for use with a DBMS are really ***programs*** which change as the application changes. They are prone to problems of multiple programmers making changes at the same time, thus losing some changes accidentally. Project leaders need to track changes to these programs similarly to a project based on a programming language.

However, few DBMSs provide the control mechanisms necessary for managing a medium to large application development team. Their menu based interface prevents you from using the existing tools. You can only use some of these tools if you do not use their development interface.

5.10 Conclusions

We examined several facilities which UNIX offers to DBMSs in this chapter. These facilities are the foundation for the multiuser capabilities of these DBMSs. They allow sharing of a database with concurrency and security control, alternative data storage options and network connections for distributed systems in the near future. They also allow DBMSs to provide vendor independent terminal support and choice of UNIX processors from several manufacturers.

Three types of UNIX activities can affect the performance of your application: type of terminal activity, number of system calls, and volume of disk I/O. We discussed the reasons for this effect and how it affects the performance.

Raw mode terminal handling is necessary for forms based interaction to accept a user's input and take action on it immediately, but increases the number of system calls. The number of system calls that can be executed is limited by the processor's capacity for performing context switches.

Disk I/O speed depends on the disk hardware capabilities. Many activities, such as swapping and heavy database access, can increase the I/O volume. You can add more physical memory and tune the kernel buffer sizes to reduce swapping and the number of physical disk accesses needed. Using the indexing facilities provided by your DBMS also improves data access speed and reduces disk I/O volumes.

UNIX is unique in its availability on processors of various sizes from different manufacturers. Its portability and that of the C language is evident from the variety of hardware supported by DBMS vendors. You can move your application to a different processor easily because of these reasons. You can also gain the advantages of advances in hardware technology without needing major redevelopment of applications.

6

Developing a DBMS Application

In this chapter, we examine how DBMS facilities affect our design and development strategies. Many of the traditional application design methods do not apply to the DBMS environment. Instead, we choose between the DBMS facilities and tools best suited to the application needs. For example, in traditional systems, each program contains the code for security needs appropriate to its functions. In a DBMS application, we apply security restrictions independent of the program to the database or *views* seen by a program.

A typical application consists of a database, screen based forms for data entry and access, and reports displayed on screens or printed. DBMSs provide utilities for developing these components as an integrated application. We cover the following topics:

- The data storage choices are different from those in a traditional application. The choice affects not only the performance of the application but also the ease of changing database structures and future enhancements.

- The choice of access methods to the data are more comprehensive than in a traditional application. You can specify the access method when creating indexes and can change them at will.

- Maintaining data integrity, a popular misnomer for concurrency control, is a major issue in DBMS applications. We describe the correct meaning of this term and the facilities that help in maintaining it.

- Locking and concurrency control needs vary for each application component. We look at methods for determining the levels needed for your application and the use of transaction based control.

- There are many facilities for building user interfaces to an application. We discuss the pros and cons of using a combination of these tools and integrating the application components.

- The last two sections discuss the pros and cons of coding choices, including a comparison of host language interface types and fourth generation languages.

6.1 Data Storage Options

DBMSs may store a database in many ways using the UNIX facilities we discussed in Chapter 5. From an application developer's point of view there are two approaches to data storage: one relation table per file and multiple relation tables per file. These implementations are transparent to application users. The key areas affected by storage approaches are

- Maximum size of a single table.
- Maximum size of the entire database.
- Maximum number of relations allowed in a join operation.
- Ease of adding new relations or modifying existing relations.
- Data access performance.

6.1.1 One Relation Table per File

DBMSs using this approach use one file for each relation and another one for each index. If they use the same storage structures for storing their data dictionary information, the data dictionary also consists of several files. Some DBMSs store dictionary, data, and index files into a directory which is created when you create a database, as shown in Figure 6-1. Others store dictionary files in separate directories from data as shown in Figure 6-2.

A typical normalized database definition leads to many individual files in this approach which fits well in the UNIX filesystem and its hierarchical directory structure. Each file changes size dynamically as data is added or deleted using the filesystem facilities. Buffering of data is done by the kernel as discussed in Chapter 5. A DBMS using this approach may depend on these filesystem features and not implement any additional buffering schemes.

This approach is perfect for small databases. However, you run into performance difficulties if a single relation contains large quantities of data. Performance degradation occurs because of the indirect blocks scheme of the filesystem which causes extra I/O for each record access. Also, large files get fragmented because of the filesystem storage scheme: that is, data blocks get spread out all over the disk. Fragmentation causes delays in retrieving data since the disk subsystem has to position the disk read heads before reading each and every data block. You could improve performance somewhat by using an index for searching. We discuss indexed access methods in more detail in Section 6.2.

You could use raw disks for specific files by simply making a special node (mknod command) with the same name as a data file and copying the data. The problem is that you have only a limited number of partitions available. On many UNIX implementations, the size of the partition is fixed. Besides, the reconfiguration process is dangerous. You will definitely need a *guru* to reconfigure your disk partitions in order to avoid a disastrous loss of the entire system by accidentally overlapping partitions.

The lack of buffering in the product may still defeat your hopes for improving performance with a raw disk. If the DBMS depends on kernel buffering for filesystem access, it may use frequent I/O calls for small quantities of data. In this case, you might even degrade performance due to the frequent physical disk access. The high volume of system calls for accessing small quantities of data also causes performance degradation.

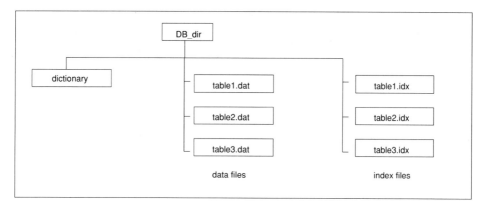

Figure 6-1 One Directory for Dictionary, Data, and Index Files

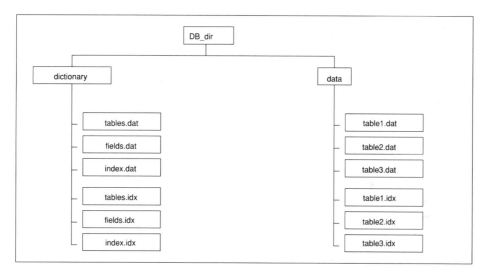

Figure 6-2 Directory Structure for Data and Index Files

The advantage of this approach is that you can create databases very easily. Creating a database consists of creating an appropriate directory and initial data dictionary files which is an easy process under the filesystem. Creating a table for a relation is similarly simple and you do not need to specify which data partition to store the table data. Thus, changing the database structure during development or for enhancements is easy.

The main disadvantages are performance degradation with large tables and the limit on table size imposed by the size of the filesystem. If the entire database must reside in a single directory, a table must share the space with the rest of the database tables. Another disadvantage is that a join operation opens each referenced table as a file. So, the number of tables you can join in a statement is limited by the maximum open files limit.

6.1.2 Multiple Relation Tables per File

In this approach, a database consists of one or more data areas. Each area associates with one or more operating system files with SQL statements or other DBMS facilities. The files which compose a data area can be either raw disk partitions or filesystem based files. Creation of a database in this approach consists of setting up at least one data area before any relation tables can be created.

Each data area can contain one or more relation tables, created with either the administrative facilities or SQL statements. When you create a table, you can specify which data area the table should reside in. A default data area is usually assigned to handle cases when you do not define the data area. Figure 6-3 illustrates a typical relationship between operating system files, data areas, and relation tables.

Creation of a database and its component tables is rarely straightforward in this approach. In some products, a relation table cannot span more than one data area, which forces you to estimate the table sizes before creating them. Products without this restriction do not allow you to control the association between relation tables and data areas. Being able to choose the association between data areas and table is essential for tuning disk I/O distribution.

SQL data definition statements in this case are also more complicated. However, most products follow the DB2 statement structures with only minor differences in syntax. Forms based data definition facilities to define the database structure, such as those provided by UNIFY, might appear attractive but tend to be less flexible than using SQL statements. In other products, such as ORACLE and INFORMIX-TURBO, you must use SQL statements.

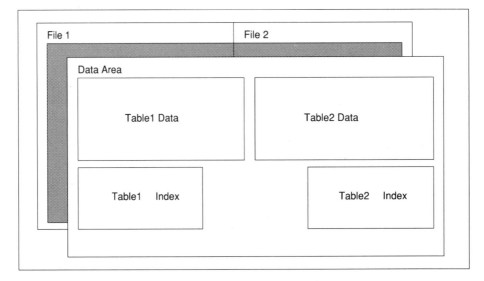

Figure 6-3 System Files, Data Areas, and Relation Tables

When you specify a data area consisting of raw disks, the UNIX kernel does not buffer any access to this area. Each access to the raw disk incurs the overhead of a system call, as well as leading to a physical disk access. Thus, many accesses to small quantities of data can degrade performance. Some products provide internal buffering to reduce disk I/O overhead. Although they let you specify the memory buffer size, changing this setting dynamically is not always easy.

Some products, such as ORACLE, use a *parameters* file containing definitions of the buffer space size at start-up time. Others, such as UNIFY, allow you to change the buffer space size from host language programs. In this case, it is up to you to implement a convenient means of setting and changing this value.

The location of the buffer space affects other considerations in setting up the database. For example, ORACLE uses shared memory space for these buffers. So you may need to increase the kernel parameters for shared memory and reconfigure UNIX before increasing the values for your application database.

This storage architecture is most suitable for supporting large databases which may span more than one physical disk. It may not be worthwhile for setting up simple databases with a few small tables, although it can support such databases. Changing the database structure frequently in this approach is also awkward.

6.2 Which Access Methods to Use?

Typical methods of accessing data include sequential access, indexed access, referential links, and data clustering. We discussed the concepts underlying these methods in Chapter 3. In this section, we examine how the choice of the access method affects your application design. In many high performance applications, your host language programs will depend on particular access methods. Changing the access strategy at a later date for such programs can bury you in code rewrites. If you want to avoid dependencies on particular access methods, you need to understand how these access methods are implied when you use certain interfaces.

The way DBMS utilities use these access methods can also have an unexpected effect on performance. For example, building a secondary index might be useless if the query processor does not use it. A complex SQL statement specifying multiple conditional clauses might use indexes to resolve only the first clause. Each product handles such decisions differently.

Some products implement different access strategies for primary and secondary indexes. You want to choose the fastest strategy for the majority of your application's data access needs. Thus, the choice of primary and secondary keys and the access methods used to implement these should be a major concern at application design time. You should also consider the relative merits of each method and use them to complement the types of access needed by the application.

Decisions at design time on choosing particular access methods can affect the application in the following areas

- Speed of search access to database.

- Add and update performance degradation due to multiple indexes.
- Program dependence on particular access method.
- Difficulty in modifying database structures.
- Disk space usage.

6.2.1 Hashed versus B-Tree Access

From our discussions of these methods in Chapter 3, hashed access is clearly faster than a B-tree search, but consider some of its drawbacks. Primarily, you should consider the suitability of the data in the key. *Pathological* data, where many items have similar values, may cause an uneven distribution in the hash table. Uneven distributions cause frequent collisions and the DBMSs collision resolution strategy will not perform as well as it would with an even distribution. Products such as UNIFY and INGRES provide administrative information which helps you determine such circumstances. You can then increase the database size to tune hash access.

Hashed access is useful only when the full key value is known. It is suitable when you need to access only one record. You cannot retrieve a set of records with a hash index because you have to specify an exact key value which uniquely identifies one row. In the customer orders and ordered items example, you could not use hashed access to retrieve all ordered items for a given customer order. B-tree indexes are best for accessing records with a repeated field value.

Hashed access works only for an exact match with unique key values. It cannot support wildcard searches or searches where partial key value is known. B-trees are inherently structured to allow searches for partial keys. They also support comparisons such as greater than and less than for which hashed access is of little use. The B-tree method also supports nonunique key values.

With B-trees, indexed sequential access is possible in a forward direction – for example, find the first instance of the key value with the index and then sequentially access the remaining instances. This feature is particularly useful in executing join operations. However, B-tree implementations do not support a backward direction — that is, sequentially access the previous instance of the key value. Thus, implementing a *previous* option for users requires considerably more work in the program.

B-tree indexes have to store the values of the key fields. Therefore, they can require a lot of storage when used on a long character field such as a customer name. Compressed B-tree indexes save space but not all products support this option. Of the four products discussed in this book, UNIFY does not support compressed indexes.

Compressed indexes only store the minimum portion of the key required to distinguish it from the previous one (in sorted order). They are most efficient on data where many keys have similar values. The danger in using them is that decoding is necessary during a search, resulting in higher CPU consumption.

The values stored in an index are frequently used by the query processor to resolve joins or where conditions. The query processor needs the full key value for handling such conditions. So, with a compressed index, it might choose to retrieve the data records rather than reconstruct the full key from the index. Thus, performance of systems using compressed rather than normal B-trees will probably suffer for join operations.

Even through some products allow direct access to an index, avoid using such access functions directly in your host language programs. Using such functions makes the program dependent on the access method. A better way is to use generic functions which can achieve the required task and allow independence from particular access methods. Programs which access hashed or B-tree functions directly are really using the DBMS as an ISAM file system, rather than using its power to provide independence from database structure. This problem does not arise in embedded query language interfaces which prevent direct access. Of course, programs using direct function call access may perform better than those using interpreted query language statements.

6.2.2 Using Referential Links

Referential links is an idea borrowed from the network data model and allows you to define *sets:* that is, an owner-member relationship between data in two tables. The definition could, of course, serve as a hint to the DBMS to cluster data.

This concept in a relational environment is similar to the concept of *foreign keys* discussed in C.J.Date. UNIFY DBMS is the only product which implements it as an access method at the time of writing this book. It provides many functions based on these links which you can use for fast access.

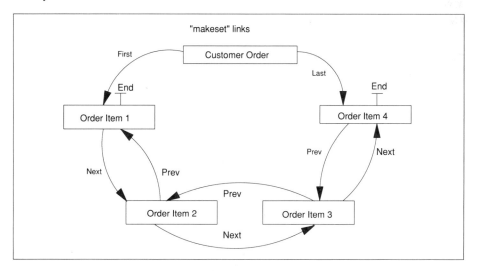

Figure 6-4 Data Access Using UNIFY Referential Links

As an access method, it requires the DBMS to implement special data dictionary structures to maintain the links. Figure 6-4 illustrates the set functions of UNIFY for access using referential links. Having found an owner record (parent), you can sequentially access member records (children) in a similar fashion to the *via* access concept in network databases. Its real worth is in maintaining data integrity, which we discuss in Section 6.3.

Using the access functions to make use of this facility directly in a program is dangerous, as the program becomes dependent on the particular relationship. However, in stable relationships such as in our customer order and ordered items example, the performance gain may override the data independence issue. Note that you can use this feature indirectly through more generalized functions provided by UNIFY.

6.2.3 Using Data Clustering

Data clustering is not actually an access method, but a way of storing data. However, it affects the way the DBMS accesses data and hence we discuss it here. Although database designers and administrators need to be aware of clustering to establish it, users of the database are not concerned with it. Users may only notice the performance improvement under heavy loads requiring a significant amount of disk I/O. Note that referential links discussed in Section 6.2.2 are one way of implying relationships and thus are useful for clustering. In Chapter 3, we discussed two types of clustering: *interfile* and *intrafile*.

The performance gain in clustering is obtained by storing data close together based on patterns of access peculiar to your application. For example, if your application always accesses customer information in alphabetic order by customer names, intrafile clustering will maintain the customer table information in alphabetic order. Thus, access to the disk retrieves several records in alphabetic sequence, reducing the need for a disk access per record.

An example of interfile clustering is the customer order and order item tables. They are generally accessed together possibly with a join operation. You can specify these two tables to be clustered to reflect this relationship and access. The DBMS will then attempt to store related rows from these tables in one physical block if possible, or separate blocks which require the minimum disk head movement. An example of such clustered storage is shown in Figure 6-5. Note that interfile clustering applies only to products based on the *multiple relations per file* approach discussed in Section 6.1.2. In the *one file per relation* approach, correspondence between relations is not possible.

Clustering data reduces the number of physical disk accesses because a single disk I/O retrieves an order and its related order items. Hence performance of such access improves. Note, however, that performance improves only in the cases where actual data in clusters is accessed; no improvement occurs when an index is sufficient to resolve a join or a conditional match. Thus, clustering will have no effect in these cases.

Changing cluster arrangements after a database is loaded with data clearly involves a significant shuffling of data on disk. Most products require you to unload the database, redefine clustering requirements, and then reload the database. This procedure can be time consuming and you can save tedious work and application downtime by including clustering needs in your initial database design.

```
┌──────────────────────────────────────────────────────────────────────┐
│                    ┌─────────────────────────────────────────────┐     │
│                    │  DBMS System Information                     │     │
│                    ├─────────────────────────────────────────────┤     │
│                    │  Cluster Key: Order Number = 1234            │     │
│                 ⎧  ├──────────────────────┬──────────────────────┤     │
│                 │  │  Customer Number     │    Company            │     │
│                 │  ├──────────────────────┴──────────────────────┤     │
│ Customer Order  ⎨  │  Name                                        │     │
│      Table      │  ├─────────────────────────────────────────────┤     │
│                 │  │  Bill Address                                │     │
│                 │  ├─────────────────────────────────────────────┤     │
│                 ⎩  │  Ship Address                                │     │
│                 ⎧  ├──────────────────────┬──────────────────────┤     │
│                 │  │  Item No. = 1        │  Catalog Number=AB-123-345  │
│                 │  ├──────────────────────┼──────────────────────┤     │
│                 │  │  2-inch Nails        │  Qty = 30 lbs        │     │
│                 │  ├──────────────────────┼──────────────────────┤     │
│  Order Items    ⎨  │  Item No. = 2        │  Catalog Number=CD-110-887  │
│     Table       │  ├──────────────────────┼──────────────────────┤     │
│                 │  │  16-oz Hammer        │  Qty = 100           │     │
│                 │  ├──────────────────────┼──────────────────────┤     │
│                 │  │  Item No. = 4        │  Catalog Number=MS-564-123  │
│                 │  ├──────────────────────┼──────────────────────┤     │
│                 ⎩  │  Heavy Duty Wrench   │  Qty = 20            │     │
│                    ├─────────────────────────────────────────────┤     │
│                    │                                             │     │
│                    │             Index Information               │     │
│                    │                                             │     │
│                    └─────────────────────────────────────────────┘     │
└──────────────────────────────────────────────────────────────────────┘
```

Figure 6-5 Example of Clustered Data Storage

6.3 Maintaining the Integrity of Data

During the design stage, you need to consider the rules for maintaining the correctness of data between relation tables in your database. For example, an ordered item cannot exist in the order items relation table if a corresponding entry in the customer order relation does not exist. We discussed these concepts of referential integrity and entity integrity in Chapter 3. Note that many products *claim* that they implement integrity facilities when they really mean concurrency control mechanisms such as transaction rollback and rollforward.

Entity integrity is commonly supported by products via the option of defining a field to be not null. But few products provide mechanisms to allow the designer to define referential integrity. One exception is UNIFY which provides the referential links just discussed. These links prevent a member record from being added if a corresponding owner record does not already exist. Thus, in our example, we might define a referential link from the order items relation to the customer order relation as shown in Figure 6-6. Once the link is defined, we would not be able to add an ordered item for a nonexistent customer order.

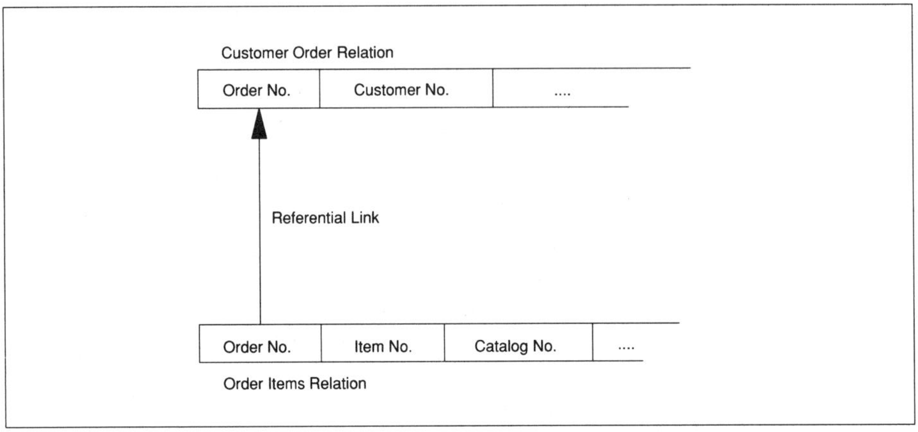

Figure 6-6 Example of a Referential Link

In products without any integrity maintenance facilities, the application programs must enforce the required constraints. In such cases, allowing users direct add and update access to individual relations is dangerous since integrity constraints cannot be enforced. For example, allowing users to use the SQL insert statements allows them to add new rows to a single relation table. We might restrict insert access which is possible with some products or, alternatively, restrict add access to the appropriate relation tables with security measures. Keep in mind that restricting access to the relations will prevent the user from adding data through other utilities and programs as well as SQL. We discuss these issues in more detail in the next chapter.

6.4 Concurrency Control Issues

In Chapter 3, we discussed the types and levels of concurrency control facilities available among the products. Your selected DBMS will provide only some of these facilities based on its architecture. During the design stage of your application you have to choose which facilities you really need.

The choice between field level and record level locking depends on the consistency needs of specific functions of your application. Field level locking is desirable in functions which update individual items in relations and in which there is no dependency between the set of items updated. For example, in a personnel table, updates to the address and salary information can be performed by two separate users concurrently without affecting the consistency of data. Similarly, name changes and address changes could be applied without affecting the data consistency. However, changes to a part description and part price may be interdependent and must match each other, so record level locking is essential.

File level locking might mean locking a single table or the entire database, depending on the product architecture. Locking a relation table is desirable when a function makes

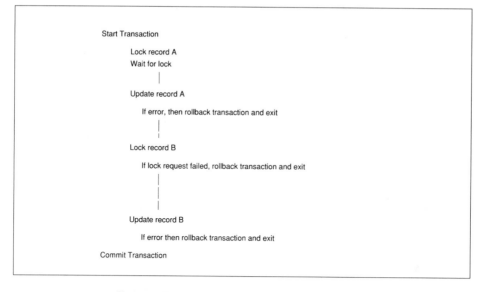

Figure 6-7 Example of Transaction Level Control Mechanisms

bulk changes to the table as in a batch update. Locking the entire database is desirable when performing a backup to prevent the backup containing inconsistent data due to a partially completed transaction.

Most products provide a facility for transaction level concurrency control with transaction start and commit facilities as illustrated in Figure 6-7. Any updates specified after the start point are not actually applied to the database until the commit point is executed. You can specify updates to multiple relations within the transaction. Thus, if one of the updates fails, you can roll back the transaction to the start point, which in effect aborts the transaction. Rollback will free any resources you have locked up to that point in the transaction so that other users can use them. Note that this facility is frequently claimed to provide data *integrity*, but it does not satisfy either of our definitions discussed in Chapter 3.

Rollback and rollforward operations are often used by DBMS products to avoid deadlocks. When all of the resources required by a transaction cannot be locked, the transaction might be temporarily rolled back allowing some other transaction to complete. Then, it is rolled forward to its commit point for completion. Your application programs can use a similar strategy when an update within a transaction fails.

A good design strategy to ensure that deadlocks do not occur is for the application functions that share some resources to always access them in the same order. Thus, failure of an update due to locking failure will indicate that another function has currently locked the resource. You can then wait until the resource is unlocked with the assurance that previously locked resources are not needed by another transaction. If resources are not accessed in the same order in different transactions, your only way of deadlock avoidance is to roll back the transaction.

Be wary of performing tasks in a transaction which cannot be rolled back. Such limitations are product specific. If you do use such operations, you have to write your own code to undo the database changes after aborting the transaction.

6.5 Facilities for Building User Interfaces

Your application may offer two major types of user interfaces: interactive and noninteractive. Interactive interfaces include menus and forms based data entry and inquiry. Noninteractive interfaces include report generation and SQL output. Note that interactive SQL access should only be given to users who are familiar with the language and the application database structures. They should know how to handle command based interfaces with their cryptic editing keystrokes under UNIX.

During interactive interface design you should aim for consistency in presentation and command handling. For example, command options presented at the top of the screen in one program and bottom of the screen in another program are very disconcerting to users and make the application difficult to learn. Using the tools available with the product often makes it easier to maintain presentation consistency than if each program were handling its own presentation.

Noninteractive interfaces also need to be rigorously consistent in format and usage. For example, report output displayed on the screen should be designed for 80 column width so that lines do not wrap. Line wrap makes reports difficult to read. Output should be divided into sections such that each section fits on one screen, with headings and titles repeated on each section.

Most report writer tools in DBMS products allow you to specify report width and length, and where headings should be repeated. Users should have the option of aborting the output using the same commands used for other programs. This can be difficult since interactive programs display the command to exit a program where noninteractive programs frequently do not have such a display arrangement.

6.5.1 Menu Interface Considerations

Menu interfaces allow you to present selection choices to the user in an easy-to-use manner. Traditionally, we built menus into each individual program. We have faced a lot of maintenance headaches with this method since each program duplicated the code for menu handling. Making any changes to the menu structure or its interface behavior required changes to each and every program.

More recently, menu tools have eliminated these difficulties by separating menu handling from application programs. They consist of two parts: a menu definition program and a menu driver program. The menu definition program allows you to define a menu tree suitable for your application. Each menu selection is associated with a program command, typically in the same format as used to run the program from the SHELL environment. The menu driver program accesses these definitions to display each menu to the user. When the user choose a menu selection, the driver starts a child process to execute the associated program. This scheme is well suited to the process based architecture of UNIX.

Most DBMS products include a menu utility which provides a consistent user interface. Some of these utilities have built-in knowledge about interfaces to other DBMS utilities in the same product which they use to make menu definition simpler. They may also include the DBMS's own login procedure and provide extra access security definitions to prevent access to other programs.

The main advantage of using menu tools is that you can restructure menus without changing any programs. Using the utility provided not only saves development time, but also provides an interface similar to that of other utilities in the package.

There are some disadvantages to using a menu utility. Menu drivers execute programs as a child process, which means there are two running processes as illustrated in Figure 6-8(a). In the traditional method, you would have only one process, since the program itself presents and drives the menu. However, each such traditional program contains extra menu handling code leading to a larger program size than those designed to run under a menu driver.

Some menu drivers allow you to specify SHELL special characters or environment variables for a selection program. They may spawn a SHELL child process which in turn creates the program child process. So you end up with three processes: the menu, the SHELL process, and the program being executed, as shown in Figure 6-8(b). The SHELL process is necessary to interpret the environment variables and special characters specified in the program command. This SHELL process is eliminated in some implementations by menu drivers that replace the SHELL process by the program to be executed.

These differences are significant if your machine lacks sufficient *real* memory, with the potential for frequent swapping. The menu utility option is still desirable as it can be swapped to disk with no perceptible effect to the user executing a program under it. Swapping of the traditional program can lead to a noticeable effect on user response. The SHELL process is largely shared code and does not require a significant quantity of extra memory. However, extra processes occupy slots in the kernel's process table and their status is examined frequently to determine whether they are ready to run. Thus, a large number of processes can affect system performance.

Another difficulty with using menu utilities is that you cannot customize their menu display and commands handling to fit your whims. For example, you cannot change a utility which presents a ring menu display, to display a full-screen style menu. Many designers actually consider this inflexibility to be an advantage since it enforces consistency in all menus. Consistent menu handling makes user training easier, while using an independent menu utility allows you the flexibility of changing menu structures without touching application programs.

The commands used by some menu utilities for standard functions such as ***exit menu program*** or ***go to previous menu*** might be cryptic control sequences. However, most DBMS menu utilities allow you to associate these sequences with terminal function keys. In the worst case, you might pay a few dollars more for a modern terminal with programmable function keys which you can set to generate the cryptic sequences. (*Do you really still use that antique ADM3A or even VT100?*)

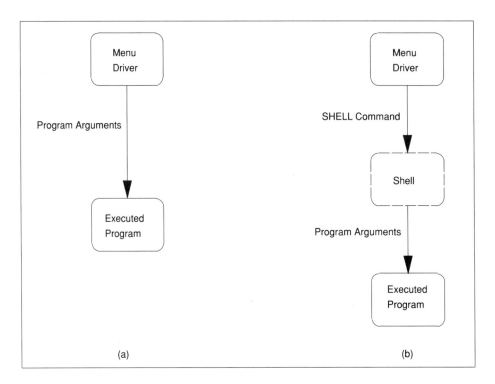

Figure 6-8 Relationship between Menu Driver and Executed Program

You should consider the facilities provided by the available menu utility early in the design stage, so that you can match custom developed interfaces to use similar commands and presentation schemes. If the utility allows you to specify access restrictions to program facilities, you should design your application to utilize these security measures. Incidentally, you could restrict insert and update access to SQL in such a menu utility to resolve the problem we discussed in Section 6.3. With such a facility, users could still use SQL to retrieve data but would not be able to add or update any relations.

6.5.2 Forms Based Interface

A forms based interface, like the menu interface, consists of two parts: forms definition and forms driver. A forms definition program allows you to define the layout of a form and the forms driver displays the form and allows a user to access data defined by the form. You can define consistent presentation of forms to a user using these utilities for the common types of access: *insert, update, delete*, and *search*.

Development using forms utilities is faster than using a programming language such as C; however, you can only provide limited functionality. Their important advantage is to facilitate *prototyping* at the early stages of analysis and design. You might even put a late-model prototype into production if its performance is adequate for your needs.

Forms definition programs can be a separate *paint* utility, such as the UNIFY PAINT or INGRES VIFRED, or may be simply a language script created with a normal text editor and then compiled, as for INFORMIX FORMBUILD. These programs often allow you to create a default form which use database field names as labels in the form. You can edit a default form to customize its layout.

Screen based paint utilities are easier to use since they prevent mistakes in database table name, field names, and sizes during the definition stage. The FORMBUILD approach requires an iterative edit and compile cycle, which is more tedious. However, in this approach, the source program is an ordinary text file and can be controlled with SCCS which is not feasible with the paint approach.

A forms driver provides, as a minimum, four types of access to data: insert, update, delete, and search. Examples of forms drivers are UNIFY ENTER, INGRES QUERY-BY-FORMS (QBF), INFORMIX PERFORM, and ORACLE SQL*FORMS (IAP). Some drivers, such as PERFORM, provide additional functions to handle multiple screens and tables, and master-detail hierarchical relationships. These commands are fixed and displayed to the user even if the user is not allowed appropriate access to the data defined on the form.

UNIFY provides security measures integrated with its menu driver to specify the types of access a user is allowed for a given form. In this case, ENTER displays only those commands associated with the type of access allowed. For example, if add access is denied to a user, the add command will not appear when that user runs the form.

Most forms drivers allow you to specify edit and validation checks on each field including valid range of values, alpha or numeric fields etc. Products such as PERFORM also allow *lookups* into another table so that you can specify data integrity rules. However, these drivers allow a user to access fields from only one table at a time, requiring a special command to change the current table. Thus, users need to know the database structure to use a form containing multiple tables effectively.

You can specify the order of cursor movement between the fields in most of these products. However, you cannot specify that a portion of the form be hidden from users until they enter a value in a particular field. For example, if a field has two possible values and you wish to present users with additional fields based on which value they enter, you cannot hide the additional fields for each case. To provide such an interface, you need to use a fourth generation language, such as UNIFY ACCELL, or your own host language interface program, to drive the form. In most forms drivers, you would achieve a similar effect by skipping over some fields based on the value entered in the determining field.

Be warned that no debugging tools are available with these forms drivers, thus making development of complex forms difficult. Their best use is for quick development of data entry and file maintenance components of your application, which is actually a significant, but tedious, portion of development. You should carefully examine the facilities available in your DBMS and experiment with them before deciding to develop more complex forms interfaces. It will probably be easier to use a fourth generation language program to drive the form instead.

6.5.3 Forms Driven by a Fourth Generation Language

You could develop a simple application entirely with the facilities provided in this language. Hence, their manuals frequently refer to developing *applications*. However, each such application is a single large program and thus could lead to swapping problems.

An important issue in designing a form driven by a fourth generation language is to make the interface match the forms driver interface. Otherwise, some of your forms will behave differently from those developed using the fourth generation language. Fourth generation languages provide more flexibility in driving forms with the following mechanisms:

- A means of specifying menu options, and actions to be taken when a user selects the option.

- A means of specifying actions to be taken before and after entry in a screen field.

- One of the actions can be displaying of the next or previous form. Some languages refer to forms by name, and chaining of forms must be explicitly coded in the program.

- You can specify actions to perform before allowing entry in the first field, or after completing entry in the form but before invoking the next form.

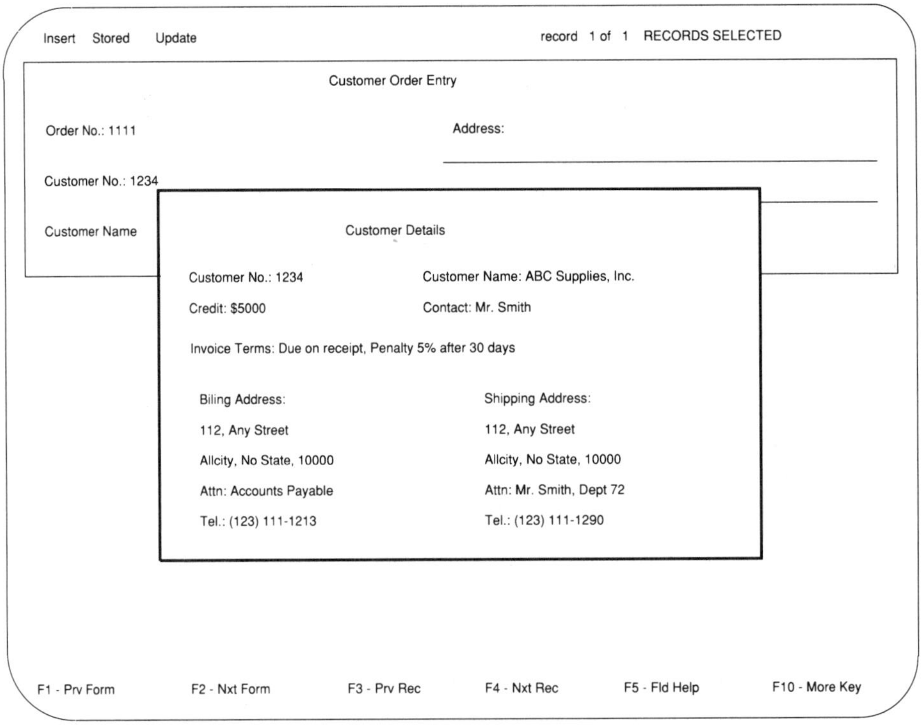

```
  Insert   Stored   Update                                    record  1 of  1   RECORDS SELECTED

                                          Customer Order Entry

     Order No.: 1111                                      Address:

     Customer No.: 1234

     Customer Name              Customer Details

                       Customer No.: 1234          Customer Name: ABC Supplies, Inc.

                       Credit: $5000               Contact: Mr. Smith

                       Invoice Terms: Due on receipt, Penalty 5% after 30 days

                       Biling Address:             Shipping Address:

                       112, Any Street             112, Any Street

                       Allcity, No State, 10000    Allcity, No State, 10000

                       Attn: Accounts Payable      Attn: Mr. Smith, Dept 72

                       Tel.: (123) 111-1213        Tel.: (123) 111-1290



  F1 - Prv Form      F2 - Nxt Form      F3 - Prv Rec      F4 - Nxt Rec      F5 - Fld Help      F10 - More Key
```

Figure 6-9 Forms Windows with ACCELL

- Actions specified can access any part of the database, not just the data referenced in the form. You can thus perform lookups in another table to satisfy integrity rules, calculations based on database data as well as screen field data, and so on. Help functions could display lists of valid values from another database field when you specify lookups to maintain data integrity.

Some of the common menu options are: *next form, previous form, help*, and *exit*. You may be allowed to specify forms which occupy different parts of the screen at the same time, as for instance in UNIFY ACCELL. In this case, you could display an appropriate second form based on the value entered in a field as shown in Figure 6-9.

A consistent design for menu options, field error handling, and help actions is essential to the success of your application. Consistent interface is enforced in the forms driver method by the utility, but you must design it in the fourth generation language driver.

Performing similar tasks using the host language interface is possible but requires significantly longer development time. This interface gives you the ability to design a host language program for speed which is not feasible in the fourth generation language. Many of these fourth generation products translate their programs into a host language interface prior to being compiled into an executable. They cannot, however, optimize code sufficiently to improve performance, and generally consume more resources than your finely tuned host language interface program.

6.5.4 Interface to Displayed Reports

In many applications, you may display short reports to the user on the screen. For such reports, you need a report page size which matches the screen size, typically 80 columns wide and 24 lines long. The DBMS report generator utility allows you to redefine the page size to match your needs. With this utility, you can also specify headers for page and data items which repeat for each new report page. Thus, you can present a report to the user in a readable format with titles and headings repeated on each page, with little extra effort.

You could filter the report output through a UNIX utility such as *more* (Berkeley) or *pg* (System V), to pause between each page. In this case, the report page length needs to be 23 lines to reserve the next line for the continuation prompt from these utilities. Some report generators, such as INFORMIX ACE, provide a *pause* statement which you can code into your report script to achieve the same effect. In this case, you could pause the report at convenient points in the report as well as every 24 lines. If you use a pause statement, you also have to handle display of report headings appropriately on the screen.

In many DBMS products, the forms driver utility interfaces to its report generator utility so a user can specify runtime parameters. You can also achieve a similar effect with a form driven by the fourth generation language or a host interface program.

6.5.5 Printed Reports Considerations

The considerations for printed reports differ from those described in Section 6.5.4. The page layout and size should match the size of printer paper used. The printed report should also include the following items to aid the user:

- A banner containing the user's name, date, and time of printing. This banner could be produced by the UNIX print spool utility.

- The report title should match the menu option presented to the user to avoid confusion.

- A list of the data selection criteria used for the report. This list should contain runtime parameters supplied by the user as well as criteria programmed into the report. Such a list is invaluable to clarify the user's expectation of the report output. Report generator utilities do not print this list automatically, so you need to include the process at the start of the report.

- A *report end* message, which signals the user that the report completed successfully. Thus, its absence indicates that the report may have aborted before its completion. You also need to include this procedure in your report definition file, as the utilities do not generate this message on printed output.

You can initiate printed reports from the menu and then run them as a background process in UNIX. Background processing is not an option under the single tasking MS-DOS operating system, although OS/2 does permit it. Think about the increase in the number of processes running concurrently when you choose to process reports in background mode. The background process might require a lot of system resources and affect the system performance. Even if its resource requirements are small, several such processes can distract the kernel scheduler from paying quick attention to interactive users.

A good way to control the number of such background processes is by using a batch job spooler, available from third party UNIX tools vendors. Then you would submit each background process to the job spooler queue and the spooler would run them one at a time from the queue. Some examples of such spoolers are UQUEUE from Unitech Software Inc. and UNIBATCH from Unisystems Software Ltd.

Finally, what happens to background processes when the user logs off before they complete? The UNIX kernel kills all active processes, including background processes, associated with the user who logged off. Using a job spooler would avoid this problem. In other cases, you need to use other utilities such as the *nohup* utility in SYSTEM V.

6.6 Developing with a Host Language Interface

As we discussed in Chapter 3, there are two types of host language interfaces: function call and embedded SQL. Each of these has advantages and drawbacks. One drawback common to both is that the resulting program is very specific to the DBMS for which it was developed. Thus, converting such programs to another product effectively requires a rewrite of the application. This is because two products may provide similar functionality but their interface methods differ significantly. For example, one product might provide an outer join but another does not. There could even be syntactical differences in the SQL language supported.

You can use the host language interface to write programs that drive a screen form. A form driven by such a program can be designed to perform faster than its equivalent written in a fourth generation language. Developing it will take longer since you need to develop several facilities which are available only in the fourth generation language. Thus, there will be significantly more source code to maintain than in the fourth generation language program. More source means, of course, more potential bugs and longer enhancement timeframes, just like our current dark ages of third generation language programming!

6.6.1 Function Call Based Interface

A function call interface allows access to the database via calls to a library of functions to retrieve data. You can specify arguments, such as a search key, by passing literals or program variables containing the value and obtain results into other variables. Note that you could choose between more than one set of functions to access data where the performance of each set depends on the database structure. You could choose the set of functions which provides the best performance for your database or you could add indexes or referential links or improve the execution speed of another set.

It is easy to make the application programs very dependent on the database structure by using functions which depend on the existence of indexes, referential links, or data elements in particular tables. Such dependency makes the application less flexible and may cause difficulties when you incorporate new versions of the DBMS product. You can only avoid dependency by choosing functions at the design stage which do not refer explicitly to particular indexes for accessing data and enforcing coding practices. If your database is properly normalized, and any referential links defined are inherent in the data, then the data elements and relationships between them are not likely to change. Thus, references to particular data elements in specific tables may be acceptable.

A major advantage of using a function call based interface is that you could use the UNIX symbolic debugger, *sdb*, for certain types of program development. For example, you could debug C programs which do not create child processes. Programs which perform screen I/O may be difficult to trace; however, you could use sdb to trace variable value changes and control flow. Using sdb, even with screen functions impaired, can save a significant amount of testing and debugging time.

6.6.2 Embedded Query Language Interface

An embedded query language interface, unlike function call interface, requires you to use query language statements for all access to the database. Thus, you cannot access indexes or referential links making your programs independent of the database structure. This interface requires you to use its preprocessor on the source code prior to compiling it into the executable.

You cannot specify which access methods the DBMS should use in this programming interface. The query language optimizer considers the available indexes and data clusters to determine the access strategy. Note that in most products the embedded query language statements are *not* precompiled, but are interpreted at runtime. Thus, the optimizer strategy for data access is determined each time the statement is executed. This processing has the following implications

- Runtime interpretation is an unnecessary overhead if the database structure is stable, as in a production environment.

- Errors in field or table names in the embedded query language statements are not detected at preprocessing or compilation stages, but only at runtime. Thus, you need to test run these programs to find such syntax errors.

Some inherent drawbacks of the embedded query language interface are the limitations of the query language itself. For example, the standard SQL language cannot output data from a join specification where one table does not contain a matching record for the joined table. Thus, a vendor record with no matching records in the supplied-items table cannot be accessed together with matching records. Some implementations of SQL, such as INFORMIX-SQL, contain language extensions to handle these cases, although using such extensions makes your programs very dependent on the particular DBMS.

With other products, you need to use multiple statements to obtain the data described in the preceding example. In this case, you have to use external sort and merge mechanisms to print the combined data. Multiple statements also increase the overhead of interpreting the query language statements at runtime.

It is possible to use a symbolic debugger for a small portion of programs written with this interface. A couple of trials in using the debugger will probably convince you that this is a frustrating exercise. The problem is that symbolic debuggers are based on programming language source code and not the embedded query language source code. The source code output by the embedded query language preprocessor often has greater resemblance to *spaghetti* than to the code you wrote. It's a pity that debugging tools cannot directly handle embedded query language statements. They certainly cannot help you in determining if the best data access strategy is used.

The most effective way to debug such programs is the traditional method of incorporating *trace* statements at appropriate points which print variable values. You could define coding standards for incorporating such trace statements in each program using this interface.

6.7 Host Language versus Fourth Generation Languages

Fourth generation language programs, in most products, convert into the lower level host language interface before their compilation into an executable program. Thus, a fourth generation language is a higher level interface than the host language interface.

Fourth generation languages use a completely different syntax and structure than the programming languages, while host language interfaces are standard programming languages with additional features to allow access to the database. For example, fourth generation languages understand data types supported by the DBMS, such as date and money. Programming languages do not support these data types, and you must use the equivalent data type supported by the language. A date data type from the database must, therefore, be converted to an integer in the programming language. The equivalence between the database data types and programming language data types differs for each DBMS product.

Fourth generation languages also differentiate between field types such as screen fields, database fields, and program variables. Such distinction exists partially in the embedded query language interface of some products and not at all in function call based interfaces.

In host language interfaces, you need to set variable naming standards to distinguish between field types. Many fourth generation languages enforce naming conventions since their preprocessors depend on the conventions for correct translation into the host language.

Fourth generation languages consist of more than just the coding language. They include the form definition, display, and driver mechanisms which are separate entities in a host language interface program. Database access through a query language, with modified syntax, and high level report formatting facilities are also components of a fourth generation language. In a host language interface, database access facilities are not integrated parts of the programming language but are additions which are hidden from you by their preprocessor. Report formatting facilities are highly dependent on the programming language and frequently are very low level such as those in the C language. Thus, more code is required to perform tasks in a host language that are trivial to define in a fourth generation language.

An important advantage of fourth generation languages is that programs can achieve a significant quantity of work with a few lines of code because of their high level facilities. Note that these facilities are provided with a number of functions, each offering a generic operation. Since each function must offer a generic interface appropriate for different application environments, they contain complex code and consume a significant amount of system resources.

The advantage of using this method is that it reduces the amount of program code an application programmer must write. However, due to the generic operation of each high level function, they contain some code which is unnecessary for your specific application. You would not write such code in an equivalent host language interface program, and hence the resulting executable programs are smaller in size and probably run faster. The moral here is that more lines of source code do not automatically imply a larger executable program!

Since host language interfaces do not provide all of the facilities of a fourth generation language, programs written with them are longer. The program size in turn implies that more effort is required to test, debug, and incorporate enhancements in them. However, you can fine tune the third generation code in such programs to maximize performance, which is not possible in the fourth generation languages. Host language interface programs allow you to perform many tasks which are not supported by fourth generation languages.

6.8 Conclusions

In this chapter, we saw how you can use DBMS utilities in the design and development of applications. You need to consider UNIX constraints and capabilities as certain design decisions affect the system performance. These considerations differ from those in a non-DBMS application environment but they give you the ability to develop flexible applications. Using the utilities provided saves you a significant portion of development and could further reduce the effort required for enhancements.

An application consists of four major components: a database, a menu interface to integrate application components, screen based forms for data entry and access, and reports. DBMS utilities allow you to develop these components to suit the needs of your application. This section lists some rules of thumb to consider when designing each of these components.

Database:

The major considerations in this component are relation or database size limitations, choice of access methods, data integrity rules, and concurrency control needs. Size limitations depend on the storage approach used, either one relation per file or multiple relations per file. The first approach provides a database which is easy to restructure but suffers from the UNIX filesystem limitation. The second approach allows you to bypass the filesystem limitations, but requires more effort to restructure.

The access methods commonly available are hashed indexes, B-tree indexes, and compressed B-tree indexes. You can only use hashed access when you know the full key value, whereas both types of B-trees can support searches with partial key values or wildcards. B-trees also allow you access in a key based sequential fashion – that is, for successive next key value, and support nonunique keys. Compressed B-trees save disk space but do not perform as well as normal B-trees, since extra processing is necessary to decode compressed keys.

Data integrity rules are application dependent. Most products can enforce entity integrity through definition of null data restrictions; however, few provide referential integrity facilities. UNIFY can support such integrity rules with its referential links facility.

Concurrency control is mostly used at field level, record level, or transaction level depending on the operations performed by each component of the application. Coding standards can make transaction processing easier and reduce the possibility of deadlocks occurring.

Menu Interface:

You can develop a flexible and consistent user interface using the menu utility provided with a DBMS. This utility allows you to change the menu structure without affecting application programs. You should consider redefining any cryptic command sequences with the redefinition tools provided with the utility or with the terminal function key programming capabilities.

Screen Forms Interface:

Forms command interface should be consistent with the menu interface to avoid confusing the user and for ease of user training. Forms drivers give you the ability to develop simple data entry and access facilities quickly but are difficult to use for developing complex programs. They do not provide any debugging facilities. You can develop application specific forms drivers with fourth generation languages or using the host language interface. Some simple rules for forms design are

- Do not crowd a screen with too many data items.
- Avoid multiple tables on a single screen with most forms drivers as they operate on one table at a time. Users have to use a special command to switch between tables.
- Avoid splitting a table across screens, unless you can make the division transparent to the user.
- Set design and coding standards for developing forms drivers in fourth generation languages or host language interface programs.

Reports:

Report generators provide most of the facilities for you to develop reports. Useful facilities for a good user interface include page layout and size definition so you can match the output to its destination. You can filter the report output through UNIX facilities for presentation on a screen or to a printer. You can obtain runtime parameters for the report by using a screen form and use the forms-driver-to-report-generator interface to run the report. Reports destined to run as background processes should be spooled in a job spooler to avoid potential performance degradation.

7

Running a DBMS Application

While designing the application, you cannot ignore issues of the production environment. Although these issues may not affect the design of individual programs in your application, they determine how easily users can perform their day-to-day functions. They have a major impact on successfully implementing your application. This chapter examines some of these issues:

- How much interaction do the application users need with UNIX itself? A well-designed application should hide the underlying operating system from the users, so they can concentrate on getting their job done. Users should not need to learn any cryptic UNIX commands.

- The performance needs of users change as they become familiar with the application. We discuss some user interface tricks which improve the user's perception of speed. This is an important issue that you must consider in the design and development stages, as correcting it after these phases requires a complete redesign of the application.

- Administration of a UNIX application is often done by users rather than an MIS operations department, especially with applications running on small computers. We discuss these administrative needs and how to satisfy them with the available facilities.

- The access control facilities of many products depend on the underlying operating system facilities. Your design should consider how these controls will operate in the production environment to achieve the desired access security. This set-up often requires a combination of UNIX and DBMS facilities.

- Applications requirements change frequently throughout the development process and after its release into production. Using a DBMS helps you to change your application easily. We also examine how the DBMS and UNIX combination helps you in porting applications to different manufacturers' computers.

7.1 How Much Interaction with UNIX?

Whether or not to give users access to the UNIX SHELL is a controversial design issue. Giving access to SHELL means that users can use many of the operating system commands and utilities. The danger is that they can accidentally delete files vital to the running of the application and thus prevent its use by others. We saw in Chapter 5 how easily such an accident can occur even with experienced technical staff. File and directory access control methods provide one way to prevent such accidental deletion. A better way is to prevent all access to the SHELL, preventing opportunities to make mistakes.

Consider whether your users can already use the cryptic UNIX commands, or if they require additional training. Application users who are primarily interested in performing their job functions may be better off with an easy-to-use menu interface. They could access all the functions they need through this interface without typing SHELL commands. Thus, you can completely hide the underlying operating system from users.

An integrated application presents the menu interface to users directly after they log in. Section 7.1.1 discusses ways to integrate login procedures and menu display. Your menu options may execute utility programs which allow users to *escape* to a SHELL process. For example, many menu drivers, forms drivers, and UNIX text editors provide such an escape mechanism. To prevent all access to SHELL, you should disable these mechanisms using the techniques discussed in Section 7.1.2. We also discuss alternative utilities provided by some DBMSs for program access control which denies access to specific programs.

To provide a comprehensive set of facilities in the application menus, you should include all administrative functions required by a user. Such administrative functions might include viewing and control of print jobs, and monitoring of batch jobs which are part of the application. If the day-to-day administration of the application is performed by non-technical users, consider providing a menu based interface to the functions discussed in Section 7.3.

7.1.1 Integrated Menu Start-up

An ideal approach is to display the application menu as soon as the terminal is powered on. Consider the success of starting up PC applications via the *autoexec* mechanism in MS-DOS. You can achieve similar effects on UNIX if you do not need security access control provided by the UNIX login and password mechanism. Achieving this effect in SYSTEM V UNIX requires replacing the *getty* terminal control program in */etc/inittab* by the application menu program. In BSD UNIX, similar procedures are possible, although actual files to be modified are different.

Note that in this approach, you can only support terminals which are directly connected to the machine with a fixed baud rate. Getty incorporates support of terminals at different speeds and over modem connections, so it starts the login process when it realizes that a terminal is on-line. Note also that without the login procedure execution, you need to specify extra processing to set up the environment needed by many DBMS utilities.

It is unfortunate that getty has the login program name hard-coded into it. You could consider replacing the login program itself with your application menu program, but be prepared to discard this notion if unrelated users share the same machine. You will have to apologize to these users, at the very least, for messing up their login mechanisms.

You can use the preceding option with security control in products such as UNIFY and ORACLE, which implement their own login mechanisms. However, other products, such as INFORMIX-SQL and INGRES, base their data access security control on the *uid* and *gid* assigned by the UNIX login mechanisms. Therefore, you cannot bypass the login procedure with these products. Note that you must assign a separate login id to each user in order to use their security measures. With these products, present the application menu after the UNIX login procedure completes.

There are two ways of defining the menu presentation after login: by specifying the menu program in the */etc/passwd* file, or by running it in each user's *profile* SHELL script. In the first alternative, the application may not terminate when the terminal is powered off depending on the terminal driver settings at the time. In the second alternative, you must disable the quit and interrupt signals during the execution of the profile. Otherwise, the user could interrupt the profile execution and get access to the login SHELL process. Both alternatives create a login SHELL process, which in turn starts the menu program. Unless you use the SHELL exec command, you get a minimum of two processes per active user. The login SHELL process will remain idle throughout the session.

7.1.2 SHELL Escape Mechanisms

Many interactive utilities such as menu drivers and forms drivers provide mechanisms to run SHELL commands using an *escape* mechanism. A designated character sequence activates such an escape mechanism, for example, the sequence ":!" in the *vi* editor. Each utility has a different means of disabling its escape mechanism. This is a necessary task if you wish to prevent SHELL access completely.

UNIFY treats the SHELL program just like an application program so its menu access control methods are useful in denying access to it. Other products such as INFORMIX-SQL do not have a way of preventing SHELL access. In this case, you may need to redefine an item in the terminal driver settings (*stty* command) such as *Quit* or *Interrupt* to the SHELL escape character. You should be careful to preserve any items providing essential functions before such redefinition. Consider as an example the PERFORM forms driver. The "!" (exclamation mark) character activates its SHELL escape mechanism, and it uses the Interrupt setting to abort current operation. Thus, you might redefine the Quit character to the "!" (exclamation mark) character which PERFORM ignores.

Text editors commonly implement a SHELL escape mechanism. Disabling this mechanism is important if any of the DBMS utilities, such as interactive SQL, allow access to an editor. In the standard UNIX editor, *vi,* SHELL access depends on whether an environment variable called SHELL exists and refers to an executable program. If you define this variable to be a dummy program, as illustrated in Figure 7-1, attempted SHELL escape causes this

```
***file: noshell.c

#include <stdio.h>

main()
{
    printf ("Access to SHELL Denied!");
    exit();
}


***compiling into an executable module

$ cc -o noshell  noshell.c
$

***Setting the SHELL environment variable

$ SHELL="noshell";
$ export SHELL;
$
```

Figure 7-1 Disabling *vi* SHELL Escape Mechanism

program to run. The dummy program might simply output a warning message that access to SHELL is not allowed. Other commonly used editors may provide a different means of disabling SHELL escape.

Another possibility for a user to gain access to SHELL is through SHELL scripts accessed from a menu selection in some menu drivers. The user might press the quit or interrupt keys while the script is running terminating the current command and thus gaining access to SHELL. Some menu drivers terminate the SHELL process as well when this occurs, but others may not. The only way to avoid this accident is by trapping these two signals either in each shell script run from the menu driver or in the user's login profile.

7.1.3 Print Jobs Interface

One of the facilities needed in an application where a user can request a printed report, is a print queue status display. A user must have a way of finding out the length of time before his requested report is ready, especially if the printer is a shared resource. The standard UNIX print spooler subsystems such as the SYSTEM V *lp* or the BSD *lpr* have utilities which display the current print queue status. However, the format of the information displayed by these may be confusing to the users. Some third party packages provide a screen based status display which may be better suited to your application.

Some of the other functions a user needs are controlling the printer to which a job is submitted if there are multiple printers, and controlling the print job already queued. For example, the user may wish a particular report to be printed on a laser printer which is not the default printer. The default printer is set for the login environment and cannot be changed from the menu driver since a script run as a menu option will be a child process. The SHELL restrictions do not allow exporting values of environment variables to a parent process. One compromise is to allow users to choose an alternative printer destination at login time for the entire session. The user also needs an easy way of moving a job from one printer to another or cancelling a job in the spooler queue.

One difficulty with the standard print utilities is the interface to options which control print features. They follow the conventions for UNIX commands so these options are specified on the command line. Standard menu driver interfaces do not allow a user to type commands in such a format, so users cannot select the particular options they wish to use. Thus, the user's interaction with print utilities is severely limited. To offer such choices to the user, consider a third party package which provides a forms based interface for users to control such print features.

7.1.4 Batch Jobs Interface

In the last chapter we discussed how reports could run as individual background processes or in a batch job queue. When you use such a scheme in your application, users need facilities to

- View the status of the job queue or their background job.
- Cancel or terminate their job.
- Obtain status of completed work.

There are no standard UNIX or DBMS utilities which provide such information. The *ps* command provides some of this information in a cryptic manner suitable for technical users, as shown in Figure 7-2. The display includes information about system processes, such as *init*, which you need to filter out. Third party job spoolers may provide batch queue specific information in a format suitable for nontechnical users.

7.2 Users' Performance Needs

Users who are new to an application often accept its speed with patience until their familiarity increases. Users familiar with another application or use of other computers, however, may have different demands. Thus, they may become dissatisfied with slower performance as the system load increases. This section examines some of their expectations to determine the application areas where you should pay particular attention to performance.

```
$ps -ef
    UID   PID  PPID   C     STIME TTY          TIME COMMAND
   root     0     0  40   8:10:20 ?           68:30 swapper
   root     1     0   0   8:10:20 ?            0:04 /etc/init
   root     0     0   0   8:10:20 ?            0:01 swapper
   root    81     1   0   8:14:44 console      0:00 /usr/lib/errdaemon
   root   101     1   0   8:15:01 tty02        0:00 /etc/getty tty02 9600
    jde   120     1   0   8:20:00 tty01        0:03 -sh
   root    86     1   0   8:14:47 ?            0:00 /etc/cron
    jde   189   120   0   9:25:23 tty01        0:00 vi /tmp/abc00068.sql
     lp    91     1   0   8:14:56 ?            0:00 /usr/lib/lpsched
   root    96     1   0   8:15:12 tty03        0:09 /etc/getty tty03 9600
    jde   214   201   0   9:31:45 tty01        0:00 ps -ef
    jde   201   189   0   9:31:30 tty01        0:00 [ sh ]
```

Figure 7-2 SYSTEM V 'ps' Command Display

We examine two categories of programs which have widely differing performance needs: interactive and background. For the purposes of the following discussion, interactive work is all tasks where the user and the system alternate their actions. Thus, users initiating a report from the menu and waiting for its completion before they can proceed to other tasks is an interactive task. Background tasks, on the other hand, are initiated by a user and continue running while the user proceeds to other tasks. An example is submitting a report to the print spooler, where the user can perform other tasks while the print job continues.

7.2.1 Interactive Program Performance

The critical time from a user's perspective is the wait time between an action and the system's acknowledgment of it. This wait time is often called *response time*. It does not always imply that the system is ready for the user's next action, merely that it recognizes the action. Appropriate messages displayed to the user after an action can reduce the wait time, thus improving their perception of application speed.

Such measures are insufficient in some applications where the need for speed is inherent in the tasks performed. An example would be a financial trading system supporting traders who complete transactions every second. The completed transaction must be posted to the application database so that the trader gets status information before starting the next transaction. In this case, the transaction is complete only after all updates are written to the database. The response time, then, includes the time taken to complete the database update.

A critical element in users' perception of speed is the time taken to display a screen form. DBMS products, which use the *curses* optimization facilities, improve this perceived speed at the cost of CPU time. These products display forms at an adequate speed over slow terminal connections such as at 1200 baud. They do not make a perceptible difference in display speed at 9600 baud or higher speeds.

Some of the important parts of typical commercial applications where you should pay close attention to performance are

- *Data entry tasks:* The speed of echoing characters as the user types is critical. This is important since professional data entry personnel type at a high speed, and the UNIX character at a time processing affects speed under heavy system load.

- *Full-screen display:* Try to eliminate perceptible pauses between clearing of the screen and the start of display, slow character-by-character painting of each line, and bursts of display with perceptible pauses. If you use DBMS utilities to display forms, these symptoms are beyond your control. However, they indicate heavy CPU utilization perhaps due to excessive system calls, too many processes, or swapping.

- *Interactive printed reports:* This task involves a user initiating a report, perhaps from a menu and having to wait until it is complete. This is a poor user interface design, although unavoidable if the type of batch facilities described in Section 7.1.4 are not available. You could define messages in the report generator script which indicate the amount of work completed. A good example is the name of the department being processed. Displaying the number of records processed is useful only if the user has some idea of the database size.

- *Successive prompts:* A program may prompt users for necessary parameters at runtime before processing starts. Significant pauses between prompts makes the system appear slow. You should group prompts and obtain user input as early in the program as possible to avoid this perception. A better way is to use a screen form to obtain runtime parameters, thus giving the user facilities to edit all parameters easily.

7.2.2 Background Jobs Performance

Many applications enter transactions but apply updates only at off-peak periods. Note that DBMS forms drivers apply all transactions to the database immediately and so are not useful to implement this method. Speed of completing each transaction is not as critical in such batch processing; instead, the volume of transactions to be completed in the available time-window is the determining factor for acceptable performance. For example, a nightly batch update that requires more than six to eight hours to run is not acceptable since it leaves little spare time for backups and recovery from problems. Unacceptable batch performance may be due to program performance or simply excessive transaction volume.

Other popular candidates for background processing are report generation tasks and data integrity checking programs. Background reports might be initiated interactively by a user or triggered automatically by the UNIX *cron* facility.

User initiated reports should be short so that processing completes in a short period, typically within a few minutes, although actual printing can take longer. Long reports prevent other users from obtaining their shorter printouts. A suitable timeframe for a printout depends on the work habits of its target users. If they walk up to the printer immediately after requesting a report, the suitable timeframe is less than five minutes. However, if they perform other tasks before checking the printer, a completion time of up to an hour is acceptable.

If you need to support ad hoc reports which could be very long, consider using multiple printers of different speeds. Users should also have the ability to inquire about the size of each job and to move their own print jobs among printers. Alternatively, you could arrange for administrative support which can respond to user needs quickly or monitor the system on a continuing basis.

7.3 Administrative Needs

One area which receives little attention during application design is application administration. *This is particularly important for applications where expert UNIX support does not exist on-site.* In the absence of user oriented administrative facilities, nontechnical users need extensive training to use UNIX facilities intended for technically oriented personnel. Applications aimed at environments with an expert systems staff also need some administrative facilities to reduce tedious tasks and prevent trivial mistakes.

In a DBMS application environment, standard UNIX administrative facilities are insufficient. For example, adding users with the standard facilities does not set up the necessary access information for the user to use the application DBMS. In the sections that follow, we discuss the integrated facilities you need to develop for administrative support of your application.

Another aspect of administration is system accounting procedures. Although UNIX facilities allow you to track usage of resources by users, you cannot enforce any restrictions. These accounting utilities are therefore rarely used. One consequence of this inability is that you need to implement a disk cleanup utility which erases temporary files created either by the DBMS or the application programs. Without an automatic cleanup utility, disk space is used up quickly, requiring tedious manual cleanup by systems staff.

7.3.1 User ID Management

One of the difficulties of implementing a DBMS application is the added complexity of *user id* management. You need to add a UNIX user id as well as perform necessary changes to the database to allow access to the application data. This additional processing depends on the security measures designed and also the directory and profile set-up needed for each user. Data access security measures require that each individual use a separate user id, so security requirements can be specified individually. Therefore, adding and deleting user ids frequently are important tasks in administering an application.

Before we examine the tasks required to add or delete a user, a note about organizing *home* directories and application directories. Separating application directories from those used by the operating system is a good idea, since changing the operating system version will not then affect the application files. In addition, it is worth separating application program directories from users' home directories.

As an example consider the directory structure for the *ord* application shown in Figure 7-1. This structure is similar to that used by UNIX itself. One of the directories in this structure could be a *data* directory holding all database related files such as indexes and data dictionary. The advantage is that you could create a duplicate test environment as a different tree. Then, reference the root directory of this structure with a SHELL environment variable from all programs. Thus, you could change a program to run in the test environment, or production, simply by resetting the environment variable value.

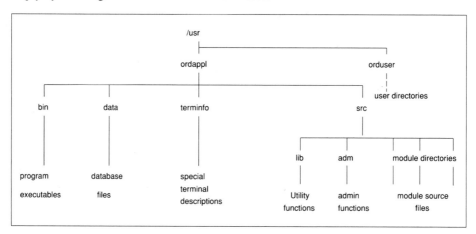

Figure 7-3 Application Directory Structure

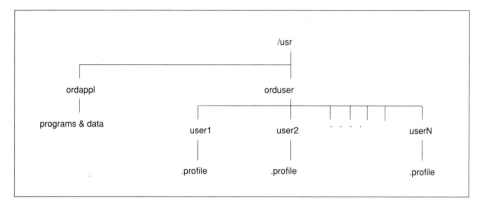

Figure 7-4 Application Users Directory Structure

Users' home directories should be different for each user and separate from the application directory structure, so that temporary files can be easily erased. Another advantage of this separation is that users' profiles could be individually customized to reflect their preferences. Figure 7-4 illustrates one such directory structure.

Many UNIX systems provide menu based administration facilities which automate the procedures for adding and deleting user ids. These procedures do not include adding the user id into the DBMS application. Also, some implementations of these cannot gracefully handle cases where the *passwd* file is write protected, or a user's home directory cannot be created. On the other side, DBMS facilities for adding and deleting users from an application do not create the necessary entries in the passwd file nor do they create a home directory. The tasks necessary to adding a user for a DBMS application are

- Create an appropriate entry in the passwd file, including a substitute start up program, if your application prevents access to SHELL in this manner.
- Create a home directory under the structure designed for your application. The owner and group of this directory must match those of the user id.
- Create a profile script in the home directory. This profile must set up the correct environment for the user to run the application, including starting up the menu driver program if required.
- Create a corresponding user id in the application database, necessary only in DBMS products like INGRES, ORACLE, and UNIFY.
- Set up security access control definitions for the user to access the application database. These may be done via SQL statements as in ORACLE or INFORMIX-SQL or by developing a program to manipulate the data dictionary as in UNIFY.
- Products such as ORACLE may require you to increase the parameters defining the maximum number of users attached to the database.

7.3.2 Database Backup and Recovery

Backup and recovery are crucial functions of any administrative system and standard methods are provided with the operating system. The important point to note is that these standard backups may be of little use for an application based on a DBMS. This is because they use the *cpio* or *tar* command which only handles filesystem files not databases stored on raw disks and can only recover if the entire backup is not corrupted. Many implementations of cpio do not handle multivolume backups and are frequently unreliable with operating system backups.

The UNIX *dd* utility does handle multivolume backups, but it creates a disk image as the backup. Its backup, therefore, includes all specified disk space even if your data occupies only a small portion of the space. For example, you might need four tape cartridges to backup using the dd utility, even though the actual data could fit onto two tape cartridges. The extra time for creating the remaining tape cartridges is clearly wasted.

Also noteworthy is that the backup facilities provided by the DBMS products are insufficient for the needs of a running application. These facilities do not recover your application directory structures and do not include application programs and system files such as passwd which are part of your application.

The essential ingredients of a backup and recovery facility for a DBMS based application are listed next in order of importance.

- *Data:* You could use the DBMS backup facility for performing this function, since it will arrange to lock the database against updates for the duration of the backup. It will also include data stored on raw disk as well as filesystem data files and include only those portions which are valid data. It will exclude any deleted data. Note, however, that it will also exclude application specific set-up information such as directory structures. This is a static backup and does not include changes to data applied up to the next backup.

  Recovering data is conceptually a simple process consisting of copying data from the backup into the existing database structure. However, you cannot recover individual database files and must restore the entire database. This recovery requires that the data dictionary contain correct information prior to attempting recovery. You also need the correct environment set-up before the application can be operational.

  Such a recovery process restores the contents of the database as it was at the point of the backup. However, many changes may have been applied since the backup was taken and you need to redo these transactions. You can either do this manually or by using the journaling facilities of the database. A manual method is suitable where the volume of transactions is quite small and reentry requires a short time. Journaling methods, discussed in Section 7.3.3, are suitable for large transaction volumes.

- *Application environment:* This backup includes all files needed for your application to operate correctly; for example, application directory structures, data dictionary files, user profiles, and any special files such as the *configuration parameters* file for the ORACLE DBMS start-up. All of these files must match the set-up at the time when the data backup was performed; however, you only need to perform this backup when some configuration item changes. For example, changes to database structure or adding and deleting users imply that this backup should be performed along with data backup.

You need restore the application environment from this backup before recovering the data so that the environment is correct for the backed up data. Keep in mind that if you choose to perform this backup only when necessary, the recovery procedure must decide from which backup copy to restore. For greater convenience, it should allow recovery of any individual file so that you restore only the necessary files. However, this method causes difficulties for nontechnical administrators who are not aware of the functions of individual files, and have no way of determining which file needs restoring.

· *Application software:* This backup includes all application programs, screen form files, report script files, and menu databases developed for your application. It is only necessary if you do not have a formal application release, and you do not use phased installation procedures where application programs are modified or developed in phases. In the absence of a formal release and installation procedure, the software backup should be performed whenever any of these items change.

In this case, the recovery procedure should determine which backup copy to restore and whether the data and environment backups match the software restored. These programs must be recovered before users can use the application. Note that if you develop your own backup and recovery programs, you must implement a scheme to bootstrap the recovery program so that other software, environment, and data can be recovered. One method that works is to put the recovery program on a floppy filesystem so the user can mount this filesystem and run the program. The program then recovers the application environment, software, and finally data.

· *UNIX configuration:* This backs up the operating configuration needed for your application to operate in the production environment. It includes the vital system configuration files from the /etc directory and its subdirectories. For example, in SYSTEM V, you would include the passwd file, the inittab file, and files in subdirectories /etc/master.d and /etc/rc.d. It should also include procedures set up to run at boot time and information on jobs triggered via at or cron facilities. They only need to be backed up when they change. A custom backup program could examine the last access date and time on these files to determine when to include them in the backup. Your procedure should take into account the ease of preserving at least two backup copies so that the restore can determine which one to use.

· *DBMS software:* You need not back up the product software since it is packaged with formal installation procedures, if these procedures are easily used by the administrator. A backup is necessary if the installation procedures are more difficult than the recovery procedure. You should recover this software prior to the application environment, so any default configuration files distributed with the standard software will be overwritten by your application specific set-up.

- *UNIX software:* The backup requirements for the operating system software are similar to those discussed for product software. This software obviously must be recovered prior to any other. You may need to provide detailed instructions to nontechnical users for installing this system or, alternatively, provide systems support to perform this rarely needed function.

You can automate all of the components into a single backup process from a user's viewpoint. However, backup of all components daily increases the total backup time required. Instead, consider setting up procedures for daily, weekly, and monthly backups. You should detail also the exact steps of recovery based on the extent of the disaster.

7.3.3 Transaction Journaling Facility

Most DBMS products offer a transaction journaling facility, which logs every data update transaction performed since the start of the process. You need to define this facility to stop every time a complete data backup is taken and restart it with a fresh log file immediately after backup. This can be difficult with some products such as INFORMIX-SQL which need journaling to be specified when creating the database. A common interface to starting and stopping journaling is via SQL statements.

A transaction log file contains information on transactions performed since the latest backup. This log file can be used to recover up to the last completed transaction prior to system failure. This method is usually faster than manually entering a large volume of transactions and therefore is suitable under these conditions. However, note that you must also back up the transaction log which matches the previous backup before performing the current backup. Otherwise, if you have difficulty recovering from the latest backup and wish to use a prior backup, you lose transactions which occurred between the prior and the latest backup. Your cleanup procedures should remove unnecessary on-line logs after they are backed up since they consume significant quantities of disk space.

Note that the journaling process does not perform proper recovery if a matching static backup does not exist. Although you can recover from a journal without first recovering the static backup, the resulting database will not reflect the correct data.

7.4 Access Security Control

In Chapter 5, we discussed the access security control mechanisms provided by UNIX. Many DBMS products depend on these mechanisms to implement further data access security. Their security mechanisms are often based on the user ids assigned by standard login procedures. In this section we discuss how these products use the underlying operating system mechanisms to incorporate the necessary data access control.

7.4.1 Login and Password Security

Most products use the operating system login procedures as the first level access control. The UNIX login procedures assign *uid* (user id) and *gid* (group id) values, which form the basis of the filesystem security measures. Any data access control facilities implemented by the DBMS use these to identify users and to determine which data items they are allowed to access.

Products such as UNIFY and ORACLE provide an additional login mechanism. In these products, the login user assignments can work independently of the operating system user ids under very restricted conditions. For example, if you design the file level access control using the UNIX security measures, the application may have difficulty in accessing the database files.

If you wish to use multiple group ids to differentiate between groups of users, only the group with a gid matching that of the database files can access it. For example, consider an ORACLE database whose server processes run under a master login id with its own administrative group, while application programs run under users' login ids and their respective groups. In this case, all database files are owned by the master login id with the administrative group. Users with their individual user ids and groups can access the database files only if access is permitted to public. This is because UNIX only defines one group id for each file and a user can only belong to one group. Thus, the login mechanisms implemented by DBMS products work under the following restrictions:

- Database files are accessible to all application user ids as well as the database administrator id, under the UNIX security measures.

- Users bypass the operating system login and only use the product login mechanism which does not require the uid or gid values. Note that this is only possible if you do not bypass the services of the getty program as discussed in Section 7.1.1.

A product login mechanism allows you to bypass standard login procedures to implement the ideas discussed in Section 7.1.1. Alternatively, you can link them to the standard login procedures so that the second login becomes unnecessary. You should choose which login mechanism your application uses, since two consecutive login procedures are annoying to users.

The method for linking standard login to the product login differ in each product. The link may be based on the uid value as in UNIFY or the login name as in ORACLE. When the link is based on the uid value, you need to implement a special program to add and delete users as discussed in Section 7.3.1. If you use such a link, you may need to disable the display of the product's login screen so that the user only sees one login procedure.

7.4.2 Data Access Control

Data access security mechanisms are primarily implemented through the DBMS facilities. Beware, however, of file level access control mechanisms implemented by the underlying operating system. These controls may interfere with your application's needs in ways described in Section 7.4.4.

In Chapter 3, we discussed the types of facilities that a DBMS provides for controlling users' access to data items and their ability to change the database structure. These facilities frequently consist of standard SQL statements such as *grant* or *revoke,* which define the access permissions to a given user. Although you can define database structure alteration rights such as *alter table* and *index,* consider their implications on the application structure before granting them. A good rule of thumb is to allow these rights only to users who perform database administrator duties or participate in the disciplined application development environment. Another candidate for such restriction is the grant option which allows users to grant their rights to other users.

You can track the use of access rights by users with the ***audit*** facility of DBMS products such as ORACLE. This facility records the date and time of the operation, the identity of the user performing it and other useful information needed to detect a security violation. Note, however, that no facility can pinpoint a security breach using a stolen user id and password.

Another popular means of access security is through the ***user views*** facility discussed in Chapter 3. Although, the primary purpose of this facility is to provide logical windows on the database regardless of the physical storage in relation tables, it also serves security needs to some extent. Note, however, that many products do not allow operations other than ***select*** on views which leads to difficulties in using the application. Where users need restricted access to these other operations, the security measures must be applied through the grant and revoke facilities just described.

Although these facilities provide comprehensive data access control, they do not affect the user interface. Users find out that they are not permitted a particular type of access only when they attempt such access. The facility described in Section 7.4.3 illustrates an active access control mechanism. Consider the following example.

Suppose your application allowed users to query the database using SQL. To maintain integrity constraints, you restrict their access to only the select operation. However, these users ought to be able to perform add, update, and delete operations using an application program which maintains the integrity constraints. Restricting data access to only the select operation means that they will not be able to perform the other operations from any other interface. This problem can be solved with the UNIFY facility described in the next section. In other products, the only workaround is to disallow access to the query language.

7.4.3 Program Access Control

Only UNIFY and ORACLE provide program access control, which is a different perspective on access control. The underlying concept is that all data is accessed via programs. The facility then consists of defining the type of access available to a user through each program. Four access rights can be defined: add, modify, inquire, and delete, for individual users or groups of users. Programs use a facility which displays the four access options to users based on rights permitted to a user. Thus, if a user is only allowed inquire rights, this facility only displays the inquire option for that user.

The advantage of this approach is that there is no inherent restriction on access to data, only access via a given program. Thus, a user can be given different types of access through each program. Moreover, the user is aware of the types of accesses allowed, since the program only displays permitted access options.

The drawback of this approach without the data access control mechanisms is that access to specific data items such as relation tables or fields cannot be controlled. Thus, we can solve the update access via SQL problem described in the previous section, but cannot restrict the user from querying specific data items in the database. Access restriction to specific data items requires the use of data access control facilities.

7.4.4 Directory and File Access Control

You could prevent database file deletion by preventing *write* access to the directory. This access control requires that the database reside in the filesystem, under one or more directories. However, many products using such a database storage structure need write permission in order to create new relation tables and index files. You may have to allow all types of access to all users on the system to overcome the conflicts described in Section 7.4.1. In these cases, users could inadvertently delete one or more database files from SHELL.

The problem with deleting parts of the database by deleting one or more files is that the database recovery procedures cannot recover just the missing portions. You have to recover the entire database and perhaps also recover from the transaction journal which is a time consuming process. During such recovery, users cannot use the application which in turn may affect their job functions.

In Chapter 5, we discussed one standard trick for quick recovery by linking all database files to another directory. Only the superuser should have permission to access this directory. These links will prevent the file contents from being deleted when a database file is deleted from the data directory. Recovery of a data file then only requires you to relink the file from the protected link directory into the data directory.

The drawback of this method is that every database file must be linked individually when it is created, a process not performed by the DBMS create facility. This link must be created each time the database structure is changed, or re-created in a complete recovery process. A complete recovery is necessary when the contents of the database are corrupted. So the old links must be removed to free any data blocks associated with the old contents.

7.5 Adaptability Considerations

In this section we discuss an important advantage of using the DBMS and UNIX combination for developing your application. It is important because applications change throughout their life, from conception through implementation and use in a production environment. The changes depend on changes in user requirements, new requirements arising from a successful implementation, software upgrades, and an increase in data volumes or number of users. This section examines what you need to do during the design and development stages to ensure easy adaptability of the application to a changing environment.

Requirements of the application change either during its development or after its release into a production environment. These changes can affect the application in the following ways:

- Extra data elements or elimination of some data elements — that is, changes to the database structure.

- Additional functionality or a change in behavior — that is, change to the application programs which may also mean a change to the database structure.

- Changes due to an upgrade of either the operating system or the DBMS product software, which may force modification to your programs.

- Growth in the application's use which in turn requires a larger database space or requires support of more users.

7.5.1 Adapting to Changing Database Structures

Ease of changing database structures depends on the storage strategy of the product used by the application. A DBMS using the one relation per file approach, such as the standard INFORMIX-SQL, provides the easiest transition in most cases. For example, adding new relation tables does not affect existing data in this approach. Adding or removing data elements from individual relation tables only affects the files containing their data. An easy restructuring method is to create a new table with the required structure, loading it from the old table's data, removing the old table, and renaming the new table to the old table's name.

In products using the multiple relations per file approach, such as INFORMIX-TURBO, ORACLE, and UNIFY, restructuring is more cumbersome. It usually requires a complete unloading of the database, changing the database structure, and reloading the old data. This extra work is necessary since the new structure affects the space used by each relation table and may require changes in allocation of tables into data areas. Another reason is that data clustering needs may change with the addition of new relation tables or data elements.

In either case, changes to the data structures are independent of the way programs access the data elements, so long as the data elements continue to exist and have not changed their data type and size. Data elements which no longer exist or have changed data types or size imply a change only to programs which use them. This is a major advantage over traditional methods which depended on the position of a data element within a record. In traditional methods, any change to a file implies a change to all programs which use that file. This *data independence* provided by DBMSs is a major reason for their popularity.

7.5.2 Adapting to Changing Functions

Changes to the functionality of an application imply changes to the application programs. Program changes include modifications as well as enhancements which add new functions to existing programs, or require new programs to support the new functions. Such changes are easy to implement if your application uses standard DBMS utilities such as forms driver, report generator, and menu driver. Programs based on these tools usually contain fewer lines of source code and therefore are easier to maintain. Fourth generation language programs are similarly smaller than traditional host language based programs and therefore are easier to maintain and enhance.

However, if you need to change the user interface behavior, programs based on standard tools are not as flexible as host language interface based programs. For example, if you want to use a tab key to proceed to the next field rather than the commonly used carriage return key, such a change cannot be made with the standard utilities. Even with host language interface based programs, you need to discard use of the DBMS function for field input, and develop your own substitute function. This choice of substituting your own function is not available in the standard utilities. Such substitutions in host language interface based programs introduces nonstandard functions which make the application less portable. Thus, the behavior of user interface related activities is difficult to change with standard tools, and should be done with caution in host language interface programs.

An important point to note is that once you have developed an application for one DBMS product, you cannot easily move it to a different product. Moving to a different product needs a complete rewrite of the application since the utilities and 4GL interfaces of each product differ greatly. Thus, selection of the product is important for new developments, and we discuss this in detail in Part 4.

7.5.3 Adapting to DBMS and UNIX Upgrades

Upgrades to the DBMS product software probably occur more often than upgrades to the operating system. However, the effects of either upgrade are similar on the application. Namely, your programs may not work without modification in the new environment. You must first determine the impact of the upgrade, make necessary changes to the application, and test the changes before implementing the upgraded application release into production. This process is easy for DBMSs since you can install the upgrade in a test environment.

Testing an operating system upgrade may not be simple, especially if you use one computer for both development and production environments. The low cost of UNIX machines should allow you to use separate object code compatible computers for development and production environments. We examine the need for object code compatible machines in Section 7.6. There are many obvious advantages to separating development machines from production machines, especially for improving performance in the production environment.

If you use a single machine for both activities, consider staying with the older version of the operating system, or attempting the change during nonworking hours. Note that installing UNIX upgrades can be a time consuming process and may require a complete system backup and restore. You probably also need to upgrade the DBMS product after upgrading the operating system. Staying with an older version has drawbacks: Namely, the DBMS vendor and the operating system vendor will eventually stop supporting it. This grace period can be as short as three months depending on the number of customers served by these vendors.

DBMS upgrades usually add extra features to the product which you may wish to use in the application, so that some programs change to gain the advantages of the new functions. Product upgrades sometimes include changes to the data dictionary format or database storage structure. In such cases, the product vendor often provides a conversion utility to convert your application database and dictionary to the new structure. Such format changes might mean that all programs based on standard utilities need recompiling, which is easy if you use UNIX tools such as *make*.

Operating system upgrades should have no effect on your application if you rigorously avoid using nonstandard facilities directly. Your programs should only use high level UNIX and DBMS facilities which are stable and unlikely to change. The DBMS software should absorb any lower level changes to the operating system and provide compatibility between product releases running on successive UNIX versions.

7.6 Growth and Portability Considerations

As the application becomes established in the production environment, more data gets loaded into the database and more users access it. This growth in the database size and functionality changes the design criteria which are the basis of the application. Such growth also results from enhancements to the application, making it useful to many more people.

You can estimate growth in the database size during the requirements definition stage of the application. Then, use this estimate in selecting the hardware, DBMS product, and your design strategy. In Part 4 of this book, we discuss the details of determining growth requirements and performance needs. Typically, your estimates and product selection should account for growth between two to five years after release of the application which is its common life expectancy. If the database grows larger than its designed size, you need to examine the tradeoffs between the following options:

- Increasing the available disk storage space, an option available only with DBMS products which allow a database to span multiple disks. We discussed the database storage architectures which allow this option in Chapter 5. It is only viable if the resulting performance degradation in data searches is acceptable, and growth in number of users is small so that your current configuration supports them adequately.

- Moving the application to a larger machine, a feasible option when using a DBMS product and the UNIX operating system. This may be the only solution if you need growth capacity without compromising performance. The simplest port is to move the application to a larger but object code compatible machine without changing manufacturers. Be aware, however, that many manufacturers' product lines are not fully object code compatible. Thus, your application requires more effort to port. You may need to recompile the entire application on the new machine and have to overcome some inconsistencies between the operating system implementations.

These potential problems are due to programs using nonstandard features of a particular UNIX implementation which do not exist on the larger machine. Your best approach is to only use standard features, preferably those common to both the SYSTEM V and BSD UNIX. Using only such facilities and those supplied by the DBMS makes your application portable not only among different machine sizes, but also machines from different manufacturers. You can obtain guidance on which facilities are standard from publications such as AT&T's *System V Interface Definition,* the IEEE POSIX standard, and the X/OPEN portability guide.

7.7 Conclusions

This chapter discussed issues of integrating your application with the operating system facilities necessary to users in a production environment. Many of these issues are peripheral to the business functions served by the application, but they are critical to its successful use and growth throughout its life. Specific areas covered in this chapter were

- *User's needs to interact with UNIX:* A good integrated system removes the need for access to standard utilities via SHELL commands. There are three methods of setting up the user interface with no access to SHELL: by replacing the getty program in inittab, or the sh program in passwd, or executing it in the user's login profile. You must also disable SHELL escape mechanisms from the application functions.

- *User's performance needs:* Needs for perceived speed differs between interactive tasks and batch tasks. The waiting time between a user action and its acknowledgment by the system, often called *response time,* must be short in interactive tasks. The nature of some applications, such as financial trading systems, dictates that response time measurement include the time required to complete the task rather than just a system acknowledgment. Critical interactive tasks include data entry, screen display, interactive reports, and tasks requiring successive prompts to users.

Batch tasks, on the other hand, can take longer to complete. Be sure to estimate the volumes of data to be processed carefully, so the total time requirements are within limits of system operation hours. Determine the *suitable* timeframe inherent in the nature of some batch tasks, for example batch report generation and printing, based on patterns of user behavior.

- *Administrative needs of the application:* An easy-to-use interface for day-to-day administrative facilities is essential if nontechnical users will perform those duties. Facilities needed are hybrid user login management and database backup and recovery subsystems serving both the UNIX and DBMS needs. Standard operating system or DBMS facilities alone are inadequate. An alternative to including the administrative functions in the integrated application is to provide a team of expert systems staff. This team should be able to respond quickly to user requests.

- *Security control needs:* Exercise caution in designing these controls, so that operating system facilities complement those of the DBMS without unnecessary restrictions. Mix and match the alternative facilities for login and password control, data access, program based control, and filesystem access control.

- *Application growth needs:* Catering to application functional growth easily is a valuable advantage of using the UNIX and DBMS combination. Adding new functions and data to your application requires minimum change to existing functions with the DBMS facilities. Growth path to larger machines for increases in database size or user loads is feasible since both underlying components run on a wide range of machines from different manufacturers. Consider using only standard development facilities to ensure easy portability.

Part 3

Four UNIX DBMSs

In this part of the book, we examine four commercial products in detail. We compare their features to the generic features we determined essential in a database management system. We also examine which unusual features they offer to both developers and end-users, and any particular issues you should consider when using them for development. The intention here is to point out features that are most useful for developing and running applications. In particular, we examine how well they integrate into the UNIX environment in light of the issues we raised in the previous parts of the book.

Although the specific versions of each product might get out of date, the concepts discussed in these chapters are unlikely to disappear for years yet. These concepts are fairly mature in the industry and will probably form the core of future technologies in the DBMS environment. DBMS vendors will probably add new tools to their range of products, or additional facilities to existing products. Perhaps they will even note some of our discussions of drawbacks in their products and rectify them.

As you will see from the discussion in the following chapters, no one product meets the needs of every application. These descriptions intend to supply sufficient information so you can select products for further investigation for your application. There are many other good products, such as EMPRESS, PROGRESS, and FOCUS, discussions of which are beyond the scope of this book. You can judge the suitability of such products based on the issues discussed in this book.

8

The Informix DBMS

8.1 Introduction

Informix Software Inc., formerly Relational Database Systems, Inc (RDS), is head-quartered in Menlo Park, California. They were founded in 1980 and introduced their first UNIX relational database product in 1981. Since 1981, they have increased their product offering to a range of products aimed at different application needs. These products run on many hardware systems, primarily UNIX and MS-DOS operating systems as well as other proprietary operating systems.

Their products are available from dealers and computer manufacturers worldwide as well as their own sales offices throughout the U.S. and Europe. The X/OPEN group has adopted some of these products as a portability standard.

Although product versions change frequently, major architectural changes occur rarely. We discuss the major features of this product family which probably won't change significantly in the near future. The versions on which we base our discussion are listed here for your information.

INFORMIX	Version 3.3
INFORMIX-SQL	Version 2.10
INFORMIX-TURBO	Version 1.10
INFORMIX ESQL/C	Version 2.10
INFORMIX-4GL	Version 1.10

8.2 Packages and Components

The packaging scheme for the Informix product line is unusual and causes confusion for a novice customer. The products will be discussed in this section from two viewpoints: packages provided by Informix Software and packages needed for different types of development. Descriptions in the first case include a list of components comprising the package. Use these descriptions as an overview of the product line to determine your specific needs. Later sections in this chapter detail the features available for development tasks.

8.2.1 Informix Software Products

The product line consists of two distinct groups: non-SQL products and SQL based products. Products in the non-SQL set are stand-alone products. For upward growth, the SQL based product set is essential.

Products in the SQL set use a common data dictionary and comprise different aspects of a comprehensive tool set. Each of these products is a stand-alone system. Each contains all of the underlying data management facilities. Confusion arises when you already own one product and wish to purchase another component. We shall attempt to clarify the role of each component in Section 8.2.2.

Each product in the SQL based set has a version number independent of the others. Incompatible versions of these products do exist. So be careful to select matching versions of different products. For example, you need INFORMIX-SQL version 2.1 or higher to use INFORMIX-TURBO. You may have to upgrade the product already owned in order to use it together with the latest version of another product.

Other products from this company are file and spreadsheet management products. File-It! is a simple file creation, data entry, and retrieval tool aimed at end-users and requiring very little development experience. C-ISAM is a library of C language routines which allows you to create and access indexed sequential files. The DATASHEET ADD-IN product allows links to the LOTUS 1-2-3 program for data exchange from an INFORMIX database. REPORT/DB2 and BATCH/SPUFI are products to connect to a DB2 database. Discussion of these products is beyond the scope of this book.

INFORMIX:

This product was the first offering from Informix Software, Inc. (referred to as ***the original INFORMIX*** from here onwards). Its basic structure has not changed over several enhancements. Figure 8-1 illustrates its component structure. The components listed are very similar in functionality to their SQL counterparts. The major differences between this set and the SQL set are the data dictionary storage structures and the query language. This product uses a proprietary structure for the data dictionary rather than using the same format as its database. You cannot access data dictionary information using the query language. Its query language is proprietary and differs significantly from SQL.

- *Menu Environment:* The master menu is a one level, single column menu which provides access to each of the other utilities.

- *DBBUILD:* This utility allows you to create or alter a database. You define the database schema in an ASCII file using a proprietary language. DBBUILD compiles this definition file to create the database. The SQL based set does not have this utility.

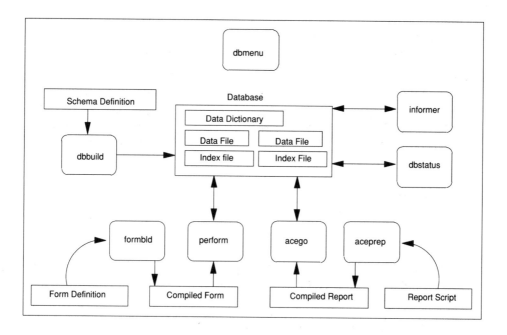

Figure 8-1 INFORMIX Component Structure

- **PERFORM and FORMBUILD:** This pair of components comprises the forms utility. FORMBUILD allows you to create and compile a default form. Alternatively, you can create a custom form definition in an ASCII file and then compile it with FORMBUILD. Compiled form definition must be run with PERFORM. We discuss these utilities in detail in Section 8.4.2.

- **ACE:** This report writer utility consists of a script compiler, ACEPREP, and a report generator program, ACEGO. Report definition scripts consist of INFORMER query language statements for data access and ACE language statements for formatting the data.

- **INFORMER:** This proprietary query language is available only in this package. It provides facilities to manipulate data in an existing database. You manipulate data dictionary structures using the DBSTATUS utility.

- **DBMENU:** This menu utility uses a special INFORMIX database to store menu definitions. You use a predefined PERFORM form to create and alter menus for your application. DBMENU then drives your application menus.

- **DBSTATUS:** This utility allows you to manipulate data dictionary structures and perform administration tasks.

- **ALL-II:** The Application Language Library provides C language functions to access and manipulate the database. You can use certain termcap and curses functions in conjunction with this library for screen handling.

- *ENTER1 and ENTER2:* These utilities are quick and easy way of creating data entry interfaces for individual files. ENTER1 is a command based interface and ENTER2 is a simple screen based interface. Their data presentation cannot be customized.

INFORMIX-SQL:

This product provides the desirable SQL interface to the database. Its data dictionary is itself a database so you can access its data via SQL. You can thus develop the custom application administration facilities discussed in Chapter 7. Figure 8-2 illustrates the structure of its components.

- *Menu Environment:* This environment is a multilevel ring menu structure which allows access to other components including a proprietary text editor and a screen based schema editing utility.

- *PERFORM and FORMBUILD:* This pair of components is essentially the same as in the original INFORMIX product. There are minor differences; for example, PERFORM uses a ring menu structure for its commands similar to those of the menu environment.

- *ACE:* The main difference between this report writer utility and its namesake in the original INFORMIX is that data access functions use SQL statements. The report formatting language is the same in both packages.

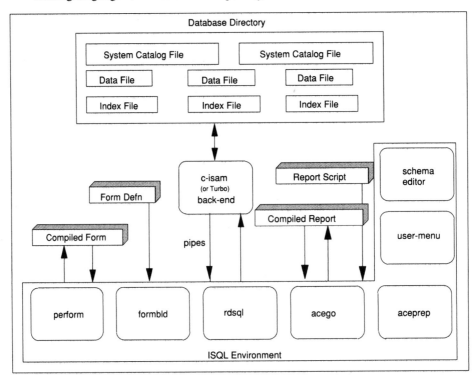

Figure 8-2 INFORMIX-SQL Component Structure

- **RDSQL:** This implementation of SQL differs somewhat from the ANSI standards due to many useful extensions, in particular the **outer join** feature. It includes all facilities for database administration as well as data manipulation.

- **USER-MENU:** You use this utility to generate menus for your application. It differs from DBMENU since it has built-in knowledge of the forms driver and report generator utilities.

INFORMIX-TURBO:

This product is suitable for use only with the other SQL based products. It replaces the normal C-ISAM back-end using one relation per file implementation with a multiple relations per file implementation. We discuss its details in Section 8.3.

ESQL Products:

These products complement the other SQL based products by providing a host language interface. They are available for C, COBOL, and ADA programming languages. You can also use them to add custom facilities to the SQL based PERFORM forms driver and ACE report generator.

INFORMIX-4GL:

You can use this package as a stand-alone or together with the other SQL based packages. It provides a programmer environment with ring menus to reduce the learning curve for novice programmers. These menus allow access to utilities such as an editor and an interface to the compiler. It supports the notion of multiple source code files and compiles only the changed source. INFORMIX-4GL is basically a programming language which is a hybrid of the FORMBUILD language, the ACE language, the RDSQL query language, and additional statements to combine these together into a single program. We discuss it in detail in Section 8.4.6.

8.2.2 Development Components

Database Storage:

The product family supports both storage approaches described in Chapter 6. The original INFORMIX and INFORMIX-SQL support the **one relation per file** approach using the C-ISAM storage method. The INFORMIX-TURBO package supports the **many relations per file** approach using the UNIX raw disk. Support of the raw disk mechanism means that the database can span more than one physical disk, whereas the C-ISAM based implementation restricts the entire database to a single filesystem.

Menu Driver:

There are two different menu drivers available: DBMENU in the original INFORMIX, and USER-MENU in the INFORMIX-SQL. DBMENU provides a SHELL command interface to all programs including the other utilities. USER-MENU knows the command syntax for the utilities and needs minimum information for these, while still providing a SHELL command interface to non-INFORMIX-SQL programs.

INFORMIX-4GL provides functions for you to build menu interfaces into your programs. They help you build a consistent user interface throughout your application, even if you mix and match 4GL programs with PERFORM. However, you lose the flexibility provided by stand-alone menu driver utilities. You must change the program if the menu needs to change.

Forms Driver:

The forms driver pair, PERFORM and FORMBUILD, is available in both the original INFORMIX and INFORMIX-SQL products. FORMBUILD is also available in INFORMIX-4GL. However, you must code the statement to run the compiled form definition explicitly in your programs written in these languages. Note that the forms defined in INFORMIX, INFORMIX-SQL, and INFORMIX-4GL are not perfectly compatible with each other. For example, to move a form from INFORMIX to INFORMIX-SQL, you must as a minimum recompile it. You may need to change certain statements in the form definition as well.

Report Generator:

The ACEPREP and ACEGO report writer programs are available in the original INFORMIX and INFORMIX-SQL products. A major difference between these products is the language used to extract data from the database. The INFORMIX-4GL report function uses a language similar to ACE.

Host Language Interface:

The original INFORMIX and the SQL based products provide radically different programming language interfaces. The Application Language Library (ALL-II) is a function call based interface for the C language available as a standard component of the original INFORMIX package. It consists of only database manipulation functions. The embedded SQL products, ESQL/C and ESQL/COBOL, must be purchased separately. They include database manipulation functions and a smattering of other useful routines for string manipulation and date conversion. You can use them in conjunction with PERFORM for screen handling support.

Fourth Generation Language:

The INFORMIX-4GL product is sold separately. It can be used as a stand-alone or in conjunction with other SQL based products, provided their versions are compatible. This language is a hybrid of the PERFORM, ACE, and SQL languages.

Query Language:

The proprietary INFORMER query language is a standard component of the original INFORMIX and is not compatible with other products. The SQL query language is supplied with each of the SQL based products.

Development Environment:

The original INFORMIX comes with a simple one level menu environment to access each of the runtime utilities. However, you must resort to the UNIX SHELL to create, edit, and compile your application database schema, forms and report definitions. The INFORMIX-SQL package includes a more sophisticated environment, ISQL, which is sufficient for most simple development activities. It includes access to editors of your choice, as well as menu options to define and compile simple database schemas, forms, and reports defi-nitions. Interactive access to the SQL query language allows you to perform several operations not provided directly in the environment. The I4GL environment of the fourth generation language package has a similar interface for creating and compiling 4GL programs.

8.3 Data Control

The product family provides different database storage strategies and allows you to switch from one to the other. Changing the strategy once you load a significant quantity of application data is a nontrivial task. The discussions in Parts 2 and 4 of this book help you to choose the strategy suited to your needs.

You may see some of our terms used in a different context in the product literature. We clarify such terms according to the common ground established in Part 1 to reduce the potential confusion when you compare DBMS products.

8.3.1 Data Types

The INFORMIX products support machine independent data types shown in Table 8-1. Notice, however, that two of these are not machine independent. This table relates our generic high level data types to the specific names used in these products.

Our Data Types	INFORMIX Data Types
Small Integer	SMALLINT (-32,767 to +32,767)
Large Integer	INTEGER (-2,147,483,647 to +2,147,483,647)
Floating Point Decimal	DECIMAL(M) where M=no. of significant digits
Fixed Point Decimal	DECIMAL(M,N) where M=no. of significant digits and N=no. of digits to the right of the decimal point
Small Floating Point	SMALLFLOAT (size depends on your machine)
Large Floating Point	FLOAT (size depends on your machine)
Money	MONEY(M,N) decimal currencies only; M and N are similar to fixed point decimal data type
Auto-increment Numeric	SERIAL, incremented on add operation to database
Three-part Date	DATE, day, month, year in any order
String	CHAR(N), fixed length

Table 8-1 INFORMIX Data Types

8.3.2 Storage Structures

You have a choice of two storage strategies for the application database with this product line:

- Filesystem based storage.
- Raw disk based storage.

You can change your application database storage strategy at any time, provided you purchase an additional product. Take this extra cost into account when planning your application budget so that further budget approvals are avoided. If you choose to use one method during development for convenience with plans to convert for production, your project work plan should include tasks for the conversion and tuning. The discussion is a guide to the scope of conversion to help you avoid an embarrassingly long implementation phase.

Filesystem Based Storage:

This strategy uses the proprietary C-ISAM method for storing data and is the default method. It uses one file for each relation table and one file for each index. All data and index files must reside in a single database directory which has the name of the application database and the .dbs extension.

The original INFORMIX and INFORMIX-SQL both use this method for storing data, although their data dictionaries are stored differently. The original INFORMIX uses a single data dictionary file with a proprietary format. In the SQL based products, the data dictionary itself is an INFORMIX-SQL database accessible with query language statements.

The relation files contain fixed length data records initially in the order of adding. The data storage scheme reuses the space freed by deleted records. Thus, the record order becomes random through add and delete activities on a file. Since the space freed by deletions is not returned to the filesystem, the file size can be larger than the space required for its records. This size difference can be significant after an operation that deletes a large number of records. You can reclaim the space by unloading the data from the file, recreating the relation table from scratch, and reloading the data. Obviously, such a time consuming task is necessary only if your application has massive data purges without a similar sized addition of new records.

Bear in mind that fixed length records mean that fields take up space whether or not they contain data. This is especially important if your application requires long character fields which do not always contain data. You can reduce the amount of wasted space through proper normalization of your database. In addition, you should put such sparsely populated fields into a separate table where records are only created when the field is populated. Figure 8-3 shows an example where such a separation is sensible.

Since the strategy uses the UNIX filesystem, files grow dynamically as you add new records. Random growth of the database files can thus lead to fragmentation of the disk. Large data files are then subject to the drawbacks described in Chapter 5. Careful use of indexes can alleviate some of the effects of the disk fragmentation, so that a large proportion

order table				ord-instruct table	
cust_no	ord_no	cust_co		c_ord_cno	instructions
1111	1100	ABC Corp.		1100	Express Freight
1212	1101	New Corporation		1111	Call for pickup

order-items table

o_cust_no	item_no	catlog_no
1100	1	123-12-1112
1101	1	123-11-4532
1101	2	123-88-3456

Figure 8-3 Table Separation for Fixed Length Records

of record access is via key values giving direct access to the required record. In desperation, you can reorganize the filesystem at appropriate intervals. However, neither UNIX nor INFORMIX products provide a simple utility to perform this task.

Raw Disk Based Storage:

You must invest in the INFORMIX-TURBO product to obtain this option. It is compatible only with the SQL based products and not with the original INFORMIX. This software replaces the filesystem based, one relation per file storage, with a multiple relations per file approach. The terminology used in this product differs from our terminology as shown in Table 8-2.

Chunks can be either filesystem files or raw disks accessed as special files in the /dev directory. Only raw disk based chunks are contiguous areas. A dbspace is made up of one or more chunks and contains one or more partitions. A partition cannot span more than one dbspace. It contains data for a relation table as well as any indexes defined on its fields. Individual tables within a database can reside in separate dbspaces, although a single table must be entirely contained in one dbspace.

Our Terminology	INFORMIX-TURBO
System Files or Raw Disks	Chunks
Data Areas	Dbspaces
Relation Tables	Partitions

Table 8-2 INFORMIX-TURBO Terminology

Each partition is further subdivided into *extents* which define the initial size of table data and the size of additional space to obtain when the table expands. Finally, an extent is made up of *pages* which are the basic units of physical disk access used by the database server.

You can set up a one relation per file environment by defining a one-to-one correspondence between a filesystem file, a chunk, a dbspace, and a partition. However, you would lose the potential performance gains offered by this product. For maximum performance gain, you should use raw disks as much as possible. Clearly, you need to put multiple partitions in each dbspace and so must estimate the size of each table and its indexes.

Creating a database using this product is different from the simpler filesystem based approach. Realize that the ISQL menu options to create tables always use the default options preventing you from choosing the physical distribution. Instead, you should consider using the product's extended SQL statements for the schema definition. These statements allow you to specify the location of the database and individual tables in terms of dbspaces and partitions. The *monitor* utility allows a database administrator to create dbspaces and partitions using a screen interface. The procedure for creating a database consists of the following:

- Define dbspaces for your application database.
- Define partitions and parameters for each table in the database.
- Use SQL statements to create and locate the database, each table, and its indexes.

The SQL data definition statements in this utility are different from those supported by the C-ISAM based SQL products. Thus, a script of SQL statements recorded for the creation of a C-ISAM based database should not be used.

This scheme also implements a one back-end server per user architecture. However, where shared memory is available, all back-end processes use it as their data access buffers so that unnecessary disk I/O is reduced. The shared memory parameters for UNIX must therefore be reconfigured appropriately before installing and using this product. You may tune also the INFORMIX-TURBO parameters to optimize usage of shared memory space.

The main advantage of this storage scheme is support of large databases. A TURBO database can span more than one physical disk. It can bypass filesystem overheads by allowing you to use raw disks. Its buffering strategy implemented via pages allows you to tune the size of disk transfers, thus alleviating the overhead of small retrievals and frequent disk I/O.

It is, however, a complex scheme to use and administer. Its sharp tools definitely need technical administrators. Backups are about the only task an untrained, nontechnical user could perform. Thus, your production system plan must allow for a technical database administrator for performance monitoring and tuning activities. A minor restriction of this implementation is that you have to start the server process deliberately before any users can access the database. This start procedure performs necessary initialization for shared memory and any necessary recovery processing. Your best bet is to include it in the system boot procedures.

You have to be careful of using temporary tables or creating ad hoc tables in this scheme. By default, these will reside in the ***root dbspace,*** causing it to overflow quickly. If possible, you should prevent most users from creating ad hoc tables and thus hogging space. Avoid keeping temporary data stored in tables for an indefinite length of time. Avoiding such differences between this scheme and the C-ISAM method should present a challenge to application designers.

Conversion between Strategies:

The concept of plug together back-end servers is an inspired strategy. Unfortunately, it could not be made as simple as a child's toy. Converting between strategies is a nontrivial process because of the differences between them. A single application database can work with only the type of back-end server it was built for. Although separate applications, on the same machine, which do not share a database can use different schemes. There are three considerations when converting from the C-ISAM method to the TURBO scheme:

1. Changing the database design.
2. Conversion of parts of application design or code.
3. Conversion of existing data.

Some developers might choose to simply purchase larger capacity hardware rather than perform the conversion process. Obviously they need plenty of spare cash! Such a decision is defensible if the application makes copious use of incompatible facilities.

1. Changing the Database Design

The following steps are necessary if you want to take advantage of the TURBO facilities. If your application is already in production, size estimates should be easy. You might even know a good way to spread your database over the physical disk space.

- Determine the tables required, including temporary tables.

- For each table, estimate its size, sizes of its indexes, and forecast of growth potentials including, of course, system overheads.

- Identify disk space for use as chunks, and reorganize existing disk partitions and filesystems to make this space available. You need to perform a *complete* system backup and restore to perform this task.

- Design the organization of chunks and dbspaces appropriate for the sizes of tables required. This design must ensure that each table fits into a single dbspace. You also need naming conventions for dbspaces and ***table partitions*** to aid their use when creating the database.

- Estimate the number of users for the application and shared memory usage parameters for the TURBO monitor.

- Estimate the shared memory parameters for UNIX and reconfigure the operating system accordingly.

- Create the database, tables, and indexes in the appropriate dbspaces and table partitions.

2. Considerations for Converting Application Code

The complexity of your application determines how much effort you need to put into this phase. For applications using just PERFORM and ACE, you might not need any modification. Use of SQL, either embedded or in 4GL, means that you need to find any incompatible statements. If estimating the conversion effort for poorly structured code takes significant time, you have only yourself to blame!

Once you create the database, you need to test the application code in case there are assumptions which are no longer suitable. Such assumptions might include the use of large temporary tables, and statements to create, alter, and remove tables which need to be modified. You might also want to use the levels of isolation mechanisms provided in this product to enhance concurrency control. Your application must be modified for the change in the database environment. Other areas of change might be the data administration procedures for application administrators and user SHELL environment to include variables such as SQLEXEC which selects the TURBO back-end server in the system.

The extent of the changes depend on whether the conversion is a planned phase of the application development project or a conversion of a production application due to its growth. In a planned conversion phase, you need to exercise care during the application design to avoid known differences. Training obtained prior to attempting the design will ensure that you have sufficient knowledge of the target system. You also need to carefully monitor the development phases, possibly through structured program reviews, to prevent use of facilities which lead to extra work in the conversion phase. In a production system conversion, the requirements phase should identify each of the modifications needed for the new environment. Then the project work plan can include these as tasks with an estimate of effort required.

3. Converting Data

This task is really a lot easier than in a traditional files environment. Appropriate tools for converting data are provided in the package. All you need is lots of spare disk space or scratch tapes. Your application users can take time off while you do this conversion. The tasks involved in this phase are:

- Unload all data from the existing C-ISAM database, using the ***dbexport*** utility provided with TURBO. You must use the utility provided in the TURBO package, since the format of the *unloaded* files is different from that of the utility provided in the C-ISAM based package. You will need to set the value of the SQLEXEC SHELL variable to force the use of the C-ISAM based database server prior to running this utility. Make sure that sufficient disk space is available if you choose to unload on disk, all in a single file-system. Unloading to a tape unit is the best way for medium to large databases.

- Make sure that the new TURBO database is correctly set up.

- Use the ***dbimport*** utility, with the SQLEXEC variable set to the TURBO back-end server before loading the data into the new database. You may need to repeat loading of some tables if any differences need to be resolved.

- Install the modified application release for users and implement any required changes to their runtime environments.

Alternatively, you can use SQL statements to unload and load tables individually so you can place each unloaded ASCII file in a separate directory or filesystem. In this case, be sure to unload the system catalog tables as well. Data conversion is also necessary if you restructure the database – for example, to move a table partition from one dbspace to another. This is not a frequent operation since you can easily add chunks to increase the size of a dbspace.

8.3.3 Access Methods

The INFORMIX products provide only B-tree indexing. B-tree index methods can support access via a given key field value which is either a complete value or may contain wildcard characters for character fields. B-tree indexing improves the speed of access to a record by reducing the number of key comparisons needed to find a given record. The conceptual structure of the binary tree is the same as discussed in Chapter 3. We also review the clustering scheme supplied in these products.

B-Tree Access:

B-tree indexes can be created on either individual fields or a combination of fields in a table. There is no limit to the number of indexes you can create; however, indexes adversely affect the speed of adding and updating records. You should design the indexes carefully to provide maximum benefit to your application while minimizing the extra overhead of updating indexes with each new key value. Note that you cannot access an index directly from any product other than the C-ISAM library. You should not use this library on indexes created via the database management system — you would be bypassing important access and concurrency controls applied by the DBMS and can severely corrupt your database.

An index in the C-ISAM scheme is stored as a separate file, while in the TURBO scheme it is stored in the same partition as the table data. The size of an index is directly proportional to the size of the key and the number of records in the table. The key size determines the number of keys stored in an index node. When a record is deleted from the relation table, its corresponding entry in the index is marked as deleted. A node containing all deleted keys is then reused at the next opportunity.

Although the underlying C-ISAM method provides compression methods for reducing the size of an index, you cannot choose these options through the SQL index statements. The database management system automatically provides white space compression without giving you the choice of which types of compression should be applied.

Clustering:

The term *clustering* is used by these products to mean intrafile clustering. This storage order is specified when creating or altering an index and you can specify it on only one index on a table. Its effect is to physically store records in a relation table to match the order specified for the index. It improves access speed when a large proportion of your access is in key sequential order.

The cluster order is not maintained as records are added and deleted, and thus is of limited use except on static tables. The time consuming process of reordering data must be repeated periodically to gain significant advantage, unless data is essentially static.

8.3.4 Access Security Control

Access control in all of these products uses the UNIX classes: user ids (uid), group ids (gid) and all others (that is, public). They do not implement internal user identifications separate from those of the operating system. The controls provided by the SQL based products are more extensive than those in the original INFORMIX product. In the SQL based products, access controls can be defined and dropped at any time, whereas in the original INFORMIX you must restructure the table to change permissions on it.

The controls applied by the original INFORMIX are different from those applied by the SQL based products. We describe each of these separately.

Original INFORMIX Controls:

The original INFORMIX product has seven types of privileges: all, none, read, update, add, delete, and control. Only the first four types can be defined at field level, and all apply at the table level. Access to the database itself is controlled only through UNIX directory and file access permissions. Table 8-3 describes the meaning of these privileges.

Privileges specified at table level apply to all fields within the table, unless specific field level privilege is granted. Privileges are defined in the database schema using the DBBUILD language.

SQL Controls:

All SQL based products use query language statements to define privileges. A database administrator can grant or revoke these privileges at any time for any user. However, a user with privileges allowing the ***grant option*** can grant or revoke only these privileges to other users. Thus, these products implement a new implicit class, database administrator (DBA), via the privilege mechanism. Table 8-4 describes the privilege structure of these products.

Privilege	File Level Application	Field Level Application
all	Full access	Full access
none	No access	No access
read	Can read records	Can read field
update	Can update records	Can update field
add	Can add records	n/a
delete	Can delete records	n/a
control	Can restructure database files	n/a

Table 8-3 Original INFORMIX Privilege Structure

Privilege	File Level Application	Field Level Application
Alter	Can change existing table structure	n/a
Delete	Can delete rows	n/a
Index	Can create indexes	n/a
Insert	Can add rows	n/a
Select [(*cols*)]	Can read all fields if none specified	Can read only fields listed as *cols*
Update [(*cols*)]	Can update all fields if none specified	Can update only fields listed as *cols*
All	All Access	n/a
Connect	Can access database, but cannot create permanent tables	n/a
Resource	Can access and create permanent tables	n/a
DBA	All administrator privileges	n/a

Table 8-4 SQL Based Privilege Structure

DBA privilege is automatic when you create a database. You can transfer administrative functions to another user by granting this privilege. The new DBA must then revoke your privilege to exclude your access.

A more subtle way to define privileges is using the *views* facility, although this is not its main purpose. However, it limits add and update operations on views. For example, suppose a view on a single relation table excludes a field which is defined to be a not null field. Adding a row through this view implies that this field must be set, by default, to a null value: violates the definition of the field! Therefore, you cannot add rows through such a view. Here is another example of restriction on update through a view: You cannot update through a view formed using joins, group by clauses, or the distinct keyword.

Implying privilege restrictions via views leads to a system which is very complex to administer and causes difficulty in determining who has which privileges. Privileges granted through the data access statements can be tracked easily by listing the contents of the *sysusers* system catalog.

8.3.5 Concurrency Control Options

Concurrency control facilities in these products are described with the term *data integrity*, which differs from our definition of data integrity. Other terms used in the product literature are *locking* and *transactions*. In our definition, these are all aspects of concurrency control.

The basic mechanism needed for concurrency control is a lock. Most of these products use a lock file with some versions using the *semaphore* facility of UNIX. The TURBO product uses shared memory area to implement its own locking mechanism. The granularity of locks differs between the C-ISAM based products and the TURBO product.

The default lock level in the C-ISAM based products is a row level (or record level). You can explicitly request a table level (file level) lock either as a shared or exclusive lock. However, at the row level, you cannot specify different types of locks such as read-for-update or shared lock allowing dirty reads in these products. Locks are only applied when an update operation occurs.

The TURBO product provides four levels of locking granularity: database, table, page, and row level. Page level locking is synonymous with our description of block level locking, except that you select the size of a page when you set up the database parameters. You must specify page or row level locking when creating or altering a table definition. The portion of a table locked by a page level lock depends on its size and how many rows fit into a single page. A locked page containing multiple rows prevents other users from accessing any of these rows, even if the lock owner is not accessing them. The tradeoff between row level and page level locks is the number of concurrent locks needed. The increase in number of locks, implied by row level locking, increases the shared memory space required to maintain these locks.

The SQL based products provide transaction level locking through three mechanisms: begin work (Start Transaction), commit work (End Transaction), and rollback work (Rollback). These facilities are only available if you define a transaction log when creating or starting your application database. Their use is similar to our description in Chapter 3. However, certain operations, including data definition and access security control statements, are always applied to the database immediately, whether or not enclosed within the start and commit statements. These operations cannot be rolled back. You can think of them as single statement operations.

This restriction of single statement operations is important when coding your application programs. For example, if you create a table within a transaction, then roll back the transaction, the new table *will not be deleted*. Another dangerous case is our example, in Chapter 6 and 7, showing how access control on data only is insufficient. In this example, we prevent a user from updating data through SQL statements by denying add, update, and delete privileges. This also prevents the user from updating this data through a program. You might think that you could temporarily change this access control within a transaction. However, since this operation cannot be rolled back, you create a potential security loophole whereby a rolled back transaction leaves the user with more privileges than normally allowed.

In conjunction with transaction level locking, the TURBO product provides the *Levels of Isolation* discussed in Chapter 3: dirty read, committed read, cursor stability, and repeatable read. You can select the level of isolation needed for each transaction. Committed read is the default type provided by all products.

The Cursor stability implementation depends on explicitly using *cursors* (pointers into result sets) to address rows. Hence, it only applies when you use either the embedded SQL host language interface or the fourth generation language.

8.3.6 Data Integrity Measures

This term is frequently used in the product literature to mean consistency obtained by concurrency control mechanisms. We will continue to use this term to mean *logical* consistency inherent in the application's use of the data. The SQL based products provide *entity integrity* by allowing you to specify whether a field can be null and then enforcing it whenever you add or update data. There are no facilities to enforce *referential integrity*. You can specify some additional data constraints for data updated through views, which will not be enforced if the underlying tables and fields are updated directly. You must enforce all other constraints through your application programs.

8.4 Utility Packages

The entire INFORMIX product line provides a range of utilities aimed at meeting the needs of developers. We shall concentrate on the major items identified in Chapter 3 as essential for application development. Other utilities that are worth mentioning are:

- C-ISAM indexed sequential access method, which is useful when the full power of the database management system is not required. Of course, you also lose out on the development tools!

- DATASHEET ADD-IN spreadsheet link, useful for exchanging data between an INFORMIX database and the LOTUS 1-2-3 program.

- REPORT/DB2 report writer for connecting to the IBM DB2 database management system.

- BATCH/SPUFI SQL processor also for the IBM DB2 product.

The development environments, included in each package, provide access to many of the utilities described in this section and provide an interactive interface which reduces the need to use UNIX SHELL commands. They aid novices in becoming productive quickly.

These environments cannot provide access to all of the facilities used in developing a complex application. For example, you cannot create indexes on field groups using the database schema editing facility in ISQL. You must use the query language to create such indexes. This is only a minor nuisance, since a DBA should clearly do such complex tasks.

An important drawback of using these environments is they do not directly support the UNIX application development tools. The I4GL component of INFORMIX-4GL does, however, implement some desirable features similar to those of the make utility. These environments cannot be customized for your project standards and cannot enforce any naming or coding conventions set by your project development methodology.

8.4.1 Menu Subsystem

The type of menu subsystem available to you depends on which package you select. The DBMENU subsystem in the original INFORMIX product displays a full screen menu. The USER-MENUS facility of INFORMIX-SQL is very similar, except that it has built-in knowledge of the command syntax for utilities such as PERFORM and ACE. This knowledge means that you do not need to know the SHELL command to run a standard INFORMIX-SQL utility. In both products, menus are defined using the familiar PERFORM forms based interface.

In these subsystems, you should consider two potential problems: the number of processes per user as a result of using the menus, and untidy menu definitions in the menu database. You should design your menus to be *shallow,* say two or three levels deep, which is a good design practice in any case. Since menus and menu selection descriptions are stored in separate tables, you can delete a menu without first deleting its selections. You thus create *orphan* data which is difficult to track and delete later.

In both menu subsystems, the only way to print the entire menu structure is via the PERFORM *output* command. This command simply prints a screen image of the form. You cannot obtain a more helpful report of all menus with one line per item indented according to its level within the menu tree.

The INFORMIX-4GL and the embedded SQL products do not provide a stand-alone menu utility. INFORMIX-4GL does provide facilities that you can embed in your 4GL programs to build a menu interface. This menu interface is a ring menu, similar to the PERFORM command menu in the INFORMIX-SQL package. Thus, you can build consistent interfaces throughout your application. The obvious drawbacks of embedding menus into your programs is that their maintenance requires access to the program source code itself. In the embedded SQL host language interface you must develop and use your own menu facilities.

8.4.2 Screen Forms Facilities

There are two ways you can drive forms: using PERFORM or INFORMIX-4GL. In this section, we discuss the standard forms driver, PERFORM, together with its forms definition partner, FORMBUILD, available in the original INFORMIX and INFORMIX-SQL packages. We discuss the 4GL way in Section 8.4.6.

The forms definition and driver programs supplied in the two packages are essentially the same. One difference is the type of host language interface you use to add custom built functions: with the original INFORMIX you use the ALL-II library, and with INFORMIX-SQL you use the embedded SQL interface. The basic steps in defining and running forms are:

1. Define the form layout and operation as a text file containing FORMBUILD language commands, using a standard text editor. Alternatively, FORMBUILD allows you to generate a default format form for given database tables.

2. Compile the definition using the FORMBUILD program. Compilation errors are written into an error file. Repeat from step 1, if you get any errors.

3. Test and run the compiled form definition with PERFORM.

You can perform these steps from the menu based environment of ISQL and I4GL.

Our Data Validation Criteria	FORMBUILD Data Validation Criteria
Range check	INCLUDE, numeric ranges, character range strings checked based on ASCII sequence.
List of valid values	INCLUDE
Required entry	REQUIRED
Lookup in other table	LOOKUP
Double entry verification	VERIFY
Field format enforcement	FORMAT on numeric fields, PICTURE on character fields

Table 8-5 FORMBUILD Data Validation Criteria

The programming language for defining forms is largely nonprocedural. Its basic syntax can be learned easily. However, predicting the effect of several combined operations can be difficult due to its nonprocedural nature. Rather than describing the syntax of this language which is better learned directly from the manuals, we examine the important features supported by this utility:

- Multiple tables; however, you can access only one row of one table at a time. You can cycle through tables with the table command.

- Multiple screens; you can cycle through these using the screen command. The limit on total number of screens in a single form definition file depends on your machine but is typically 20 or more.

- Fields corresponding to fields in the database.

- Fields that do not correspond to any database fields. Such fields allow you to display data calculated from other fields, for example, sales commission for a given order value. You can also use these fields for input of data that might be used in calculations; for example, shipping quantity used to update the quantity in hand in a stock control application.

- Data validation criteria shown in Table 8-5.

- Field editing criteria shown in Table 8-6.

- Two-level hierarchy where one table is the master, the other detail. This facility is useful in handling relation pairs such as customer order and order items relations. In this example, customer order is master of the order items relation.

- Look up into another table for a value entered by the user. You can use lookup to check existence of the value in the other table. For example, in an order entry application, you can look up a customer number entered on an order entry screen in the customer table. You can thus prevent entry of orders for a customer not recorded in the customer file.

Our Field Editing Criteria	FORMBUILD Field Editing Criteria
Case control	UPSHIFT, DOWNSHIFT
Default value	DEFAULT
Field format	FORMAT for numeric fields, PICTURE on character fields
Field display attributes	REVERSE, depends on definition in termcap or terminfo
Justification	RIGHT
Field padding	ZEROFILL, numeric fields only, pads with leading zeros

Table 8-6 FORMBUILD Field Editing Criteria

- Joins between several tables defined in the screen form. This facility used with multiple tables allows handling of matching data from each table in the join. For example, defining a join on customer number in an order entry application causes a *query* operation to retrieve data from both the customer order relation as well as the order items relation.

- Actions to be performed before and after each screen field or table row is changed. Actions can change the order of cursor movement between fields, assign values to fields, display messages, or abort the current operation. You can conditionally define different actions based on an *if-then-else* clause.

When running a compiled form, PERFORM provides several commands. You cannot customize these commands or prevent their display. These commands can make user training difficult as the operation of some of these changes based on the form's definition. The commands are:

- *Query:* Starts an inquiry operation, which lets a user enter search values or conditions into screen fields. You have to train users to enter only the values necessary to locate the required data. Their initial tendency is to enter all known information even if much of it is redundant. For example, in an order entry screen, specifying an order number is sufficient to find a particular order. You need not enter additional information such as customer name, address, and so on into the fields displayed on the form.

- *Next, Previous:* After a query retrieves several matching records, these commands let you browse through the results.

- *Add:* This command allows you to enter data into the fields for a single table. Data is not added into the database until you signal completion with the esc key. This scheme means that you can only add one record at a time, which is annoying and can reduce data entry speed. All data validation and field editing criteria are enforced.

- *Update:* After finding the required record with a query operation, you can use this command to change values in fields. PERFORM enforces all data validation and field editing criteria.

- *Remove:* After finding the required record with a query operation, you can remove it. Your intention is verified before the record is deleted.

- *Table, Screen:* These commands allow you to cycle through tables and screens as appropriate. The table command causes confusion if you defined either a join or a master-detail relationship between tables, as it merely sets a new table to be the current table. The data displayed in your previous table changes under these circumstances, but not otherwise.

- *Current:* This command is one of the most confusing as it does nothing in most instances. It applies only in forms with multiple tables joined in some manner and only after you search and browse tables separately. In this case, you can restore on your display the record you were looking at in that table before you changed tables and performed another separate query. When tables are joined, this changes the data displayed in the previous table.

- *Master, Detail:* These commands let you change between tables defined with a master-detail relationship. There is no actual relationship implied in the database data itself.

```
PERFORM: Query Next Previous Add Update Remove Table Screen . . .
Searches the active database table.                    ** 1: cust-order table**
_____
                                  Order Entry
   Customer Number:    [     ] Company:   [                    ]  Order #:   [     ]
   Name:            [                              ]
   Bill Address:    [                              ]
                    [                              ]
                    [                              ]
   Ship Address:    [                              ]
                    [                              ]
                    [                              ]
_____
                                  Order Items
   Order #:              Item #:           Catalog #:
   Description:                                 Unit price:
   Quantity:                              Order Item Price:
_____
```

Figure 8-4 Order Entry with PERFORM (INFORMIX-SQL)

- *Output:* This command allows users to print a screen image of the currently selected data. If the printing options are not set, you need to provide extra options to allow users to queue the output to the print spooling system. In this case, you also need some way to clean up the files created by this option.

With these comprehensive facilities, defining and running forms are sometimes too complex, causing frustration in both developers and users. Inability to customize commands for application specific terminology is a drawback. You cannot hide the database structure from users since they must be aware of individual tables in a screen form. It does, however, allow the definition of field level help messages for the benefit of the user.

You can only access one row of one table at a time, which leads to tedious command input during data entry. In our order entry example, shown in Figure 8-4, the user must first add an order record, then change tables to the order items table, and add each item ordered one at a time. You cannot automatically calculate the order total since all order items are not accessible at once. To provide multiple order items on one form, you must resort to the host language interface link. You may find it easier to simply develop the entire order entry program in the fourth generation language.

8.4.3 Report Generation

The ACE report generator utility consists of two programs, ACEPREP and ACEGO, which are available in both the original INFORMIX and INFORMIX-SQL packages. The difference between these packages is the query language used in ACE to extract data from the database: In INFORMIX, you use the INFORMER language; in INFORMIX-SQL you use SQL. You can also generate reports from the fourth generation language as discussed in Section 8.4.6.

The basic steps, which you can run directly from the ISQL environment, for defining and running reports are:

1. Define the report script using the ACE language as a text file using a standard text editor.
2. Compile it using the ACEPREP program. Compilation errors are written to an error file. You may need to repeat from step 1 in case of errors.
3. Run the compiled report script with the ACEGO program.

You can also generate default format reports which use database field names as labels and print all records, one field per line. Like our generic report generator, this utility uses a fixed execution cycle with parts of your report script commands executing at specific points in the cycle. Table 8-7 shows how its commands relate to our list of generic functions.

It has some unusual facilities which are useful. You can specify multiple data extraction statements which means that you can save results from one statement into a temporary table and use it to formulate the next statement. So you can break down a complex data extraction statement into several individual statements improving program maintainability.

You can pass values as command line parameters into the report at runtime, or prompt for them from within the script. Thus, your report can use different criteria for selecting data based on user input at runtime. Keep in mind that if you choose to prompt for runtime values, you cannot run the report as a background process.

Generic Report Writer Facilities	ACE Facilities
Page Size Control	Left Margin, Right Margin, Top Margin, Bottom Margin, Page Length
Page Layout	First Page Header block, Page Header block, Page Trailer block, Pageno, Skip to Top of Page, Need \<lines\>
Line Format Control	Skip, Column, Spaces, Lineno, Every Row
Field Format Control	Using "*format-spec*", Clipped
Data Control	Read (INFORMIX), Select (INFORMIX-SQL), sort option
Control Blocks	Before [After] Group Of block, On Every Row block, On Last Row block
Conditional Branch	If-Then-Else
Loop Control	For-Do, While-Do
Internal Variables	Define Variable (database data types), Let
Date and Time functions	Date, Day, Mdy (day of month), Month, Weekday, Year, Time, Today
Group Calculations	Count, Percent, Total, Average, Min, Max
Run time Interaction	Param (command line parameters), Prompt For, Pause
Output Control	Report To (pipe, file, printer)

Table 8-7 ACE Report Writer Facilities

Another useful facility when displaying reports on screen, is the *pause* statement. You can then control the size and content of each screen to make sure that entire records are displayed, important if the width of your report causes line wrap on the terminal. If you use the UNIX *more* or *pg* utilities, you can display partial records because of line wraps.

On the output side, you can use the *report to* statement to force output redirection via a pipe into another program, into a file, or directly to the printer. This facility means that you do not have to write a short SHELL script to redirect output, and cause an extra process to run the script.

8.4.4 Query Language

The original INFORMIX provides INFORMER query language, which differs from SQL provided by all other packages. The INFORMER relational language includes only data manipulation statements, while data administration statements are available in the DBSTATUS utility. You perform data definition functions only through the DBBUILD utility.

INFORMER provides data retrieval, add, update, and delete statements. Except for the add command, all statements operate on sets of data, thus conforming to the relational concepts. You can join more than one table when retrieving data; however, the add, update, or delete operations apply only to one relation table. Thus, you cannot specify changes to more than one table in a single statement, a restriction similar to the SQL data manipulation statements.

The retrieve operation supports joining of several tables (limited by the UNIX *open files* limit), the use of wildcard characters in selection criteria, and sorting of results. You can save results in temporary tables, or in an operating system file. You can specify synonyms (*Aliases*) useful for *self-join* operations on a table. INFORMER also provides date manipulation and group calculation facilities including *count*, *total*, *average*, *min,* and *max*.

DBSTATUS facilities include commands to manipulate indexes, transaction logs (*audit trails:* a combination of the audit trails and transaction log facilities provided in the SQL packages). You can perform data administration functions such as printing database schema and status, checking and repairing indexes, and erasing the entire database or some files. No backup facilities are provided; you use the UNIX facilities or build your own.

Parts Table

p_no	p_desc
A12	2-inch nails
B24	2-inch screws
C01	2-inch nails
D21	hammer

Suppliers Table

s_no	s_name
AAA001	Hardware, Inc
AAB110	ABC company
ABC110	New Company
BBD001	XYZ, Inc

part_supp Table

part_no	supp_no	min_qty
A12	AAA001	1000
A12	ABC110	1500
B24	BBD001	1500
D21	ABC110	200
D21	BBD001	100

Figure 8-5 Parts, Suppliers Database

The SQL products provide all of the features of the language discussed in Chapter 4. They include extensions to SQL features which provide some data administration facilities and enhance the usability of the language. A noteworthy extension is the **_outer join_** facility.

To understand the importance of the outer join facility, consider this simple example query from the parts and suppliers problem illustrated in Figure 8-5. Suppose we wish to list part numbers and suppliers of two-inch nails. The SQL query is as follows:

```
SELECT  part_no, supp_no
FROM    part, part_supp
WHERE   p_desc matches "2-inch nails*"
AND     p_no = part_no
```

Result:
```
part_no   supp_no
A12       AAA001
A12       ABC110
```

This result does not contain part number "C01" since no supplier currently supplies it. However, we still needed that part to be listed since it meets our part description criteria. The outer join facility allows us to list part numbers for all two-inch nails and any supplier who supplies it. The new SQL query with outer join is

```
SELECT  part_no, supp_no
FROM    part, outer part_supp
WHERE   p_desc matches "2-inch nails*"
AND     p_no = part_no
```

The result of this outer join, shown here, is what we wanted.

```
part_no   supp_no
A12       AAA001
A12       ABC110
C01        -
```

8.4.5 Host Language Interfaces

There are two types of host language interface available: the ALL-II function library in the original INFORMIX package and the ESQL products. These interfaces are not compatible with each other, as they assume different database structures.

The ALL-II library consists of a set of C functions to access and manipulate data in individual database files. These functions allow you to set indexed access mode, and add and remove indexes. You cannot access these indexes directly; instead, you use a high level search function called DBFIND, passing either a single search value or a composite value in a structure. This function will automatically utilize appropriate indexes to aid its search. Thus, your program can be independent of the underlying access methods.

Other useful facilities to make your program independent of the physical storage are the functions DBSETFILEVIEW and DBSTRUCTVIEW. These functions allow you to associate variables in your program with fields in a file. Subsequent calls to ALL-II functions use this association to obtain and forward data to your program. Additional functions provide you with the ability to find information about files, single and composite fields, indexes, and predefined synonyms.

The embedded SQL interface consists of a preprocessor which converts the embedded statements into special functions calls in the host language. This interface hides many of the complex structures which a programmer needs to know. The database access tasks are expressed in the familiar SQL language with some adaptation to handle program variables. Embedded SQL facilities make your programs easier to maintain than a function call based interface due to the high level of SQL data access statements.

One frustrating drawback for developers is that trivial typographical errors in the SQL statements are not always detected at compilation time. Errors such as misspelling database field names are detected only when you try to run the program. Normal debugging utilities such as sdb, are of limited use because the output of the preprocessor is significantly different from the code you write. Besides, such utilities only understand C; they do not understand SQL.

You must use ESQL/C programs to hook into the version of PERFORM supplied with the INFORMIX-SQL product; you cannot use the ALL-II library. This restriction is because of the different data dictionary structures assumed by the ALL-II functions.

Neither product provides any screen handling functions; instead, you have to use the standard curses library functions to build your own screen interface. Alternatively, you can use the hooks in PERFORM to run custom C functions from the forms driver. However, these hooks are provided only at specific processing points and may not fully satisfy your needs.

8.4.6 Fourth Generation Language

The INFORMIX-4GL product provides a high level programming language to develop your applications. Its advantage over a third generation language is that it provides statements which perform a task that requires many lines of code in a lower level programming language. However, it is substantially a procedural language whose similarities to a third generation language are obvious. There is no formal definition of what constitutes a fourth generation language: This language is yet another variety, different from other vendors' products.

Programs written in earlier versions of this software are preprocessed first into ESQL/C, secondly into C programming language, and finally into executable code. Later versions compile directly into a proprietary format intermediate code, which is interpreted at runtime. This partial interpretation mechanism allows support of the INFORMIX-4GL interactive debugger utility with many features desirable in a development environment.

One of the major differences between the embedded SQL interface and this fourth generation language is the mechanism it provides to structure your programs. Its control is based on a ***main*** controlling function, any number of subsidiary functions, special purpose ***report*** functions, and mechanisms for handling error conditions. Execution control starts with the main function and passes to subsidiary or special purpose functions through a call mechanism. Error handling code is executed usually when an error occurs, or you must occasionally check the return status for error.

You can add custom functions to a 4GL program, which are written either in 4GL itself or in C. You can link any other modules at the final compilation stage (only in version 1.10 software), provided they are first compiled into the standard UNIX object file format. Note that linking functions written in ESQL/C to 4GL programs can cause difficulties, if you need to use embedded SQL statements in both.

One advantage of using this package is the high level screen handling functions it provides, rather than lower level curses functions. You can define forms using the familiar FORMBUILD language and drive them with a program written with the 4GL package. Keep in mind that you must now explicitly code some of the features of FORMBUILD language into your program. For example, in an application program dealing with multiple screens, you must explicitly code the movement between screens. The commands available in PERFORM are no longer displayed, and your program must explicitly define and process the commands offered to the user. If you need to join tables for some combined processing, your program must do this explicitly; FORMBUILD definitions will not perform this task.

An important feature provided by this package is a screen *array*, which you can consider as a display table of multiple records on the screen. You use this feature in screen forms where you need to let a user access multiple records from a single table. PERFORM cannot provide this type of form handling directly. Another facility provided by this package and not available in PERFORM is *windowing,* which allows you to display a different form temporarily, either for reference, help, or optional data entry.

You still define forms layout using the FORMBUILD language; however, some statements such as join are ineffective. You must explicitly perform such operations in your program. Your program must contain appropriate statements to display forms with or without windowing, interact with users for input, handle menu selections, and access the database explicitly. Unlike PERFORM, 4GL separates user interaction from database access, thus providing a more procedurally oriented language. Another minor difference is that attributes for fields are now defined in special system catalogs using an interactive definition utility, rather than as statements in the attributes section of the forms definition file.

The special purpose report function uses a formatting language just like that of ACE report writer. However, you obtain and set up the data to be printed in the report in some other function and pass it to a report function one record at a time. The structure of code in the report function contains the same control blocks and sections of an ACE report script, with the exception of the INPUT and SELECT sections.

The fourth generation language hides from the programmer many of the details such as conversion between data types, improving development productivity. It supports the higher level database data types which make the resulting application portable to INFORMIX-4GL in another environment. If you dislike writing *code*, albeit in a high level language, you can try program generation utilities supplied by third part vendors such as FourGen Inc. Such utilities allow you to interactively define specifications in addition to a FORMBUILD screen definition and generate a 4GL program for you.

8.5 Integration with UNIX

This database management system depends quite a lot on the facilities provided by UNIX. Its architecture takes advantage of the process based architecture of the operating system, with one front-end and one back-end per user. Its standard data storage method implements an indexed sequential access method on a UNIX filesystem, while the TURBO product uses the raw disk facility to improve disk I/O performance. All products depend on SHELL environment variables to determine runtime parameters such as location of database files, programs, and changes from assumed defaults such as currency symbols and date formats.

The dependence of these products on UNIX facilities raises many issues in implementing your application in a production environment and including administration functions for end-users. We have already examined most of these issues and some workarounds in the discussions of Chapter 7. So this section will simply point out the important considerations relating to this product line.

8.5.1 Login Access Usage

All INFORMIX products depend on the user identifications set up by the UNIX login procedures. So do not even consider bypassing these login procedures. They use the operating system uid and gid values, as well as login name, to determine who you are when you access the database. Its access security features all require you to use login and group names when specifying access restrictions and determining the owner or creator of database tables. They do not implement any internal login mechanisms which could substitute for the operating system procedures.

You cannot ignore the login procedures, even if you do not use any access restrictions. This is because to access the application database files and to run programs, you must have access to the files and directories in which they reside. UNIX itself determines this access and thus requires that you have appropriate user and group identifications.

8.5.2 File Access and Administration

As described in the previous section, your user and group identifications are very important in obtaining access to data and program files. The internal security mechanisms can often be thwarted by operating system mechanisms, unless you carefully set directory and file permissions either explicitly or through the *umask* settings when you create the database. For example, granting connect permission to a user does not guarantee access to the database. The user must also have at least read permission on the database directory and data files for successful access. Thus, the owner and group permissions must be chosen carefully at design time, and in production, user login and groups must match appropriately. Your administrative facility for user login management must reflect this consideration.

The C-ISAM based products do not include any utilities for data backup and recovery. You must backup either the binary files themselves, or unload data into ASCII files before backing up. Clearly, using an operating system utility for incremental backup is dangerous, since it may not ensure that any pointers internal to the files match after recovery. This forces you to perform full database backups each time.

You must prevent all users from changing the database while the backup is in progress, to guarantee that the backup is a consistent image of the data. Otherwise, the backup may contain partially completed updates. In some cases, this consideration may not be important, for example, if the administrator is the only user performing updates and all other users merely retrieve data. In all other cases, you must prevent access during backup by either locking the entire database, or performing backup in the UNIX single user mode.

The TURBO product does offer its own backup utility through its *monitor* environment. This is essential as backing up multiple raw disks with UNIX utilities is difficult. The monitor puts the database into a single user mode (that is, not accessible by any other user) during backup. It also provides separate back-up of transaction logs so you can match them with the appropriate backup. The only drawback of this scheme is that it is interactive, so backups cannot be scheduled to run unattended.

8.5.3 Process Architecture

The utilities in the original INFORMIX run as individual processes, which means that there are short delays when you access them especially from the menus. On the other hand, front-end utilities in INFORMIX-SQL are combined into one executable so load delays disappear, but the executable itself is very large and hogs a large amount of memory.

The SQL based products also use one back-end process per user, which is transparent to the application user. This separation of front-end and back-end processes is the reason why you can discard the C-ISAM storage strategy and plug in the TURBO storage strategy. Differences between storage strategies affect developers and administrators but are transparent to application users. They might simply see a performance improvement.

8.5.4 SHELL Access

Many of the utilities provide access to the SHELL environment and are triggered by the user typing a "!" (exclamation mark). As we discussed in Chapter 7, this trigger is one of the most difficult to bypass. If you provide interactive SQL interface to the users, you have to use the ISQL environment. This environment allows access to a system editor, an essential facility for editing of files larger than a single screen. Thus, your application design should also consider SHELL escape via your selected editor.

If your application uses SHELL scripts to run any application menu options, then substituting a dummy SHELL program is not a feasible alternative. The menu driver needs the SHELL program to run SHELL scripts defined in menu options.

8.6 Conclusions

The INFORMIX product line offers comprehensive facilities catering to the needs of many different applications. Their product breakdown allows you flexibility in purchasing only the components you need, although you can only decide which components you need if you have prior experience with them. Customers with little prior experience are frequently confused by the overlapping facilities in the packages. This chapter attempted to reduce this confusion by clarifying the potential uses of each facility.

You can be certain that no single package will meet all of your needs, unless you develop a significant quantity of functions in libraries of your own. There will also be irritating but minor differences that you have to take into account as you add new packages for meeting specific needs.

A C-ISAM based database probably suffices only for small quantities of data — say a database size of under 20 megabytes. You must use the INFORMIX-TURBO back-end for larger databases. This chapter discussed some of the important tasks involved in converting between these storage strategies. Such conversion is tricky, but can be done if you understand the differences.

There are few project management aids for tracking the development of a project built into the product line. The menu driven environment components make it difficult for you to custom fit the existing UNIX tools such as SCCS. The discussion in this chapter attempted to point out to you other issues and tasks you should consider in your project plan. Attention to incompatibilities between products during your application design will make your project run more smoothly.

9

The INGRES DBMS

9.1 Introduction

The Berkeley public domain DBMS called INGRES is widely known and discussed in academic circles. However, the commercially available product INGRES, supplied by Relational Technology Inc. (RTI) is of more interest to application developers. This product was introduced in 1981. Its development has diverged from its academic namesake since its introduction to the market, moving towards satisfying business needs. RTI'S INGRES is available on many UNIX machines as well as several other operating systems such as DEC VMS, IBM VM/CMS, and MS-DOS.

RTI operates from Alameda, California and has sales channels worldwide. The product is also available from several computer manufacturers. INGRES supports both its own query language, QUEL, and the industry standard SQL. The product can run on a single machine or in a distributed mode over several machines connected with a network link. We discuss the distributed capabilities in Part 5. In this chapter, we discuss the following versions:

INGRES   Version 5.3

and a garnish of INGRES Version 6.

9.2 Packages and Components

INGRES offers a variety of facilities as evident in the large number of its components. It is one of the few DBMS products that provides administrative tools rather than depending on the operating system facilities. Since the UNIX operating system rarely provides adequate tools in this area, INGRES tools fill this gap.

INGRES consists of many components which you can mix and match according to your needs. The relationships among the components are illustrated in Figure 9-1. Note that though INGRES supports the SQL and its own QUEL query languages, the basic utilities are

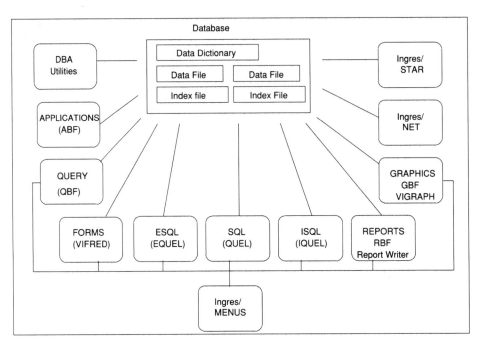

Figure 9-1 INGRES Components

common. The only difference you see is the syntax you would use whenever a query language statement is needed. You do, however, need to choose which query language you want to use.

Some of the components not discussed in this chapter include the INGRES *gateway* products which allow access to products such as VAX RMS and dBASE.

9.2.1 INGRES Software Products

In this section we discuss the component products of the INGRES DBMS. Section 9.2.2 contains a description of which of these components you need for development. Some of these products have been known by different names, so their older names are listed here.

- *INGRES/Menu:* This is a one level menu which allows you access to each of the other components.

- *INGRES/QUEL:* This is a line oriented interface to the QUEL query language. It includes commands for data definition, data manipulation, data integrity, and security functions. This is the original query language provided in INGRES.

- *INGRES/IQUEL:* This component is a screen oriented interface to the QUEL query language which was designed for end-users. It does not require you to learn the syntax of the QUEL language.

- *INGRES/EQUEL:* This embedded query language interface is available for a variety of third generation programming languages including C, COBOL, and FORTRAN.

- *INGRES/SQL:* This line oriented interface allows INGRES users to use the industry standard SQL language. There are, however, some nonstandard extensions.

- *INGRES/ISQL:* This end-user interface is the screen oriented counterpart of the SQL query language. Its implementation is very similar to the IQUEL component.

- *INGRES/ESQL:* This interface is the SQL version of the embedded query language for third generation programming languages.

- *INGRES/FORMS (VIFRED):* This utility allows you to develop custom forms for use with either the QBF or the ABF components. It allows you to define screen fields which are associated with database fields and specify their display attributes. Validation criteria can be defined to edit user input. It also allows you to define forms to display multiple records from a single table.

- *INGRES/QUERY (QUERY-BY-FORMS: QBF):* This forms driver utility has some unusual features. It can handle display and scrolling of multiple records from one table on the screen. Its *joindefs* facility allows multiple tables on one form to be related in any suitable manner, as well as allowing master-detail relationships.

- *INGRES/REPORTS (REPORT-BY-FORMS (RBF) and REPORT-WRITER):* This end-user utility allows you to define and generate simple reports using a screen based interface. You do not need to learn the language for defining report scripts. For more complex reports or sophisticated formatting, you would define your report scripts using the *report writer*.

- *INGRES/APPLICATIONS (APPLICATIONS-BY-FORMS: ABF):* This optional component is the fourth generation development facility. You can develop forms based interactive applications driven by the OSL language provided in this component.

- *INGRES/GRAPHICS (GRAPH-BY-FORMS: GBF, VIGRAPH):* This component allows you to generate business graphics objects such as histograms, bar charts, and line graphs. A screen oriented editing utility allows you to edit the resulting graph. These optional utilities are available only on hardware capable of graphical display; for example, SUN workstations and CALCOMP plotters.

- *Data Administration Utilities:* There are several utilities to manage data security, data integrity, backup, and restore of a database. INGRES implements a checkpoint facility in addition to transaction journaling to save snapshots of the database. It includes utilities for monitoring and improving the performance of query language based access.

- *INGRES/NET:* This component allows you to network individual INGRES databases so that you can exchange data between them. It is supported using TCP/IP protocols and so is available only on certain hardware. We discuss its capabilities in Chapter 15.

- *INGRES/STAR:* This distributed database management component provides additional facilities to allow you to distribute your database on more than one machine. It also uses TCP/IP protocols and is available only on supported hardware. It can provide seamless inquiry capabilities. We will discuss its capabilities in Chapter 15.

9.2.2 Development Components

Database Storage:

INGRES supports the one relation per file approach discussed in Chapter 6. An individual relation table must reside in one filesystem. However, you can distribute relation tables comprising a single database over more than one filesystem. You can thus use more than one physical disk to store your database.

Menu Driver:

INGRES does not provide a generic utility for developing application specific menus. You can use the capabilities of the fourth generation facility to develop menus. Most INGRES utilities display the names of the objects (such as forms or reports) they operate on, so that users can select the desired object from a list. Users do not need to remember the names of forms or reports. They would need to access the query or reports utilities via the INGRES/MENU utility which means that you could not prevent access to specific tools.

Forms Driver:

The forms definition utility, VIFRED, and the driver, QBF, are necessary for fast development of screen oriented forms applications. They also support default form formatting, so you do not need to custom define every form. Unfortunately, they only support single screen interaction.

Report Generator:

For end-user development of straightforward reports, you need the RBF utility. However, some user training is essential before they can make effective use of it. For more complex formatting of reports, you need the report writer utility. We discuss the capabilities of each utility in Section 9.4.3.

Host Language Interface:

The approach implemented for host language interface is the embedded query language approach with a precompiler. You can choose either the EQUEL interface or the standard ESQL interface. We will discuss some of the nonstandard extensions to this interface in Section 9.4.5. INGRES supports these interfaces for a number of programming languages, including C, FORTRAN, COBOL, ADA, PL/I, and PASCAL.

Fourth Generation Language:

The INGRES/APPLICATIONS facility is an optional package. You will also need a C compiler which can be an optional package on some UNIX systems. Note that you can link in your own subroutines in any supported programming language; however, the C compiler is always necessary.

Query Language:

INGRES supports the ANSI standard SQL language in addition to its own proprietary QUEL relational query language. This component is an essential interface for all data management activities.

Development Environment:

The INGRES/MENU utility can be used by novice developers to gain access to development utilities. However, experienced developers might prefer direct access from the Shell. The ABF facility provides a comprehensive development interface, including built-in compilation intelligence similar to **make**.

9.3 Data Control

The INGRES data control strategy is a two-tier hierarchy: a master **database of databases** (**dbdb**) and the individual application databases. The dbdb database contains information about all application databases, administered by a super-DBA. Each application database can have its own DBA. Registering new user ids and transferring special DBA privileges for any application database must be done by the super-DBA. The dbdb uses the same data structures as any other INGRES database, and so its interface is very similar to an application. Some special utilities, such as **accessdb** security management utility, are available only to the id used for dbdb access.

INGRES uses its own data storage methods for storing most of the system and application objects. For example, the data dictionary, information about application forms, and report definitions are stored in tables as part of the application database. This consistent use of relational structures makes it easier to develop a consistent application, and the DBA needs a familiarity with fewer extra commands and interfaces.

You can customize the directory structure for storing application objects by defining SHELL environment variables for individual applications, although there are system default directory definitions for these objects. Since each type of object could be placed in a different directory, you need to set several SHELL environment variables which might appear to be complex. Novice users might find it easier to simply use the defaults as a start. Later, you can relocate the different objects to suit your own set-up.

We discuss the details of data storage in Section 9.3.2. The important point is that INGRES provides several utilities to change your usage of directories and devices and to relocate data tables. These utilities make reorganization of the database easy, without requiring tedious unloading and reloading of the entire database.

9.3.1 Data Types

The product supports many of the generic data types discussed in Chapter 3. Internal representation of these data types may differ from other DBMS packages, leading to different restrictions. Table 9-1 relates our generic data types to those supported by INGRES.

9.3.2 Storage Structures

INGRES uses the UNIX filesystem for storing database tables and data dictionary files. System files are divided into four major components: INGRES system code, database files, checkpoint files, and journal files. Each of these components occupies an **area** — that is, a filesystem directory – called the INGRES root directory. One or more **locations** can be mapped to an area, and thereafter used for accessing objects residing in that area. Figure 9-2 illustrates the relation between an area, locations, and an application database.

Our Data Types	INGRES Data Types
Small Integer	INTEGERn, where n=1 for 1-byte integer (-128 to +127) and 2 for 2-byte integer (-32,767 to +32,767)
Large Integer	INTEGER4 (-2,147,483,648 to +2,147,483,647)
Small Floating Point	FLOAT4 (7 decimal digit precision, $-10**38$ to $+10**38$)
Large Floating Point	FLOAT8 (17 decimal digit precision, $-10**38$ to $+10**38$) (differs for IEEE standards conforming floating point hardware)
Money	MONEY, (8 bytes), decimal currencies only, total of 16 digits, precision after decimal point specified with a SHELL environment variable
Three-part Date	Date (Day, Month, Year in any order) (Limits 1-Jan-1582 to 31-Dec-2382)
Three-part Time	Date, defined in format, based on time zone *Time interval* between -800 years and +800 years.
String	Cn, where n is between 1-255, fixed length, blanks, and control characters ignored on matching. VCHAR(m), where m is between 1-2000, variable length, blanks, and control characters are relevant when matching.

Table 9-1 INGRES Data Types

You can think of locations as just names for an area. For example, you might have locations called *stock_dev* and *stock_prod* in the same area, since they share the same database. Different location names could also be used for different application databases. Area and location management is done by the super-DBA using the accessdb utility.

When you create a database, you can specify the locations to use for database files, checkpoint files, and journal files. You can place all components in one location or in any combination. Each location contains a data directory which contains a subdirectory for each database using that location. Thus, a location can be shared between many databases.

A single database could reside entirely in one location or can be *extended* over several. Thus, the size of your database is not limited to a single filesystem. The only restriction is that any one relation table must reside entirely in one location. This scheme works well for small to medium sized tables which are not likely to exceed the size of a single filesystem. However, you need careful calculation to make sure that a large table is likely to fit in a given filesystem. Alternatively, you could wait until the table gets large enough to overflow the space available and then relocate it on another filesystem.

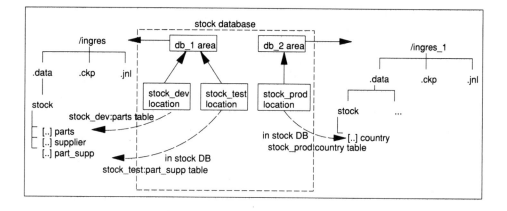

Figure 9-2 Relation of Areas and Locations to Database

Database creation is done via the ***createdb*** utility from the SHELL level. Once this process is complete, you can create database tables and indexes at any time using the INGRES/MENUS forms based facilities. For complex definitions, such as access security and integrity specifications, you have to use the query language facilities.

INGRES uses the one relation per file approach discussed in Chapter 6. Thus, each table is a separate file under the database directory under the INGRES data directory. Each index is also a separate file. INGRES, like many other products, allows users to create their own tables as part of the application database. These tables are wholly owned by the creating user and are inaccessible to other users. This is a frequent source of headache for a DBA. You probably want to prevent users from creating their own tables in an uncontrolled way. You can simply make sure that users do not have sufficient privilege to create tables, or you can periodically purge such private tables. Developers really find this facility useful for trying out new ideas without affecting other developers.

If any tables in your application are large, you need to watch out for the overhead of using a filesystem. This overhead is particularly acute if most of the access to the large table is random. Using indexes for access does not reduce the overheads of indirect blocks. You might also trip the ulimit file size limit, requiring you to reconfigure the UNIX kernel.

Apart from the ***.data*** directory, there are also ***checkpoint*** and ***journal*** directories in the database. Checkpoints are simply backup copies of a database which has journaling turned on. Each checkpoint file has a matching journal file which contains a log of database updates since that checkpoint. These pairs of files allow you to recover the database up to the last completed transaction prior to some disaster. Checkpoint files need not reside on disk; they can be written directly to tape. The journal file should reside on disk since it changes each time an update occurs. The speed of writing to the journal file in turn affects the speed of completing a transaction.

9.3.3 Access Methods

INGRES allows you to create and drop indexes at any time without requiring changes to the programs using the data. Its index creation commands allow you to control compression of key data in the index to reduce disk space usage on very large tables. You can also specify how full the index pages can be, and how full the data pages can be before overflow chains occur. Indexes for both primary and secondary keys are supported. Each key can consist of one or more fields which need not be consecutive within the record.

The utilities for optimizing the actual access path used by a query statement are noteworthy. Using the *Query Execution Plan (QEP)* facility, you can display the actual access path that INGRES would use. Based on this information you can use the optimization facilities on the database itself. You can tune the access path by changing the type of index specified for a table or by reworking the table statistics. Since the query language is the common means of data access, this facility is useful whether using the embedded host language interface, ABF, or the query language interactively.

Watch out for overflow in data and index pages since INGRES uses a chaining strategy to handle it. Overflow chains increase the amount of disk I/O that INGRES must do to satisfy a query. It, therefore, provides utilities to measure overflows in data tables and index pages to provide distribution statistics. You can then decide when to run the *optimzedb* function to reduce overflow chains and to reuse space freed up by deleted items.

Heap:

This is the default storage structure – that is, sequential data access. There are no keys defined in this method.

Hash:

This method creates and maintains access based on hashing the key value. This method minimizes disk I/O provided you supply an exact key value for fast, direct retrieval. It does not support partial key matches, or wildcard pattern matches on keys.

ISAM:

Data is stored in sorted order based on the key fields. This concept is similar to intrafile clustering discussed in Chapter 3. It allows partial key matches and pattern matches on key values. Note that sort order is not maintained after insertion of data record; that is, the index is static. Hence, it is best used on tables which change on rare occasions. You must rebuild the index after each modification.

B-Tree:

This method is the most versatile of the access methods. Though retrieval is not as fast as with the *hash* method, it is fairly good. Unlike the *isam* method, indexes are not static but are updated automatically whenever you insert a new record, or modify a key value. It supports partial key matches and pattern matches on key values. This method is best used for tables that grow or change frequently and for large tables.

9.3.4 Access Security Control

INGRES implements a three level user hierarchy: *super-DBA, DBA,* and *user*, within which all privilege structures are contained. The access control facilities are based on the simple philosophy of ownership: A user who creates an object owns the object. If the object is a database, the user automatically becomes its DBA. Access permissions are usually based on the user's login id only. However, it is possible to define *groups* of users using the facilities provided in the query language *permit* statement.

The super-DBA level has all access to all databases created with INGRES. Essentially this level of privilege allows you access to the dbdb database. Thus, any information in this master database can be changed only if you have this privilege.

DBA privilege, the next level down from super-DBA, is automatic when you create a database. By default, a newly created database is accessible to all. You can optionally create a private database and then give access to selected parts of it to other users.

Users of a publicly accessible database can create their own private tables — that is, accessible only to themselves. This can complicate the task of administering the database, especially if users create their own duplicate data. Fortunately, the DBA can control which users are allowed to make such unwelcome additions, or delete them via a special *impersonation* facility — that is, the DBA impersonates the owner in order to delete such files.

The access security controls also extend to application objects such as forms, reports, QBF names, and joindefs. They are owned by the developer who created them. To make them publicly accessible, you have to change ownership to DBA. Keep in mind that any tables accessed by these objects must also be accessible to a user before they are useful. INGRES provides many utilities, such as *copydb* and *copyapp,* to enable you to change ownership of different objects.

Super-DBA and DBA privileges can only be granted by using the accessdb utility. However, individual user level access permissions can be specified in both the QUEL and SQL query languages. The access security information is stored in an INGRES database, so either query language can modify it. Table 9-2 illustrates the types of permissions that can be granted to individual users.

Privilege	File Level Application	Field Level Application
QUEL: Retrieve SQL: Select	Can read all fields in the table.	Can read only those fields listed explicitly.
QUEL: Replace SQL: Update	Can update all fields in the table.	Can update only those fields listed explicitly.
QUEL: Delete SQL: Delete	Can delete any record in the table.	n/a
QUEL: Append SQL: Insert	Can add new records.	Can add new field values.

Table 9-2 INGRES Privilege Structure

Note that the permit statement (in either query language) can be qualified with a where clause, unlike the standard SQL grant statement. This facility allows you to define access privileges on a cross section of a table. For example, to enforce an access restriction such that department manager "Mary" can only access the employee records for her department the permit statement in QUEL would be

```
define permit retrieve of employee (emp_name, age, salary)
to mary
where employee.dept = department.dept and department.manager = "Mary"
```

Access can also be limited to a time period or a specified device.

9.3.5 Concurrency Control Options

INGRES supports *page level* and *table level* locking, with two types of locks: *shared* and *exclusive*. We have already discussed the pros and cons of page level locking versus record level locking in Chapter 3, so we won't go into it again in this chapter. The only notable point is that INGRES practices *lock promotion;* that is, it escalates a user's page level locks to a table level lock when the maximum threshold for page locks is reached. The saving grace is that you can customize the threshold as appropriate to your tables. A maximum threshold of 50 locked pages might be reasonable in a 10 megabyte table but is ridiculously small in a 100 megabyte table.

The INGRES terminology is somewhat different from our description of Levels of Isolation in Chapter 3: you have to choose the locks appropriate to the level of isolation you need. You can set locking defaults for a session, a particular transaction, a single statement, or the entire system. You can also specify *timeout* periods — that is, return to the user with an error condition if a lock could not be acquired within the given time period.

A dirty read is possible if you set no locks at all (*readlocks = nolocks*). This may be suitable for report programs which take a long time to complete. You probably would not lock the company president out of the database just because the monthly stock inventory report is being produced! However, you would want the data to remain unchanged while entering an order — that is, you want a committed read. To obtain this, you should choose a shared read lock (*readlocks = shared*). In this mode, many users can concurrently read data; however, it can only be updated after all locks are released.

By setting the lock mode to shared or exclusive before a multistatement transaction automatically guarantees the cursor stability level of isolation. This is because INGRES always obtains an *intended shared* (or *intended exclusive*) lock on the table before obtaining a page level lock. Note that a shared lock is simply a *read* lock, that is, other users can read locked data but not update it; whereas an exclusive lock is a *write* lock, that is, other users cannot access the data at all.

An additional option, provided for backward compatibility with older INGRES versions, is the *set deadlock/nodeadlock* command. Setting nodeadlock causes INGRES to obtain all locks prior to starting a transaction. This means that you need fewer program measures to avoid deadlock: the transaction does not start until all resources are locked. The default setting, deadlock, acquires locks as it proceeds through the transaction. When a deadlock occurs, the transaction is rolled back and an error condition is reported to the user.

There are syntactic differences between the ANSI standard SQL and its INGRES implementation. But its extensions such as where clauses in access control statements highlight the deficiencies in current standards.

9.3.6 Data Integrity Measures

INGRES allows flexible definition of data integrity constraints. Using the query language statement, ***create integrity***, you can specify an integrity constraint on a table. This statement accepts a where clause in a format common to other query language statements. You could consider this to be a flexible extension of the entity integrity rule.

As an example of this flexible facility, consider an employee database. Suppose we require a constraint that no one can earn a salary more than $10,000. We use

```
create integrity on employee where salary < 10000
```

Integrity specification cannot involve more than one table. INGRES does not support referential integrity.

9.4 Utility Packages

INGRES provides a tightly integrated set of development tools which present a remarkably consistent user interface. It also provides screen oriented interfaces to its two query languages rather than the usual line oriented interface. These interfaces allow you to browse through the results back and forth at will, as opposed to seeing them once on the screen only in a forward direction. Unfortunately, they do not relieve you from the task of learning the query language commands and syntax, which would really make them suitable for nontechnical users.

An unusual tool is the forms based report definition utility, RBF, which is easier to learn than the report writer language. Section 9.4.3 discusses some of the pros and cons of this interface together with the more common interface provided by the report writer tool.

One of the tools which deserves a mention as a report generation tool is INGRES/GRAPHICS which only works on graphics hardware. It allows you to present report data in graphs and charts rather than as just numbers. You can edit these created graphs using the VIGRAPH utility.

9.4.1 Menu Subsystem

The INGRES/MENUS product is merely a utility to access the standard INGRES components. It does not allow you to develop application specific menus. Thus, its name can be misleading. This utility is a menu based development environment, not a menu driver.

Application specific menus can be developed using ABF or the embedded host language interface facilities. Since you are defining a form to represent a menu, there are no restrictions on the layout of your menu. You may format it exactly as you wish. You can even define the application components in a special database table, including the invocation commands, so that changing a menu item associated with a particular program is easy. This is actually a very simple ABF application.

In the host language interface, you are hard-coding the menu names into your program. Although the facilities provided make it easy to identify menu items from all other entities, any changes require recompiling the program. This is why the approach of using a special database table to hold menu information is generally a better idea.

9.4.2 Screen Forms Facilities

The INGRES forms definition utility, VIFRED is a screen based paint tool. Forms defined with this utility can be driven using QBF, an embedded host language interface program (ESQL or EQUEL), or the ABF facility. In this section we discuss only the forms definition and QBF utilities. The embedded host language interface is described in Section 9.4.5 and ABF in Section 9.4.6. The *copyform* utility, to copy a form definition to another database, and utilities to print form layouts, complete the toolbox of INGRES forms handling facilities.

The basic steps, which you could also run from INGRES/MENU, for defining and running a form are:

1. Use VIFRED to define the form layout, associate form fields with database fields, and define field validation criteria.

2. Specify the form as a QBF form by selecting a QBF name for it. If you want to use this form with an embedded query language form, or with ABF, you need not perform this step.

3. Run the form with QBF.

There is no programming language involved in forms definition. The VIFRED interface consists of painting the screen layout, and filling in forms to define fields and their attributes. The most important facilities provided by VIFRED are:

- Form fields can correspond to a database field, or can be display only. Display only fields allow you to perform some calculation on other fields and display a value.

- You can specify any of the validation criteria specified in Table 9-3, or field editing criteria specified in Table 9-4. Validation criteria are free-form specification of the constraints similar in syntax to the where clause of an SQL statement.

- You can define multiple tables with some join relationship between them. Tables can be joined as any combination of a master-detail relationship.

- You can define a *tablefield* consisting of multiple rows from a table. This feature is useful in conjunction with a master-detail relationship. Thus, in a customer order example, you would display one row from the customer order table and multiple rows, with a tablefield, from the associated order items table.

- For each table in a multiple table form, you can define rules for deletion and update. These rules allow you to specify whether the displayed data from one table should be deleted when you delete the data from another table.

- The sequence of accessing form fields can also be defined. The default order is left to right and top to bottom.

Our Data Validation Criteria	VIFRED Data Validation Criteria
Range check	Numeric fields - any comparison operator (=, !=, <, <=, >, >=), Character fields - pattern specification (regular expression)
List of valid values	*field-name* in *list-of-values*
Required entry	Mandatory field attribute
Lookup in other table	*field-name* in *tablename.column-name*
Double entry verification	-
Field format enforcement	Via pattern specification (regular expression), field display format definition

Table 9-3 VIFRED Data Validation Criteria

Forms information is stored in the INGRES database and is catalogued by its name. You can use supplied utilities to delete a form, rename it, or print its layout. If you develop using a test database, putting the form into the production database requires copying it into a text file and loading the text file into the new database.

Although you can define field validation criteria in the form, keep in mind the integrity constraints defined on the database itself. The integrity constraints will prevent updates where the data fails these checks, even if it passes the validation checks of the form.

A confusing part of forms definition in a multiple table form is defining the ***joindef*** definition for the tables. A joindef must be defined using the QBF utility prior to using VIFRED for editing layout. In a joindef, two or more tables can be joined with each other in any combination of master-detail relationship (that is, master-master, detail-detail, or master-detail). The deletion and update rules are also defined for each table in the relationship. After you complete this definition, the joined tables are treated essentially as a single table by VIFRED and QBF.

Our Field Editing Criteria	VIFRED Field Editing Criteria
Case control	force upper case, force lower case attributes
Default value	default value, keep previous value
Field format	field display format definition
Field display attributes	box field, reverse video, blinking, underline, brightness change, color, no echo
Justification	-
Field padding	-

Table 9-4 VIFRED Field Editing Criteria

You can invoke QBF in development mode, allowing you access to table and joindef catalogs, or in a run mode specifically for data entry or query. You can invoke it for only one function — for example, query only mode — by specifying this option on the command line. The runtime command menu on the screen form then suppresses all other commands.

The commands available at any point in QBF execution are displayed as a ring menu on the screen. The major execution modes are *Retrieve*, *Append*, and *Update*. The update mode allows you to modify or delete rows. Additional menu items include commands to move between tables, scroll and insert functions on a multiple record display.

The update mode essentially starts in a query mode, allowing you to first select the rows to operate on. You can then browse through the results to select rows and change data in them. Alternatively, you can delete selected rows. New rows are added in the append mode. The retrieve mode is only for querying the database and browsing through the results. You cannot switch to the update mode from this mode.

9.4.3 Report Generation

There are four components to the INGRES report generation system: *sreport*, *Report-By-Forms (RBF)*, *report*, and *copyrep*. The first two utilities allow you to define reports. Sreport, the report specifier, can generate default report definitions. You can also create the report definition as an ordinary text file and use sreport to put the definition into an INGRES database. RBF provides an easy to use screen-based interface for creating and editing many of the simpler reports. You can use a default report, generated using sreport, as a starting point. Since report definitions are stored in the INGRES database, a utility to copy these definitions, copyrep, is available to propagate a report to other databases.

The sreport facility to generate default reports in *column style* (fields across the page) is unusual, although it can also generate reports in *block style* (one field per line). These column style reports are common in typical applications so that high productivity gains are possible with default reports. Obviously, column headings are the field names from the data dictionary.

More complex reports require the use of the sreport formatting commands. Table 9-5 illustrates the functions performed by these commands as compared to our generic report writer interface. This table lists complete command keywords which can be abbreviated to one or two characters in most cases. In fact, if you abbreviate all commands, the report definition script becomes as cryptic as a document containing the UNIX *nroff* commands. Thus, you can make it cryptic enough to satisfy even the most seasoned guru but maintenance is then, of course, almost impossible. You really would do better to avoid abbreviations altogether.

This report definition language has some unusual features for handling the sequence of formatting commands. You are not restricted to defining one line completely before moving down the page, as with most report writers. The *.block/.endblock* commands enclose formatting commands which allow you to define several print lines down the page before moving up to the top of the block for further output on the first line. Such a block can span control blocks started with the *.header* command. Thus, within a .block/.endblock delimiters you can move up or down to compose the report as appropriate.

Generic Report Writer Facilities	INGRES/REPORTS Facilities
Page Size Control	.Pagelength, .Leftmargin, .Rightmargin
Page Layout	.Header page, .Footer page, .Formfeeds, .Newpage, .Need
Line Format Control	.Tab, .Newline, .Left, .Right, .Center, .Lineend, .Linestart, .Top, .Bottom
Field Format Control	Apply to columns and blocks of data: .Format "*format-spec*", .Position, .Width, squeeze(), trim(), uppercase(), lowercase(), concat()
Data Control	.Data, .Query, Select (SQL version), Retrieve (QUEL version), .Sort
Control Blocks	.Header *field-name* or *report*, .Footer *field-name* or *report*, .Detail, .Block, .Endblock, .Within, .Endwithin
Conditional Branch	.If - .Then - .Elseif - .Else - .Endif
Loop Control	-
Internal Variables	w_column (within the current column)
Date and Time Functions	Current_date, Current_day, Current_time, Date(), Dow()
Group Calculations	Sum, Count, Minimum, Maximum, Average
Runtime Interaction	Specify runtime parameters on command line, automatic prompt
Output Control	.Output *path-name*, *path-name* can be changed on the command line

Table 9-5 INGRES/REPORTS Facilities

The .within/.endwithin commands, together with the .block/.endblock commands, allow you to format columns of data one column at a time. You can then conveniently calculate totals and subtotals of columns and place them appropriately at the top or bottom of the block. Thus, you could count the number of items printed in a group as you print them one per line and place the count at the top of the group block. For example, in a report of employees grouped by their departments, you could print the number of employees in each department as part of the department header line. An excerpt from such a report is shown in Figure 9-3.

```
/* Employee report excerpt showing number of employees in each
department followed by a listing of their names. */

.header department
    .need 4
    .block
    .print "Department:", department .newline .newline
.detail
    .tab .print employee(c30) title(c15) .newline
.footer
    .top .tab+5 .print "No. Of employees:", count(employee) (f3)
    .endblock
```

Result:

```
Department: Data Processing        No. Of employees:  5

Mary Jones                         Systems Analyst
John Smith                         Systems Analyst
Betty Smith                        Programmer
Jack Warner                        Programmer
Harry White                        Project Leader
```

Figure 9-3 Excerpt from a Report

Several commands are provided to define the position, width, and format of columns in a report. The *.position* command allows you to define these attributes together with a column name. You can then use the line positioning commands such as *.left* and *.center* with the column name to position within the width of a column. These column based formatting commands make the report definition less procedural than many common report writer languages.

9.4.4 Query Language

Initially implementing the proprietary QUEL query language, INGRES now supports the de facto standard SQL. You have to choose which query language products to purchase. Support of SQL will allow heterogeneous database access, to products such as DB2, via the *gateway* utilities. In this section, we do not repeat the well known features of SQL, which we have already discussed in Chapter 3, but only the differences between the standard and the INGRES implementation. We concentrate instead on a description of the QUEL language.

Before we dive into the details of the query language, it is worth noting the *Query Execution Plan (QEP)* utility provided by INGRES. This utility displays the planned access path chosen by INGRES for a query statement. The path aims to minimize the number of pages to be searched based on the where conditions, the type of index, the storage structure, and known statistics of values in each table involved in the query.

The statistics are collected by a DBA utility, *optimizedb*, and stored as part of the database. This collection process is static for obvious performance considerations. You can run optimizedb on a specific field of a table to collect statistics about the actual distribution of data values. Appropriate parameters indicate the types of selection conditions you are likely to use in predefined queries. On tables that get updated frequently, periodic reexamination and tuning of statistics is necessary. These tools are useful even if most of your application is written in a programming language or with ABF, since you are still using the query language. The query language is the primary interface for all data access functions.

The QUEL relational query language is similar to SQL in its structure. It provides data definition statements to create tables, indexes, and views; data manipulation statements to retrieve, insert, update, and delete data; and data administration statements to define integrity constraints, checkpoint, and restore databases.

It provides all of the relational operations: projection, restriction, join, and cartesian product. It supports table join operations in the where clause similar to SQL. A separate statement, *range*, allows you to assign synonyms (aliases) for table names which are then effect until you disconnect from the database. This is a better way than SQL where aliases are only in effect for a single statement. The usual group calculation facilities are available with additional functions to operate on unique occurrences of values.

The conventions for *nesting* are rather more flexible in QUEL than in SQL. You can nest selection conditions even within a group calculation function occurring in a where clause. For example, to obtain a list of all customer numbers and their order values where an ordered item is worth more than the average item value, you might use the following statement:

```
range of c is cust-ord
range of o is ord-item
retrieve (c.cust-num, ord-value = sum(o.tot-price by c.cust-num
             where c.cust-num = o.cust-num
             and o.tot-price > avg(o.tot-price))
```

Clearly, such nesting can make your queries arbitrarily complex. Gurus would certainly be essential (*job security!*) to decipher the more complicated compositions. Fortunately, you can always use multiple statements to obtain the same result. In our example, you might first obtain the average item value with one statement into a temporary table. A second statement would select all customers who ordered an item worth more than the average, saving the resulting customer numbers in another temporary table. The third and final statement would list customer numbers and the calculated order values of these customers.

QUEL supports transaction controls with the **begin transaction** and **end transaction** statements. You can rollback the transaction with an **abort transaction** statement. In addition to these basic facilities, you can declare **savepoints** within a transaction, which are especially useful when the transaction contains a lot of statements. An abort then need not roll-back the entire transaction, but only up to a named savepoint. Note that an abort does not undo any data definition statements that have completed successfully prior to it. Thus, when you abort a transaction which created a table, you must explicitly drop the table.

QUEL also provides a number of data type conversion functions such as converting a character representation of date into internal date format, numeric values into character strings. Date functions allow you to extract parts of a date or time allowing you to compare quarter-year date, weeks, hours, and so on. String manipulation functions allow you to shift characters left or right in a string, concatenate two strings, trim leading or trailing blanks, and compress spaces throughout a string. Mathematical functions such as *sin(), cos(),* and *log()* are also available. In addition to built-in functions, you have symbolic constants to access operating system information such as direct I/O requests, CPU time, and cache usage information for the INGRES data cache.

The SQL implementation in INGRES is very close to our description of the query language in Chapter 4. There are, however, several extensions which provide the extra facilities available in the QUEL implementation. An example discussed in Section 9.3.6 is the integrity specification statement, *define integrity*. Since the facilities already exist in the underlying database, these extensions must have been easy to add. As with any extensions to a standard, your portability needs dictate whether or not to use them.

Other differences include syntactical variations on the SQL language, though the functions performed are the same. For example, access security specification uses the syntax *create permit* and *drop permit* rather than grant and revoke. A wildcard match in a select statement uses the = *(equal)* operator rather than the *like* predicate. Thus, the INGRES SQL implementation supports all of the functions we discussed in Chapter 4, with some syntactic differences. The only operator not supported in this version is the *union* operator.

9.4.5 Host Language Interfaces

INGRES supports the SQL and the QUEL query languages embedded into a third generation programming language. Languages supported include C, FORTRAN, PL/I, PASCAL, and COBOL. These interfaces use a preprocessor to convert the embedded statements into calls to the back-end server process. Call parameters are statements which are interpreted at execution time. Thus, you cannot detect mistakes in the statements during compilation.

Version 6 extends the query language so that you can save a set of statements which are compiled. When you execute such a saved set, no interpretation overheads are incurred. In addition, you can use runtime parameters in the statements for flexibility.

The embedded SQL implementation follows the DB2 conventions of preceding each embedded statement with the keywords *EXEC SQL.* The normal use of select statements is when the result retrieves only a single row. In this case the order by or group by clauses are not available, for obvious reasons. For queries which result in multiple rows, you can use the conventional cursor structure which behaves just like a pointer to a record in the result set. Statements based on using the cursor structure can have the order by or group by clauses.

An extension to the standard select statement, the *repeated* keyword, helps to reduce the cost of run time parsing. Using this keyword implies that the statement is used repeatedly in the program and so the runtime system should save the access path plan for it. Thus, it is parsed once only: when it is first encountered at run time. Subsequent execution will simply use the saved access path plan. The version 6 *compiled transactions* save even on the one-time parsing overhead.

The *forms runtime system (FRS)* facilities are an unusual extension to the host language interface. It allows you to drive a form from a third generation programming language. Statements for these facilities are prefixed by the keywords *EXEC FRS.* Forms in this interface are also defined with the VIFRED painting utility. They can then be used directly from the database tables, or precompiled and linked into your program. There are obvious performance advantages to precompiling the form definition.

The FRS provides a high level interface to screen handling from a third generation programming language. You can display a form, define menu items associated with the form, and allow the user to move around the form, all with a few lines of code. A particularly nice feature is the ability to prefill values in the form before it is displayed. These values might be field default values specified in the VIFRED definition or in the *initialize* code block in the program. Prefilling the data before form display is more pleasing to the user in a multiple screen query application, rather than seeing a blank form on screen which then gets filled one field at a time.

The FRS capabilities allow you to handle tablefields (a display of several rows from one database table) with high level commands. You can define a data selection statement and associate its result to a screen tablefield. The FRS then handles scrolling of the rows of data according to the user interaction. You can define your own specialized scrolling functions, such as scroll to a specific record. You can control deletion of rows in the tablefield with the deleterow statement so that a deleted row causes compression of the remaining rows on the display. Row insertion similarly generates a blank row in the display table.

Most of the embedded SQL facilities derive from the original EQUEL implementation. Thus, the same functions are supported by both embedded host language interfaces. Some syntactic differences in their implementation exist. For example, QUEL statements are identified in a program with ## (two hash signs) in the first two columns rather than the EXEC SQL keywords. Form manipulation statements do not have EXEC FRS keywords, only the hash sign identifiers. All other facilities are conceptually the same, except that the syntax for query language statements follows the QUEL conventions.

Handling of multiple row retrievals in EQUEL is slightly different: You do not need to explicitly declare a cursor. Cursor functions are implicit in the {...} (curly brackets) enclosing the processing loop. You do have to do some mental juggling when writing the code within the loop, because you can only move forwards through the resulting rows. There are no facilities to scan backwards in the result set. This restriction also holds true for the ESQL interface.

Note that this version of INGRES does not support dynamic assembly of embedded statements. Thus, you have to hard-code names of tables and fields into each statement. Future implementations will undoubtedly rectify this limitation.

9.4.6 Fourth Generation Language

The INGRES/APPLICATIONS (ABF) facility implements the frame based approach we discussed in Chapter 3. It is the obvious culmination of the facilities available in the embedded host language interface. As you would expect, it is intended to be a productivity improvement tool for typical screen based interactive data processing functions. This facility is best suited for quick development of functions like data entry, interactive query on the database, reports with parameters specified on a screen form by users, or data displayed as graphs on a graphics screen.

The ABF interactive forms based development environment is impressive. It is an excellent example of the consistent interface you could achieve in your own application. It allows you to create and populate database tables, define the frames which comprise the application, and run these frames even if you have not yet developed the complete application. There are obviously some limitations. For example, you cannot specify indexes on table fields. However, these are issues that should be dealt with separately by a database administrator anyway. The programmer need not worry about it for quick development.

As implied by the frame based approach, there are two major components in each ABF frame: a nonprocedural part and a procedural language called *Operation Specification Language* (OSL). The nonprocedural part might be a QBF form, a report writer component, or a GBF component. You might also define a custom frame consisting of a form defined with VIFRED. Connected with this custom frame would be a procedural component specified in OSL. Figure 9-4 illustrates the relationship between an application, a frame comprising the application, and components of a frame.

The procedural language, OSL, comes in two flavors: SQL and QUEL. Both flavors implement the same functions, though the syntax of each resembles its base language. The SQL data access statements start with the keywords EXEC SQL and forms manipulation statements with EXEC FRS, just like the embedded SQL syntax. QUEL based OSL simply uses ## (two hash signs).

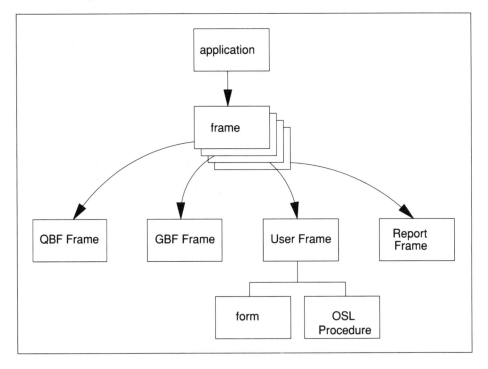

Figure 9-4 ABF Application Components

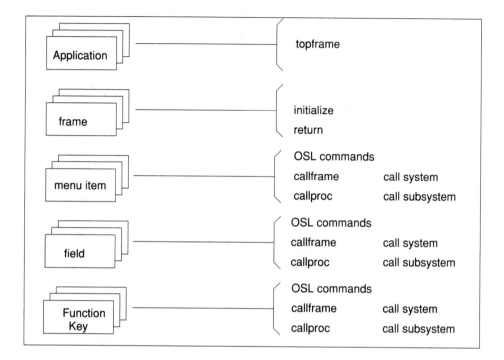

Figure 9-5 ABF Processing Control Points

A procedure associated with one frame is coded in an ordinary text file, just like a program. The development environment provides access to your favorite text editor and keeps track of whether you change the file. You can then compile the procedure and link it, together with others, to create your application. The ABF environment only recompiles procedures which have changed, thus exhibiting some make-like features. One nice feature is that you can link and run partially defined applications – that is, with one or more frames – to test and debug it. This facility has great value in impressing management and colleagues with your high productivity.

OSL procedural code associates with certain control points such as menu items and fields. Figure 9-5 illustrates the ABF components and control points for OSL code. Execution of code associated with these control points depends entirely on user actions. For example, code associated with a particular field would not be executed if the user does not move the cursor into the field and then on to the next or previous field. Thus, you have to be careful to avoid any dependence on the order in which the user might fill in the form. You can use VIFRED validation and default value facilities to enforce mandatory field entry.

OSL is a complete programming language. It therefore contains the usual components of any programming language such as variable declaration, assignment statements, mathematical functions, constructs such as if-then-else and while. Its difference from a third generation language lies in its database access and forms manipulation capabilities. The database access capabilities are high level query language statements rather than record-at-a-time access. The forms manipulation statements operate on high level forms objects such as fields, and tablefields instead of issuing low level terminal commands to move the cursor, display characters, and so on.

You can call any of the standard INGRES utilities directly from an OSL procedure. You can also connect one frame with another using the OSL *callframe* statement. Other *call* mechanisms allow you to execute SHELL commands, call your own host language subroutines, or subroutines written in OSL. It is possible to develop many applications without resorting to a third generation programming language.

9.5 Integration with UNIX

Although INGRES originated on a UNIX system, it now runs on several other operating systems. Its architecture still reflects its use of the process based architecture. It implements its storage strategies and access methods using the UNIX filesystem. SHELL environment variables abound, indicating the directories where the data dictionaries, data files, and application files reside. They also indicate user preferences at runtime such as date formats and currency symbols. Evidence of its good integration with UNIX rests also in its philosophy of supporting different terminal types via the *termcap* and *terminfo* mechanisms.

All of these dependencies lead to many administrative issues in your application's production environment. In this section, we relate issues detailed in Chapters 6 and 7 to this specific implementation.

9.5.1 Login Access Usage

INGRES secures the directory where dbdb resides using the UNIX login id and group id of the super-DBA. Similarly, the application database owner is the login id of the creator. Each data (and associated index file) is owned by the creator's login id. Thus, INGRES depends on these UNIX user identification mechanisms to determine who you are and what you are allowed to access. So, you have no chance of success in trying to bypass the standard operating system login procedures.

Your only choice in preventing users' access directly to the SHELL is to use their profile to start-up the application. This special profile set-up must now be part of your custom *add user* administration function. You might be tempted to skimp on developing this function by simply using one user id for all users. Prepare to overcome it, however, as you are likely to run into several other obstacles like confusion on audit trails: How can you determine which person deleted those vital employee bonus records?

9.5.2 File Access and Administration

Since INGRES uses the UNIX login ids and group ids to secure files and directories, it is best if you don't interfere with its choice of access security on these. Your backup and restore mechanisms must integrate with the *chkpointdb* facility offered by INGRES. You could use a directory accessible to the operating system backup utility for keeping checkpoint files and then backing them up as part of your routine backup. Alternatively, the checkpoint function can write directly to backup media such as magnetic tape. Bear in mind that for use by end-users you will need to build a menu front-end to such administration utilities.

A further obstacle is that you cannot simply copy database files, or application definition files, as you please. INGRES's internal mechanisms will prevent any use of such unauthorized copies. Its designers anticipated your need to move applications from a test database to a production database. INGRES, therefore, provides copy utilities such as *copyapp* to move an ABF application, *copyform* to move application forms definitions, and so on.

Tackling the database growth problem in INGRES, even though it uses the filesystem, is relatively easy. Your database need not be restricted to a single filesystem. You can allocate a new INGRES *area* in another filesystem, and relocate some of the tables from the problem database there. The only restriction occurs when a single table grows to the maximum size of a filesystem, unless you consider buying a larger disk.

9.5.3 Process Architecture

INGRES uses a two process architecture: Its utilities act as front-end interfaces and the database access is controlled by a back-end server process. In version 5, there is one back-end server per user — that is, two processes per user. Version 6 changes this architecture to use multithreaded multiple servers. Thus, several front-end interface processes can share a multithreaded server, and there can be as many servers as you choose. Thus, version 6 will be able to take advantage of multiprocessor hardware architectures.

The front-end interface and the back-end server communicate with each other via *pipes*. A memory cache scheme allows the front-end interface to store blocks of data to reduce communications traffic with the back-end.

On SYSTEM V UNIX, the concurrency control mechanism uses shared memory segments accessed by all back-end processes. Where shared memory is unavailable, alternative implementations include a *lock-driver* which is compiled into the UNIX kernel, or a *lock-daemon* process. Having a separate process to manage locks, as in the lock-daemon implementation, obviously has some performance degradation over other approaches.

9.5.4 SHELL Access

SHELL access for end-users is possible through a couple of the utilities in INGRES, so be careful how you set-up access to these. The INGRES/MENUS utility provides the command SHELL which creates a SHELL process for executing commands. You can disable this command only by renaming the SHELL executable. Since this menu interface also provides access to development tools, you might not want end-users to access it anyway.

Another potential access is via the ISQL and IQUEL utilities. These utilities allow you to edit query language statements by entering a standard system editor such as *vi*. As we discussed in Chapter 7, the vi SHELL escape mechanism is easily disabled with the environment variable called SHELL.

If you provide menu access to application functions, in a typical application perhaps developed with ABF, you should not face any significant difficulties. Giving each user a separate login id, with its own *home directory,* probably avoids most of the potential accidents.

9.6 Conclusions

INGRES has by far the most impressive development facilities of the four UNIX DBMS products discussed in this book. It provides comprehensive administrative tools for managing the database, and for achieving high development productivity. These productivity improvement tools do exact a performance penalty (not unlike the other products). Your choice then becomes whether the productivity gains, allowing faster satisfaction of user needs, are sufficient to offset the higher hardware costs due to the necessary extra CPU horsepower.

Project management for a team using INGRES utilities is difficult although some of the necessary features exist in the ABF environment. Since many application components reside in an INGRES database, some protection against multiple simultaneous updates exists. It is a lot easier however, if each team member simply uses a separate login id during development — allowing INGRES to naturally separate and protect them from each other.

A commendable feature of all of the INGRES utilities is their consistent interface. They also provide exactly the same interface to the applications you develop using them. Thus, you need to pay little attention to which components you can combine when developing a well-integrated, consistent application.

10

The Oracle DBMS

10.1 Introduction

Oracle Corporation has its headquarters in Belmont, California. The company was founded in 1978. The first UNIX version of the ORACLE DBMS product was offered in 1984. The product also runs on a range of hardware and operating systems from micros to mainframes. It is available from their own sales channels worldwide as well as from computer manufacturers.

A major feature of the ORACLE database management system is its high degree of compatibility with the IBM DB2 SQL. This compatibility means that you can port an application developed on DB2 to ORACLE with relatively little effort. It is possibly the first step towards heterogeneous distributed databases.

In this chapter, we discuss the following facilities provided by the ORACLE DBMS. Its networking facilities and distributed features are deferred until Part 5.

ORACLE RDBMS	Version 5.1 with a garnish of Version 6
SQL*Plus	Version 2.0
Easy*SQL	Version 2.1
SQL*Forms	Version 2.3
SQL*Report	Version 1.0
PRO*C	Version 1.1
SQL*QMX	Version 1.1
SQL*Report Writer	Version 1.0

10.2 Packages and Components

The ORACLE product line includes a large variety of software, from the RDBMS kernel to a spreadsheet, and from data analysis tools (CASE) to preprocessors for programming languages. We restrict our discussion to DBMS tools and facilities; discussion of spreadsheets and data design tools are beyond the scope of this book. Section 10.2.1 provides an overview of each of the ORACLE components. In Section 10.2.2 we examine which components are needed for the different development tasks.

10.2.1 ORACLE Software Products

The central theme of all ORACLE DBMS products is the SQL language. Figure 10-1 illustrates how these components are structured around the DBMS kernel. Note that you need not purchase all components for an application: You can mix and match the components you need. We also list the older names for these components where appropriate.

RDBMS:

The kernel of the ORACLE DBMS implements the relational model. It allows you to use UNIX filesystem files as well as raw disk partitions. The SQL*Plus component provides the interface to create and maintain tables in the application database.

SQL*Plus:

This component is the primary interface to accessing the database. It provides commands for data definition, data manipulation, and administrative facilities based on the SQL query language. It includes other commands for setting up headers and simple formats for obtaining reasonable output from a query.

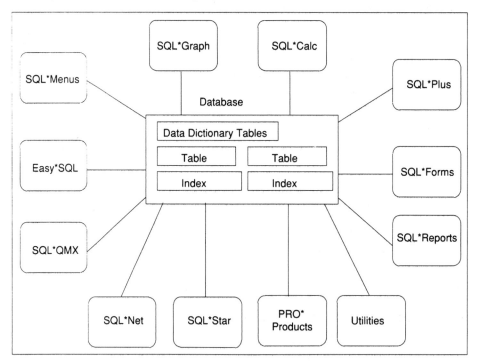

Figure 10-1 ORACLE Components

SQL*Menu:

This utility allows you to define application menus items for an integrated end-user interface. You can specify access security privileges for the programs so that any items not accessible to the user do not appear on the menu.

Easy*SQL:

This utility is a forms interface to the database. It allows you to create, change, store, and retrieve data in the database. You can format data as reports or graphs such as bar charts and line graphs. It is very useful for novice users, but experienced developers may prefer the SQL language or the forms utility.

SQL*Forms:

This forms driver subsystem consists of a forms definition utility (IAD), form generation programs (IAC and IAG), and a forms runtime driver (IAP, RUNFORM). You can create default forms or custom layouts, and define the correspondence of form fields to database fields and data validation criteria.

SQL*Report:

This utility includes two components: a report generator (RPT) and a runtime report formatter (RPF). Its formatting commands allow you to define reports which could not be formatted with the SQL*Plus facilities.

PRO*products:

These products consist of preprocessors for programming languages such as C, PASCAL, FORTRAN, COBOL, PL/I, and ADA. They are based on embedding SQL statements into your programs. These statements are then converted to function calls which pass the embedded statement to the kernel for processing.

SQL*QMX:

This utility provides easy query and simple reporting facilities for ad hoc access to the database. You can retrieve data using either the Query-by-Example (QBE) interface or via an interactive SQL session. Retrieved data can be scrolled on the screen in default format. Alternatively, you can use the report formatting facilities for custom formats including calculation of subtotals and totals, definition of report headers, footers, and column titles.

SQL*Report Writer:

This recent addition to the ORACLE toolbox is a forms based report definition program. It is completely non-procedural, but can accommodate most types business reports.

ORACLE Utilities:

ORACLE also includes many utilities to save work during development. The performance monitoring utility, ODS, provides a continuous display of system resource usage by ORACLE. You can monitor resource consumption, such as disk I/O requests, for the entire system as well as for individual users. The SQL*Loader utility facilitates loading and unloading of data into files in different formats. You can, of course, obtain information on the data dictionary itself using SQL statements.

10.2.2 Development Components

Database Storage:

ORACLE allows you to use either the UNIX filesystem or raw disks for data storage. It implements the ***many relations per file*** approach discussed in Chapter 6. It allows you to choose the distribution of database tables between different files. Note that files and tables are not directly related, so it is possible to have a really large table spread over several files. We discuss the details of this set-up in Section 10.3.2. You can use multiple physical disks for one database, and hence there are no restrictions on the size of the database.

Menu Driver:

You can define application specific menus using the SQL*Menu utility. You can also define access privileges at the menu level in this utility to prevent specified users from running particular programs.

Forms Driver:

One of the forms based interaction facility is the Easy*SQL utility. You might also consider the Query-By-Example interface of SQL*QMX as a forms based query interface which does not allow updating or deleting data from the database.

The SQL*Forms utility provides a forms based interface to developing an application. It assumes that your application is based on forms. So then you can lay out your forms, associate forms fields to database fields, define input validation, and processing commands. These processing commands are procedural and use SQL syntax as the basis.

Report Generator:

For ad hoc reports, you can always use SQL facilities to quickly format data retrieved from the database. Interactive report formatting facilities are also included in the Easy*SQL and the SQL*QMX utilities. Reports in the form of graphs can be produced from Easy*SQL provided you have graphics display hardware such as workstations and plotters. For more complex or routine reports, you can use the SQL*Report utility: RPT to define reports and RPF to run them. Alternatively, you can use newer SQL*Report Writer tool which involves less tedious development than the older SQL*Report language.

Host Language Interface:

This interface is necessary if you wish to add custom functions to the forms driver, or the report writer utilities. You can, of course, develop an entire batch application using this interface. The PRO*products support programming languages such as C, COBOL, FORTRAN, PASCAL, PL/I, and ADA.

Fourth Generation Language:

ORACLE does not provide a fourth generation development facility. However, its SQL*Forms subsystem provides much of the functionality seen in other fourth generation products. Its one major restriction is the lack of a comprehensive procedural component to match its nonprocedural component. It also does not provide an interface to the other components of the RDBMS.

Query Language:

The ORACLE implementation of the SQL query language is compatible with DB2. There are some extensions to the language to allow you to examine the data dictionary information and obtain help on your application database structure.

10.3 Data Control

This section examines the data storage and access strategies implemented by ORACLE. Where possible, we relate these features to the common ground established in Parts 1 and 2 of this book.

10.3.1 Data Types

The data types implemented by ORACLE are fairly simple as shown in Table 10-1. A notable point is that an ORACLE data type has one or more synonyms to provide compatibility with the names used by DB2 and SQL/DS. When creating tables, you can specify field data types using either ORACLE's data type or the appropriate synonym.

ORACLE stores all data in a hardware independent, variable length format. Internal character data storage consists of a *length* field and a *string* field, though this representation is completely transparent to the programmer. Numeric data storage simulates, in a hardware independent manner, the way floating point numbers are stored — that is, in two parts: an *exponent* and a *mantissa*. Integers and floating point numbers are both stored in this format. The exponent is base-100 and ranges from 0 to 127. The mantissa consists of up to 38 decimal digits.

Our Data Types	ORACLE Data Types
Small Integer	NUMBER (SMALLINT for DB2 compatibility)
Large Integer	NUMBER (INTEGER for DB2 compatibility)
Floating Point Decimal	NUMBER(m,n) (DECIMAL(m,n) for DB2 compatibility
Small/Large Floating Point	NUMBER (FLOAT for DB2 compatibility)
Money	NUMBER
Three-part Date	DATE, Century, Year, Month, Day, Hour, Minutes, Seconds
Three-part Time	Included in DATE
String	CHAR variable length, max length 240 characters, LONG variable length, max length 65,536 characters
Bit Map	RAW variable length, max length 240 bytes, LONG RAW variable length, max length 65,356 bytes

Table 10-1 ORACLE Data Types

10.3.2 Storage Structures

Consistent with all of its interfaces, ORACLE database tables are created, dropped, or changed using SQL statements. Query language statements also let you create and drop indexes at any time, provided you have the appropriate access privileges. The software, as distributed, also contains several administration tools at the SHELL level, so you can avoid having to type SQL statements.

ORACLE implements the many relations per file approach described in Chapter 6. Each operating system file used in a database can be either a filesystem file or a raw disk. Thus, ORACLE allows you to mix the use of raw disks and the UNIX filesystem. It also provides mechanisms that allow you to choose where each table resides.

Table 10-2 illustrates the relationship between our terminology, described in Chapter 6, and the corresponding terms in ORACLE. An ORACLE database storage structure actually breaks down into further subdivisions. Figure 10-2 illustrates this breakdown. Note that version 6 changes some of the terminology associated with the storage structure to match DB2 terminology more closely.

Each *partition* can consist of one or more files or raw disks, in any combination. When you first create a partition, you must add at least one file to it before using it in any manner. Later, you can add more files to the partition as the need arises. Note that each file comprising a partition could reside on any disk. Thus, the size of the partition is not restricted, except by the available disk space on your machine.

Relation tables relate to a partition only via a *space.* A partition can consist of one or more spaces, but a space belongs only in one partition. A table must reside in one space. ORACLE manages the allocation of *real* resources from the files belonging to a partition into the spaces that a partition contains. Hence, a space can span several files.

A space is further broken down into *datapages,* which define the space for data in tables, and *indexpages,* which define the space for indexes on the tables. The description of datapages and indexpages each takes parameters for the size of the *initial* and *increment* extents. The initial extent size is space that ORACLE reserves when you first create a table. After this extent is full, ORACLE will obtain an increment extent to extend the table. The same principle applies to the allocation of space for indexes except that the sizes used are based on the indexpages parameters.

Our Terminology	ORACLE Equivalent Term
System Files (filesystem or raw disk)	System Files
Data Areas	Partitions
Relation Tables	Tables

Table 10-2 ORACLE Data Storage Terms

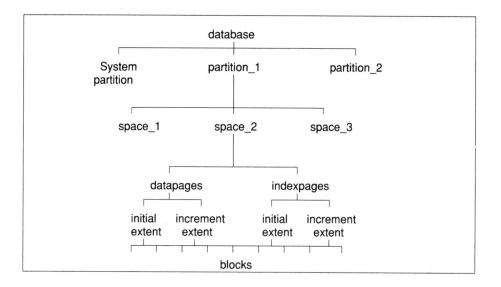

Figure 10-2 ORACLE Data Storage Breakdown

The relationship between a space and a relation table is straightforward: You specify the space for a table when creating the table. The default space definition, in the *system* partition, is used whenever you omit specification of a space for a table. Thus, you can choose where a new table should reside, but once defined you cannot easily relocate it. When you define a space, you are really providing hints to ORACLE on how to allocate the space in a partition. The sizes for the extents in datapages and indexpages are in terms of number of blocks which relate directly to ORACLE's basic unit of disk I/O. This is why you need to choose carefully the parameters for datapages and indexpages in a space definition. You can, of course, change these parameters at any time, but they do not affect tables already created with the older parameter values. The new parameters only affect tables created after the change.

It should be obvious from this discussion that before you use any partitions, you need an existing empty file. If you use raw disks for your database, you would simply use one of these as the existing file. For UNIX filesystem files, ORACLE provides the *ccf* (Create Contiguous File) utility to create empty files of a specified size. The name of this utility might be confusing, since the file it creates might not be physically contiguous at all. It might only be contiguous if the filesystem is newly created, or recently reorganized.

A common blunder is to assume that filesystem files will automatically keep extending as you add more data (provided that you escape the dreaded ulimit problem!). Not so with ORACLE: it does not extend a file once it is added to a partition, and nor should you! Attempting to run ccf on an existing database file to increase its size *zaps* all of its contents, bringing down the wrath of users on your head.

You can, of course, simply use default settings for all tables in the database. The defaults will always use the system partition, which you can grow by simply adding more files. However, to optimize performance you might wish to distribute database tables selectively over several physical disks. One way of creating a database with custom table distribution might be according to the following steps:

1. Estimate the size of each table and each of its indexes, allowing for the ORACLE overheads.

2. Using the convention that a partition corresponds to one physical disk, create the appropriate number of partitions with suitable names in the ORACLE database. For example, suppose the filesystems */db1* and */db2* represent two separate disks. You might create two partitions called *part_1* and *part_2.*

3. Determine how you wish to distribute the tables on physical disks.

4. Use the ccf utility to create at least one file to be used in each partition. If you are using raw disks, you can simply use their node names instead, provided that you change their ownership and access permissions for access by the database. Add these files to the partitions as appropriate.

   In our example, we create the file *data1* in the /db1 filesystem and *data2* in the /db2 filesystem. Then we add data1 to part_1 and data2 to part_2 partitions. For optimal space usage, you should make these initial files somewhat larger than the total size of the tables you intend to store in them.

5. For each partition, create a space definition with parameter settings appropriate to the tables to be placed there. Ideally, most of the table should fit into the initial extent.

6. Create each table and its indexes specifying the chosen space definition.

Once a table is created and associated with a space definition, you cannot relocate it at will. You can add more files to the partition to provide extra space for the tables. If you want to relocate a table from one partition to another for some reason, you will have to save the data from the table, drop it, re-create it using a different space definition, and then load the data back.

10.3.3 Access Methods

B-Tree Access:

The standard ORACLE indexes are B-tree indexes. This type of an index is very versatile as we discussed in Chapter 3. It also supports compressed B-tree indexes.

ORACLE stores indexes together with the table data in a space. Remember that the space definition, discussed in Section 10.3.2, included parameters for indexpages. ORACLE uses these parameters when you create an index. Thus, for optimal access, an index should fit mostly into the initial extent. Making the size of the initial extent sufficiently large for an index ensures that the index occupies contiguous blocks. Each increment extent might not be physically close to the initial extent on the disk.

An index can consist of several fields concatenated to form a composite key. The maximum limit on the size of an index key is 240 bytes including one-byte separators between each field. The fields comprising a composite index need not be in any particular order within the record. Each field can be ordered in either ascending or descending order; by default they will be in ascending order.

There is no limit on the number of indexes you can create on a single table. But, assess the performance tradeoffs between improved speed of data retrieval versus degradation in speed of insertion and updates. Each time you insert a row or update one, ORACLE has to update all of the corresponding indexes.

Clustered Storage:

ORACLE provides interfile clustering which we discussed in Chapter 3 – that is, storing data from more than one table close together. Typically, tables which share a column are ideal for clustering. Storing this data close to each other minimizes the amount of disk I/O ORACLE needs to perform when accessing the data from both tables together.

ORACLE implements clustering by means of a *cluster key*. This key can consist of up to 16 fields corresponding to the appropriate fields in the tables to be clustered. In our customer orders example, we might choose order number as a cluster key to join the order table and the order items table. ORACLE can cluster a maximum of 32 tables in a single cluster. The steps in creating and using a cluster are:

1. Create a cluster using the SQL *create cluster* statement. Note that you can associate a cluster with a space definition.

2. Create each table to be clustered with the *create table* statement including the cluster clause. Note that you have to specify the table's cluster key in the cluster clause.

3. Load data into the clustered tables.

Given enough spare space in the database, you can cluster an existing table. The basic principle is to create the desired cluster definition, followed by creating each table under a different name. In this case, steps 2 and 3 can be combined into a single SQL statement to load the data from the existing table into the new table during creation. Then, you can drop the old table and rename the new table to the desired table name. You need extra spare space because until you drop the old table, the database actually contains two copies of the data.

It is possible to cluster just one table with this clustering scheme — that is, intrafile clustering. It is useful only when the key columns can contain many duplicate values. Thus, clustering one table whose key is always unique is really not worthwhile.

Clustering data really involves rearranging the way data is stored. Thus, changing existing tables to a cluster involves a significant shuffling of data. Clearly, you perform this type of database restructuring while others are using the database at your own peril.

10.3.4 Access Security Control

ORACLE implements its own scheme of user ids protected by passwords. You can specify access privileges to data based on these user ids. They can also be linked to the UNIX login ids by using the OPS$ prefix when declaring the ORACLE user ids.

ORACLE user ids get created when the DBA grants the connect privilege to a new user id. You can also associate a password with this user id at the same time. To link a UNIX login id called *jsmith* to an ORACLE user id, you would use the following statement:

```
grant connect to ops$jsmith identified by <password>;
```

Note that the ORACLE password is distinct from the UNIX password. ORACLE cannot use the same password as the UNIX login procedures. You might, alternatively, omit the ORACLE password completely. This will work so long as the user automatically enters the application on login so that direct access to system files is not possible. Section 10.5.1 covers the pros and cons of this approach and some alternatives in detail.

You can also make use of the UNIX file access control mechanisms for filesystem files. File access control can also be made to work for raw disks if you move their *special nodes* into a secure directory and remove all references to them from the */dev* directory. We will discuss ways of setting up UNIX file access security measures in Section 10.5.2.

Privilege	File Level Application	Field Level Application
Alter	Can change existing table structure (not on views)	n/a
Delete	Can delete rows	n/a
Index	Can create and drop indexes (not on views)	n/a
Insert	Can add rows	n/a
Select	Can read all fields	n/a
Update [(*cols*)]	Can update all fields if none specified	Can update only fields listed as *cols*
All	All access	All access
Connect	Can access database, but cannot create or change table structures	n/a
Resource	Can access database and create table and index structures	n/a
DBA	Access any part of the database, grant and revoke privileges, perform database administration	n/a

Table 10-3 ORACLE Privilege Structure

Table 10-3 illustrates the types and levels of access you can define on database data. One notable point is that most privileges apply only at the table level, except for the update privilege. Thus, you cannot prevent users from accessing parts of a table, say only a few fields, via the access control mechanisms. You can only achieve this effect by using views which exclude the protected fields.

Keep in mind that a table created by a user is owned by that user. Other users gain access to it only if the owner grants them access. Generally, letting users create their own tables in a database shared by many users is not a good idea. Managing space usage in this case becomes hairy, never mind administration of access security. For example, a user authorized to access sensitive data could copy this data into a personal table and let unauthorized friends access this table. So, work out your access control strategies carefully if you want to prevent easy breach of security. At the very least, you ought to make breaking security very difficult to discourage casual or unintentional breaches.

A noteworthy feature of ORACLE is its security audit trail facility. A DBA can start monitoring of the types of access performed by each user on the database. You can choose to monitor specific types of accesses on selected tables. For example, you can monitor only successful attempts to insert rows in a particular table, but on another table you might monitor unsuccessful attempts to select data. Audit trail information is saved in a special database table called **audit_trail**. The collected audit trail information can be formatted into a report using normal report formatting utilities, or using SQL.

10.3.5 Concurrency Control Options

ORACLE implements its own concurrency control mechanisms using the shared memory segment, SGA, under UNIX. It provides explicit and implicit locking mechanisms for a transaction, at table and row levels. The default locking level on SQL*Forms update is row level. Internal ORACLE functions, such as the data dictionary cache, also use locking.

ORACLE provides three types of locks: **shared, exclusive**, and **share update**. Let us relate these terms to our description of levels of isolation in Chapter 3. By default, ORACLE provides committed read level of isolation. It implements a **before-image** file which contains a copy of the data at the time of query for each user. Hence, a user always obtains a consistent view of data even though others might have updated the same rows in the database. A dirty read level of isolation is not possible in the ORACLE implementation.

The cursor stability level of isolation is rather more complex. You have to use a share update lock which operates at row level. You would obtain this type of a lock using either of these statements:

```
LOCK TABLE table-name IN SHARE UPDATE MODE [NOWAIT]
or
SELECT ....... FOR UPDATE OF column-name
```

This type of a lock prevents someone else from updating the data you are reading and from explicitly locking the entire table in exclusive mode. It does not prevent others from reading the selected data. Other users can obtain share update locks on the same tables.

There are two ways of achieving the repeatable read level of isolation. One way is by using the shared lock which only operates at the table level. In this case, you are preventing other users from performing any updates to the table, although they can read it, until you release the lock. The other way is by using a share update lock which operates at row level. With this lock, other users could still obtain a share update lock on different rows, but their updates will not be applied to the database until you release the shared lock on the table.

You would only use an explicit exclusive lock on a table if you wanted to make extensive changes affecting a lot of rows. Obviously, while a table is locked no one can update any data in it, so you would not do this at peak database usage times. Note that even with an exclusive lock, other users can still read data from the locked table. Implicit exclusive locks occur automatically whenever you change anything in a table; that is, when you use an insert, update, or delete statement. ORACLE locks the entire table for the duration of the change.

If you cannot obtain the lock you want, ORACLE normally just waits until the lock becomes available. You can control this default, however, by specifying the *nowait* option. There is no way of specifying a *timeout* period; that is, wait for the specified time and then, if the lock does not become available during this period, return. You can simulate this yourself with a *busy-wait* loop in your program.

ORACLE also provides mechanisms for transaction level controls based on the use of locks and the SQL *commit* and *rollback* statements. Note that ORACLE does not supply a specific start of transaction statement. The start of a transaction is implied by the first executable SQL statement. The end of the transaction can be a commit statement, a rollback — that is, abort transaction — any data definition statement such as create or rename, or when you log off from ORACLE. ORACLE can also automatically unravel transactions in progress when errors such as deadlocks, or abnormal terminations occur.

An *after-image* journaling facility supplied by ORACLE can be used to keep a continuous record of changes to the database. With this facility, you can recover from disastrous situations such as disk head crashes which destroy all database data. Remember, from our discussion in Chapter 3, that such a facility must be used in conjunction with regular backups of the database. After a disastrous loss of your database, you will consider the effort expended in backups and journaling well worth it! Even users who complained of the overhead of using journaling will appreciate not having to manually repeat all transactions since the latest backup.

10.3.6 Data Integrity Considerations

ORACLE implements the entity integrity rule by letting you specify the not null option for a field when you are creating a table. This option will enforce that the field must always have a value; that is, it cannot have a null value.

There is no way to enforce referential integrity at the database level. Version 6 does promise to support it. In the meantime, you must specify any interdependencies between tables using the facilities provided in utilities such as SQL*Forms.

10.4 Utility Packages

ORACLE DBMS is packaged together with many utilities, some of which are optional purchases. In this section, we discuss only the basic utilities such as forms drivers and report generators. The utilities beyond the scope of this book include SQL*Calc, ORACLE's spreadsheet, and SQL*Graph, ORACLE's business graphics utility (mentioned briefly in

Section 10.4.3). ORACLE also has an interface to LOTUS 1-2-3 which allows transfer of data between this popular spreadsheet and an ORACLE database. Details of these products are beyond the scope of this book.

For the purposes of our discussions in this chapter, Easy*SQL is considered to provide basic forms facilities. SQL*Forms is described in Section 10.4.6 as a fourth generation language. This classification does not really conform with the assumptions laid out in Chapter 3 because SQL*Forms facilities are restricted to forms based access. Strictly speaking, a fourth generation language should also include integrated batch processing and report generation facilities.

Not all ORACLE utilities are available on all hardware, so your first step should be to ascertain whether your chosen utilities are available on the target hardware. This, unfortunately, is the price you have to pay for the very large porting base offered by ORACLE. The database kernel and basic utilities are, of course, available on all supported hardware.

10.4.1 Menu Subsystem

SQL*Menu is an optional product which allows you to develop application specific menus. It uses a full screen display style but some of its facilities are based on the SQL*Forms interface. Although it initially stores menu information in data dictionary tables, at runtime it uses this information from a *menu library* file. Functions to create and maintain the library file are part of the menu definition utility.

It has some nice features, such as control of access to menu selections based on the ORACLE user id. Users only see those menus and selections which are accessible to each; inaccessible selections are not displayed. Another nice feature is the ability to define a screen form to prompt users for runtime parameters. The screen form is essentially a SQL*Forms object, but is integrated into the menu driver. This facility means that you can obtain runtime parameters, such as a range of dates for a report, from the user. The consistent forms interface makes it easy to learn.

10.4.2 Screen Forms Facilities

In this section we discuss the forms based facilities of Easy*SQL and SQL*QMX. These components are not, strictly speaking, forms drivers. Although they both include simple forms definition and driver utilities, each of them is really an environment intended for end-users, providing menu based access.

Easy*SQL:

Easy*SQL provides facilities for database maintenance as well as database access utilities. It does limit the functionality available to its user, so you have to resort to using other ORACLE components for more complex functions. It would be an ideal interface tool for novice users creating and using a private database.

The basic facilities provided by Easy*SQL are:

- Creating, modifying, and deleting relation tables.
- Defining and running forms for access to the database.

Our Data Validation Criteria	SQL*Forms Data Validation Criteria
Range check	Specify Validation Window: Range Low–High
List of Valid Values	-
Required Entry	Specify Attributes Window: Mandatory
Lookup in other table	Specify Validation Window: List of Valid Values - Table, Column (must use *trigger* if you want enforcement)
Double Entry Verification	-
Field Format Enforcement	-

Table 10-4 SQL*Forms Data Validation Criteria

- Forms based data entry and update.

- Report generation: textual reports and graphs on supported hardware.

- Database administration including backups, data format translation to other popular formats such as DIF.

All of these facilities are started from a menu and use special purpose forms to perform the appropriate function. The query option allows you to choose up to three tables on which to base your query on. The selection conditions are very similar in syntax to the SQL where clause. What you are actually doing with this function is composing an SQL select statement.

The data entry and update facilities, unlike the query function, do let you define a screen form. You must use the default layout provided. Two types of default form layouts are available: *single* and *multiple*. A single form works with one row at a time and a multiple form works with several rows on the screen at once. A multiple form displays columns across the screen and allows horizontal scrolling for access to columns when all columns will not fit on one screen.

Obviously, before you can update existing records you have to find and display them on the screen. You can use standard comparison operators in the field itself to specify the selection conditions. For example, to find all employees who earn more than $10,000, you would enter **> *10000*** in the salary field.

The forms definition tool in this package is actually the same as in SQL*Forms. So, you could use its powerful forms definition capabilities. Data validation and field editing criteria provided by SQL*Forms are illustrated in Tables 10-4 and 10-5. However, these criteria are defined in Easy*SQL when you create a table.

SQL*QMX:

This utility provides facilities for:

- Querying the database and formatting the results.

- Simple data entry with only default input validation.

Our Field Editing Criteria	SQL*Forms Field Editing Criteria
Case Control	Specify Attributes Window: Uppercase
Default Value	Specify Validation Window: Default
Field Format	Specify Attributes Window: Fixed Length
Field Display Attribute	-
Justification	-
Field Padding	-

Table 10-5 SQL*Forms Field Editing Criteria

- Data update facilities using QBE or SQL interface.

- Interactive access to all SQL statements including data definition, data manipulation and administrative commands.

The Query-by-Example (QBE) interface basically allows you to *draw* a table on your screen. Each column in this table corresponds to a field (or a column) in the database relation table. Figure 10-3 illustrates a typical QBE table drawing for our customer orders example.

The first column in the drawing represents the relation table itself. You would select specific columns to be *presented* in the results of a query by typing *P.* in the appropriate column. To select all columns, you would type *P.* in the first column. Conditions for selecting rows are typed in the *condition* box using a similar syntax to the SQL where clause. Similarly, you can insert rows by typing an *I.* in the first column. Table 10-6 lists the commands which you can type in a column.

This interface allows you not only to manipulate individual rows in the table, but also to perform multiple row operations, join tables, use group calculation functions, and sort the result on columns. Each of these functions is achieved by simply typing an appropriate command in columns on the screen table. In essence, it is a powerful visual interface to most of the SQL facilities.

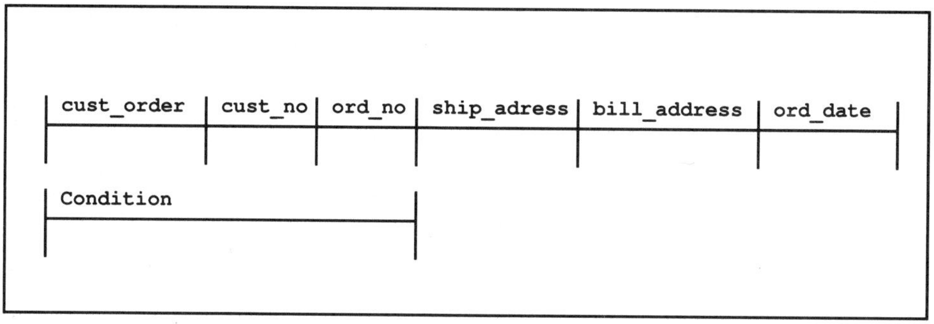

```
| cust_order | cust_no | ord_no | ship_adress | bill_address | ord_date |
|            |         |        |             |              |          |

| Condition  |
|            |
```

Figure 10-3 A QBE Drawing for Customer Orders

Command	Description
P.	Present: display values from this column in the result, if entered in first column (table name) all columns are displayed
I.	Insert Row(s) - in first column (table name) only
U.	Update Row(s) - in first column (table name) only
D.	Delete Row(s) - in first column (table name) only
G.	Group: group values in this column to produce a summary
UNQ.	Unique: only display unique values in this column
ALL.	All: displays all column values
AO.	Ascending Order: sort values in this column into ascending order before display
DO.	Descending Order: sort values in this column into descending order before display

Table 10-6 ORACLE QBE Commands

```
                              SQL QUERY

    Top line # 1                                            # of lines 5


UPDATE cust_ord SET
 -- Column name              Enter Values below       Datatype   length   Nulls
   cust_no=                                           --- NUMBER   6 0      NO
   ,ord_no=                                           --- NUMBER   6 0      NO
   ,cust_co=                                          --- CHAR      25     YES
   ,ship_address=                                     --- CHAR      50     YES
   ,bill_address=                                     --- CHAR      50     YES
   ,ord_date=                                         --- CHAR      10     YES
WHERE



    1=Help        2=Run Query      3=End         4=Delete      5=Duplicate
    6=Proc        7=Backward       8=Forward     9=Insert      10=Report
    OK DRAW performed
    COMMAND ===>                                      SCROLL ===> HALF
```

Figure 10-4 SQL*QMX: Sample Update Template in SQL Interface

The SQL interface in SQL*QMX is an interactive interface to this query language. In this interface, you can work in two ways: simply type in any SQL statement, or use the *statement type* option to the draw command to obtain a template of the statement desired. Figure 10-4 illustrates the usefulness of this feature in an update statement.

Whether you obtain your results using the QBE interface or the SQL interface of SQL*QMX, they are formatted using default formats. You can, of course, tailor the formats to your needs by changing the settings in the associated forms.

10.4.3 Report Generation

You can generate reports in a variety of ways:

- Using the SQL query language formatting facilities.
- Using the Easy*SQL report formatting facilities.
- Using the SQL*QMX report formatting facilities.
- Defining and running a report script with SQL*Report facilities.
- Defining and running a report with SQL*Report Writer.

We defer the discussion of the query language formatting facilities until Section 10.4.4. In this section, we briefly describe the facilities available in Easy*SQL and SQL*QMX for ad hoc report generation. The rest of this section covers in detail the facilities of SQL*Report which is the tool for generating reports as part of an application. The SQL*Report Writer utility is a recent addition which may replace the SQL*Report utility eventually. We discuss this tool briefly.

Easy*SQL Reporting:

The report facility works together with a query which you develop with other Easy*SQL components. For a given query, it displays the typical format of the result, surrounded by entry fields. The types of formatting you can define in these entry fields include header and footer information, columns whose values to group and sort, columns to total, and page size. Clearly, this utility handles most of the formatting requirements for a typical business report. It cannot handle unusual reports such as letters; instead use the SQL*Report utility.

You can also present query results in a graph form: as a bar graph, a line graph, or a pie chart. The graph option of Easy*SQL allows you to select the columns to graph; specify titles, labels and legends; and change the display attributes of the graph. For obvious reasons, you need graphics display devices, such as workstations and plotters, for this option.

SQL*QMX Reporting:

Report formatting in this component is more complex than in Easy*SQL since it allows many more formatting options. It handles only typical business reports.

The basic structure of this tool is similar to our description of a fixed cycle generic report generator described in Chapter 3. The difference is that for each part of the formatting process, SQL*QMX provides a form to fill out rather than you writing program-like statements. Table 10-7 shows the types of forms available and the formatting options you can specify.

SQL*QMX Form Type	Formatting Options
FORM.MAIN	Commonly used components from other forms, sufficient for many reports. Changing these also causes them to change in the appropriate other form.
FORM.COLUMNS	report width, column headings, aggregate function on column including grouping, column indent, column width, display format per column
FORM.PAGE	page header, page footer, up to 5 lines of text for header and footer, alignment of each line of text
FORM.FINAL	report summary, last page format including up to 12 lines of text, alignment for each line of text; text can include aggregate functions
FORM.BREAKn	n specifies control level (break level), up to 3 lines of text for level header, up to 5 lines of text for level footer, text alignment for each line of text, repeat column headings at start of level
FORM.OPTIONS	line spacing, handling of repeating values in grouped columns, overall spacing at control levels, page numbering

Table 10-7 SQL*QMX Report Formatting Forms

These forms constitute a powerful interactive report format definition tool. For typical business reports, it should enhance developer productivity severalfold over a script oriented report definition tool like SQL*Report.

SQL*Report:

This utility is a programmer oriented report generator which can handle the standard business reports as well as unusual formats. You define the data selection, any literals to include in the report, and formatting commands in an ordinary text file created with a system editor such as *vi*. This script is run by two processors: RPT and RPF.

RPT extracts data from the database and generates an intermediate file containing data interspersed with formatting commands. RPF takes this intermediate file and produces the formatted report. Since these are two independent programs, you could write your own program to generate the intermediate file for processing by RPF.

The assumption made by this utility is that a report consists of four parts: a data extraction part, an optional header (beginning), a report body (middle), and an optional footer (end). This concept is recursive; that is, each part might in turn contain a ***subreport*** consisting of four parts. Thus, your report definition might be structured like a tree with the complete report at its root and subreports as branches. The only exception is that the data extraction part can only be a leaf, although you can have any number of data extraction routines in the main report body as well as in each ***subreport***.

Generic Report Writer	SQL*Report Facilities
Page Size Control	Command line device switch: Diablo printer or VT100 screen, #PAGE *top-line bottom-line*, #HS horizontal spacing in 1/60 inch, #VS vertical spacing in 1/60 inch
Page Layout	#APN (page no. position on even pages), #SPN (specify page no. formats), #F (leave blank pages), #FR (flush left and right), #RR (ragged right), #R (right justified, ragged left), #NP (next page), #TTL (centered title), #TTLU (centered, underlined title)
Line Format Control	#DT (define table of columns), #B (one blank line), #S (skip n lines), #SP (line spacing) #L (literal — no format), #UL (underline)
Field Format Control	Within column: #CEN (center), #CL (literal — no format), #CS(skip n lines), #CUL (center and underline), #I (indent), #N (new line in column), #NC (next column), #P (new paragraph), #T (invoke table), #TE (end table), .DECLARE <variable> <format>
Data Control	.DEFINE <SELECT macro>, .EXECUTE <SELECT macro>, using SQL SELECT statement, .ROLLBACK, .COMMIT
Control Blocks	.REPORT <SELECT macro> <body macro> <head macro> <foot macro>, .<procedural macro>, .EXECUTE <SELECT macro>
Conditional Branch	.IF-THEN <label1> -ELSE <label2>, IFNULL <variable name> <label3>
Loop Control	.GOTO <label name>, .&<label name>
Internal Variables	.DECLARE <variable> <format>, .SET, .EQUAL
Date & Time Functions	TO_CHAR in SELECT, $$DATE$$, $$TIME$$
Group Calculations	Use SQL aggregate functions: Count, Min, Max, Avg, Sum in a SELECT macro, Arithmetic in report definition: ADD, SUB, MUL, DIV, DSUB
Run time Interaction	.ASK, .TELL, #PAUSE, command line W switch
Output Control	Specify output file, spool to line printer, or direct device on command line

Table 10-8 SQL*Report Facilities

Each part must be defined as a *macro,* which is similar to a subroutine in a programming language. There is a special macro type called a *select macro* in which you define an SQL select statement to obtain data. All other macros are *procedural macros.* A select macro constitutes a data extraction part, but can be deliberately executed in any procedural macro. The concept of macros makes this report definition language much more like a programming language. You can define each logical unit of processing as a macro and then execute it at the appropriate point.

The facilities to execute a procedural macro at any point, statement labels, conditional and unconditional branches to labels make this definition language almost too flexible. It does not prevent you from writing *spaghetti* code just like in a normal programming language. So, with an unstructured definition script, you would suffer familiar maintenance problems. The problem is aggravated by the abbreviated formatting commands and the lack of the debugging tools which developers take for granted with normal programming languages. You would need to enforce the same development methodology for using this tool as you would with a normal programming language.

Table 10-8 compares the facilities of this language with our generic report generator terms. A notable feature is the variety of powerful formatting facilities for column based reports. With these facilities you could handle almost any type of report, from a columnar document, a form letter, to a typical business report.

This utility also allows database *updates,* even though it is supposed to be a report generator. Thus, it is used as a procedural programming language in many instances. Unfortunately, its interpretive nature makes such programs very slow, especially for calculation intensive processing. Some of its idiosyncrasies — for example, if a header macro exists, it must process the first record since the first record is not available to the body macro — lead to more coding than initially apparent.

SQL*Report Writer:

This recent addition to the product line is a forms based interface to developing reports. It incorporates the concept of control break processing, which is absent in the older SQL*Report product. During definition, the report data is stored in the database. It can then be *generated* into a binary output file which is used at runtime. The development interface encourages you to test incomplete definitions frequently, lending itself to a evolutionary prototyping environment.

This product is flexible enough to handle most of your reporting needs. You can use it for columnar reports, block style reports, matrix reports, and form letters. Matrix reports, a style unique to this product, is simply a spreadsheet style report; each data cell associates with a row item as well as a column item.

The development interface is based on *objects* which comprise a report; for example, query, group, field, summary, text, and so on. The query object definition consists of defining one or more SQL select statements. The group object definition allows you to define control blocks. You use the field objects to define formats and positioning of data fields on the report. Headers, footers, and body are concepts essential to defining a report with this product. In addition, it incorporates the concept of a *panel*, which lets you define reports wider than a page. Panels are pages pasted side by side.

This product is intended for use by programmers. Experience with its concepts and its completely nonprocedural interface is necessary before tackling any complex reports. Its object oriented nature means that a little preparation on paper — to determine how a given report fits into its objects — might save a significant amount of effort. Without such preparation, you might find it difficult to determine which of its components to use to achieve a certain end result. In addition, there is no utility to obtain a printed copy of a report definition. You need to devise your own report based on its database tables, perhaps using SQL*Report Writer itself.

10.4.4 Query Language

The SQL*Plus query language component is the heart of the ORACLE DBMS. As mentioned earlier, ORACLE's aim has been to maintain an almost 100% compatibility with the DB2 implementation of this query language, and is likely to also stay compatible with ANSI standards. This aim has not stopped ORACLE from adding their own extensions however. One of these extensions, the *array access* capability, only becomes obvious in the host language interface and so is discussed in Section 10.4.5. This section concentrates on the *outer join* and *tree retrieval* extensions.

We discussed the concept of outer joins in Chapter 3 with a specific example in Chapter 8. ORACLE also implements this facility with a minor syntactical difference, at least until some standard syntax is defined. Refer back to our parts and suppliers database example in Section 8.4.4. One query which requires an outer join is to list part numbers for all two-inch nails and any supplier who supplies it. Keep in mind that we want the part number for two-inch nails in the result, even if no supplier currently supplies it. ORACLE uses a plus sign enclosed in parenthesis, *(+)*, to indicate outer join after the join condition in the where clause.

```
SELECT  part_no, supp_no
FROM    part, part_supp
WHERE   p_no = part_no (+) and
        p_desc = '2-inch nails'
```

ORACLE's tree structure refers to data in a table that is related to itself in some manner — for example, a parts table which contains information on the smallest individual unit, parts — and assemblies which are made up of these parts, which in turn may be part of bigger assemblies. Basically, a tree structure refers to any data that could be arranged in a hierarchical nature, whether the data is stored in one table or more.

ORACLE provides two related clauses, *connect by* and *start with*, which allow you to obtain data from tree structures in a hierarchical grouping. The connect by clause specifies the field values to connect to generate the tree. The start with clause provides the value for the *root* record of the tree. The result of a query using these clauses is still printed as a table, not as a tree or an organizational chart. To illustrate the use of these clauses, let's query the parts table shown in Figure 10-5 as a tree structure.

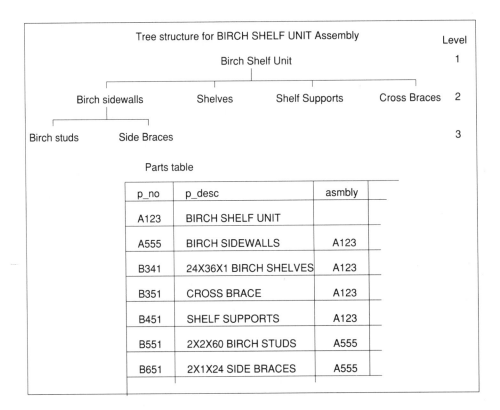

Figure 10-5 ORACLE's Tree Structured Data

The query statement, including ORACLE's *level* pseudocolumn, would be

```
SELECT level, p_no, p_desc, asmbly
FROM    parts
CONNECT BY PRIOR p_no = asmbly
START WITH p_desc = 'BIRCH SHELF UNIT'
```

```
Result:   level   p_no    p_desc                  asmbly
          1       A123    BIRCH SHELF UNIT
          2       A231    BIRCH SIDE WALL         A123
          3       B551    2X2X60 BIRCH STUDS      A231
          3       B651    2X1X24 SIDE BRACES      A231
          2       B341    1X24X36 BIRCH SHELVES   A123
          2       B441    CROSS BRACE             A123
          2       B351    SHELF SUPPORTS          A123
```

This query language also plays a major role in ORACLE's ad hoc reporting capabilities since it implements many formatting commands. These formatting commands allow you to specify report headers, footers, field labels, page layout, and field formatting commands prior to running a select statement. In fact, using its break commands to define groups of data, you can even include subtotals and totals in your report. Thus, its report formatting capabilities are quite sufficient to produce impressive looking ad hoc reports very quickly.

The PL/SQL component of version 6 promises procedural extensions to this query language. Procedural extensions would allow conditional branching similar to if-then-else, and loop constructs. Storing such transaction definitions could save the amount of coding needed in other utilities such as SQL*Forms.

10.4.5 Host Language Interfaces

ORACLE implements two forms of host language interface: embedded SQL (PRO*SQL) and PRO*ORACLE. It supports a large variety of languages including C, FORTRAN, COBOL, PL/I, PASCAL, and ADA, though it may not support all of these languages on your hardware.

The PRO*SQL interface depends on using a preprocessor which converts embedded SQL statements into internal calls to the ORACLE run time system. A single embedded statement frequently converts into several internal calls. Note that the preprocessor does not actually parse the statements. The statements are instead passed as a parameter to the runtime system for later processing.

The embedded PRO*SQL interface follows the normal conventions of using the EXEC SQL prefix to identify embedded statements. There are no restrictions on the types of SQL statements supported: All statements are supported for embedding into the host language program. You can compose an SQL in your program with runtime information, including table and field names, and execute it. ORACLE also supports the cursor convention to allow you to access the records resulting from a query.

There are, however, several extensions which are ORACLE specific. Some of these provide greater control over the runtime behavior of embedded statements. For example, you can control whether a statement should be parsed each time it is encountered, or whether a cursor structure, allocated at runtime should be reused. Some of these optional features use the EXEC ORACLE prefix to identify the statement when it is embedded into your program.

A particularly notable facility, which has a significant impact in improving performance, is ORACLE's *array access* feature. This feature enables you to work with several records in an array structure. When dealing with a select statement which results in multiple records, this feature can save a tremendous amount of repetitive processing. When adding or updating records, you can reduce the number of times you invoke the runtime system.

Such extensions make using ORACLE's embedded SQL host language interface very convenient. Using the power of SQL statements within your programs dramatically reduces the amount of code you have to write. Although reducing the amount of code improves productivity, you may well find the tribulations of debugging preprocessed code even out the score. After all, your system debugger, such as sdb, cannot work at the embedded SQL level: You must depend on using the code generated by ORACLE's preprocessor.

As an alternative to embedded query language, ORACLE offers the PRO*ORACLE (OCI) interface. The two alternatives are not mutually exclusive; that is, you can mix their use in one program under certain conditions. For example, your program must explicitly coordinate the initialization of the data areas used by each of these interfaces, especially when logging in to the ORACLE runtime system.

This call interface still uses SQL statements to interface to the ORACLE runtime system. Thus, instead of embedding the query language statements into your program, you pass them as parameters to an OCI routine. The only advantage of using this interface is that you do not have to debug your program using code generated by the preprocessor. You really do not get any control over retrieval access paths, or memory usage by ORACLE routines.

10.4.6 Fourth Generation Language

ORACLE's SQL*Forms subsystem does not conform entirely with our expectation of a fourth generation development system, although it does provide some powerful features. Its basic functions are actually comparable to a forms driver. What differentiates it from other forms drivers is the procedural code that you can define in SQL*Forms. You cannot define procedural code in many forms drivers.

One of the reasons for not calling it a fourth generation language is the limitation of its procedural commands. These commands follow SQL syntax, which makes certain trivial functions unnecessarily awkward. It also does not implement some of the common concepts, such as master-detail relationships, by default. You have to write similar code for every screen which involves such a relationship. A fourth generation language should also incorporate batch and reporting functions as well as forms based interactive functions. SQL*Forms performs only forms based interactive functions.

SQL*Forms consists of four components: the Interactive Application Designer (IAD), the Interactive Application Converter (IAC), the Interactive Application Generator (IAG), and the Interactive Application Processor (IAP). SQL*Forms, alias IAD, stores your forms definitions in special tables in the database. Before running the application, you must **convert** the form with IAC; that is, convert it from the database into an INP file. This INP file must be **generated** into an FRM file using IAG. The main window in SQL*Forms provides the generate option to perform these two operations. The RUNFORM, alias IAP, program is the actual forms driver which takes its input from an FRM file. In the main window, the **run** option represents this driver. To avoid confusion, you should probably stick to using the main window options, although the sequence of operations is very important and not always intuitive.

An application in SQL*Forms is made up of **forms**, each of which can be one or more **pages** that is, screens. A form consists of one or more **blocks** each relating to one database table. A block can span multiple pages. You can also have **control blocks** which are not associated with any database table. These blocks might be used for displaying custom menus, help screen, and so on.

A block is, in turn, made up of *fields* each of which may relate to a database field or a display-only field, or be a hidden field. A display-only field is commonly used for displaying data when some change occurs in some other field. For example, when a user enters a customer number, you might use a display-only field to display the corresponding customer name. A hidden field is not displayed on the screen at run time, but might be necessary to perform some calculation. For example, you might use a hidden field to hold the sales tax rate.

The forms definition utility, IAD, provides an interactive interface to define the different items in an application. It uses *windows* to allow you to choose operations appropriate to the stage of form creation you are in. It provides extensive facilities to paint the layout of your form, define validation criteria, and input editing criteria and processing control points. Access to these facilities is not always intuitive as some are accessed from windows and others from the screen painter. You will need to spend some time learning your way around this utility.

This forms definition utility is also used by the Easy*SQL component of ORACLE. We described its validation and editing criteria in Tables 10-4 and 10-5 in Section 10.4.2 earlier. Another feature you can define is restricting the type of operations a user can perform on fields and database tables. You can, for example, restrict users only to update database records so that they cannot add new records. Unfortunately, you cannot tie this facility into an access security feature which is different for each user.

The procedural language in SQL*Forms consists of three types of commands: SQL commands, macros, and *user exits.* SQL command syntax is slightly modified to include an *into* clause similar to the embedded host language interface, except that variables named in this clause are screen field names. Macros simulate actions which could be performed by a user. They allow you to reduce operator keystrokes if you can find a suitable procedural control point and automatically perform the action. User exits are your own third generation language subroutines linked into the forms driver. Figure 10-6 illustrates the processing control points where you can specify procedural code. SQL*Forms calls this procedural code *triggers*.

There are two types of triggers: program and event. Program triggers include key triggers and any user-named triggers invoked by a key trigger. An event trigger includes all other types of triggers. The reason for this break down is that event triggers can only perform certain limited functions which do not interfere with the basic SQL*Forms function in progress. Program triggers are completely flexible; that is, you can define any type of procedural commands in it. Event triggers can define any SQL commands and user exits, but can only include certain limited macros such as *call, callqry* to display another form, and the null command. This restriction means, for example, that you cannot change the user from an insert mode to an update mode as they type values in a field.

A notable feature is that the SQL commands are not restricted strictly to database access. You can use a dummy table and field in these commands to achieve some astonishing tasks. For example, you might use a dummy in a select statement just to specify a where clause for validating a field. As another example, you can specify a calculation on form fields and

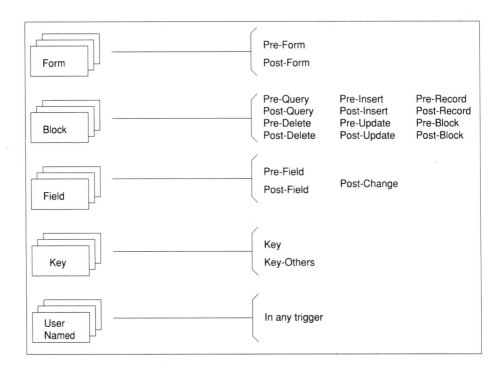

Figure 10-6 SQL*Forms Processing Control Points

display the result in another form field by using a select statement on a dummy table. Such statements can be a little disconcerting since the use of the dummy table is not really intuitive. However, it allows you to specify tasks which would otherwise require writing a user exit subroutine.

10.5 Integration with UNIX

The ORACLE database management system has minimal dependency on the peculiar ways of UNIX. It depends largely on its own scheme of obtaining run time parameters from *profile* files, though it does use a few SHELL environment variables. This minimized dependence is probably why ORACLE is so portable to many different operating systems.

Its basic data storage scheme is free from worries of filesystem or raw disk. It uses a file of either type and implements its own storage management and buffering schemes. One ORACLE feature that is unusual in the UNIX environment is its start-up procedure. The ORACLE database manager processes must be running before anyone can access a database. Thus, each time the UNIX system is booted, you must start these ORACLE processes before the database becomes available to users. Section 10.5.3 discusses the process architecture and their operation in detail.

10.5.1 Login Access Usage

ORACLE implements its own user id and password scheme which can be linked to the UNIX login id. Note that you always have to identify yourself to ORACLE before you can access a database. Even programs must execute the connect SQL statement with an appropriate user id and password before they can perform any database manipulation. ORACLE security control mechanisms depend on the use of this user id information. Although you can link a UNIX login id to an ORACLE user id, you cannot similarly link passwords. Thus, the ORACLE password, if used, must be specified separately.

The requirement for logging in to ORACLE means that all programs must use a hard-coded id and password, or use the UNIX login id linkage facility with no password. You could, of course, set up a mechanism to request users to enter a login id and password before entering their application. This scheme would result in users having to log in twice, which they might find tedious.

You can set up access security on ORACLE data files using standard UNIX user and group ids. We will discuss techniques for these measures in Section 10.5.2. The impact of these measures is that you cannot discard or bypass standard login procedures, without which a user will not be assigned an appropriate login and group id.

One workaround for this dilemma is to use the UNIX login id linkage facility of ORACLE and come up with some scheme for composing an associated ORACLE password. This makes for complications in adding new user ids to the ORACLE application. For security, you do not want the password composition scheme to be commonly known. You have to develop an *add user* administrative function which includes the same password composition scheme to transparently add users to both UNIX and the ORACLE application database.

10.5.2 File Access and Administration

As mentioned in the previous section, you can use the UNIX file access security measures to secure ORACLE data files. These measures mainly prevent unauthorized copying of database files. We examine techniques for securing the two types of files ORACLE uses: filesystem files and raw disks.

Files used in an ORACLE database are accessed only by the data manager processes. The front-end interface processes do not access database files directly — only by passing requests to these manager processes. Therefore, all data files must be owned by the same login id from which the ORACLE software was installed. You must also set read and write permissions only to this master login id with no permissions to others. A similar permissions structure for the directory ensures that users cannot inadvertently gain access to these files.

To set directory level permissions when using raw disks, you must ensure that the only access to the raw disk is via the protected database directory. In other words, do not use the node entry in the /dev directory. Create your own special node for the raw disk in the databases directory using the *mknod* command. Make sure it is owned by the master login id, with permissions just like all other files. Then, remove all references to it from the /dev directory for both the character (/dev/rdsk/..) and block (/dev/dsk/..) device. Even if no damage is intended, some harried systems administrator might accidentally create and mount a filesystem on your raw disk, resulting in disastrous loss of data and system downtime.

You must also set the *oracle* executable to be owned by the master login id and set its *setuid* bit to on. You can do this with the standard *chmod* command. This means that oracle will always run under the master login id regardless of the id running it. Similarly, the database administration utilities, such as *ior* and *ccf,* should have permissions set to prevent unauthorized users from running them. Typically, you would use one DBA login id to perform all administration functions such as increasing the size of the database, creating files to include in the database, and so on.

If non-ORACLE users share your system, you might create a special group id indicating users of the ORACLE based application. All authorized users must belong to this group. Your permissions set-up then must reflect your use of the group id. For example, ORACLE utilities must belong to the same group id to be accessible by these users. You can have only one such group id, since a file cannot have more than one group id associated with it. You, therefore, cannot set up one group id per application with only one copy of ORACLE executables.

10.5.3 Process Architecture

ORACLE uses a process architecture that is unusual in the UNIX environment, even though it does use the advantages of separate processes. Figure 10-7 illustrates the processes used by ORACLE version 5. Note that the *data manager* processes shown must be running before a user can access the database. One set of these processes exist for each application database. Typically you might start these processes at UNIX boot time by including the start-up procedure in the boot time SHELL scripts. Alternatively, you can start them manually at will by running the ior utility. Version 6, the release optimized for transaction processing changes the process architecture to obtain performance improvements.

ORACLE uses shared memory to implement the *system global area*. As shown in Figure 10-7, all user processes access this area indirectly through the back-end server process. In addition, communication between the front-end and the back-end processes can be via another shared memory segment, though you can choose to use either message queues or pipes. This choice is made once for the database in ORACLE's initialization parameters file, *init.ora*. Parameters in this file can be changed at any time but take effect only when the ORACLE data manager processes are started. Keep in mind our discussion in Chapter 5 about the system call overheads of messages queues and pipes. Shared memory does not have these overheads though it does reduce the amount of memory available to other processes.

Multiple databases, one per application, can be set up on one machine. However, you cannot easily use more than one database from one program. When multiple ORACLE databases exist on one machine, users choose the one they wish to use by setting the SHELL environment variable, oracle_sid. One system id, sid, is associated with each application database.

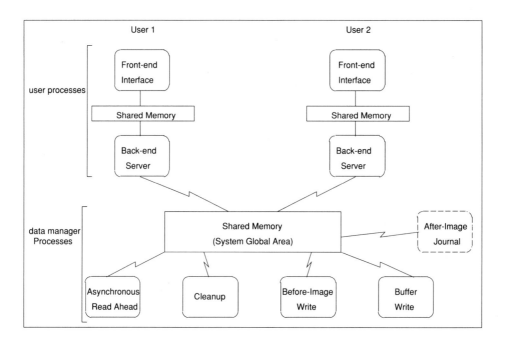

Figure 10-7 ORACLE Process Architecture

UNIX reconfiguration is necessary to set-up the required space for shared memory. If you choose to use raw disks, you will probably have to rearrange the filesystems on your system. ORACLE uses the *system global area* to buffer data and to share it between users. You can tune the allocation of memory in this area to each of the ORACLE buffering and locking functions by changing the *init.ora* parameters file. You can determine the effectiveness of the memory allocation using the ORACLE performance monitoring utility, *ods*.

10.5.4 SHELL Access

ORACLE makes some use of SHELL environment variables which can be set in a user's profile. In addition, we saw in Section 10.5.1 that it would be quite difficult to set up ORACLE to bypass UNIX login procedures. You could, however, set up a user's .profile to drop them directly into an application, as well as preventing them from access SHELL. This way you could still use the UNIX access security measures for data files.

It would be a good idea to prevent users from accessing the SQL interface directly, if you intend to prevent them from accessing SHELL commands. This interface creates a subshell to execute SHELL commands interactively. Though it also uses a specified system editor, such as vi, we discussed in Chapter 7 how SHELL access can be prevented from this editor.

Some of the other utilities, such as Easy*SQL also permit users to execute SHELL commands within the environment. However, since these utilities are best used for managing private databases rather than an application shared by several users, preventing SHELL access is not a serious consideration.

10.6 Conclusions

ORACLE did not originate on UNIX, although it clearly uses its facilities quite intelligently. It may be a little disconcerting to change various settings in one or more of ORACLE's profile files rather than the common way of setting SHELL environment variables. Its interactive facilities use function keys, or terminal numeric keypad keys, rather than the single character commands, such as vi commands, common in a UNIX environment. However, a user, with some training in the use of such keys, should not be affected. After all, a well-designed application should hide the underlying operating system from the user.

You will need careful assessment of your needs when you choose which ORACLE components you need. Packages such as Easy*SQL and SQL*QMX are really aimed at end-users and may not be useful in a specialized application. They allow users a lot of flexibility in managing and accessing their own databases and producing their own reports. They are very good for ad hoc databases. Keep in mind the training necessary for nontechnical users to understand the DBMS concepts involved and to use these tools.

You may find some of the ancillary tools which were not discussed in this chapter also useful in your development team. An example is the ORACLE's CASE product which allows you to draw entity-relationship diagrams for data analysis and design. There are also third party products based on ORACLE for project management and development methodology. They may not all be available on your UNIX machine.

ORACLE's implementation of the SQL language is quite impressive. Don't lose sight, however, of the fact that many of its facilities are extensions to the standards. Although SQL gives you the flexibility in moving to a different DBMS in the future, using ORACLE specific extensions will increase the effort. Even to actually use ORACLE's advertised compatibility with DB2 requires that you restrain yourself from using such extensions. Perhaps the easiest way to use ORACLE is as the common product on all your machines rather than trying to connect disparate databases. The range of environments supported by the product certainly makes this feasible.

11

The ACCELL Application Development System

11.1 Introduction

Unify Corporation, formerly North American Technology, Inc, is headquartered in Sacramento, California. It was incorporated in 1980 and released its first product, UNIFY database management system, in 1982. This product was the first to offer two features highly desirable for large application databases under UNIX:

- The de facto standard SQL language.
- Database that could span more than one physical disk.

Their most recent product, the ACCELL application development system, incorporates a fourth generation development facility with windowing capabilities and uses the UNIFY DBMS as its core function. These products run primarily on UNIX and MS-DOS and are available worldwide, directly through their sales offices as well as value-added resellers and computer manufacturers. In this chapter, we discuss the following versions of their products:

ACCELL	Version 1.3
UNIFY	Version 4.0

11.2 Packages and Components

The packaging scheme for the Unify products is straightforward. UNIFY is a subset of ACCELL facilities, including a function-call based host language interface. Both products use the same database structures as the basis and are therefore compatible. In Section 11.2.1, we examine the components of each product and in Section 11.2.2, the facilities provided for development tasks.

11.2.1 Unify Software Products

The products provide comprehensive coverage of development utilities for a database environment. Your basic decision about which package to buy depends on whether you need the fourth generation facilities provided by ACCELL. ACCELL includes all of the components provided in UNIFY.

ACCELL:

This package provides a fourth generation language and an environment for application development, in addition to the UNIFY DBMS facilities. We therefore restrict our overview to the additional features in ACCELL in this section. Figure 11-1 illustrates the relationships between these components and we detail their operation in Section 11.4.6.

ACCELL follows a frame based approach. This approach, described in Chapter 3, breaks an application down into separate modules which are then easy to develop. The ACCELL development environment enforces the modular breakdown.

- *ACCELL/Environment:* You use this environment to access all utilities needed to develop applications. It enforces the frame based approach underlying the development philosophy. The environment tracks accesses to particular frames so that only one person can change a given frame at a time.

- *ACCELL/Manager:* This runtime environment manages interaction with a user running an application. It is responsible for displaying screen forms, running precompiled instructions written in the 4GL, and managing database access.

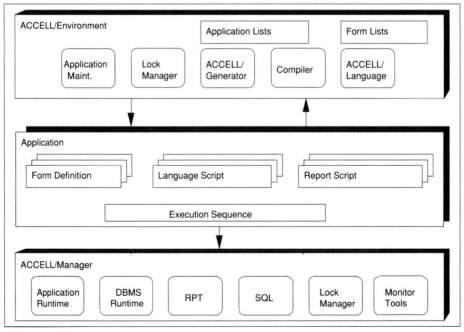

Figure 11-1 ACCELL Components

- *ACCELL/Generator:* This interactively development utility lets you define the characteristics of a form and its contents. Form characteristics define which operations are allowed, the target database table, links to next form, form size and window definition, and form fields. These definitions are the nonprocedural portion of this 4GL.

- *ACCELL/Language:* This language component provides the procedural facilities of this package. It is organized into separate *sections* which the runtime Manager executes depending on user actions. Thus, the instructions they contain are procedural, but execution of the sections themselves is nonprocedural.

UNIFY:

This product is the basic DBMS package. It stores its data dictionary in the same format as its database, allowing you to access it with standard functions. Figure 11-2 illustrates the structure of its components.

- *Menu Environment:* This menu driver is central to the UNIFY facilities. It provides access to all of the development utilities and your application programs. Since you use the same menu driver for both application programs and UNIFY utilities, the application and its administration interface are consistent.

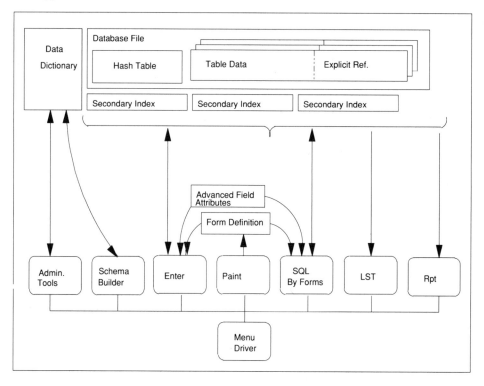

Figure 11-2 UNIFY Components

- *Schema Builder:* This is a forms based interactive utility which you must use to define or change your database schema. You cannot define and create your database in batch mode. An associated utility prints the database schema and index information. We discuss this utility and the index creation utility in more detail in Section 11.3.

- *Paint:* This screen-based forms definition utility allows you to define custom format forms for use with either ENTER or your host language programs. We discuss this utility in more detail in Section 11.4.2.

- *Enter:* This forms driver utility allows you to perform data entry, update, and simple query operations. It works on one row of one relation table at a time, although secondary table data can be displayed. It can be customized to handle many additional functions. We discuss its features in Section 11.4.2.

- *RPT:* This report writer can generate reports either independently or linked to a front-end such as the ENTER forms driver. Stand-alone report definition scripts consist of SQL for data extraction and its own language for formatting.

- *SQL:* The query language provides only the data manipulation statements of SQL. Extra statements allow you to list the database relation and field names to aid in formulating your query.

- *LST Listing Processor:* You can use this interactive utility to select and format data from the database. It is a proprietary, easy-to-use alternative to using the SQL and RPT utilities. It allows you to carry results of a query into the next query statement.

- *Host Language Interface:* This library consists of functions you can call from C programs. It provides extensive functions to access and manipulate forms, data items, and indexes. We discuss its features in Section 11.4.5.

- *Administrative Tools:* The UNIFY package includes many utilities for you to perform administrative duties such as defining access security, tuning the database, creating or changing indexes, checking and repairing the database, and database backup and recovery.

11.2.2 Development Components

Database Storage:

You can store the database either as a single UNIX filesystem file or using multiple raw disks. The two options are mutually exclusive. All relation tables in the database are stored as a single file under the filesystem, but are divided into segments for even distribution when you use raw disks. Thus, it uses the multiple relations per file approach for storage. Primary keys are indexed via a hashing scheme and secondary indexes use the B-tree access method. Indexes can be built on single fields or a combination of fields.

Menu Driver:

You use the same menu driver for your application that UNIFY uses to provide its development environment. You can define access restrictions for each user to access selections and menus. Thus, you can control the menu seen by each user or group of users. Items to which a user is denied access simply do not appear on the menu at runtime.

Using the ACCELL/Generator, you automatically define a menu whenever you define a **next form** link to more than one form. This type of menu, however, is built into your program and is not a separate utility. It is equivalent to hard-coding the menu options into a program. We discuss this feature and the menu driver utility in Section 11.4.1.

Forms Driver:

You create forms definitions using the screen based PAINT utility. The standard forms driver, ENTER, allows you to manipulate data from one row of one table at a time. It cannot handle forms containing multiple rows from a single table, or those requiring data access from multiple tables. You can drive the same form by writing a host language interface program.

The form creation and driver mechanism in ACCELL is more sophisticated. ACCELL forms are not compatible with PAINT forms, although you can mix these forms by host language functions linked to ACCELL programs. We discuss these utilities in Section 11.4.2.

Report Generator:

There are two report generators available, RPT and LST. They are both fixed execution cycle utilities, using program-like statements. You can run RPT stand alone or link it to other programs such as an ENTER form or via a UNIX **pipe.** We discuss both utilities in detail in Section 11.4.3.

Host Language Interface:

A library of functions which you can call from a C program is included in the packages. These functions can also be linked to COBOL programs through an optional package. We discuss the extensive features of this interface in Section 11.4.5.

Fourth Generation Language:

This feature is only available with the ACCELL package. It consists of a nonprocedural component for linking forms, form fields, and a procedural language to describe the processing of each form item. It provides a sophisticated environment for developers which facilitates team development efforts. We discuss the facilities available in Section 11.4.6.

Query Language:

UNIFY was the first product to provide SQL language under UNIX. This implementation includes only the data manipulation facilities of the language. Some extensions allow you to list the database relations and field names, which help in composing your query.

The LST listing processor, also a standard component of the packages, is a proprietary data extraction and formatting language. It is simpler to use than SQL. It also allows you to save the results of one query and use them in successive queries in the same interactive session. We discuss both utilities in Section 11.4.4.

Development Environment:

ACCELL provides a very sophisticated development environment which caters to team development. You develop the nonprocedural components interactively and link them into a complete program through this environment. The UNIFY package provides a menu system to access its administrative utilities for database development functions and standard utilities. Any development in host language interface is done primarily at the SHELL level.

11.3 Data Control

UNIFY presents a relational interface to users, although its internal storage structures use pointers to support its *explicit reference* facility. It allows you to use either the UNIX filesystem or raw disks. One notable feature is its Advanced Field Attributes facility, which allows you to define field characteristics centrally. This scheme promotes consistent validation of data regardless of the utility used to update the data. We discuss this facility in Section 11.3.6.

11.3.1 Data Types

An important feature when you choose a database management system is the types of data you can store in it. Table 11-1 associates our generic data types, described in Chapter 3, to those supported by UNIFY. These data types are machine independent and you need to know their internal machine dependent representation only when using the host language interface.

11.3.2 Storage Structures

UNIFY implements a multiple relations per file storage strategy. You can choose to use the UNIX filesystem to store the database or choose raw disk areas; you cannot mix the use of both storage types in a single application. You might use the filesystem during development and change to raw disk for the production system. Converting from a filesystem database to one using raw disks does not change the internal storage scheme for tables. It merely uses different portions of the disk.

UNIFY uses three file entries for each application database: *file.db*, *file.dbr*, and *file.dbv*. If you use the filesystem to store your database, file.db and file.dbr are two links to one file. If you use raw disk storage, these files are links to the special device *nodes* in the /dev directory. file.db is the file name for the block interface and file.dbr is the file name for the character interface (raw disk). The third file, file.dbv, contains any variable length data such as text or binary fields. The application data dictionary is always called *unify.db*.

Your application data dictionary, database files, and index files must all reside in one directory on a filesystem. Note that when you use raw disks, the database file names (file.db, file.dbr, and file.dbv) appear in the filesystem, but since they are special device nodes, the data is not stored in the filesystem. The terminology differs from our descriptions in Chapter 6, as illustrated in Table 11-2. Although this table shows that data areas are not available, they are used by the internal mechanisms; the designer may not access or control their size or division. The advantage is that you also do not have to worry about whether an entire table fits in a data area. The database creation mechanisms divide a table, even across physical disks, provided there is sufficient space for the entire database.

Our Data Types	UNIFY Data Types
Small Integer	NUMERIC (specify up to 4 digits)
Large Integer	NUMERIC (specify between 5 to 9 digits), use FLOAT for numbers with more than 9 digits
Floating Point Decimal	FLOAT (up to 19 significant digits + decimal point)
Fixed Point Decimal	FLOAT (lln where ll=total digits in number, and n=no. of digits to the right of the decimal point) or AMOUNT if two digits after decimal point is sufficient
Money	AMOUNT (up to 11 digits before decimal point, 2 digits after) decimal currencies only
Auto-increment numeric	Advanced Field Attributes - Unique, only if you use these attributes
Three-part Date	DATE (Year between 1900-1999), LDATE (Year between 1752-9999), Day, Month, Year in any order
Time	TIME, 24 hour clock, hours and minutes
String	STRING (Fixed Length, max 256 chars), TEXT (Variable Length, min 12 chars)
Bit Map	BINARY (Variable Length, min 64 bytes)

Table 11-1 UNIFY Data Types

You can only specify multiple system files when using raw disks. Otherwise, databases are stored in the filesystem as a single file and cannot span more than one filesystem. Raw disks from separate devices are allowed in one database. UNIFY does not support temporary tables. Its database structure is essentially fixed. In other words, you cannot create new tables at will; you have to reconfigure the entire database.

Our Terminology	UNIFY Terminology
System Files	Volumes (raw disks only)
Data Areas	n/a
Relation Tables	Record Types

Table 11-2 UNIFY Terminology

During the database design, you must estimate the number of records in each table, as UNIFY requires you to define these when you create the database. The total database space should actually be 50% larger than needed to allow for spare capacity. Hash tables for primary keys are stored in the database, so you must allow space for these as well. Each explicit relationship defined requires space in the database proportionate to the size of the fields involved.

When you design and set up your application database, there are additional considerations specific to a UNIFY database. With other vendors' products, you would enforce some of these considerations in your application programs. In UNIFY, they are enforced by the database itself; you must therefore include them in your database design. They are called *explicit relationships* and *combination fields* in UNIFY terminology.

Explicit relationships define the dependence of the values in a field in one table to those of a field in another table, similar to that of a *foreign key*. Defining this dependence allows you to specify referential integrity of the data. For example, consider the case that you cannot have an order item for a part which does not exist in the parts table. You would define this restriction by creating an explicit relationship from the part number field in the order items table to the part number field in the parts table. This definition designates the parts table as the parent, and parts in the order items table as children. Parent fields must be primary keys of their table. Once you have defined this relationship, the database will not allow you to add a part number in the order items table, unless it first exists in the parts table. Your database design should define all such restrictions applicable to your specific data.

A combination field is simply several fields defined to be a group. In UNIFY, you access combination fields as a single entity, especially from the host language interface. This is an important issue as it determines whether you have to access each field individually or as a group. Keep in mind that the UNIFY host language interface only has field access functions; it does not provide any functions to access an entire record. Accessing data via a combination field causes a single disk access, as opposed to a disk access for each individual field. Thus, you can reduce the number of disk accesses required to obtain all fields in a single record. The performance improvement you gain is not only through fewer physical disk accesses, but also the reduction in number of system calls executed as discussed in Chapter 5. A parent field of an explicit relationship is not allowed in a combination field.

During development you might use a smaller database, stored in a filesystem for convenience. Changing from such a database to a larger production database which uses raw disks involves several tasks which you should include in your project plan:

- Update the size estimates for each table as appropriate for the production system requirement. Include forecasts of potential growth in the size estimates.

- Estimate overheads for each primary key (for hash table estimates) and each explicit relationships (for internal pointers maintained by UNIFY).

- Identify raw disks for use as database *volumes,* and reorganize existing disk partitions and filesystems to make this space available. You need to perform a *complete* system backup if you have to rearrange any filesystems. You may also need to reload the entire system, after reorganizing the disk partitions, and in some cases, may need to reload UNIX itself.

- Use the screen based utilities to revise the sizes of database tables and to define the raw disk partitions (volumes) to be used for the database.

- Run the database creation utility. You must be a superuser when creating a database using raw disks.

If you want to keep the development database as a test system, you must copy the data dictionary file, unify.db, to the production database directory. Any changes for the production system must be made on this copy. If you make changes on the development dictionary itself, you lose the development system when the new database is created. Once you have successfully created the database, you should disable all access to the corresponding raw disk nodes in the /dev directory. You thus ensure that the only access is via UNIFY, rather than one of the UNIX utilities such as *mount* and *volcopy.*

Apart from these database reconfiguration tasks, you do not need any other changes to your application. This is because the internal database structure has not changed at all. Only the estimated size of tables and the storage space used is different. If you changed the structure of the database, changes may be necessary in certain cases. For example, changing the data type of a field means changing all programs which use the field. With forms definitions, you may simply need to recompile to incorporate the change. Host language programs require more extensive changes.

11.3.3 Access Methods

UNIFY provides four types of access methods: hashing, B-trees, explicit relationships, and buffered sequential access. Hashing only applies to a primary key — that is, a field or a group of fields which uniquely identify a record. You must use an exact key value for access to a record. This method is suitable whenever you need to access individual records in random order, and when you know the exact key value. This method provides the fastest random access regardless of the number of records in the database, as we discussed in Chapter 3. You imply hashed key access when you define a primary key for a table. Changing the primary key requires reconfiguration of the database.

Hash tables are most effective when they are approximately 50% full. A usage rate greater than 50% means more likelihood of conflicts with consequent chaining of hash table entries, as we discussed in Chapter 3. An administrative utility prints out the statistics on the hash table usage. You can use this information to decide whether to increase the size of your hash tables (by increasing the number of expected records), or if hashing is not suitable for the type of data in the field. Symptoms such as a low usage rate with very long chains indicate that the data is unsuitable.

B-tree indexes are provided on all secondary indexes in the database. They can be built on one or more fields in a table. This method is suitable whenever you access a set of records without knowing the exact value of the key in each record. It is particularly useful for accessing records in a sorted order on the key, locating records in a given range, and locating records by using wildcard characters when you only know the beginning part of the key. B-trees are kept as separate files in the database directory, and thus use space in the filesystem. You can create and drop B-tree indexes at any time.

Explicit relationships between fields in separate tables are defined when you create the application database. Changing explicit relationships requires reconfiguration of the database, but should be necessary only if the earlier database design needs correction. The DBMS maintains these relationships as pointers internally in the database, transparent to the users. The internal pointers supply a fast access method when accessing related sets of data as described in Chapter 6. You can use this access method through functions in the host language interface. Although such use may appear to make a program severely dependent on the database structures, the dependence is inherent in the data itself and is not likely to change.

In addition to the usual manner of sequential access, UNIFY also provides a buffered sequential access. The buffering scheme reduces disk I/O when you access all records in a table. You can use this scheme on any table without any prior preparation.

The standard utilities dynamically determine which access method to use for a particular search. Keep in mind that utilities such as SQL base their decisions on the phrasing used to specify the search criteria. Thus, if the order of your selection conditions forces the use of a particular access method, they may not use the optimum access path. In such cases, you can improve the performance of a search by rephrasing the selection conditions in a different order, or by building a B-tree on the fields in an appropriate order.

With ACCELL, you can use the *list_scan* utility to find out which access method is used in particular searches. The information provided by this utility allows you to experiment with different ordering of selection conditions, and to decide whether you should build a B-tree index on the fields involved in the search.

11.3.4 Access Security Control

UNIFY provides two basic types of access control: access to programs and access to data. You define the types of access shown in Table 11-3 to menus and programs for either individual users or groups of users. UNIFY provides its own login mechanism, or you can link the UNIX user and group ids and ignore the internal login mechanisms. The menu driver enforces these controls at runtime, by simply not showing the user any menus (or programs) to which the user is denied all access. Privileges allowed to an individual user supersede those defined for that user's group.

You also define the starting menu for individual users or groups when specifying their privileges. They will then only see menus and programs accessible from the starting menu or its lower level menus. Higher level menus are not accessible. You can define a menu tree for each group of users, with only the system administrator having access to all menus. For

Privilege	Menu Level Application	Defined for a Program
Inquiry (Read)	Displays the menu, program level privileges have no meaning without this.	Displays menu item and Inquire prompt in program. Data cannot be changed.
Add	n/a	Displays menu item and add prompt in program.
Modify (Update)	n/a	Displays menu item and update prompt in program. New records cannot be added.
Delete	n/a	Displays menu item and delete prompt in program. Data cannot be added or updated.

Table 11-3 UNIFY Privilege Structure

example, in an accounting system, define separate starting menus for accounts receivable and accounts payable users. The accounts receivable users will not even see the accounts payable menus.

If the user is allowed only certain types of access, say inquiry access, the program can show only the *inquire* prompt. You implement such a control by using certain host language interface functions, or interpret the parameters passed to your program to define your own meaning. You can control access to all UNIFY menus and programs, including the SHELL access program through the menu mechanisms.

You can control access to data by defining read and write passwords on either individual fields or groups of fields. Note that ENTER and the *database test driver* programs ignore these restrictions. You can enforce password protection in your programs by using certain host language interface functions. You can either hard-code access passwords in the programs (strongly discouraged!), or prompt the user at runtime for the password. Entering a password for protection applied on field groups allows access to all the fields in the group.

11.3.5 Concurrency Control Options

UNIFY implements field level concurrency control by default. You can also request locks on either the entire database or individual records. This method applies a representative lock to a lock file using the record locking facility of UNIX, if available. If an implementation of UNIX does not provide this facility, it writes the record information in a lock file. Locks prevent other users from updating or deleting the record, but not from reading it.

ACCELL implements a more sophisticated lock manager using shared memory. Any host language interface programs linked to ACCELL use this *lock manager's* facilities rather than UNIFY DBMS locking.

ACCELL provides two types of locks: exclusive (*XLOCK*) or shared (*SLOCK*). If you lock a record with an exclusive lock, no other user will be granted any type of lock on it. They also cannot read data from such a record, although they can determine whether the record exists. If you lock a record with a shared lock, other users can request a shared lock and read its data, but requests for exclusive locks are denied.

These ACCELL controls apply at transaction level only. A transaction can be interactive and form based, running with the ACCELL/Language statements, or running with code written with the host language interface. The Levels of Isolation, described in Chapter 3, it provides are: dirty read, committed read and cursor stability. Since these terms differ from ACCELL's terminology, we discuss their correspondence below.

You perform a dirty read when another user has a shared lock on the record and you do not lock it before reading. A dirty read is most suitable for including data in a report where updates performed after you use the data are irrelevant. Using this level of isolation means that other users with a lock can update records at any time.

Obtaining a shared lock prior to reading guarantees a committed read; that is, no one can update or delete the record until you release the lock. However, two users can obtain a shared lock on one record concurrently, in which case neither can update the record. An exclusive lock guarantees that no other user can either read or update the record during this committed read.

You can choose two types of isolation level of cursor stability: record level consistency and set level consistency. These types apply to records in a selected set – for example, when you search for a range of records. With record level consistency, the selected set includes all records which match the selection criteria whether or not they are locked by other users (shared or exclusive). The owner of the lock may update the record at any time you do not have it as the current record. When you attempt to make an exclusively locked record your current record, you may get an error message if the record still has an exclusive lock. With set level consistency, the selected set does not include records which match the selection criteria but have exclusive locks by other users. Thus, you can protect all selected records from updates by other users.

Exercise care in choosing the type of lock and consistency level in your ACCELL transactions. The most suitable use of record level consistency is when you find and update individual records, typically on a form which only shows one record at a time. For example, data entry and updates on customer information can use record level consistency. Use set level consistency when you select several records which logically belong together as a set, typically on a form showing multiple occurrences of these records. For example, order items for a particular order belong together as a set. Other users are not likely to want to update one order item without looking at the entire set for an order. Individual programs in your application which access the same data should use mutually compatible lock type and consistency level, otherwise you will get undesirable lock conflicts.

ACCELL *promotes* record level locks to table level when the number of record level locks on a single table exceeds a defined threshold (*lock promotion*). This threshold is one of the ACCELL tunable parameters, and its setting affects the amount of shared memory needed for maintaining lock information.

11.3.6 Data Integrity Measures

You define data integrity measures at several different levels. You define partial *entity integrity* when you choose a primary key for each table. The integrity is partial because you can actually add exactly *one* record where the primary key is a null value. The uniqueness requirement of primary keys prevents addition of further null value keys.

You also define *referential integrity* when you create the database by defining explicit relationships. The restriction placed by these relationships is enforced by the database itself, and is thus common to any utilities accessing it.

You can define several additional restrictions through the *advanced field attributes* mechanism, which are enforced by the standard utilities such as ENTER and SQL. They are also available to programs written with the host language interface. Table 11-4 shows the data validation criteria supported by this mechanism as they correspond to the criteria we established in Chapter 3. You define these criteria in a text file which is then compiled with either an interactive utility or directly from SHELL.

Our Data Validation Criteria	Advanced Field Attributes Definition
Range Check	Legal values (Numeric data types: using an expression involving constants, String data type: a regular expression)
List of Valid Values	Legal Values (All data types)
Required Entry	Any non-null Legal Value definition
Lookup in other table	checkreference
Double Entry Verification	-
Field format enforcement	Legal Values — regular expression on character fields only
Default Value (Field editing)	Default Value section (with constant or key-words unique, today and hour, and any *offset* to default value)

Table 11-4 Advanced Field Attributes Data Validation Criteria

The advanced field attributes scheme is the ideal way to enforce any constraints on your data. Defining these at the database level means that you only specify validation criteria once rather than in each individual form. The additional advantage is that all utilities, including the query language, obey the restrictions. In other products, you have no way of enforcing data validation for user access via the query language.

11.4 Utility Packages

The UNIFY and ACCELL products provide a range of utilities targeted at developers. In this section, we discuss the details of each utility identified in Chapter 3 as an essential component of a database management system.

Since it is an integral part of the fourth generation language, we cover the ACCELL product in Section 11.4.6. But the features of its development environment deserve a mention here. This environment provides access to most components you define in an application, except functions written in the host language interface. You perform a majority of the development tasks in writing host language functions from the SHELL environment. It has some desirable features, such as locking a form when you start development on it to prevent concurrent changes by other developers. It also maintains information about applications such as which forms belong to which application, and which procedures belong with which form. It interfaces to the UNIX make utility, and hence, indirectly, to the SCCS facilities.

The tunable parameters of ACCELL are also worth noting. These parameters can be either environment variables or limits set by default in the master data dictionary. Environment variables define memory usage for items such as the stack of forms and sort buffers, and display limiting parameters such as maximum number of windows and message displays.

The master data dictionary is also a UNIFY database. It is, therefore, limited by the expected number of records for each of the dictionary tables. Dictionary tables contain application information such as menus, screen forms, and user privileges. The most important limits are the expected number of explicit relationship entries, B-trees, record types, and field descriptions. If your application database requires more B-trees or field descriptions than this default, you can reconfigure the master data dictionary to increase these limits. You can then apply the master data dictionary changes to your application data dictionary using the utilities provided.

11.4.1 Menu Subsystem

UNIFY's standard developers' menus are driven by the same menu driver which you use for your application menus. The menu display is a full screen style menu. You can define menu selections to run any of the standard utilities including ENTER, custom programs written with host language interface, ACCELL applications, or any other UNIX executable program.

The menu handler can display a screen as part of its program load time initialization. Utilities such as ENTER use this facility to improve the user perceived performance by displaying the first screen quickly. You can also design your custom programs to utilize the menu driver to display the first screen at load time. The first screen for your program is associated with your program when you define the program run command in the menu definition utility. The menu driver then displays this screen automatically before passing control to your program.

The menu handler also provides a login mechanism, which you can disable if you choose to use the UNIX procedures. We discussed the access security mechanisms enforced by this menu handler in Section 11.3.4. These are probably necessary, if you want to avoid using the password mechanism for field level security.

11.4.2 Screen Forms Facilities

There are two ways to create a form: with the UNIFY PAINT utility and from within ACCELL. You can drive forms created with PAINT using ENTER, or host language programs, or by associating them with a SQL script. In this section we discuss the PAINT and ENTER utilities. The SQL association is described in Section 11.4.4, host language driver functions in Section 11.4.5, and ACCELL facilities in Section 11.4.6.

PAINT is a screen based forms editing utility. Associated utilities allow you to create default screen forms, print a form layout, compile a form definition, edit the form, and test the display of a form. Default forms are based on fields from a single table and list one field on a line.

Editing functions provided by PAINT include the ability move the cursor around the form screen, editing text and video attributes of the form trim items — for example, form title, field labels and so on — and defining field data spaces. You can move or copy these components on the screen. Editing commands are a sequence of keystrokes, which you can customize using the *unicap* definition file.

A form field has a unique name and can associate with a database field. Screen fields associated with database fields automatically assume the data type and length definitions from the database. Fields not associated with a database field — for example, display fields — must be defined with a UNIFY specific data type and display length. PAINT places no restrictions on which tables the fields belong to or the number of tables involved in the form. Thus, you can repeat database fields on a single form, or define multiple occurrences of records from a table.

Forms definition, the ENTER forms driver, the report formatter, and the menu definition utility are tightly integrated. Before you can use ENTER to drive a PAINT form, you must register the form so ENTER knows about it. During registration, you can associate one or more formatting programs (for example, RPT scripts) with that form. A registered form becomes immediately available to the menu definition utility. Removing a registered form automatically removes the associated menu selection definition.

ENTER is a simple data entry and query utility that works on one record of one table at a time. You can only add, update, or delete records from one target table, but you can display data from secondary tables which are linked to the target with explicit relationships. Results from an ENTER query can be passed to an RPT report generator script for formatting.

ENTER obeys any field validation or editing criteria defined in the Advanced Field Attributes file, described in Section 11.3.6. In addition, it uses other descriptions from this file. It displays the *FYI* message before data entry into a field, the ***error message*** if invalid data is entered, and allows the user to display the *help* information. Thus, you do not need to include separate validation criteria in each form containing a particular field. Messages and help information associated with the field are always consistent.

The runtime operation of ENTER uses four main operations:

- *Inquire:* This command allows you to search for data. You can specify exact values on any field, or use wildcard characters with partial values. You can browse through the results, one record at a time, with convenient prompt commands displayed by ENTER.

- *Add:* This command allows you add one record at a time to the table. When you finish filling out one record, it clears all fields ready for the next record. It stays in add mode until you request an exit from this mode. You must always enter the value in the primary key fields first, unless the Advanced Field Attributes define a default value.

- *Modify:* In this command, you search for the required record in the same way as the inquire command. Once the record is found, you may change any field as in the add command.

- *Delete:* Similar to the modify operation, you need to first locate the record to delete. Then, you can use the delete prompt to delete the record.

In each of these operations, you see error messages if either access to data is denied, another user has locked your current record, or an attempted operation fails due to violation of integrity rules.

When you associate formatting programs such as RPT scripts, ENTER allows a user to request a report options screen. This screen allows you to choose one of the formatting programs, since you can define several, and also decide where the output should go. You can request output either on the screen, directly to the printer, or into a file. The user can also choose to run the report formatting in foreground or background at this point. Output redirection to one or more of these can be suppressed by the designer when registering the form with ENTER.

11.4.3 Report Generation

The RPT report generator can run stand-alone or can be interfaced with ENTER, SQL scripts, or other programs which extract data from the database. Like our description of a generic report generator, it has a fixed execution cycle. One peculiarity of this utility is that since it interprets the report definition scripts directly, compilation is not necessary.

A report definition script is a text file containing commands written in the RPT language. Table 11-5 shows how its commands relate to our list of generic functions. The unusual feature of RPT is that its data extraction process is separate from the data formatting process. This feature is the reason behind its ability to receive input from any of the standard utilities as well as your own programs. This feature allows you to write a data extraction program,

Generic Report Writer Facilities	RPT Facilities
Page Size Control	Left Margin, Width, Top Margin, Bottom Margin, Length
Page Layout	Header block, Footer block, Before Report block, After Report block, Pageno, (start new) Page, Need (# of lines)
Line Format Control	Skip, Column, nn[*Char-to-repeat*] (*nn* is count of repeats), Centered, No Newline
Field Format Control	Using '*format-spec*' (numeric and amount data types), Using *%printf-format* (float data type), + & /+ (concatenation and space clipping), Substr.
Data Control	Separate data extraction SQL script, Input section (input data format), Separator (between fields in input), Sort
Control Blocks	Before [After] Report block, Before [After] *name* block, Detail block
Conditional Branch	If-Then-Else
Internal Variables	Set (no declaration, all data types)
Date and Time Functions	Comparisons and Math operations, Dow (day of week), Mdy (day of month), Today, Hour, Formats defined by environment variables
Group Calculations	Count, Total, Avg, Min, Max
Run time Interaction	Through front-end interface with SQL-by-forms and ENTER
Output Control	Redirect using UNIX SHELL facilities

Table 11-5 RPT Report Writer Facilities

if the facilities of SQL are inadequate, without the need to format the data in your program. Interfaces to ENTER and the SQL screen input program allow the user to enter runtime parameters in an easy-to-use manner.

The LST processor is a much simpler report generator. It has a minimal set of facilities for formatting a report which include report heading and field format specifications. Database field names are used as column headings, and default spacing is used between fields. You can also sort and total on given items. A significant advantage of LST is that data extraction can be done in several steps, saving intermediate results in temporary *subsets*. This utility is useful as an interactive database query facility; however, it does not have sufficient facilities for complex report formatting.

11.4.4 Query Language

UNIFY supports only the data manipulation statements of SQL — that is, the *select, insert, update,* and *delete* statements. It supports the standard form of these statements as discussed in Chapter 4. Its peculiarities include using *long field names* (defined when creating the database), and a lack of temporary table facilities. Without temporary tables, your SQL scripts consist of multiple subqueries which are complicated to understand and develop. UNIFY does not implement a solution equivalent to the *outer join* facility.

Several extensions to the standard language allow you to load and unload data from ASCII files, get help on field and table names, and edit statements with a standard text editor such as vi. The most notable extension is the interface between the report generator and a screen form for obtaining runtime report parameters. The basic steps in setting up this interface are:

- Create a form with PAINT; the form fields have data types defined but are not associated with database fields.
- Create the SQL script using parameters in search criteria instead of constant values.
- Create one or more RPT report definition scripts to format the appropriate input data.
- Register the form, SQL script, and report definition with the SQL-by-forms utility.

The user can then enter the runtime parameters on the screen form using an interface similar to ENTER. These parameters are substituted in the SQL script to execute the search. The user then selects a report program on an options screen similar to that in ENTER, and chooses whether output is to screen, printer, or a file. You can also choose to run the program in foreground or background.

The data extraction part, *selection processor*, of the LST listing processor is worth mentioning here, even though the utility is a report generator. This selection processor does allow you to save the results of a query in a file called a *subset* and use it in subsequent queries. You can thus accomplish complex queries by using several small steps. The SQL implementation does not allow you to create temporary tables and so forces you to write complex nested query statements.

11.4.5 Host Language Interfaces

UNIFY provides an extensive library for a function call based host language interface. Most of the standard utilities use these library functions, so you can match their user interface behavior closely in your programs. You also customize the standard utilities, such as ENTER, RPT, and ACCELL, by adding your own functions written with this interface. The basic classes of functions are:

- *Data access:* These functions allow you to find, read, and write the required data from the database.

- *User interaction:* These functions let you interact with the user through forms, prompts, and commands on screen, or aid you in formatting reports.

- *Utility functions:* These functions facilitate conversion between data types, give you access to Advanced Field Attributes for data validation, and provide information on database structures and transaction facilities.

An important feature of the interface is the way table and field names are incorporated into your programs. When you create the database and compile forms definitions, the process creates header files assigning integer values to table names, database field names, and form field names. The integer values are the keys used to access information about these items. Adding new tables or fields to the database or form does not change these values, but deleting some items before adding new definitions can change them. If the key values in these header files change, you must recompile all programs with the new header files.

It is dangerously easy to treat a UNIFY database as just an indexed file storage method. You can ignore many of the fast access utilities it offers, perhaps through a lack of experience in using them. Do not be surprised, in such cases, if your performance objectives are not achieved and your programs become difficult to modify. Sharp tools are best used under the direction of knowledge and experience.

Data Access:

These functions operate on the concept of a current record in each table which is similar to our description of a cursor, in Chapter 3. Thus finding an individual record results in it becoming the current record. You can locate records from a single table by:

- Giving the exact value of the primary key.

- Giving a partial value, with wildcard characters, for a secondary index. This process is quite complicated: First, you find the appropriate B-tree, search it to find the first match, and then step through each matching record. You can determine whether a B-tree exists on the required fields in the appropriate order before choosing it.

- Locating the parent (or child) record in an explicit relationship with one the above methods, then use the *set* functions to find its child (or parent) records. You can sort child records, if needed, and step through them one record at a time.

- Sequentially accessing each record in the table, with or without buffering.

Clearly, all of these functions make your program code very dependent on the database structure. To avoid this dependence, you could use the higher level search functions which operate on one or more fields. These functions determine which access methods are available in the current database structure and choose the one best suited for each search. Their results are stored in a *selection* file containing pointers to matching records. You can search individual tables on a single field, or, given a selection file of parent records, find the children in another table with these functions.

When more than one field is involved in the search criteria, use the *unisel* function. This function requires you to set up a table of selection conditions: Each entry in the table corresponds to one condition. There is an assumed logical AND relationship between conditions. If you need logical OR relationships, you can use the *De Morgan* Boolean logic rules to convert your conditions. Alternatively, you can write your own functions to perform AND and OR processing on selection files. The results of the selections can be sorted and sequentially accessed one record at a time.

This may appear to be a complicated process, but its advantages are the data independence they give your programs. They also provide a compact way of specifying your search conditions. Note that the resultant records must be all from one table, which is not a major restriction since from these records you can directly locate other required data. For most of the access, you would probably use only the primary key access and explicit relationship access functions. Both of these methods use characteristics inherent in the application data, and are therefore unlikely to change often.

Record level functions, such as insert and delete records, depend on using the primary key. But, data read and write functions operate only on individual fields in the current record, except for combination fields which operate on all components of the group as a single unit. These functions work with or without buffering. Without judicious definition of combination fields, field level functions can lead to a significant amount of physical disk I/O and associated system call overhead.

User Interaction:

The high level screen interaction functions allow you to display forms defined with PAINT, read field values entered by the user either directly into a database field or into a program variable for processing. You can use supplied functions to validate field values against definitions in the Advanced Field Attributes file or to obtain default values. You can also prompt the user with the UNIFY standard prompt for inquire, add, modify, and delete commands, with the access security maintained by the menu driver. Fields on the screen can belong to one or more tables, and more than one record can be displayed. To handle multiple records from a table, your program must handle scrolling and cursor movement operations using the terminal control utility functions provided.

The report formatting functions allow you to use predefined layout definitions containing fields and their column position information. You can also use the buffer composition functions to format one line at a time. Output can be optionally piped to the print spooler.

Utility Functions:

Utility functions are provided to manipulate string data types, since UNIFY keeps this data with space padding rather than the null terminated string format of the C language.

Dates are internally stored in Julian date formats, so a number of date format conversion functions exist. You can obtain dictionary information such as *short* and *long names* of fields and tables, size of fields and tables, and primary key fields for given tables.

Locking and unlocking functions operate at record, database, or resource level. A resource is simply an item, usually a device such as a printer, which all programs agree to lock or unlock. Note that non-UNIFY programs do not check the lock, so the resource should not be shared with such programs. In addition, you can manipulate the transaction log file — that is, read or write log records. However, higher level functions such as start transaction, commit transaction, and rollback are not provided in this host language interface. They are available only in ACCELL.

11.4.6 Fourth Generation Language

In this section, we describe the ACCELL development facilities. Although it contains a procedural language part, the system is largely nonprocedural both during development and at runtime. To understand the operation of the system, let us look at the components of what ACCELL calls an *application*.

An application consists of one or more forms linked together in some manner such that users can view and manipulate data contained in them. Each form may constitute a single logical transaction, or several forms may be involved in one logical transaction.

You can associate procedural language code at certain control points: an application, a form, each form field, user actions, and database accesses. Figure 11-3 illustrates some of these relationships. If code is not associated with any of these processing points, the system uses default processing.

Since an application consists of related components, consider this term to mean a module or function within your application. A typical application will consist of several ACCELL applications.

A form defined with ACCELL/Generator differs from a PAINT form, since it can contain multiple occurrences of records from a table, and fields from separate tables. Unlike PAINT forms, the field data entry area can have a video attribute. You define field characteristics such as display format and video attributes, entry required, informational messages, and associate a help form and file. You can also specify automatic processing such as case conversion for a field. Field display size can be smaller than the database field; the runtime manager will allow horizontal scrolling in the field.

The form itself need not occupy the entire screen; you define its size and position. Forms can be overlapped for a windowing effect, especially in conjunction with the *zoom* facility. The runtime manager keeps track of the screen display and form windows. You also define the sequencing of forms within an application, which the user can override with the zoom facility, or you can override in the language code sections associated with a form or field component.

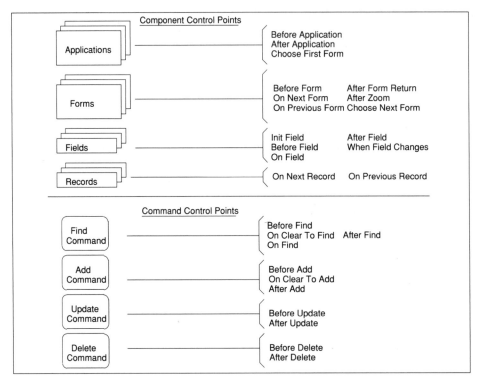

Figure 11-3 ACCELL Components and Processing Control Points

An unusual feature of ACCELL is the number of ways forms can link to each other. Forms can link sequentially, so that a user can use next form and previous form requests to flip from one to the other. You can also force a change of form from the language code with the ***choose next form*** capability and zoom from a field in one form to another form. A suitable use for this facility is to offer a ***pick-list*** of values for a field, where the choices are in a database table. The user can then zoom from the field to view and possibly select a value from the choices listed on the zoom form.

You could also use this facility to allow users to temporarily enter or update data in a table not included on the current form. For example, in a order entry application, you might zoom from the customer number field to a form containing all information for the customer. You might then update a field on this form, say correct the address, before continuing entry on the order entry form.

These facilities allow you to develop a very flexible user interface, which can reduce the need to exit from a transaction (or application) to choose another menu option. Be careful, however, that the number of active forms at any time does not overwhelm the available resources on your system. The ACCELL runtime manager stacks each active form in memory until the transaction is completed or restarted. Use great care in defining the transaction span, form sequencing within a transaction, and level of isolation for the transaction (consistency level).

Inquiries using a form containing multiple occurrences of a record can use the **browse** feature. With this feature, matching records are retrieved from the database in batches. Each batch contains the number of records that can be displayed at once on the form. Users can scroll forward or backward through the batches. This feature is especially efficient when a search retrieves a large number of records.

Some important points about ACCELL are its method of processing the language statements and its report production facilities. It precompiles the SQL statements embedded in the application, thus reducing the overhead of runtime parsing of such statements. Pre-compilation is feasible because ACCELL applications are not processed into C code before compilation. They compile into proprietary intermediate code which is executed by the runtime manager.

ACCELL's main focus is to provide high level facilities for interactive portions of the application. It does not provide statements to produce reports directly. You must pass data to be formatted to the RPT utility using the **pipeline** facilities.

Including functions written in the host language interface in ACCELL applications involves relinking ACCELL runtime environment with these functions. You pass parameters and return values in these functions using specific data structures and functions.

You may find yourself repeating ACCELL procedural code in several application sections. If the task is time consuming, occurs frequently, or occurs in critical sections such as the **on find**, **on next record**, and **on previous record**, it can cause performance degradation. Writing C functions in such strategic cases will help to improve the performance of your application.

Batch systems in ACCELL are simply applications with dummy blank forms, with the display redirected to **/dev/null.** You can run these applications in foreground or background using the SHELL facilities.

ACCELL operation is very amenable to translation from a detailed data flow analysis, using modern Computer Aided Software Engineering (CASE) tools, into an application. You must, however, define your data flow analysis diagrams and process descriptions with enough detail to determine which language sections you need to develop for each application, form, or field component. Such detail is rarely defined in an application design.

11.5 Integration with UNIX

UNIFY products were built for the UNIX environment and therefore provide many facilities to integrate your application into this environment. The products' use of directory hierarchies, and the usage recommended for your applications, reflect their understanding of the environment. The object archiving facilities of the UNIX **ar** utility are commonly used when compiling and linking UNIFY programs.

One notable facility is ACCELL's interface to the UNIX **make** utility and ACCELL's **makeamake** utility. You can control the portions of an application to recompile with the link into make, which also gives you SCCS facilities for change tracking. The makeamake utility generates a **makefile** including any ACCELL forms and scripts necessary to build your application. The ACCELL environment uses this makefile when you generate the application.

11.5.1 Login Access Usage

UNIFY can use either the UNIX login procedures or its own login mechanisms built into the menu driver. If you use the operating system procedures, you must specify the resultant user and group id (uid and gid) values to the menu driver security controls as the user and group identifications. In this case, administration of user login ids requires you to add or remove users in two steps, at the operating system level and at the database management system level. You also need to know the correspondence between the login id name and uid and gid values.

You may find it easier to build a single program which performs the two step login and figures out the correspondence using the *passwd* file. Such a program must run as a superuser program to be able to update the passwd file. You can write it using functions from the *stdio* library which manipulate the passwd file, and update records in the application data dictionary directly.

If you use UNIFY's login mechanisms, you can choose to bypass the operating system processing in any of the ways discussed in Chapter 7. If you choose to bypass UNIX procedures, you need to allow all users all types of permissions to the required database files and programs. Without access permission at the public level, users cannot access the database and run application programs. In addition, you should disable all access to the SHELL preventing accidental erasures of vital files and potential security breaches.

Note that the products use several SHELL environment variables to determine runtime parameters such as the database directory and memory usage parameters for performance tuning. If you bypass the use of users' .profile file, you must set the required environment variables in some other manner.

11.5.2 File Access and Administration

As described in Section 11.3.2, UNIFY depends on the filesystem permission structure for all the database files. If you store the database in the filesystem, you can set up the permission structure as needed for your user and group set-up. If you use raw disks for storage, the corresponding special nodes created in your database directory must be owned by the superuser. In this case, you may have to set all permissions at the public level so users can manipulate data in the database. Another factor you should consider is whether you bypass the operating system login procedures. We discussed the implications of bypassing in Section 11.5.1.

Recognizing the difficulty in backing up data from raw disk with UNIX facilities, UNIFY provides its own backup and recovery mechanisms together with an optional transaction log. These utilities are screen based interactive facilities which can be easily used by end-users. They only operate on the data in the database, so consider some other means for saving the data dictionary file. You only need to save a copy of this file after restructuring the database, which occurs infrequently. Consider the discussions in Chapter 7 about when to back up files such as the data dictionary and your application programs. You can, alternatively, write your own backup and recovery procedures, using UNIFY's standard host language interface, which would consolidate saving and restoring of application programs, screen and report definitions, dictionary information, and database data.

11.5.3 Process Architecture

UNIFY uses a single process per user architecture, which avoids the overhead of process switching inherent in the front-end and back-end approach. This process may appear to be large compared to other vendors products, unless you compare it with the combined size of both the front-end and back-end processes.

Note that you get multiple processes whenever you link multiple utilities together — for example, when you link SQL-by-forms and RPT. ACCELL processes use the low overhead shared memory, when available, for its lock manager. All other cases, including stand-alone host language interface programs use pipes, sockets under BSD UNIX, and lock files for communicating lock information.

ACCELL running on MS-DOS offers the option of cooperative processing with a back-end server process. This offers the opportunity to unload the system call intensive terminal handling to the PC local processor, which reduces the load on your UNIX machine. The higher cost of PCs should be justifiable in terms of the larger number of users the back-end could support.

11.5.4 SHELL Access

Although the menu driver provides access to SHELL by default, you can deny this access in the same way as any UNIFY program or utility. Standard utilities do not allow access to SHELL directly, except for the interactive SQL utility. If you deny SHELL access, this utility obeys the restriction. It is probably necessary to provide access to an editor from the interactive SQL, so users can edit statements if any mistakes occur. In this case, you must take steps to disable SHELL access from your chosen editor.

We discussed another case where you should disable SHELL access in Section 11.5.1. If you have to set public access to the database and associated files, disabling SHELL access is safer than risking corruption of the entire database.

11.6 Conclusions

UNIFY products offer the potential for developing high performance applications for large databases. To achieve high performance, you have to invest a significant effort in designing every part of your application, and you need in-depth understanding of both UNIX and the database management system. Using the products inefficiently is easy if you mis-understand the tradeoffs inherent in their design and their limitations.

For improving productivity, you have to use ACCELL. However, avoid the temptation to turn an ACCELL prototype into a production system. A prototype concentrates on *what* functionality to provide and is usually built with little attention to underlying design issues. Use a prototype together with utilities, such as ***list_scan*** and ***lmpeek***, to investigate areas of an application where you should invest special design effort. You also need a good understanding of the tuning parameters provided in almost every utility to set up the production system in an efficient manner.

It is easy to develop casual applications using these products if performance is not important. The standard utilities are all screen based and menu driven, except for the report generator. You do not need knowledge of SQL to create a database, perform standard data entry and inquiry operations, or set up program access security controls. Using the built-in facilities for prompts, errors, and help message display in the tools, you can build a very consistent user interface to an application with a minimum of effort.

Part 4

Selecting a DBMS

This part of the book guides you through the difficult process of choosing a product to meet your needs. The basic premise is that all products are not created equal. A product that meets the needs of one application can be totally unsuitable for another. Part 3 gave you a flavor of the bewildering variety of features available in just four commercial products. This part of the book attempts to arm you against the temptation of succumbing to the best sales pitch.

The three chapters are arranged in the order of performing the evaluation tasks. You really need to determine your requirements before trying to evaluate products. These requirements are the core of your defense against a hard sell. Trying to perform both of these tasks concurrently might result in loosing sight of your needs. You might end up choosing a product with many fancy features, but which does not satisfy some essential requirement. Poorly evaluated choices only lead to embarrassing consequences!

*An important theme of this part revolves around the popular buzzwords: **performance and response time**. These vital issues are often poorly defined leading to ill-considered product evaluations. Chapter 12 offers some techniques for determining whether you have critical performance requirements, and calculating response time parameters. Chapter 13 discusses how DBMS features affect these parameters, and Chapter 14 guides you in the methods of testing products to decide if they meet the performance needs.*

12

Determining Your Requirements

DBMS selection is an important part of application design. As we saw in Part 3, product implementations vary widely. Although the four products examined are relational database management systems and support the same conceptual facilities such as forms drivers, detailed implementations are quite different. Your design must take into account the specific features and drawbacks for a particular product. The fewer drawbacks you have to work around, the simpler your application will be to develop and to maintain.

In any application, the cost of the DBMS product is small compared to the cost of labor to develop the application and the even larger cost of maintaining it. Thus, any savings in development and maintenance costs must be realized through choosing the product best suited to the application requirements. If you choose a product before determining your requirements, you will probably need to find workarounds during development. These late workarounds may lead you to sacrifice efficiency, maintainability, or portability of the resulting application.

Ideally, your application design should closely match the chosen products' facilities. Only with a close match can you achieve the productivity gains claimed for these products. Novice DBMS developers definitely benefit from obtaining training on the chosen product before designing the application. And, of course, using the prototyping capabilities offered by the DBMS utilities helps you to produce a better application design.

In this chapter, we discuss ways of quantifying and prioritizing application requirements. The next chapter will suggest ways to correlate these requirements to specific features supported by DBMS products. Note that the techniques discussed here pertain only to the tasks to be performed by your application. Techniques for estimating development and maintenance implications of these requirements are raised in the next chapter.

12.1 Data Volumes

A proper estimate of data volumes provides three items of information vital to designing and planning of your application:

1. It provides you information on the initial size of the database required by your application. This information helps you to choose the type of storage strategy needed, and the effort required to load the initial data before releasing the application into production.

2. It provides information on expected growth in the database size. This is also a factor in choosing a suitable storage strategy.

3. It provides information on the machine resources needed by the application for a development system, initial production release, and forecasts for short term and long term needs. These resource estimates provide valuable planning input for higher management as well as supplying justification for project budgets. In Section 12.2, we similarly estimate resources needed to support users.

So, the aim of measuring data volumes is to provide these three items of information. To estimate these items, you must first identify each data item, its data type, and estimate its size. We call this list of data items a data *dictionary* for now. You should be able to identify the data for the main parts of your application easily, either through a data model, or through data flow diagrams which describe the functional requirements.

Once you have developed this dictionary, normalize the data, as discussed in Chapter 2. Whether you choose a relational database management system or not, normalization gives you an accurate picture of dependencies between data items and which fields need to be duplicated in more than one relation. In products based on other data models, this duplication exists as *pointers* which are hidden from you. They still impose an overhead which you need to consider in your size estimates.

The types of estimates you should also include in your data dictionary are:

*   Identify fields which will be indexed, and type of access needed via these fields, based on our discussions in Chapters 6 and 7. This information is necessary to decide whether you can use hash indexes or you need a B-tree index. B-tree indexes impose more space overhead than hash indexes. For each B-tree index include the size of field plus one long integer, once per record in the estimate for the overhead. For each hash index include an arbitrary measure, say two long integer fields per record.

*   Estimate the space required by *reference data* which is needed for standard lists. For example, in a car information database, you might decide to code color as an integer value which indexes into a list of actual color descriptions. The integer value may be internal — that is, the user only sees a *pick-list* of colors. The application programs convert the user's choice to its associated internal code.

In addition to the total size of these items, you should include the overhead of the DBMS data dictionary. This estimate is based on the total number of fields in the database, the contents of the data dictionary, and an estimated number of different user ids. Chapter 3 provided some guidelines on the contents of the data dictionary. For each field in the database, the data dictionary will contain its name, the name of the table it belongs to, and other internal information. For each user the data dictionary will contain the user name, access control information such as database tables or fields, and other internal information.

Good data volume estimates are much harder to obtain. You may have to monitor the existing system over a period of time to obtain data volume estimates. If the existing system is already computerized on UNIX, you could use UNIX tools to measure the number of records for each table in the new database. Standard tools for manipulating UNIX files assume an ASCII *newline(NL)* as a record terminator. Hopefully, your data is in ASCII printable characters with newline characters as record terminators, or these standard tools will be of little use to you! Alternatively, you could write your own programs to count the number of records from the existing files. Such programs obviously need to take into account the difference in record structures of the proposed database. In a manual system, you might need to count data records from paper forms.

The base data volume estimate, then, is the total size of all data items including their expected number of occurrences, and the estimated size of the data dictionary. A good practice is add at least a 50% overhead to this estimate (for items not yet identified for the application database) to obtain the estimated initial size of the database. This is the first item of information needed for initial resource requirements planning.

The second item, growth estimate, needs collection of further information. For each table identified in your initial database, you need to identify the users responsible for maintaining the data. These users can supply information on the number of new entries, and the number of entries deleted in some fixed period of time, such as a week. Make sure you obtain details on any seasonal high or low activities in entering the data. You can average these figures and project them over a period of one year, to obtain a working estimate.

You should back up these estimates with evidence collected by monitoring the existing system. Significant discrepancies between verbal estimates from users and documentary evidence are a fact of life in the data processing business! In a manual system, you might need to collect paper forms and count updates, additions, and deletions.

At this point, you have to estimate the amount of increased activity you expect once users start using the new application. This figure can range between an additional 10% to 50% of the working estimate, if you expect the new application to make significant improvements over the existing procedures.

Before you can estimate the machine resources for your application, you must have obtained all of the preceding information. Once you have determined the first two items of our volume estimates list, you can use these figures to calculate the disk resources needed for the initial database. The growth figures allow you to estimate how quickly the allocated initial disk space will be consumed. You could then impress your management by predicting when a strategic decision on expanding system resources will be necessary.

You should ensure that the chosen hardware supports your initial needs as well as allowing for short term growth needs. Typically, the maximum resources available on your chosen hardware should be at least two to three times your initial estimates. Availability of a smaller amount means that you will probably run out of resources even before development is complete. Some of the extra resources will be used up by the DBMS software, your application programs, and ancillary functions which cannot be estimated in advance. Note also that your chosen hardware should allow expansion of resources such as disks, without requiring a processor upgrade. If your initial estimates are close to the hardware expansion capabilities, you can only hope for an expensive upgrade at the end of development!

12.2 Transaction Volumes

An estimate of transaction volumes is important for two reasons:

- To determine the rate of growth of the database as discussed in Section 12.1.
- To provide information on the patterns of use of the database.

A transaction for these estimating purposes is any task that accesses a record in one table. Thus, we consider a logical transaction which accesses several tables to be several transactions in the volume estimate. Note that, in this definition, a report program also generates several search transactions, at least one per line in the report.

You should estimate volumes for each type of access, such as search, add, modify, or delete. The relative ratio of search transactions versus the others tells you whether the application is biased mainly towards inquiry or towards record keeping. Applications biased towards inquiry need a DBMS with fast and efficient access methods. An example of a inquiry biased application is a telephone directory system, where additions are infrequent, but retrieval is very frequent.

Applications biased towards record keeping — that is, storage of data records for occasional search — need flexible data storage capabilities. Access to records in such applications is often straightforward. An example of such an application is an accounting application, where you frequently add new data, but search is simply based on account numbers.

Gathering information on transaction volumes can be difficult, as you have to obtain general estimates from users. These estimates need to be backed up with evidence by collecting documents from the existing system, or by soliciting multiple opinions. Accepting user opinions without any evidence can lead to your volume estimates being wrong by an order of magnitude, possibly with embarrassing consequences.

You need to break down transactions represented by the documents into individual record accesses. Treating logical transactions the same as one record access transactions is dangerous, as it leads to underestimating the volume. Remember that each record accessed in a relation table could potentially be a separate disk access. Logical transactions, involving multiple records and tables, could cause an indexed search or table joins, thus requiring more disk accesses than single record transactions.

Transaction activities can be seasonal and vary through daily, weekly, monthly, or yearly cycles. Your estimate should reflect not only the average transaction volume but also the peak volumes, which are important in a performance critical application. For example, in an accounts receivable system, a large number of records are added close to the books' closing date which could be daily, monthly, or yearly depending on the business. In a payroll system, however, a large proportion of the accesses take place close to the pay date. Other variations may depend on external conditions such as holidays, or even the weather! Your application must cater to the peak loads if performance is critical.

Underestimating peak volumes could lead to serious effects on the business needs supported by the application. It is safer to overestimate volumes, since in this case, your application can only perform better than expected. Obviously, you cannot foresee all circumstances. For example, no one could have predicted the unprecedented volume of transactions during the Wall Street crash of October 1987!

Another necessary estimate is the number of users actively involved in executing transactions at a given time. As we discussed in Part 2 of this book, interactive forms based terminal handling consumes significant CPU resources under UNIX. Terminal activity volume also affects the performance and reduces the number of active users which specific hardware can support.

Having estimated the volume of transactions, you need to ensure that the selected hardware can support these needs. You could perform benchmarks to test the appropriateness of the hardware. However, benchmark evaluation is time consuming and can only be done if project funds permit the expense. You can use the following technique as a simpler but less accurate measure. Note that if performance is critical to your application's success, this technique is inadequate, and you must perform benchmarks. If you can obtain the funds, benchmark testing is always preferable.

The technique involves calculating the average time for a single record access transaction. If the distribution of transactions is fairly even, your calculation consists of simply dividing the number of transactions by the amount of time available for running them. An average time of seven to ten seconds per transaction is an acceptable range for users on a small machine.

If there are peak transaction traffic periods, you need to estimate the volume for just that period. You then calculate the average using only the peak period estimates. The acceptance range of seven to ten seconds allows sufficient time for any terminal display required as part of the activity.

If the required time range per transaction is lower then seven seconds, you need to take into account the number of simultaneous users your machine must support. You can connect many more terminals to a machine than it can support as active users. A rule of thumb commonly used is the number of simultaneous users is a quarter, or less, of the number of terminals the machine allows to be connected. In addition, you have to account for the size of the programs run by these simultaneous users. You must have sufficient memory to avoid swapping or significant amount of paging, since these activities cause performance degradation. The number of large processes typical in a DBMS application means that memory space can be a critical factor in performance.

If the required time range per transaction is very small — that is, less than one or two seconds — you have to take into account the speed of the disk used in the machine. The effectiveness of the disk throughput depends on whether disk head movement is necessary between reads, the size of the information passed to the application, and the efficiency of the DBMS search techniques. Since there is no easy way to relate disk throughput to your application's behavior, a benchmark test is recommended. Of course, the ***equal share*** philosophy of the UNIX scheduler means that transaction completion times cannot be *guaranteed*. This technique can only provide an estimate of the *average* completion time.

12.3 Performance Requirements

You use much of the information gathered for data and transaction volumes in determining performance requirements. Bear in mind that you need to determine the response times needed by your users, rather than simply measuring the speed of the product. Thus the selection process is not simply a matter of choosing the fastest product, but choosing one that meets the requirements of your particular application. For this reason, generic benchmarks of products are an insufficient guide to the best choice for your application. Chapter 14 discusses when to perform application specific benchmarks and provides guidance on how to measure and interpret benchmark results.

Response time for an activity depends on the activity itself. You need to define the tasks to be completed before the user considers the activity complete, even if the changes may not have been applied to the database. For example, in a telephone directory application, you might consider an address correction activity to be complete as soon as data entry is finished. The actual update to the database could occur at a later time, even overnight as a batch update. In a stock trading application, however, a change to a trader's net position must be applied to the database immediately, since further activities involving this data depend on up-to-date information. Thus, response time needs vary for each activity.

The types of activities you need to define fall into two categories: interactive and batch. Each category has different characteristics. Response time for an interactive activity is measured per transaction, whereas that of a batch activity is measured for completing all transactions. For example, in a telephone directory information application, an inquiry for a telephone number consists of entering the subscriber's name, searching the database for a match, and displaying the result. However, a nightly batch update of directory listing information must complete all of the several hundred changes to the database in the available time of up to eight hours. Thus, transaction volumes are very important in a batch activity, but component tasks are more important in an interactive activity.

Typical components of an interactive activity are data entry, database search, database update, and screen display. The data entry component must display the user's input instantaneously as a visual response. Small delays in this display cause user frustration and can cause entry errors. Screen display of the results of a database search, on the other hand, can take several seconds.

Response time needs for a database search activity depend on what use is made of the results. For example, a database search to answer a customer inquiry when the customer calls on the telephone must complete within a few seconds. The complexity of the search changes the user's expectation of response time. For example, a user requesting a statistical summary of data involving many calculations accepts a response time measured in hours. Requirements for fast response are often related to the simplicity of the search, such as display information for a given customer number.

Response time needs for a database update activity are similar to those of the database search activity. If the user has to provide an order total to a customer placing an order by telephone, the response time must be within a few seconds. Sending an invoice to a mail order, on the other hand, could take a day or two. Note that, in this example, a telephone order need not update the stock inventory in the database. Updates to the database and back orders can be handled as separate tasks at a later time.

Another factor in defining performance requirements is the number of users active at a given time. Note that the important estimate is users active concurrently, not the number of users with terminals connected to the system. You can have a larger number of terminals connected to a machine than it can support concurrently within the performance constraints. The actual performance is always dependent on the number of users actively using the system at one time. You should particularly note any peak times in this estimate, since the performance of your application needs to be within the acceptable range during the high activity period.

Thus, you define performance requirements for your application by identifying each user activity and the characteristic use of the results of the activity. You can quantify response times by the types of characteristics discussed here. To obtain realistic estimates, you need to list the components tasks of each activity and define which components must be completed for the user to consider the task complete.

If performance of certain activities is critical for the application to be acceptable, you need to perform benchmarks before selecting a DBMS product. The benchmark would model critical activities to measure response times achievable with each product. We discuss some ways of building a model and measuring performance in Chapter 14.

12.4 Security Requirements

There are two reasons for access restriction mechanisms:

- The application database contains confidential information; you need access restriction mechanisms to prevent unauthorized access.

- Access security control helps in maintaining the integrity of data by preventing updates from an uncontrolled interface such as the query language. This is important if a DBMS product provides no central mechanisms for maintaining data integrity.

In Chapter 3, we discussed the types of access control mechanisms available in a DBMS. Chapters 6 and 7 outlined techniques for using these mechanisms under different circumstances. You need to determine which types you need from the DBMS product for your application. Keep in mind that restrictions for the purposes of maintaining data integrity are tedious, but will reduce the opportunity for corrupting the database. If users can access the database only via application programs, you may not need any security facilities.

The first step is to identify which specific data items contain sensitive information. You should also determine which types of users need access to each of these items and whether they need search, add, update, or delete access. A matrix of the type shown in Figure 12-1 is useful in recording this research.

Data Item	Payroll				Personnel				Administration				Managers			
	S	A	U	D	S	A	U	D	S	A	U	D	S	A	U	D
Name	✓				✓	✓	✓	✓	✓				✓			
Address	✓	✓			✓	✓			✓				✓			
Employee #	✓				✓	✓	✓	✓	✓				✓			
Salary	✓	✓			✓	✓	✓						✓			
Department	✓				✓	✓	✓		✓	✓						
Nationality					✓	✓	✓									

Access Types:

S = Search and Read
A = Add
U = Update
D = Delete

Figure 12-1 Example of an Access Privilege Matrix

The data items in this matrix are listed from the data dictionary developed for data volume estimates. You can then refer the individual data items to the normalized tables to determine if a particular type of access should be restricted at the table level, field level, or database level. Since most products support access restriction for the data items only, this analysis is usually sufficient. It is important, however, to ensure that you can meet all security requirements by restricted access to data.

In some instances, you have to implement additional constraints through application programs. For example, if a manager can view the salary data only for employees in the department, but not for employees in other departments, you may need to implement this restriction via your application program. You could use views to implement such a restriction if you can establish a connection between the user id and the data item to be restricted.

Access restrictions for maintaining data integrity can be more complex. You need to determine the integrity requirements by analyzing your normalized data. Keep in mind that if you choose to denormalize data to improve performance, data integrity requirements increase in complexity. You may need to prevent users from performing additions, updates, and deletions on certain fields and tables through the query language. If users are not permitted to use the query language at all, maintaining data integrity is not a problem. Otherwise, preventing access to the data update facilities of the query language is necessary. Users could still retrieve data via the query language, but should update only via an application program which maintains integrity needs.

The requirements should identify whether users or systems staff perform database administrator functions, such as granting and revoking access privileges, and adding or deleting user ids. If users are to perform such tasks, you may need to restrict them from performing data restructuring functions.

Your analysis should also include needs for login security control. This requirement determines whether you could use the login mechanisms provided by the product or UNIX system procedures. The analysis should include needs for preventing access to the SHELL to prevent accidental damage to the database and application program files. Chapter 7 discussed these issues in detail.

12.5 Routine Administration

The requirements for day-to-day administration depend on whether a nontechnical user will perform these duties or not. Such a user will need a significant amount of training to use query language based facilities than if administrative facilities are menu based. Some DBMS products provide screen based administrative facilities, whereas others only provide query language statements.

Typical routine administration involves adding new users to the system, changing user access privileges, deleting users, printer management, periodic backup, and restore of the database. Users may create and manage their own database tables, if your application requires it. In this case, you should note the ease of creating and handling the database as a requirement. You will also need some means of controlling resource usage by individual users. UNIX only provides a few simple facilities to monitor this consumption, and none to control it.

You need to satisfy the administrative requirements with an easy-to-use interface which also protects users from accidental damage to the application. For example, the administrator should not grant privileges to users which allow them to delete a table vital to the operation of the system. Imagine if someone accidentally deletes an index!

You need to define the types of activities the administrator needs to perform and the mechanisms needed to restrict other activities. You may find it preferable to start by providing a very restricted subset of simple administrative activities, adding more complex facilities later. However, in your product selection process you need to define all potential tasks. When you have defined the scope of your administrative requirements, you then decide whether to use a UNIX facility, a DBMS facility, or to build your own. As discussed in Chapter 7, you may have to build an application specific hybrid facility. In this case, the DBMS must provide you access to the appropriate information in its data dictionary.

12.6 Enhancements to the Application

Important parts of the requirements definition are the expected enhancements to the application. If your choose a DBMS product based only on the requirements within the scope of the current development, you might choose a product which cannot handle future expansion. For example, suppose the size of the current application database is such that it fits on a single filesystem. So you choose a product which can only support database storage under the UNIX filesystem. After a few enhancements involving changes to the database structures, the database size increases so you need larger disk space, which you can only obtain as several physical disks. Your chosen DBMS prevents such distribution of the data.

Other types of enhancements might also affect the choice of DBMS product. A typical example is the need for security control mechanisms, which might be unnecessary initially, but become essential as new functions bring in new users of the application. For example, a new function for department managers to access a personnel system means that some data must now be protected from access. Adding extra users to the application obviously invalidates the performance criteria for product selection.

When you define the scope of your application, you should also identify functions to be implemented later as enhancements. For the purposes of selecting a DBMS, you need to know the requirements of these foreseen enhancements. In particular, find out if they might increase the database size or transaction volume!

There are other enhancements which could be easily made to the initial application. For example, a time recording system could be added to a personnel system, or a customer orders function might be added to an accounts receivable system. It is much more difficult to foresee the effects of such potential enhancements, which may or may not be undertaken in future. However, you could identify some of the DBMS facilities that would aid their development. Some of the considerations are:

- Could you *prototype* user interfaces during the design of your application? The facilities required for quick prototyping include an easy-to-use interface for forms definition and easy restructuring of the database. Screen based forms paint utilities integrated with an interactive fourth generation development facility are the most useful. A fourth generation programming language, where you write a program using normal editing tools, compile, then link, is less useful.

- The types of changes required for enhancements, such as changes to the database structures, multiple separate databases and so on. If the enhancements are highly desirable, you need to choose a DBMS that allows you to change database structures easily. To allow development of integrated systems, the product should be capable of supporting databases many times the size of your initial application. Keep in mind that ad hoc exchange of data between disparate DBMS products in the UNIX environment is often difficult. Thus, choosing a different product for each application in an integrated system is not practical.

- If enhancements mean program changes, the ease of program modification is a requirement for the product. Consider also whether programs have to change due to a database structure change.

- Frequent modifications and enhancements mean that you should increase your disk resource estimates to allow extra space for a test environment. You could then set up a parallel test environment, where modifications and enhancements can be tested thoroughly before going into production.

Ideally, the development and test system should be on a separate machine from the production system. Failing this, you should organize the test system on a disk separate from those used for the production system. In this way, you will minimize the performance degradation due to disk contention between development and production. Keep in mind, when production system performance is important, that development activities such as compilations consume a large proportion of CPU and disk resources. The UNIX *equal share* scheduling means that you cannot specify a high priority for production users.

12.7 Future Portability

One of the important considerations is whether the chosen DBMS product provides a growth path to another machine. This requirement is important if your hardware supports the initial implementation of the application, but you foresee outgrowing its expansion capabilities. Note that an application based on a DBMS usually requires more resources than a non-DBMS application. Thus, your tradeoffs are better data management and faster development versus cost of hardware resources. Bear in mind that the cost of hardware continues to drop as technology advances. Therefore, getting a larger machine to accommodate growth and performance requirements is a feasible approach.

The portability considerations in developing an application were discussed in Chapters 6 and 7. In the requirements definition phase, you should determine whether you might port to another UNIX machine or if management considerations might require you to port to a proprietary operating system. To continue with UNIX, you should ensure that machines with larger capacities are available. If the initial application hardware is already the top-of-the-line model of one manufacturer, consider if other manufacturers have larger UNIX machines.

There are two types of upgrades you might need when moving to a larger machine: disks for faster throughput or more space, or more CPU power. More disk space on your initial machine might be available, perhaps at the cost of some degradation in throughput if disk controllers are loaded to capacity. If you configure a disk controller at maximum capacity, you might experience a bottleneck for disk I/O.

In such a configuration, a DBMS that allows you to tune the placement of data across disks is useful. You could then distribute the application database evenly between multiple disks and controllers to maximize throughput. The data distribution should take into account user access patterns so that the disk I/O load is equally distributed. Since user access patterns can change over time, you may have to periodically repeat the throughput monitoring and tuning effort. A DBMS which does not allow you control over the placement of data is not useful for tuning.

An alternative to complicated tuning of the application might be to use a larger machine with faster disks. Moving the application to a larger machine is probably cheaper in the long term, because of the portability of UNIX DBMS products, than the effort of repeated tuning.

If the CPU power of the initial machine becomes insufficient, you have fewer tuning options. One of the common bottlenecks in applications under UNIX is the number of system calls a processor can execute. Note that this number is only loosely related to the *mips* rating of a processor. For example, a *RISC* based processor can execute more mips than a traditional processor, but it may not perform a system call any faster. The actual implementation of system calls influences execution speed more than a processor's mips rating.

The only tuning you can perform when your application exceeds the system call limitation is to redesign program logic to use fewer system calls. This task is significantly more difficult than porting the application to a larger machine. If the DBMS itself uses a large proportion of system calls, you cannot reduce these. In this context, a machine is larger if it can execute more system calls per second than your initial machine.

You can port your application to a larger UNIX machine more easily than porting it to a proprietary operating system. The behavior of the DBMS remains very similar even though the hardware configurations vary between manufacturers. Thus, you do not need to make significant changes to the architecture of the application, and can avoid major retraining of users as well as systems development staff.

If, however, your initial system is at the top end of the available UNIX machines, you could consider porting to a proprietary system. In this case, a DBMS product which runs on several different operating systems is vital. Note that this is a common trend amongst products which currently run on UNIX. Some of these products, such as ORACLE and FOCUS, originated on other operating systems. Products, such as INGRES and INFORMIX, which originated on UNIX have been ported to other systems.

Keep in mind that changing operating systems might require architectural changes to the application, unless the initial design considered this possibility. The types of changes that might occur include administrative interfaces, the look and feel of the screen forms interface, and possibly programming language changes. Major changes might be necessary if your application depends on a process based architecture and your new operating system has a different architecture. For example, the IBM VM/CMS architecture does not allow a normal application program to control multiple processes. Its multitasking approach is significantly different.

12.8 Conclusions

In this chapter, we discussed the characteristic runtime requirements of an application that you need to define and how they relate to DBMS facilities. We also discussed some of the techniques for quantifying these requirements. Requirements for development and maintenance characteristics are described in the next chapter. You need to define the following items.

Data Volumes:

Determining data volumes provides information about the size of the database, its growth requirements, and disk resources required to support the application. Estimating the size of the database requires that you define all data elements and their sizes, sizes of key fields and indexes, and all reference data. In addition, you should estimate growth in the database over short and long term periods. Your machine should support disk resources for approximately two to three times the size of your initial estimate.

You need to identify whether the application database size is small, medium, or large. A small database is one where majority of the heavily accessed tables are small enough to not require second and third level indirection blocks of the filesystem. The absolute size requiring second level indirection blocks depends on the *logical* block size used by the filesystem on your machine. A medium size database contains some heavily used tables which require second level indirection blocks of the filesystem. A database containing tables which require third level indirection blocks in the filesystem is considered to be large. The choice of whether to use the filesystem or raw disk for medium and large databases depends on other performance requirements.

Transaction Volumes:

Transaction volumes are measured in terms of individual table accesses. Your estimate should include interactive and batch transactions. You should categorize these estimates into search, add, update, and delete tasks, to determine whether the application bias is toward inquiry activities or toward update transactions. Inquiry biased applications require fast access methods, whereas update biased applications require flexible data storage.

You should backup volume figures obtained from user interviews with evidence to avoid significant errors in the estimate. You can obtain evidence from an analysis of the existing system by measuring paper forms and documents or by using operating system facilities if the application is currently computerized. Seasonal peaks in transaction volumes are particularly important as the application must adequately handle activities during these peaks. The number of simultaneous users that the application must support is an important factor of estimating transaction volumes and peak period traffic handling.

Response Time:

This item is very important in a performance critical application. You should define the activities where performance is critical. For each of these activities, carefully specify which components must be complete for the user to consider the transaction as complete. Response time measure is the time to complete these components. Typical noncritical response times vary in the range of seven to ten seconds per transaction.

For a high performance interactive application, you should defer the execution of as many components of a transaction as possible, without affecting the user's perception of a complete transaction. A typical candidate for deferring is the task of applying updates to the database. For applications which depend on up-to-date database information, you must apply updates to the database as an integral part of the transaction.

You cannot guarantee absolute response times for each transaction due to the equal share philosophy of the UNIX environment. You can only estimate the average response time over hundreds of transactions. An implementation providing a priority based scheduling enhancement to UNIX is essential before you can speculate on any guarantees. DBMS products in this operating system rarely provide an architecture that can guarantee response times on every transaction.

Security Needs:

Access security mechanisms can be used for protecting access to sensitive data, or for preserving the integrity requirements of the database. You have to determine which DBMS security mechanisms the application needs. In addition, you should consider whether you need to control users' access to the SHELL.

Routine Administration Needs:

You need to define which types of administrative activities a nontechnical user might need to perform. Important requirements include whether to use a DBMS facility or a UNIX facility to support these activities. If you need to build your own hybrid facility, define the types of database dictionary information which you need to access.

Enhancement Considerations:

You need to identify foreseeable enhancements to ensure that the selected DBMS supports mechanisms necessary for them. Enhancements might affect the database structure, its size, the number of simultaneous users, access control, or concurrency control requirements. If you foresee frequent enhancements, the selected product should provide easy changes to the database structure and programs. In addition, it should allow you to maintain a test environment in addition to the production environment without a significant effect on the production system performance.

Portability Considerations:

Two types of growth requirements can force you to consider porting your application to a larger machine: faster or larger disk capacity needs, or a more powerful CPU. If the bottleneck is disk throughput, careful consideration of the disk and controller configuration is necessary. A larger machine, in this context, is one which provides faster disk throughput. You can tune the data distribution over disks to improve throughput, and repeat the tuning periodically as disk usage patterns change. A CPU bottleneck is often due to exceeding the processor's capability to execute system calls. In this context, a larger machine is one which can execute more system calls per second, a capability only loosely related to its mips rating.

Porting the application to a larger machine which also runs UNIX is significantly easier than tuning the application programs to run within available resources. Most DBMS products retain their behavior under UNIX even though hardware configurations and characteristics change. You can consider porting to a proprietary operating system since many DBMS products run on these disparate environments as well as UNIX. The interface behavior of the product may change to suit the operating system environment. Porting your application to a proprietary operating system is probably more difficult than porting it to another UNIX system.

13

Assessing the Tradeoffs

In this chapter, we correlate the needs determined in the previous chapter with the available DBMS facilities. It is important to separate the requirements definition from the product evaluation phase so that you do not get overwhelmed by the available facilities. If you perform these two phases concurrently, it is easy to lose sight of practical needs. You might be tempted by a fancy feature offered by one product, even though it plays a small role in the application.

The discussions in this chapter frequently refer to the estimates derived in Chapter 12. We examine how these estimates affect our decisions on which features of the DBMS are crucial for the application. In particular we look at:

- *Data volume estimates*: To help us to determine whether the DBMS should support filesystem files or raw disk.
- *Transaction volume estimates*: To help us determine which interactive facilities and concurrency control mechanisms are necessary.
- *Response time estimates*: To determine whether performance is critical.
- *Enhancement estimates*: To determine if we can use fourth generation development facilities.
- *Administrative needs*: To determine the type of integration needed from the product.

13.1 Which DBMS Facilities are Crucial?

Determining how important performance is in your application is a necessary first step. Most application requirements put fast performance as the foremost requirement. Naturally, we would like all applications to run as fast as possible, but if performance is not critical we can sacrifice speed for faster development or easier maintenance. Whether performance is critical depends on our estimates of *response time*.

If certain activities require a short response time — that is, less than seven seconds — performance is critical in your application. In this case, the bias of your application determines the DBMS features needed. In inquiry intensive applications, you need a product which provides fast data access. You would make maximum use of indexed access methods in search activities. If a product provides its own buffering mechanisms together with support for raw disk configuration, its disk access speed is likely to be better than products that only support filesystem files.

In record keeping applications, speed of update is important. You still need a DBMS with fast data access, but you would minimize the use of indexes. Each index is updated with every addition and deletion activity on the database which slows down updates. A DBMS product supporting a raw disk configuration together with its own data buffering will often run faster than those using the filesystem. Of course, if your database is relatively small, you could simply tune the size of kernel buffers so that majority of the database resides in memory. So, filesystem based data storage is reasonable for small databases.

When performance is critical, you need to use a third generation programming language. It should allow you to optimize the application programs for performance. The type of host language interface support, in this case, plays an important role. A typical function call based interface allows you to control the data access paths. Except, of course, function calls which simply pass a query language statement as an argument which are equivalent to an embedded query language interface.

With an embedded query language interface, you have to depend on the product's query processor. These processors can be sensitive to the wording of statements and might not choose the fastest path. Without any tools for optimizing the actual access path, you cannot be sure that the query processor used the fastest path or what your options are for improving it. Some products do provide monitoring tools which describe the chosen access path and tools for optimizing it.

There are two types of embedded query language interfaces: compiling or interpretive. A compiling interface generates the compiled query statement when you compile your program, and stores it for later use. You can identify such an interface since it detects mistakes in database field names at compile time. A compiling processor can detect such mistakes because it needs to use field names to reference the dictionary in determining the access paths. Thus, a precompiled query statement has the access path determined at compile time. The processor might recompile the statement at runtime if the indexes on the database change so you do not need to recompile your program.

An interpretive embedded query language interface processes the data access statement at runtime. So, it does not find syntactical errors in the statements until you execute the program. Your best bet is to test these statements using the interactive query interface before including them into your program. Such interfaces tend to be slower than compiling embedded query language interfaces since they must determine the access path each time they are executed. Some products attempt to speed subsequent execution by storing the parsed statement when it is first encountered during the execution of a program.

Implementing security requirements does impose an overhead, even though you think of them as independent of your performance needs. This overhead is due to the extra runtime checking to prevent unauthorized access. For a performance critical application, you need to minimize the restrictions implemented. The best way is to implement security checks once at the start of user session. Data level restriction results in security checks for every data access. Thus, a DBMS product that provides menu level or program level restrictions will probably impose the least execution time overhead. You can also minimize security checking by specifying restrictions at table level. To achieve table level restrictions, you may need to denormalize the database by defining sensitive data fields in separate tables which can then be restricted.

Do not think that DBMS productivity tools are mutually exclusive with the requirement for fast performance. This restriction does apply to fourth generation languages, but not to all screen forms drivers. A form requiring straightforward handling — for example, a data entry form for a single table — can be sufficiently fast to meet performance requirements. Complex data validation in screen forms drivers can cause performance degradation or fancy display mechanisms such as overlapping windows on a dumb ASCII terminal.

Performance is not critical in your application when the time available for a single record transaction is typically seven seconds or more. In this case, other requirements can take precedence. You should give security control requirements a higher priority than development productivity improvement features. If a DBMS product does not cater to your security needs, you have to build necessary restrictions into each of your programs. This task can increase the complexity of your programs, thus offsetting any improvements in productivity. A DBMS with a large variety of security control mechanisms is therefore desirable. Keep in mind, however, that a product with only a few, but pertinent, mechanisms can also meet your needs.

The order of the remaining DBMS utilities depends on the specific needs of your application. The following discussion relates some of the utilities to typical requirements. You must prioritize them as appropriate.

Development productivity improvement tools are important if you need a short development timeframe. These utilities are of two types: application development tools and database management tools. Application development tools include screen forms drivers, report generators, and fourth generation application development facilities. Database management tools include data definition facilities, export/import facilities, and administrative utilities.

You can use the screen forms drivers available with most products to develop straightforward data entry and file maintenance programs. However, if you need complex data validation support – for example, lookup checks from other relation tables – you might need the fourth generation language components of some products. Fourth generation languages are very versatile and can accommodate special processing via a third generation language routine.

When performance is not critical in your application, the choice of the most suitable utilities should be based on the features offered. Appendix A summarizes the commonly provided features. You often need the host language interface component for a few of the application functions even if other utilities satisfy the bulk of your requirements.

If you foresee several enhancements after the initial development, you should give priority to the ease of restructuring the database. Many products require you to unload the entire database before changing the structure and then reloading the data into the new structure. This process can be time consuming for all except small databases. The time required for unloading and reloading is directly proportional to the number of records in each table and the number of indexes involved.

If your data volume research indicates significant growth in the database size after implementation, you might give priority to the ease of increasing the database size. Some products allow you to increment the database size without requiring you to unload and reload the database. If the anticipated database growth leads to hardware upgrades, you need to ensure that the product supports the upgrade path. Being forced to rewrite the application for a different DBMS just because of upgrading the hardware is only one of the embarrassing consequences of overlooking this consideration. *(Even if you have moved to greener pastures by the time the upgrade becomes essential!)*

You should also consider the ease of modifying application programs. Fourth generation programs are easily modified if all you need are additional screen forms. However, changes to field processing sequence within a screen form are more difficult due to the nonprocedural nature of fourth generation languages. Forms drivers and report generation scripts obviously are easily modified.

Note that proper use of DBMS utilities can make the programs easier to enhance. Using them in the procedural style of third generation languages means you carry over all of the difficulties associated with third generation language programs. Development with non-procedural tools means changing your coding practices and hence significant training for staff with little prior experience in such tools. Testing such programs also differs from traditional methods, since they cannot control the sequence of users' actions.

13.2 Batch or Interactive Operation?

Most applications contain an interactive portion and a batch portion. In performance critical applications, you should defer as many tasks as possible to batch processing in off-peak hours. Individual transactions in batch mode run slower than in interactive mode: acceptable as long as all transactions complete within the time window allotted for the batch run. Typical batch activities can consist of database updates and report generation for complex or predefined reports. Periodic reports, such as daily or weekly, are especially good candidates for batch runs.

Update tasks deferred to off-peak batch processing typically involve multiple tables where integrity constraints must be maintained. If the query language available is sufficiently sophisticated, you could use it to perform these tasks. Remember that the update transaction information needs to be in a database table for access in a query language. You might also need transaction journaling during the batch updates. These mechanisms can recover the database state at the last completed transaction, protecting you from corrupted database if a system crash occurs in the middle of an update.

To maintain referential integrity when the DBMS does not provide any mechanisms, the query language should support the *exists* relational operator. You can use this operator when checking the existence of a value in one table at the time of adding it to another table. Incorporating such checks means that a multiple table update might consist of several query language statements, all encompassed by transaction level concurrency control statements. If you do not overlap interactive and batch access, concurrency control mechanisms become irrelevant.

Interactive functions of an application require good screen management tools. Keep in mind that if end-users are to use query languages, they require extensive training and need to know the structure of the database. Menu and screen forms interfaces are most suitable for nontechnical users and are easiest to learn. Consistency between the different screen interface utilities is an important criteria for a good user interface.

Facilities such as form windows allow nice looking interfaces. However, their support requires significant CPU resources. They are really not suitable for supporting the fast typing needs of data entry tasks. They are good for sophisticated query interfaces which can be popular with end-users if they are designed for ease of use. For performance critical interactive tasks, you need simple interfaces which allow fast display and response to user actions.

For data entry tasks where typing speed is very fast, you need the ability to remain in the add mode. Records can then be added without having to repeat the command after entering each record. If you need to incorporate validation checks into the speedy data entry interface, it is preferable to perform data validation and reporting errors at the end of entry on the entire form, rather than on individual fields. Speed of data entry becomes significantly slower if errors are reported after individual fields and must be corrected before proceeding further. Note that many UNIX based products report errors after individual fields. This style of error reporting is suitable for casual data entry — that is, where only a few records are added at any one time.

Speed of cursor movement between fields is directly proportional to the complexity of the validation check that has to be performed after each field and on the system load. In most products, you need to press a specific key, such as Carriage Return, Enter, or Tab, after entering data in a field. To reduce keystrokes during data entry, some products offer a feature to automatically move the cursor to the next field as soon as you type a character in the last position of a field. This feature is only useful when data entered in each field occupies all characters in it. For example, this feature is useful for entering data in a telephone number field, but not in a name field.

A useful feature, necessary in many interactive functions, is the ability to define a screen form field which is not associated with a database field. Such fields might take their values based on other form fields, for example, an order total field in a order screen form. Most products provide such a facility in their screen forms interface. Some products can display a value which is not related to any other field — for example, the user's name.

13.3 Development Constraints

If you have to develop the application under severe time or staff constraints, plan to make full use of any productivity improvement tools. Utilities such as forms drivers, report generators, and fourth generation development facilities aid speedy development. Keep in mind, however, that such development cannot cater to high performance requirements. Neither can you later fix such an application to improve its performance. A high performance application must be designed and developed for speed from the ground up. For example, developers have had to rewrite an entire application, initially developed in SHELL, in C to achieve performance goals. The rewrite effort required an extra year to complete: triple the time estimated at the project planning stages.

Most standard utilities provided by DBMS products restrict the complexity of the application functions. These tools aim to satisfy only the typical interfaces and data access needs. You can work around these restrictions by changing the formatting requirements in the case of reports, and user expectations in the case of forms based interfaces.

As an example, consider a report listing each part number and a comma separated list of customers who ordered it. A typical report generator allows you to obtain this report, but it can only be formatted as one customer per line. The lack of a look-ahead facility in a report generator also makes it difficult to determine whether you have reached the last customer name, so that you can avoid putting a comma after it. You may also have difficulty determining whether you have sufficient space remaining in a line for another customer name, so that you can print the entire name on the next line. Some products can automatically wrap such lines, although the line breaks may not be at some logical point such as after a comma.

Attempting to make standard report generator utilities perform such unusual tasks requires a significant effort. However, if modified formatting — say listing one customer name per line — is acceptable, then you can develop the report very quickly.

Many standard forms drivers restrict access to database tables not displayed in a screen form. They might provide facilities for lookup validation of a value entered in another table. However, most forms drivers prevent you from updating a table not displayed in a screen form. For example, you might consider using a table to temporarily store input transactions for stock updates. You develop a form based on this table, but wish to update the stock master table as soon as the user enters a valid transaction. Most standard forms drivers lack the facilities for such an update, except by using your own custom developed host language interface functions. Alternatively, you could use their fourth generation development facilities for performing such updates.

Note that the approach of using a *input transaction table,* as distinct from the *master table*, is contrary to the philosophy of typical forms based update utilities. These utilities are intended for directly updating the master table with no intermediate transaction storage tables. Thus, the traditional approach of collecting transactions and updating the master files as a batch operation at a later time cannot be easily implemented. Clearly, the techniques used in traditional batch transaction processing, such as batch totals as validation and error detection methods, are meaningless for direct updates.

In some instances, you might wish to preserve the data entered in each modification to the database, possibly for audit purposes. The traditional method of an *input transactions file* provided such information. The journaling facility of some DBMSs might provide an alternate method for you to produce such audit reports. This facility tracks actual values involved in an update. Most products do not provide facilities for you to access the transaction journal for custom reporting: These facilities are intended for recovering the database after a system crash. If a product does allow access, you probably cannot use any standard utilities to produce the required reports. Note that the *audit* facility of a DBMS provides only security information such as *who* updated *which* part of the database. They rarely provide information on the value before and after the update.

Standard utilities and fourth generation development facilities do speed development, but only if you are already familiar with their nonprocedural programming techniques. Your first attempt at developing with such tools will require more time for learning the necessary techniques, than subsequent development.

Using a host language interface for a third generation programming language might be easier for first time developers. This interface allows you to use prior experience of developing in a procedural manner. It allows you significantly more flexibility in manipulating screen forms and data entered by users and from the database. However, you gain little development speed over traditional methods, since you still use a third generation programming language. Enhancements, in this case, also require more effort to implement.

Fourth generation facilities offer the potential for fast development after you gain experience in their use. These development facilities provide the end-user with control over the sequence of events: Your procedures are executed only when particular events occur. If you need to impose any restrictions on the sequence in which the user performs a task, you have to include checks to enforce it in every procedure which might be invoked.

For example, suppose you need the user to enter the customer number in a customer orders form before allowing any other action. You have to check that the user actually does so in every other field procedure in the form as well as any procedures associated with an exit from the form. On the other hand, if you simply required a value in this field, with no assumption about when it might be entered, you can simply define the field to be an *input-required* field. Thus, you have to discard all notion of sequence when developing with a fourth generation development facility. Until you gain experience in using it, this facility cannot demonstrate the substantial development time savings claimed.

Note also that testing a fourth generation program can be more time consuming than a third generation program. You need extra testing because of the numerous execution paths possible due to its nonprocedural nature. Extra testing is essential if you enforce any restrictions on the sequence of events.

13.4 Frequency and Ease of Program Modification

Using DBMS utilities allows you to develop programs which are easier to modify than third generation programs. They also have fewer lines of code than typical third generation programs. These utilities make the DBMS programs more readable because they have a closer association with database data. Thus, simple enhancements such as handling a new field added to the database are easy to incorporate.

Utilities also provide data independence since a change to the database does not require you to change all programs, only those which need to use the changed data. This benefit is also available in the host language interface if the interface avoids assumptions on the order in which data is physically stored. Typically, interfaces based on an embedded query language provide this benefit.

Complex enhancements, such as changing the processing logic of a program, is more difficult to incorporate into the nonprocedural fourth generation programs. You need significant experience in the utilities and fourth generation development facilities, to identify the sections where the change in logic needs to be incorporated. Since it is impossible to predict the sequence of events in the actual use of the program, any change to the processing logic requires the programmer to fully understand the *entire* transaction, not just the piece to be changed. In some cases, you might find that redeveloping the program from scratch is faster than trying to modify an existing one. Keep in mind that a fourth generation program developed with procedural concepts can contain significant quantities of code to fix errors. This code can make it difficult to understand the processing logic implemented by the program.

Some of the enhancements may not be possible in programs developed using standard utilities. For example, changing the format of a report to list individual customer names into a comma separated list, requires significant effort. It may be faster to use third generation programming languages to perform such tasks, rather than attempting to develop custom functions using the hooks provided in the utilities. Incorporating multiple record display forms with a forms driver which does not support this feature is significantly more work than using host language interface facilities to implement these features.

13.5 Administrative Control

Developers of applications based on a DBMS product need several administrative tools. Some of these tools are supplied as part of the product, but others have to be custom developed for your application. An important point is that completing the application development is only the beginning of the application life cycle. The application database size grows throughout its life, and needs tuning to maintain its performance levels.

Performance monitoring and tuning should be ongoing activities after the application is released into production. The DBMS product should provide monitoring tools which show the disk I/O, CPU usage patterns, and query optimization either for specific users or for the entire system.

User specific monitoring information is useful for optimizing query language statements which are either embedded into a program or are stored as a script for repeated use. The information provided should include which particular indexes were used to resolve a query and at which stage of query execution. You can use such information to determine whether it used the best access path. You can rearrange the query statements to obtain optimal access or create new indexes which improve the query execution speed.

Systemwide monitoring information is useful to determine where the bottlenecks affecting system performance occur. Bottlenecks could include disk I/O, excessive locking activity, or CPU resources. A monitoring tool provided by a DBMS isolates disk accesses due to database activities from those caused by operating system activities. They can indicate areas where you could tune the DBMS memory buffers to improve throughput. In operating system monitoring information, disk I/O bottlenecks are not as easily resolved, since increasing memory buffers might increase paging or swapping activities. CPU bottlenecks can be resolved only by making programs use fewer CPU resources. This is clearly a difficult task, requiring you to develop more efficient algorithms for your programs.

If you intend to prevent application users from accessing UNIX directly, the DBMS products should provide mechanisms for this. A product allowing you login time access security control will aid the performance needs we discussed in section 13.1. Products which implement their own login mechanisms should allow you to automatically link to the operating system mechanisms, so users do not see multiple login procedures. Alternatively, you should be able to disable their own login procedures in order to use only UNIX login mechanisms. When preventing access to the SHELL, you should be able to disable SHELL escape mechanisms from all DBMS utilities.

When you plan to release enhancements to the initial application, you need to plan for any database restructuring necessary to the production database. Most products require you to unload all data, implement the changes, and then reload the data. Clearly the application will be unavailable to users throughout this period.

Some products are slower than others at the process of reloading data. Your only concern, however, should be whether unload and reload can be completed in some reasonable time frame — for example, over an eight-hour period. If the unload and reload process requires longer, consider the effect of the longer downtime on users. You should allow sufficient time to perform the process at least three times, so you can recover from any mistakes.

Few DBMS products provide tools to set up and control releases of applications into production. Formalizing the release process is essential for you to control the testing, debugging, and maintenance of the application. Without such a procedure, you quickly lose track of which programs are in production and which bugs have been corrected. The UNIX system provides SCCS utilities which you could use to custom build your release control mechanisms.

With each release of the application, consider the training needed by the users. The DBMS utilities should allow you to provide a consistent interface to minimize training needs. Consider also the user documentation provided with the product, to judge its adequacy for your application users.

13.6 Conclusions

In this chapter, we examined the relationship between the requirements determined in Chapter 12 with the facilities provided by DBMS products. The order of importance of your requirements determines which DBMS features are useful in your application. This order is:

1. *Performance:* For a performance critical application, you have to account for any extraneous overheads imposed by nice DBMS features. You should minimize their use for those components of the application which require short response times. You may also have to abandon the use of some productivity improvement tools such as fourth generation languages.

2. *Security:* If the product does not provide the types of security mechanisms that you need, you have to build the necessary restrictions in your programs. This need may prevent you from using standard utilities to perform most of the straightforward work.

3. *Productivity improvement tools:* These tools provide the next most important benefit of using a DBMS product. You may have to adjust your formatting needs in order to use standard forms driver and report generation facilities. Fourth generation development systems are more flexible than standard utilities, but consume significantly more machine resources. The use of these tools should be minimized in the performance critical components of your application.

4. *Growth:* Remember when you sign the purchase order for a product that limits the growth of your application, you commit yourself to rewriting your application. Growth considerations should include increase in data volume, increase in number of users, growth in application functionality, and hardware upgrades. A limited functionality product might be cheap to buy initially, but expensive in the long run if growth requires extra effort.

An important conclusion of this chapter is that if performance is critical in your application, you may have to sacrifice some of the nice features of DBMS products. This caveat is consistent with our earlier discussion that you have to pay a performance penalty for development convenience and nice interfaces. In practice, a simple solution to this dilemma is to overengineer your hardware requirements — which could provide excess power for the nice features you need. The continuing drop in the cost-to-power ratio encourages this approach.

14

Benchmarking Tips and Traps

When performance is critical in your application, you ought to benchmark the DBMS product to ensure that it will satisfy your performance criteria. You could simply test each of the products to choose the *fastest* one. However, sheer speed at any particular benchmark test is not an indication that the product will live up to your needs in a production environment!

A benchmark test is time consuming. To remain popular with your management, select two or three products based on their functionality, and then compare their performance. Generic product comparisons are definitely useful in this preliminary selection.

We examined some of the ways to determine whether performance is critical in Chapters 12 and 13. This chapter concentrates on how to set up and perform benchmark tests. We examine the following topics:

- *UNIX tools:* You can use some of the utilities provided by the operating system to measure process times and system activity during a time period. We discuss when to use these tools and when the traditional method of stopwatch timing is necessary.

- *Test model:* You need to build a model of the performance critical components of your application to conduct the tests. We examine the essential features of such a model and how to set up the test environment.

- *Interpreting test results:* We discuss how to interpret the results and extrapolate from them the likely performance of the application in a production environment. This extrapolation is tricky as you have to take into account the effect of reaching hardware limitations as the number of users and database size increases.

14.1 Getting Started

Generic comparisons of DBMS products, such as those published in trade magazines and journals, are a useful aid in choosing two or three products for your own test. They are a good starting point for determining which products might meet your needs. Keep in mind that such comparisons only cover the typical needs of applications. You would not want to be in the embarrassing position of spending your project budget on a product only to find out later that it does not permit a 132-column forms display! For such unusual requirements, you have to do your own investigation.

Most published benchmark tests only measure single user performance, so you cannot estimate the multiuser performance profile. They may not contain any transactions applicable to your requirements. Data presented by a benchmark conducted on hardware different from your configuration can be meaningless due to the differences in hardware speeds and limits. For example, benchmarks on a system capable of executing 6,000 system calls per second show significantly different results than a system capable of only 1,400 system calls per second. Such wide variations show up even on different systems all based on the same processor chip! If performance is critical in your application, you should conduct your own tests.

The main objective of a performance benchmark test is to discover the factors which govern multiuser performance with a given DBMS product. You collect measurements to gauge the trend of performance degradation with each additional active user. The performance degradation is often linear initially, with a nonlinear degradation trend starting as various system limits are exceeded.

The obvious measure in a test is the length of time taken to execute a set of transactions. This set should be large enough to provide a reliable measurement; that is, the total length of time should be consistent with very small variations no matter how often we execute it. A small set of transactions would typically take a short time to execute. It would therefore be likely to show wide variations in the total time. A good set size is such that the total execution time will be at least 10 minutes.

During execution of a test, here are measurements we might collect:

- **System calls:** The processor can only execute a limited number of system calls per second, as we discussed in Chapter 5. The number of system calls requested by the test process can indicate how many processes, similar to the test process, the processor could support before reaching the limit.

- **Disk access activities:** Read and write requests from the executing processes which cause physical disk I/O. This activity increases as the number of users increases, and will lead to performance degradation on reaching the throughput limits. You might use these measurements to initially optimize the DBMS product's use of memory buffers.

- **Swapping or paging activity:** This measurement shows use of memory by a process. By running several copies of the test simultaneously, you can determine the number of users your system could support before swapping or paging activities occur.

- **Terminal I/O:** Measuring terminal I/O in **raw** mode and **cooked** mode provides information on the overhead of the interactive interface used in the test. Relating these measurements to the total number of characters transferred indicates efficiency of the terminal interaction. Since these activities are included in the system calls measurement, they contribute towards reaching the system calls limitation as the number of users increases.

- *CPU utilization:* You need to measure the elapsed time for executing the test (real time), the CPU time used, and the percentage of time the CPU was idle during execution. This measurement indicates the amount of CPU time available for additional processes (that is, more users), provided that some other limit is not reached.

14.2 UNIX Tools

The UNIX operating system provides several tools for measuring different aspects of process performance. These utilities include *time*, *timex*, and *sar,* which you can use for benchmark measuring activities. We mentioned the sar utilities earlier in Chapter 5 as a tool for determining system bottlenecks.

The *time* utility reports three measurements for a given command: *real* time, *user* time, and *system* time. The command supplied to this utility would be the benchmark test program you wish to measure. Real time is the elapsed time for executing the command. User time is the percentage of the time spent in executing the code excluding any time spent in executing system calls. System time is the time spent in executing system calls requested by the command. Note that user and system time does not add up to the real (elapsed) time! You have to infer that the difference is idle time.

The timex utility also reports these three time measurements. In addition, it can also provide information on system activities, such as disk accesses and paging activity, for the entire system during execution of the command. Note that the system activity measurements are reported as averages over the execution time period and include activities caused by other processes running during the time period. Thus, these measurements are useful only when you run the test on a dedicated machine.

Using timex alone, it is difficult to find the baseline activity measures when the system is idle. The measurements reported by timex include unusually heavy activity caused by the initial program loading, which skews the calculation of the average. When you run multiple copies of a test simultaneously, the activity caused by second and subsequent program loading is significantly smaller due to sharing of code (*text*) segments of the program. For this reason, it is difficult to interpret the overhead due to an idle system from timex output.

Sar utilities report all of the system activity measurements at specified sampling intervals for a given period of time. In addition to the measurements we discussed as desirable, it reports on activities such as average process queue length and file access system routines, which are of little interest to application developers. The utilities consist of several programs: activity data collector, data formatter for a printable report (*sar*), and data formatter for a graphical report (*sag*). These programs may be presented under different guises in each implementation of UNIX. For example, the data collector might be started using the sar command on one implementation, or the *sadc* command on another.

Typical steps in activity data collection and reporting from collected data are:

1. Start the data collection utility and store its data in a file. Define the sampling interval to a reasonable period — say five or ten seconds — to keep the overhead of data

collection low. The total number of samples should be sufficiently large to cover the execution time of the test. Let the collector run for a little time allowing the system activities to settle down into idle mode patterns.

2. Run the test program.

3. When the test program completes, *kill* the data collector utility. Then, use the reporting utility (*sar(1)*) to obtain reports on the items of interest.

Note that the report formatter utility calculates averages between the start and end times you specify. You might find it helpful to use the ***date*** command just before starting the test program and after it completes, to obtain the period for which averages should be calculated by the report formatter utility. To exclude the unusually heavy activity during initial program loading, you need to estimate the number of intervals to ignore from the program start time.

In some types of tests it may be meaningless to time a function using system utilities. For example, in timing a test of a print job, you are interested in the total time required for the printer to complete printing, rather than the time required by the system to send all the print data to the printer. The system task will always complete long before the printer completes printing. In such cases, the only way is to use the traditional stopwatch method.

14.3 Designing DBMS Benchmarks

The most important part of a benchmark test is the function selected for testing. This function should have several attributes:

- It has a strict requirement for fast performance. For example, an account balance inquiry function in a banking system, which might have a required maximum completion time of seven seconds.

- It is sufficiently simple to prototype for a given product very quickly. Remember that with each product you have to first learn to use the product before you can build the prototype. The trial period for each product is usually too short for lengthy development even if your manager is willing to pay your salary!

- It represents a typical function from the performance critical portion of your application. For example, testing a new account creation function, when the majority of transactions involve account balance inquiry, does not yield a useful performance measurement.

- It is a task used by the maximum number of simultaneously active users. If a task such as order entry requires fast performance, but only one user is likely to perform it at any given time, multiuser benchmark tests for this task are meaningless.

It is a good idea to select two functions for testing: an interactive function and a batch function. This mix allows you to exercise the terminal intensive portion of the DBMS product as well as the disk access intensive portion. For the interactive function, you will need to prepare input scripts appropriate to the product's operation and the function being tested. Pacing the input of this script to the running program is very important for a realistic benchmark, as discussed in Section 14.4.

Testing a batch function is simpler since you need not account for the speed of human interaction. This test concentrates on the speed with which a DBMS can perform the transactions against the database. Note that you might initially prototype such a function using the query language or the fourth generation language, and consider accepting the product if it performs satisfactorily. If the performance is not satisfactory, you might then attempt the test using a program written with the host language interface.

Two key considerations in designing benchmark tests are:

- How much data should be loaded in the test database?
- How many users should the test simulate to obtain the performance trends?

14.3.1 How Much Data?

Most DBMS products slow down as the volume of data increases. With a large data volume, the size of indexes increases and they need to perform extra disk I/O for indexed searches even if you retrieve only one record. Thus, retrieving one record from a 1,000-record table is likely to be faster than retrieving one record from a 1,000,000-record table. Time taken by sequential searches increases proportionally to the number of records in a table.

For realistic benchmark tests, you should use a data volume close to your initial application database size. Does this mean that you need to load your entire application database? The answer depends on two issues: whether your chosen test needs the entire database, and the size of the entire database. Let your research on data volume requirements, as we discussed in Chapter 12, guide you in choosing the number of records to load into the required tables. Keep in mind that for tests involving inquiry operations, you need a sufficiently large number of records. However, an artificially large (or small!) database is likely to produce unrealistic measurements.

Consider practical limitations such as availability of disk space for conducting the benchmark. Your UNIX system administrator would not be too pleased to have to reconfigure the disk partitions just for your test. If the test program needs only one or two relation tables, you only need to load these. Products that implement a one relation per file approach will not be affected by data contained in other relation tables in the database. Products that implement a multiple relations per file approach might be affected, if some of the other relations share a file with those required for the test. Of course, you might not know at the time of test which relations would share files.

If you are rewriting an existing computerized system, you should be able to extract data from the existing files. Most DBMS products provide a utility to load data from a printable text format file into the database. This extracted data might need delimiters between each data field, such as a ASCII *tab* character or the vertical bar (|); the actual requirements depend on individual products.

Alternatively, you need to find some way to generate reasonable test data in sufficient volume. Generating such data can be tricky, as it has to produce patterns representative of your application data. Repetitive patterns, particularly on indexed fields, can result in an unreasonable load on the index search algorithms, and thus produce unexpected measurements. For example, if your test condition consists of a search for a particular customer by name, generating pathological patterns such as "AAAAAAA," "AAAAAAB" for customer names is unkind to the index algorithms. You would obtain better results by using a list of names such as "John Doe," "Mary Smith," and so on and composing customer names by a random combination of first and last names.

14.3.2 How Many Users?

In Chapter 12, we gathered information on the number of simultaneously active users of particular tasks in the application. We can use this information now to choose a suitable set of multiuser tests to obtain meaningful performance trends. The chosen test, clearly, must represent one of the tasks performed by many of these users. It is important to decide on the maximum number of users before starting your tests. The testing stops when you reach this maximum, even if you do not encounter any system limits!

Our objective is to discover the trend of performance degradation. So, you need to progressively test more and more simultaneous users, up to the maximum limit. Clearly, repeating the test with one extra user in each round takes a very long time and might not yield observable differences between each round of tests.

One way to arrange multiuser tests is to double the number of users in each round of tests. For example, start with a single user test for baseline measurements, then test with two users, followed by a four user test; and so on up to the maximum required number. You should see dramatic changes in measurements between each round as various limits are reached. For example, the four user test might take twice as long to complete as the two user test.

The problem is deducing which limits led to the degradation in speed. We need to know if we exceeded limits which can be rectified with more hardware or by tuning the software. For example, excessive swapping (or paging) can be rectified by simply adding more memory. Others, such as system call limit, mean that you require a faster processor which can execute more system calls per second. Sometimes, you do not see any unusually high figures for any measurement, which might mean that the degradation is due to reaching a combination of limits.

A workable alternative is to keep doubling the number of users until something breaks, then backing off by half of the increment. In this method, you would double the number of users in each round, until you notice an unreasonable increase in the test completion time. Then, you repeat the test with a smaller number of users to discover the causes. For example, say the test completion time of the eight user test was triple that of the four user test; you would repeat the test with six users.

If the task with strict performance requirements is not used by many users, you might need to combine its testing with a second task. This second task must be one that is performed in the same time period as the critical task. It might not have critical performance require-ments, but because it runs simultaneously with the first task, it affects the overall performance of the system. Ideally, you should not combine more than two tasks. Otherwise, your benchmark will go on for a long time, which would not make you popular with management or anyone else!

A benchmark test involving a combination of tasks lends itself to the second testing approach. The maximum number of users in such a test would be the maximum number of simultaneous users for each task. Doubling the number of users for each round might mean that you double users of each task equally until you find a dramatic change in completion time. Then you might try different combinations of users for each task within the range to discover the causes of degradation.

Remember to run at least one round of tests with the maximum number of users for the test task. After all, you need to know whether the product will support the performance critical portion of your application adequately. You might need to temper the results of this test based on the rectifiable causes of performance degradation. So, running this round on its own is not sufficient; you still need the intermediate rounds to discover causes that can be rectified. We discuss details of interpreting sar information in Section 14.6.

14.3.3 Generating Test Scripts

Typing input manually to an interactive test is really out of the question if you intend to test more than two or three concurrent users. Not only is the labor expense high, but obtaining people with sufficient free time is just too difficult. Off-hours dedicated machine access only increases your problem. So, you need to develop input scripts which let you simulate users.

Input scripts for interactive tests should represent the typical activities of the task. For example, for an interactive order entry task, you might need a script that enters a customer name, which automatically retrieves the associated customer number, then proceeds to input each field in the order. Another type of activity might simply retrieve a previously entered order, either by customer name or by order number. The test script would reflect both types of activity.

There are two ways to generate such input scripts:

- By manually typing all data and key sequences involved using a standard editor such as vi.
- By capturing input as the user types into the screen forms of the application.

Manual creation of scripts can be tricky. You need to input data in the exact order of form fields, and the escape and control sequences (generated by keys such as carriage return, arrow keys, and so on) must be correct. You need to be aware of the interpretation of these keys performed by the terminal device driver, due to the settings used by the product. For example, the terminal raw mode setting might result in the carriage return generating only the ASCII *CR* character, not the usual sequence *CRNL* (*return* character followed by a *newline* character). The input script must, in this case, only contain the CR character. Similar considerations hold for other ASCII control characters and escape sequences generated by other keys.

The alternative of capturing input as the data is typed into the screen form requires the use of UNIX utilities. The idea is to divert a copy of every character as it is received by the

DBMS product into a file, and also into the test program itself. The *tee* utility allows you to create a T-junction in a *pipe* for diverting data into a file. Thus, you might collect the input script by using the following command to start the test program:

```
$ cat -v < /dev/tty | tee -a in-script | testprog ...
```

This method works with products which are not fussy about their input (*stdin*) being redirected. You need to make sure that the initial capture utility does not buffer input, therefore we use the *-v* option to the *cat* command.

For an inquiry test, you need more diverse data to reflect typical activities. Try generating search field data from the database data itself. You will avoid spelling mistakes. If you created a printable text file for loading your test database, you can extract test input data from it. UNIX utilities such as *cut*, *paste*, and *grep* can be combined to extract specific fields from the file, and then manipulating them. You might sort the file, using the *sort* utility on a different field to randomize the sequence of values in the required search field. Then you could extract the required field and choose some number of records, say the first 1,000, as your test input data.

Remember that the number of transactions in an input script should be sufficient to meet the length of test time requirements we discussed earlier. If you choose too few transactions, the test will not run long enough to yield meaningful measurements; that is, it will be vulnerable to minor differences due to the asynchronous execution of processes. However, choosing a nice round number of transactions makes later calculations simpler, so don't get carried away trying to match the length of test time requirements.

14.4 Testing with *Realistic* I/O

Human typing speed is important in an interactive test. Many benchmark tests are conducted without considering the effect of human interaction. For example, an interactive test might simply obtain its input by utilizing the SHELL input redirection mechanism, and its output may be redirected to a file or discarded to the */dev/null* bit bucket. The SHELL redirection mechanism provides no controls to simulate human input speed. Input is fed as fast as the system can read the input script file, which is several orders of magnitude faster than a human can type.

Such a test goes against the principle assumed by most multiuser operating systems: A process needs to wait for I/O, and the operating system can use this waiting period to serve another process. If a process obtains its input as fast as the operating system can provide it I/O waiting periods will be unrealistically short. After all, a human user can never type as fast as a computer can!

Output to the terminal might similarly lead to waiting periods while the terminal actually displays data. Terminal display speed is significantly slower than the speed of disk I/O. /dev/null is, of course, the fastest output device of all! Some generic benchmarks completely disregard this consideration: They exclude all terminal activity overheads from their measurements. Such benchmarks are only useful if you intend to use intelligent workstations as terminals, not the common dumb ASCII terminals.

Some factors which might relieve bottlenecks on terminal I/O are intelligent I/O controllers. These controllers perform *direct memory access* (DMA) to relieve the central processor from character-at-a-time processing. Bypassing the terminal controllers — by redirecting output to files — creates an unrealistic test environment which is more suited to testing the hardware capabilities than a DBMS software product.

The typical typing speed of users varies for different types of functions. For example, the typical speed for a data entry function might be 10 characters per second (assuming a typing speed of 70 words per minute, and average word length of eight characters). In this case, the input script should be fed at the pace of 10 characters per second. In an inquiry function, however, a user performs a search which might yield several records, and then browses through the resulting records. In such a function the typing speed might only be two or three characters per second. In a browse mode, the user might take two to five seconds to examine the displayed record, before moving to the next record. The pacing of the input should reflect such activities.

You can make input feeding predictable by using a program which must pace its output to match the typical typing speed of users. You might then *pipe* the output from this *pacer* program into the interactive test. A sample pacer program written in C is shown in Figure 14-1. Note that this pacer program generates its output in bursts. Ideally you need a program that can pace output evenly over the specified period. However, UNIX does not provide any utility to allow you to build even pacing, since you would need a *sleep* function with a subsecond granularity.

Note that the screen based forms utilities of some DBMS products might behave differently if they set the terminal to raw mode. Depending on the actual raw mode settings used, you may have problems in using our simple pacer program. You may have to modify the pacer program to replicate exactly the raw mode used by the utility before starting up the utility as a child process. You can find the exact settings required by the utility as follows:

1. Run the utility on a terminal with a known device name, say *tty01*.
2. Login as superuser (*root*) on another terminal, and use the following command to list the terminal settings while the forms utility is running:

```
stty -a < /dev/tty01
```

Our simple pacer program needs modification to include code to set the terminal characteristics to handle such uncooperative utilities. Typically, we would use the *termio(7)* descriptions to change the terminal mode settings from within the program. These utilities can differ between UNIX implementations so we do not illustrate their use.

Some DBMS forms utilities behave differently if their output is redirected (*stdout*). For example, they might not output the terminal control sequences, such as cursor movement sequences, when they discover their output destination is not a real terminal (*isatty(3)*). Such sequences are an essential part of the processing performed by the terminal, and make a major contribution to degrading its speed of display. Thus, output without them again creates an unrealistic I/O environment. The only solution, in this case, is to send the test output to a real terminal. In Section 14.5 we discuss a way to preserve this connection to a terminal in an automated start-up procedure.

```
/* Sample program to pace input to an interactive forms driver
*/
/*                    Command line:
*/
/* pacer -f <script filename> -c<# of chars speed> -t<per # of sec-
onds>*/

#include <stdio.h>
#include <fcntl.h>
#define   TRUE    1
#define   FALSE   0

main(argc, argv)
char **argv;
int *argc;
{
     extern int optind;
     extern char *optarg;

     int no_char;                  /* typing speed: no of chars */
     int no_sec;                   /* per no of seconds         */
     char *file;                   /* pointer to script filename*/

     char buf[1024];               /* read buffer               */
     int wch;                      /* no of chars written so far*/
     int actch;                    /* actual no of chars read   */
     int done;                     /* loop completion variable  */

     /* set defaults */
     no_char = 1;
     no_sec = 1;

     /* get command line options */
     while ( (c=getopt (argc, argv, "f:c:t:")) != EOF) {
         switch (c) {
         case 'f':                 /* file name */
             file = optarg;
             break;
         case 'c':                 /* no of chars */
             no_char = atoi (optarg);
             if (no_char < 1)
                 no_char = 1;
             break;
         case 't':                 /* no of seconds */
             no_sec = atoi (optarg);
             if (no_sec < 1)
                 no_sec = 1;
             break;
         case '?':                 /* any other arguments*/
             fprintf (stderr, "pacer: command line error; usage \n");
             fprintf (stderr, "pacer -ffile -c# chars -t# seconds\n");
             exit(1);
         }
     }
```

```
    /* open and read script file */
    if ( (fd = open (file, O_RDONLY)) < 1) {
        fprintf (stderr, "pacer: cannot open script file %s\n", file);
        exit(2);
    }
    if ( (actch = read (fd, buf, BUFSIZE)) < 1) {
        fprintf (stderr, "pacer: empty script file %s\n", file);
        exit(3);
    }

    /* initialize counters */
    wch = 0;
    done = FALSE;

    /* loop writing the paced output until the end of script file*/
    while (done == FALSE) {
        while ( (wch+no_char) <= actch) {
            if (write (1, buf+wch, no_char) < 0) {
                fprintf (stderr, "pacer: error writing to stdout\n");
                exit(4);
            }
            wch += no_char;
            sleep (no_sec);      /* wait for specified seconds */
        }

        /*write remaining chars in buffer then read again from file*/
        if (write (1, buf+wch, (actch - wch)) < 0) {
            fprintf (stderr, "pacer: error writing to stdout\n");
            exit(4);
        }
        if ( (actch = read (fd, buf, BUFSIZE)) < 1) {
            /* successful completion */
            done = TRUE;
        }
        /* reset counters and continue */
        wch = 0;
    }
    exit(0);                        /* Done at last! */
}
```

Figure 14-1 A Simple Input Pacer Program

14.5 Running the Benchmarks

There are two basic phases in the test plan: single user performance measurement and multiuser performance measurement. Both phases ought to be carried out on a dedicated system — that is, with no other work being performed on the system. Remember that the sar utility measures activities on the *entire* system, not in an individual login session. With a dedicated system, you could obtain more accurate performance trend measurements. Unpredictable activities by other users during your benchmark test will skew the measurements.

Finding a dedicated system might be difficult only if your normal environment requires sharing a large machine with several other projects or applications. Even in such a case, you should be able to reserve a time period when you get the sole use of the machine for a benchmark test. In most cases, a UNIX machine is dedicated solely to one application, so you might not experience such problems.

Single user performance test are the easiest to conduct requiring no synchronized start time with other processes. This test establishes the baseline measurement for the benchmark. You need to collect all of the sar data for this test for comparing later with the multiuser tests. Examine these measurements to make sure that your hardware configuration is not underengineered. Remember that programs using a DBMS product can be very large and can consist of more than one process. If you see indications of swapping (or paging), your machine has too little memory. For a single user test, the process queue length (*-q* option of *sar*) should be almost nonexistent.

To conduct multiuser tests, you could use the *at* utility to synchronize start times. Typically, you would create a SHELL script to run the program with its input filtered by the pacer utility, and submit this SHELL via the *at* utility to run at some specified time. All jobs that are part of the same round of tests are submitted to run at the same time.

Since you will use the same test input script for each of you simulated users, you are likely to suffer from contention for the same data. To avoid concurrency contention, each job in a multiuser test should use its own copy of the database. Otherwise, the concurrency control locking scheme of the product might defeat your test purpose. Thus, for a four user test, you should create four separate copies of the database. Think about the amount of disk space you need to make duplicate copies of the test database. You might be able to use a single test database and still avoid major concurrency contention if you use distinctly different input values for each simulated user. Setting up such a test is rather tricky and so is frequently avoided. If your application is likely to involve a large number of locking conflicts, you ought to try simulating these in your test. Although determining the percentage of conflicts likely and then simulating them is no easy task.

The default security mechanisms of the product can also foil your plans for running all test jobs from one login id, unless you keep each copy of the database in a separate directory. These mechanisms might prevent you from simply copying the loaded database. One way to avoid these issues is to use a separate login id for each job in the multiuser test, with its own database. You will then need to create each individual database and load the data into each copy separately.

There are several steps in getting ready to run a multiuser test using our suggested plan:

- Create one login id for each user in the multiuser test. If you intend to test a maximum of 10 users, you need to create 10 separate login ids.
- Create a copy of the database for each login id, unless you plan to use a single large database.
- Load the same set of data into each copy of the database.

- Set up the profile of the login id to use the environment appropriate to the DBMS product.

- Create a SHELL for each type of test you intend to perform. This script should print the job start and stop times, using the UNIX date utility. Then, it should run the test program with the pacer utility to feed the input to the test from an input script.

- Make sure each login id has access to the SHELL scripts necessary to run the job.

It is easy to automate the entire benchmark test by simply writing a few SHELL scripts. You can use the *at* utility or the *cron* utility to automatically perform the steps for running a benchmark test. These utilities allow you to synchronize multiple tests so that you can simulate multiple concurrent users. Simultaneous tasks could start within a second of each other, probably a better precision than manually synchronized starts. If the test program is an interactive function, you can feed input via a pipe, or the input redirection mechanism of the SHELL. Don't ignore, however, the importance of pacing input to an interactive program which we discussed in Section 14.4. Running each round of tests then requires you to:

- Start the system activity data collection program in the background, to collect its data into a file.

- Login as each login id on separate terminals, so that the display output of each job goes to separate terminals.

- From each terminal, use the *at* command to schedule the job with sufficient time for you to schedule all jobs in a particular round of test. By scheduling the test from each individual terminal, you are establishing that terminal as the *control terminal* for the job. The UNIX kernel uses the control terminal mechanism to decide which processes should receive a *signal* such as *interrupt* or *quit*. Thus, any signals used internally by the DBMS product under test will be restricted only to that job and will not interfere with any other job in a round of tests.

- When the test is complete, *kill* the data collection program.

- Record the start and stop times of each job. To obtain sar data only when all jobs were running concurrently, note the latest start time and the earliest end time between jobs. Data collected for a period before and after these times only reflects some of the jobs, not all.

Automating these tasks is a fairly trivial task: It just involves writing a few SHELL scripts. Time spent in developing such SHELL scripts is probably well worth the trouble. You may even be able to run all of your tests unattended at some ungodly hour of the night!

Figure 14-2 illustrates a form for recording data as you perform each round of tests. You ought to record the measurements for each test immediately after the test to avoid later confusion. You can also examine the data as you record it for any unusual figures. Section 14.6 discusses some of the unusual measurements which indicate that some system limit has been reached. You can then modify further rounds of tests to find the causes.

Test Results Record

Test Type	No. Users	Start Time	End Time	(CPU Utilization)			(Process)		(System Calls)			(ttyio)	(diskio)		
				%usr	%sys	%other	pswch	pswap	scalls	sread+ swrit	rchar+ wchar	rawch+ canch+ outch	bread+ bwrit	lread+ lwrit	rcache+ wcache

Figure 14-2 Test Results Record Form

14.6 Interpreting Test Results

As you record the averages calculated by the sar reporting utility, you should examine the figures for unusual indications. Whether you test an interactive or a batch function, you should watch for subdued increases in: system calls per second, terminal I/O calls, disk I/O calls, and operating system overhead indicators. Initially you would examine these indicators to see if the associated cause can be rectified by adding hardware or by tuning the kernel. At the conclusion of the benchmark test, these indicators will help you to project the results for the entire application.

The indicators fall into two broad categories: I/O and CPU. I/O limits are reached when the maximum limits for system calls, disk access, or terminal I/O are exceeded. CPU limits can be attributed to CPU utilization such as when running computation intensive tasks and process overhead. Running too many processes can also limit the CPU due to the amount of process switching, swapping, or paging activities necessary.

14.6.1 I/O Limits Indicators

Reaching the system calls limit is often the first indicator of I/O limits. This is because all read and write calls, whether to disk or terminals, are system calls. Some of the system calls might be caused by the DBMS using UNIX facilities such as pipes and *message queues*. Thus, to rectify the causes leading to this limit you need to examine its components, namely disk and terminal accesses.

One indicator of reaching the system calls limit is when the sar figures stop rising between rounds of tests. Another way is to measure the maximum system calls capacity of your system with a simple test. Write a small program which loops indefinitely, counting the number of times it makes a system call, say *ctime(2)*. This program must set an alarm to interrupt this loop after one second. The count of system calls made during this one second period is an approximate maximum that your system can execute, though some system calls take longer to complete than others. This measurement does give you an idea of when the sar data on system calls is approaching the limits.

A typical interactive program performs a large number of reads and writes to the terminal, and hence a large number of system calls. The number of system calls per terminal input and output access is greater if the interactive application uses raw mode access than if it runs in cooked mode. As we saw in Chapter 5, screen form interaction requires the terminal to be in raw mode. Command based interaction, such as when using a query language, might run in cooked mode terminal access, thus making fewer system calls.

The majority of the I/O performed by a batch program are likely to be disk accesses, to read and write files and databases. Therefore, these accesses will probably account for the majority of the system calls in your test. After all, the program would not be a batch program if it interacted with a user! Storing the database in filesystem files might lead to extra reads and writes as the kernel accesses indirect blocks for large files.

System Calls Measurements:

The *sar -c* option reports total system calls, a breakdown of read, write, fork, and exec system calls, and the number of characters read or written on average by read and write calls, respectively. The total system calls figure stops rising when the maximum system calls limit is reached. The read and write figures include both disk and terminal I/O, and so are of rather limited use. These numbers are frequently large. What you really need is an individual breakdown by terminal or disk I/O, given by the *-b* and *-y* options.

An important figure to examine is the average size of read or write calls. If this size is large, you might benefit by tuning the kernel or by using a raw disk for your database. The decision depends on the ratio of logical read/write to physical read/write figures in the buffer activity report (-b option).

Terminal I/O Measurements:

The items of interest reported by the *sar -y* option are the raw input characters, canonical (cooked) input characters, and output characters rates. Large raw input character rates are common on an interactive forms based test. Keep in mind that a large number in this case equates to a large number of system calls. If you redirect input and output for the test program, you may not see any figures reported here.

Disk I/O Measurements:

These measurements include buffered read/write (bread, bwrit), logical read/write (lread, lwrit), cache hit ratios (rcache, wcache), and raw disk read/write (pread, pwrit). Transfers into and out off buffers (bread, bwrit) are the number of read/write calls which had to access the disk to be satisfied. They show similar limiting patterns to the overall system calls; that is, there is a definite maximum limit due to the disk hardware throughput limit. If your test reaches this limit, you probably need faster hardware or more physical disk units (and controllers) to spread out the load.

Logical read/write measurements indicate the actual number of read/write system calls made by the test, some of which were satisfied from kernel buffers, and others required a disk access (bread, bwrit). Remember that accesses to the indirect blocks in a filesystem file are also read/write calls, which are included in this report, although the test did not directly make these calls. If you notice the test reaching the limits on logical read/writes, you may need a larger processor capable of executing more logical read/write system calls.

The ratio of logical read/write figures to the buffered read/write figures indicates the overhead imposed by using the filesystem. If the average size of transfer (reported in the system calls section) is large, you can reduce the filesystem overhead by using a raw disk, if allowed by the DBMS product. Using a raw disk allows you to eliminate the overhead of indirect blocks inherent in the filesystem structure.

Cache hit ratios (rcache, wcache) indicate the efficiency of kernel buffering. If these figures are low, say less than 50%, you can increase the kernel buffer size to obtain a higher hit ratio. A higher hit ratio means that more read/write calls are satisfied from the memory buffers, thus avoiding the overhead of actual disk access. Notice that if your test involves sequential access, such tuning can yield a significant performance improvement. For sparse access involving random disk accesses, you could explore the benefits of interfile clustering provided by some DBMS products. This will not improve the access speed for individual searches, but makes a difference to the speed of reading the data found as a result of the search.

14.6.2 CPU Limits Indicators

CPU limits indicators are often the easiest to interpret, since they relate to the horse-power of your processor. There are very few interdependencies as are evident with I/O indicators. The two broad categories of these indicators are: CPU utilization, and process overhead. Both categories help you determine whether the test is I/O or CPU bound.

CPU Utilization:

The *sar -u* option reports CPU utilization as percentage of time spent in user mode (*%usr*), system mode (*%sys*), idle with some process waiting for I/O (*%wio*), and idle with no work (*%idle*). The %idle figure approaches 0 (zero) only for computation intensive tests requiring very little I/O. A 20% idle time is quite reasonable in most data processing activities. If the idle time is not zero, and you still experience performance degradation, your test is I/O bound and the %wio figure will be proportionately high.

High idle time, say 40% to 50%, indicates that either you are not stressing the system enough, or your test is severely I/O limited. In such instances, you may notice that actual throughput to the terminal is lower than its baud rate setting. Under such circumstances, adding more terminals to the same terminal controller will only make matters worse. You would be better advised to spread the terminal load over more terminal controllers. A similar argument holds for disk I/O. Spreading the database over several physical disks on several controllers can improve the I/O throughput, until you reach the I/O bus throughput limit.

Process Overhead:

Process overhead includes process switching, swapping, or paging, and process run-queue length measurements, reported by the *sar -w* and *-q* options. Process switches (*pswch*) indicate the number of times the kernel had to schedule changes to running a process, which increases as the number of processes on the system increases. Keep in mind that each individual test can, and frequently does, consist of several processes, even if you only see the front-end interface to one user.

Related to process switches is the run-queue length (*runq-sz*) consisting of processes which are ready to run but are waiting for their slice of CPU time. A run-queue length of two or fewer processes indicates that the system is I/O bound. In this case, reducing I/O will improve system performance. A longer run-queue length, say four or more processes, indicates a lack of CPU horsepower. In this case, your only solution is to buy a bigger machine!

We have already discussed swapping and paging overheads many times in this book. This limitation is often the easiest to overcome by simply adding lots more memory to your system. A simple rule of thumb is to keep adding more memory until swapping or paging stops, then add some more for luck! Note also that there is hidden I/O involved in these activities, so reducing them also alleviates, to some extent, your disk I/O bottlenecks.

14.7 Conclusions

This chapter concentrated on the techniques of setting up and running benchmark tests for evaluating DBMS products. The key issues in a benchmark test are:

- *The test model:* The chosen test function is representative of a performance critical portion of your application. You clearly cannot perform benchmarks for the entire application without first building it, which would be a time consuming process. Let's face it: An evaluation requiring a significant amount of time, months perhaps, is not going to aid you in keeping your job!

- *Realistic I/O:* Your test environment has to simulate I/O speeds representative of a human user. The speed with which a user types is several orders of magnitude slower than disk I/O. Factors which affect I/O speed include not only a typing speed suitable for input to the task being tested, but also the output being displayed on a screen. Ignoring these issues turns your benchmark test into a test of hardware speed, rather than a test of the performance of a DBMS product.

- *System activity data:* You can use the comprehensive tools provided by UNIX, such as sar, to monitor the activities during the test. You can use miscellaneous tools to automate many of the tedious tasks of running benchmark tests. Some effort spent in designing your use of these tools allows you to run the entire benchmark without requiring several hands, and possibly even entirely unattended.

- *Activity trend monitoring:* The primary purpose of the data collected during the benchmark test is to identify the trend as the number of users increases. This trend information allows you to detect the system limits which cause performance degradation, some of which might be easily rectifiable by adding more hardware. Thus, just testing for the maximum number of users is insufficient.

- *Test results:* You need to collect and record test results as each test is run, to avoid confusion. The sar report formatter can do most of the averaging calculations for you, if you record the start and stop times of each test. You would establish the baseline figures from a single user test, to compare with multiuser tests. Sar provides comprehensive measurements for you to detect and rectify limits which are amenable to additional hardware, kernel tuning, or DBMS product tuning facilities.

An important point in benchmark tests is to establish meaningful requirements first. Arbitrary statements, such as needing one second response time, are likely to cause you severe disappointment.

Response times perceived by users are definitely the key factor in deciding whether a product is suitable. The benchmark tests give you hard numbers from which you can estimate overall load on the system. But, in the end, a chatty product which puts out lots of messages is likely to be more popular with your users, than a uncommunicative product which actually runs faster.

Part 5

Future Directions

Finally, this part of the book vents some wild (but not so woolly!) ideas about what we are likely to see in the future. Although the DBMS technology itself is fairly mature, it holds some exciting prospects for changing our interaction with computers! Since computer databases are more and more involved in our daily lives, these potential developments have far-reaching implications.

It is unlikely that we will remain in today's stone age of computing where humans have to adapt to the style of computers, especially when using DBMS products. Tools to easily adapt database interfaces to the human way of working will be here (real soon now!). We already see the early attempts of implementing these technologies, although they are not likely to be used extensively in everyday business for some time to come.

Don't become complacent that we know everything there is about building database applications. There is work out in the real world which we have not even thought of as a DBMS application yet! These challenges will probably show shortcomings in our current thoughts. So, take these flights of fancy with a little grain of salt: They are based on what we know today. Tomorrow will probably be different!

15

What's Next?

In this chapter, we take up the discussion of several topics which we deferred in earlier parts of the book. You may wonder why such important topics as distributed databases and expert systems have been deferred to the final chapter. The reason is they are quite involved and really deserve a separate book. So we cannot do them justice by mixing them with the principle concerns of this book. This chapter will simply point out the chief issues in these areas.

The topics in this chapter center around two main themes: multiple machines and advanced tools. In the multiple processor theme, we examine:

- When and why you might consider building an application that needs the database to reside on more than one system.

- Products that allow you to distribute your database on more than one machine with a view to the types of access they can provide.

The advanced tools theme, on the other hand, concentrates on newly developing technologies and their connection to DBMS products. The obvious relationship is that these new tools also attack problematic areas in the application development process. In particular, this chapter reviews two of the emerging technologies: Computer Aided Software Engineering (CASE) tools and Expert Systems technologies.

Realize that successive topics in this chapter go further and further into the realm of research subjects. Even some of the hot topics of today, say Expert Systems, are still in their embryonic stages as far as everyday business use is concerned. There are many problems associated with these areas which we have not yet resolved. Others we simply have not encountered. Remember that it took nearly 10 years for the research on relational data models to develop into mature commercial products\mand we are still finding new problems to solve!

15.1 Why Use Multiple Machines?

Most applications share data amongst several users. Some users update the database, others extract data interactively or as reports to serve some business function. The database for such applications, in most cases, can be stored on a single machine since UNIX based machines cover the entire range from personal computers to mainframes. DBMS products, even in the late 1980s, are really intended for a centralized database, although a few products advertise the ability to support *distributed databases*. Before you get carried away with these developments, let us examine when and how you might distribute your database over several machines.

15.1.1 Geographic Locations

A classic reason for distributing a database over several machines is geographic distribution of application users. It clearly applies only to corporations with geographically distributed offices. A further requirement is that these geographically distributed offices have a need to share some data. For example, a company with warehouses and sales offices in many locations. If each location runs as a separate entity — for example, as a subsidiary of the parent company — no data sharing is necessary. Each location can simply run the application independent of others.

With a single centralized database, you have to use complex communications networks connecting geographically distributed terminals to the central application. Such databases have traditionally been the domain of mainframe systems. With UNIX terminal handling procedures, the networks simply consist of dial-in public telephone lines or multiplexed connections over dedicated lines. So you might try to save the cost of communications by building the application to run locally for each group of users.

But cost savings is not a sufficient condition to use multiple machines. The nature of your data must also support distribution of data. Consider for example what happens to your cost savings if users at each location have to frequently connect over some network to access data generated by another location. Distributing the database is really only achievable if you can minimize the cross-location data access.

Ideally, most of the access by a group of users should be to their local database. They may need the ability to obtain data from another location. However, a facility to use this cross-location connection should be necessary for only a small proportion of time. One of your choices for this cross-location connection might be occasional transfer of data — for example, transferring overnight summaries of data to a higher supervisory level. This scheme can be very efficient in terms of communications costs. Think about the fact that the transferred data might be out of date by the time the transfer takes place or the higher level supervisor reads it!

For access to up-to-date information, you might use an interactive connection method to download data on an ad hoc basis. This method obviously needs to be *very* easy to use, or it will simply be ignored. Downloaded data obviously still gets out of date if it stays around for an appreciable amount of time, just like data in printed reports.

Alternatively, you might use a distributed database management system which allows you access to data on remote machines as if it was part of your own database. Note that the type of network connection between geographically distributed machines has a profound effect on the performance of such products. Remember that the throughput over a typical network is an order of magnitude smaller than the throughput of a disk I/O subsystem. In long distance communications, there are small delays, simply because of the distances involved, delays which we do not notice in voice communications. Such delays become traumatic in data transfers. There can be further delays in data transmission due to error detection and correction processing.

In some of the products, the network connection must be active all of the time the application is active. It is difficult to see how this solution could be justified in terms of communications cost savings. It is probably better suited to the case where the different machines are still located in a single facility or perhaps distributed in a small area, using private communications networks or even short pieces of cables. Maybe, if access to up-to-date information is so essential to your company then communications costs are not a major factor.

15.1.2 Processing Load Distribution

Another reason for wanting to use multiple machines might be to distribute the processing load of an application, so that you could support a large number of users of the application. After all, buying and running several smaller machines is quite a bit cheaper than running one large mainframe. For example, compare the cost of a network of a few dozen SUN or APOLLO workstations to the cost of a single large AMDAHL or IBM mainframe. So, why don't we have more such networks in normal business use?

One of the biggest problems with a network of small machines is how to administer them in a sensible manner. Consider, as an example, the simplest administration activity: backups. To handle this activity without the system administrator backing up each workstation individually, you need to use a server to control all of the disks. In this case, you are still really using a centralized database, with possibly the interactive processing distributed on the individual workstation. Although this distribution relieves a significant load from the central database server, access to the database is still a bottleneck.

Alternatively, we could distribute the data on to several workstations. Of course, this distribution has to ensure that most of the data access is local if we are to avoid overwhelming the network with data transmissions. Taking backups becomes a very difficult activity. For example, we could take backups of each workstation from a single console. But what happens when users power off their machines before going home, disabling access to their disks?

You could, perhaps, simply teach users to take their own backups. *(What about their backups when users are on vacation?)* The problem with a distributed database, then, is how to obtain a consistent copy of the entire database. The strategy for recovery becomes so complex that we leave it up to you to imagine. There are several other administration problems along similar lines: access security, user id administration, and so on. Administrative activities, necessary for a production application, are so much easier to tackle in a centralized database environment.

Alternative ways of distributing processing load include loosely coupled architectures like the VAX clusters, or tightly coupled architectures of multiple processor machines like the UNISYS high-end UNIX machines. These architectures basically support several processors for running the applications while sharing the same disks. You increase the number of processors, or machines in a cluster, to support more users. Such configurations work well from the administrative viewpoint, but are really not a distributed database architecture in the sense discussed in Section 15.2. What they do instead is just add more mips at the central facility, even though they might be cheap mips.

15.1.3 Departmental Distribution

This option could actually be an ideal combination of advantages from the topics discussed in Sections 15.1.1 and 15.1.2. Departments of a large corporation are often distributed geographically. Each department's data is usually autonomous; at least a major portion is used only locally. They could therefore run their own machines, each with a local database, its own DBA, and application administrator. Each department's machine might be connected with some network, Local Area Network (LAN), or a long distance communication network, as appropriate to their location.

In some distributed applications using this departmental breakdown, you might want to divide relational tables horizontally – that is, each department has rows pertaining to that department. In this scheme, the *union* of all departmental tables provides the corporate view. Other ways of department level breakdown might require different ways of connecting to obtain a corporate view. In other circumstances, you might simply use independent tables containing data particular to each department. The corporate view, then, is simply the collection of these individual tables, referenced by their individual names. There might be no connection at all between these tables in the corporate view.

Some of the commercially available products provide some of the functionality needed to support such a set up. Section 15.2 reviews the types of facilities available with reference to the data distribution strategies you might consider.

Most of the bigger corporations fit this mold; they all have a hierarchy of departments. But planning and implementing such a distributed system is not a trivial task. A corporate level systems plan is of paramount importance in order to understand the relationships between departmental and corporate level data. The key to successful implementations is to provide for autonomous local needs while maintaining the relationships to the corporate view of the data.

Despite the similarity of activities between multiple departments, each department invariably manages to work in some different manner or use different aspects of data, different DBMS products, even different hardware. The plan has to cope with all of these dissimilarities, maybe with heterogeneous distribution. A plan that mandates a standard method of departmental activities has a high probability of failing (or of its use simply fading out over a period of time).

15.2 Distributed Systems

In Chapter 5, we listed three types of distributed access methods. Since there are no formally accepted definitions of these types, this section describes the author's view of these facilities in more detail. We also examine, in reference to these methods, the facilities available in commercial products.

Research in the distributed access techniques is in a ferment right now. We informally discuss some of problems this research has discovered. We are not likely to see large-scale business use of some of the research schemes for some years. The real challenge of this emerging technology is the many unknown problems of developing applications for distributed systems.

We have barely mastered the art of designing and developing comparatively straightforward applications on a single machine. We are still struggling with corporationwide data: Never mind developing an integrated plan for managing this data when it is distributed over different machines! Besides, the techniques implemented by products for distributed systems will probably be different tomorrow, in light of some new research theory.

There are many practical problems involved in maintaining a distributed database architecture. For example, what happens when the DBMS software version on the local machine does not match that on the remote machine? Some commercial products, such as RTI INGRES, make specific allowances for compatibility of different versions. Others take the view that you should use the same version of software on all machines, so that the problem does not arise. Unfortunately, imagine the problem of coordinating even 10 sites spread out over the continental U.S. especially when upgrading to a new release of software.

By the way, hard luck if you are trying to connect existing applications developed with diverse products. Most products only allow distributed databases if you use their product throughout. Even products with published interfaces are of little use: You need a massive development effort to connect your existing applications to a database with such an interface.

DBMS products are in the same stage of operation as the early railroad companies, when each railroad had its own track gauge. We can only hope that DBMS vendors will standardize their *tracks* as their railroad counterparts did early in this century. The ideal distributed system is really not possible until then.

15.2.1 Network Database Systems

Network database systems are essentially a collection of *individual* databases which reside on two or more machines where each machine is connected to others by some network. Note that there may not be physical connections from one machine to each of the others, but some logical mechanism to access all of the other machines exists. The details of how networks are set up and protocols are used for communications are subjects needing their own book. So, we won't go into these details. We concentrate, instead, on the data management and access aspects as viewed by users and DBA.

You can access any database on a network system by specifying the database name. A user does not have to specify literal addresses involving network types, protocols and so on. There is generally a logical name for the remote database location involving a ***node-name*** and a ***database-name***. So you do not need to know *where* the database is, only *what* it is *called*.

Once connected to the database, you proceed with your access just as if it resided on your local machine. You can perform any operation that you might perform on a local database, provided you have the appropriate access security permissions. A user is not aware that the access data is actually being transported from a remote system over a network, except that it is slower. This scheme is quite sufficient for cases where you merely need to access a remote database or to download data from it to a local database. Unfortunately, you have to know which database you wish to access and deliberately connect to it.

Clearly, network database systems might run on different DBMS products, different hardware, or a different operating system, not necessarily UNIX. The INGRES Gateway products, ORACLE SQL*CONNECT, INFORMIX REPORT/DB2 and BATCH/SPUFI, and FOCUS connectivity products are examples of heterogeneous network database systems. They allow you to access databases created by other products, possibly on dissimilar operating system environments.

Typical implementations of such a scheme use the front-end interface and back-end server architecture. When accessing a local database, both of these processes run on the local machine. When accessing a remote database, the front-end interface process still runs on the local machine, but the back-end server runs on the remote machine where the data resides. Thus, the network traffic between these processes is minimized to a few messages and the data resulting from some operation. Without this architecture, all of the necessary data for an operation, including perhaps the data dictionary and indexes, would have to be transported over the network.

Products such as INGRES/NET from RTI and SQL*Net from ORACLE provide network facilities. You may be restricted to accessing one database at a time, or be allowed simultaneous access to many, depending on the product. Obviously, you can extract data from a remote database and import it into your local database. But, by the time you get to use this downloaded data, it may well be outdated.

Many products are trying to minimize even the access request traffic by providing procedural extensions to SQL. They allow you to define a set of statements which is treated as a single processing unit by the database server. The server then receives the entire set as a single request and returns only the final result to the requestor. The ORACLE PL/SQL, SYBASE TRANSACT-SQL, and INGRES *Compiled Transaction* facilities are examples of such interfaces.

Users of network databases do not need to know the low-level details of which network, or which protocol is used. They simply use a logical name to refer to the remote database. A DBA, on the other hand, is responsible for setting up the definition of the logical names for remote databases. This definition usually involves specifying the type of network connection and the protocols used such as TCP/IP. Users cannot access a remote database without such a definition being set up first. Obviously, setting up meaningful *logical* names is a great help towards making this scheme easy to use. For example, basing node-names on geographic locations and database-names on departments helps users to remember them. Node-names such as "sysa" or "sysb" are difficult to relate to applications and are really leftovers from the historical use of codes in the computer industry.

15.2.2 Distributed Database Systems

A distributed database presents the view of a single database to the user, even though the data might be spread over several machines. Connecting to the database does not require knowledge of where any of the data might reside. The DBA, of course, has to define the location of each part of the database and specify the method of communicating with remote machines. Keep in mind that throughput of network components is still a bottleneck. So data distribution should be such that the majority of the access is to the locally stored portion of the database. Some commercial implementations of a somewhat limited distributed database system are the INGRES/STAR and ORACLE SQL*STAR architectures.

An ideal sought by distributed database systems is to provide a view of the database transparent of the underlying data distribution and hardware components involved. For example, if one machine participating in the distributed database system fails, the loss should be completely transparent to users. When this machine comes back on line, it should be able to continue to participate seamlessly. Clearly, this objective is similar to those of a fault-tolerant computer systems. However, there are many obstacles to achieving this utopian goal.

Providing a single view of the database requires that the DBMS use a data dictionary which is extended to include the distributed database. The extended data dictionary might contain information on the location of each portion of the data. Details of network protocols need only be set up once when a machine is linked into the distributed database. The difficulty is whether to maintain a single *master* dictionary which is used by all at runtime, or whether each machine should maintain its own copy of the entire extended dictionary, or some mixture of both. These extended dictionaries are sometimes called *common data dictionaries*. There are problems to be solved with each approach.

Keeping a single master copy of the data dictionary means that there is one major point of failure. If the machine containing the master copy is down, the distributed database is inaccessible, except perhaps the local portion. Keeping one copy of the dictionary on each machine means any change to the database structure has to be reflected on all copies. This task is tedious at best, prone to human error, and must be done when all machines participating in the distributed database are on-line. However, loss of any single machine in this scheme is less drastic, amounting to possibly losing only a portion of the database.

Data storage strategy is a complex subject in the distributed database technology. To provide full transparency, data cannot be stored as a single copy. Single copies of data mean that failure of one machine impacts the user's view since some data becomes unavailable. Suppose then that data is replicated into several copies without the user being aware of it. Maintaining consistency among these copies becomes a complex task. Consider, for example, the problem of bringing a crashed machine back on-line. The copies of data maintained on this machine must be brought up to date with machines maintaining other copies. Of course, new transactions keep pouring in during the recovery process. These types of problems ought to be handled by the DBMS and should not concern a user.

Queries in a distributed database ought to hide data location and routing details from the user. Since users see the distributed database as a single entity, their queries have to be decomposed into component parts where each component refers to the appropriate remote portion of the database. Each component of the query must then be passed to the appropriate remote server process, and the results collected and consolidated before they are presented to users. Both INGRES/STAR and SQL*STAR support such facilities.

Concurrency control for updates in a distributed database is an exciting area of research which is not yet resolved. If an update involves data distributed over more than one machine, the update must be decomposed into its component parts, similar to the query decomposition. Obviously, a *commit* cannot succeed until each component update is completed successfully. This means that the appropriate remote parts of the database must be individually locked prior to starting the update and kept locked until all update components complete. There is a clear increase in the requests for number of locks, acknowledgments of granted locks, update messages, acknowledgments of successful updates, and finally unlock requests. The difference in the amount of work between a distributed system and a centralized database could easily be two orders of magnitude. Completion of all components might take an appreciable time depending on network traffic and load on the remote systems.

It would not be difficult to imagine one of the remote machines going off-line in the middle of a distributed update. This would lead to further work in rolling back the transaction, even on those machines where updates completed successfully. One of the popular schemes used is a *two-phase commit.* The first phase in this scheme consists of completing the individual components, the second phase merely finalizes the updates after every component completes successfully.

Data replication simply increases the complexity of concurrency control. For example, should all copies of the data be successfully updated before the update is considered successful? In this case, how should machines temporarily off-line be treated — should updates involving their data fail? If we only update one copy successfully before considering the update successful, then how should the change be propagated? The database is left in an inconsistent state if the machine containing the single up-to-date copy fails before propagating the change to others containing replicated data. Again, these are problems which a DBMS ought to handle.

Distributed database systems are still in their infancy. Much more research and development is needed before they can meet their ambitious objectives. There is much to be learned on the part of application developers, too. Planning, analysis, and design techniques for corporate level business models have emerged only in the 1980s. These techniques need further refinement to take into account strategies for distributed database systems. Corporate level systems planners need to consider methods for local autonomy while maintaining an integrated corporate model based on distributed database systems. Planners have a tough job ahead unless they can read a crystal ball.

15.2.3 Heterogeneous Distributed Systems

Heterogeneous distributed systems combine databases created by dissimilar DBMS products running on dissimilar operating systems. In the IBM operating systems' environment, access between databases created by dissimilar products has been fairly common. Under UNIX, connection between dissimilar product databases is a new concept. Many UNIX DBMS products do, however, have heterogeneous network links to other operating systems. They are a first step towards heterogeneous distributed databases.

The principles and consequent problems of heterogeneous distributed systems are the same as with any distributed system. There are actually additional problems that must be resolved in producing a single view of databases residing on different operating systems.

One of the problems occurs between ASCII based machines and EBCDIC based machines. The collation sequences of these character set definitions differ significantly. Thus, query results sorted by a back-end server on an EBCDIC machine and presented to a user working on an ASCII machine, or vice versa, would not make sense. The front-end interface process, therefore, must sort the final results before presenting them to the user. The problem of dealing with different character sets can only get worse as we take this concept logically further: What if the front-end interface works in Japanese?

Clustering of data for improved performance in a relational system will clearly have different effects on physical data storage sequence. The designer would have to evaluate the beneficial effects of this procedure in a new light.

Although automatic conversion between most EBCDIC and ASCII is possible, a few printable characters in one set have no representation in the other. DBMS products do not impose any restrictions on the characters you can use in the data fields. However, you might simply disallow the use of such characters for the sake of preserving the meaning of translated characters. Note that the DBMS itself performs the actual character translation and may not allow you any control over it. Additional problems arise if the translation requirement involves non-English characters.

A completely different set of issues arise in providing a seamless view of a database if some of its portions reside under a different DBMS product. The easiest combination is, of course, if all portions use a relational data model, even if implementation architectures differ. Combinations involving products based on other data models are rather more tricky.

Support of SQL by many different products will go a long way towards making support of nonrelational products possible. Without this unifying language, the data dictionary for a heterogeneous database needs to become a great deal more complex. It needs to include not only location and network protocol information, but also information on the database structure used under each particular DBMS product. Such information, of course, makes keeping the data dictionary up to date much more difficult, since it will have to be updated passively after the product's own dictionary has been updated.

15.3 Analyst's Tools

Computer Aided Software Engineering (CASE) tools go a long way towards helping you use the development methodology of your choice. With their graphics oriented data and process representation they make it easy to build visual application models, which was a mammoth task when all we had was paper and pencil. CASE tools already provide data dictionary generation facilities suitable for many commercial DBMS products.

One of the nice features of CASE tools is their prototyping facility for user interfaces. This facility is advocated to save many specification changes in the later stages of development by involving users in the early stages of design. But, DBMS products already provide prototyping tools: forms drivers and fourth generation languages. There is no reason to consider DBMS facilities as merely fast coding aids! So, the obvious development is to interface CASE analysis tools with DBMS fourth generation languages rather than having yet another prototyping separate tool.

The advantage of such integration is that users could evaluate not only the layout of screen forms and reports, but also the *feel* of the interface. They could actually try using the prototype on a test database, say for inserting data, or querying the database. In cases where performance of the DBMS fourth generation system is sufficient, we could simply adopt a late model prototype as the production module. Where faster performance is necessary, we could use the code generation facilities of CASE tools for generating third generation programming language programs for better performance.

The problems in achieving this integration are really due to the different levels at which the two technologies operate. DBMS fourth generation facilities expect you to prepare and define a great deal of detailed information such as field validation and editing criteria. CASE analysis and design tools are usually too cumbersome to use at such level of detail. Practitioners of these tools frequently stop using the tool long before specifying such details.

The integration then is more complex than imagined at first glance. CASE data dictionaries (not to be confused with DBMS data dictionaries which are really database schemas) contain quite a lot of information about individual data items. Small extensions to these data dictionaries could probably provide the details needed by DBMS fourth generation facilities. Similarly, standardized process descriptions, such as those using *action diagrams,* might provide information on how different screens plug together, and other miscellaneous information such as appropriate help messages.

CASE tools serve an important function in the future of UNIX in the application development environment. UNIX machines with their advantages of portability and low price are suitable environments for departmental distribution of data. However, some changes to UNIX become important to support integrated graphics, prototyping, development, and production system environments.

Traditional UNIX text terminals are insufficient and cannot handle the graphical interface necessary for CASE. We really need the types of terminal interface supported by UNIX systems based on workstations and personal computers. A UNIX filesystem scheme has too high an overhead for developing large application models, but DBMS products already fill in this deficiency.

15.4 Natural Language Interfaces

Recently, a few third party products providing a ***natural language*** interface to DBMS became available. The concept is, of course, not new: The RAMIS product had its ENGLISH even in the very early 1980s. What significance do these interfaces have on DBMS technology? The potential for a significant impact is not immediately obvious.

Briefly, these natural language interfaces replace the function of query languages for interactive data access. They are *natural* in the sense that they are closer to the English language than any query language like SQL could be, and much less structured. You could view them as just another query language. Realize that these languages are like English only in the context of accessing the application data in a particular database. For example, you would not get a useful response with a query regarding employees if the current database only contained marketing data. The interface functions strictly relate to database access such as inquiry, print, update, and delete. Although they allow you to use many different sentence constructions to perform these functions, you really could not request a cup of coffee using any of them!

Establishing the context is an important facet of the ability to use a natural language in accessing a database. The DBMS application database provides this context. This requirement is essential because of the ambiguities of natural language. As an example consider a question any manager might ask: *How well is Mary (or some person) doing?* In normal conversation between sales managers discussing a salesperson, this question most probably refers to the sales achievements of Mary. On the other hand, the question posed of a medical patients database by a physician, might easily refer to Mary's current state of health. In yet another case, the same question posed of a payroll database might mean how well are Mary's career goals being met in terms of salary or promotions. The types of ambiguities of the word *well* and how some of these natural language interfaces handle them should be abundantly clear from this example.

There are other problems these interfaces also have to deal with. The construction of the sentence can generate ambiguities. For example, in the context of a particular discussion the shortened sentence: *How is Mary doing?* might still have the same meaning as the construction including the word *well.* Good natural language interfaces have to deduce your meaning from more than just the single sentence. Such topics are an area of much research under the guise of ***Computational Linguistics,*** an area which contributes to many other artificial intelligence fields such as machine translation, natural language understanding, and information systems for libraries.

The potential these interfaces portend is the possibility of being able to ***talk*** to the computer, albeit in the limited sense of getting data in and out of a database. Invariably these interfaces will combine with the advances in the ***voice recognition and synthesis*** technology to provide such a facility. The potential change to our methods of communicating with a database application implied by this scenario are almost unimaginable. Human-computer interface specialists will be hard at work figuring out the principles of this new method for many years to come, just when they thought they understood the principles of good interaction using a screen and a keyboard.

This real change in our method of communicating with a computer database will probably mean that typing skills (even those two-finger typists amongst us technical people) might become obsolete! Imagine it: No more clutter of terminal keyboards on our desks, or massive computer printouts! A display screen and voice input mechanism might be all we need, and the physical size of these is getting smaller day-by-day! Such a science fiction-like scenario is closer in the technological developments than you might think.

15.5 Expert Systems

A simplified description of an expert system is a system that holds *knowledge* of experts in a particular field. A widely known example of an early expert system is MYCIN, a medical diagnostics expert system. In the 1980s many commercial products, called ***expert system shells***, gained popularity in business applications. These shells are building tools for certain types of business applications, just like DBMS products are building tools for data processing applications. An expert system developer gathers knowledge about a particular area from the human experts and composes it into a database for the Shell to store. This knowledge can then be retrieved by users when performing functions relating to the subject, just as if requesting the advice of an expert.

The early implementations of expert system applications are obviously very primitive from our rather simplistic description. However, our description serves to illustrate, in an informal manner, the hopes and aims of expert systems. The difference between a DBMS application, even one with a natural language interface, and an expert system application is fundamentally the nature of what they store. A DBMS application stores data without attaching any meaning to it, though some meaning is implied by names used to identify records and fields. Its natural language interface uses these identifying names, together with their common synonyms, to provide you with data access facilities.

An expert system also needs data of the type stored in a DBMS application. In addition, however, it needs a database of rules which define how that data might be used. A common format of rules might consist of a condition and action pair (sometimes called ***production rules***), similar to the if-then-else statement in many programming languages. In an expert system application, groups of such rules define the reasoning process that might be applied by an expert, in a given set of circumstances, to decide on some plan. You can think of these rules as defining different aspects of knowledge of an expert.

As a trivial example, consider the stock inventory strategies in a warehouse operation. The stock inventory levels are determined by a business expert based on straight forward data such as sales volumes of each particular item over the past years. Such data is easily available from a DBMS based application. However, the figures produced by the application itself do not decide the final stock level. The expert might take into account such factors as planned advertising, seasonal sales impact of the item such as forthcoming holidays, and so on. The aim is to provide fast delivery to customers but without excess costs in warehouse storage — that is, customer satisfaction while minimizing costs. Such considerations could be expressed as a set of rules overlaying the data that can be obtained from the normal application database.

Rules are frequently stored as programs of a special type, such that a user's request itself drives which rules are chosen for execution. So, the expert system shell might try to match the pattern of a user's request against the condition portion of rules. The rule with the best match is executed, which alters or decomposes the request into a different pattern. This process repeats until the action part of some executed rule specifies that the result items be displayed to the user.

Usually expert system shells use some proprietary method for storing and searching rules for execution. But could they not equally well be stored in a commercial DBMS? After all, rules are also data. They are really data about the application database and, in a sense, the meaning of data under a specific set of circumstances. Using a DBMS for storing both the application data and usage rules might pave the way towards an integrated environment.

Integration of normal data and expert system data offers several advantages. Expert systems sometimes run on special purpose equipment dedicated to running LISP, PROLOG, and other languages peculiar to artificial intelligence. Integrating the data storage brings these expert system shells into the environment of data processing computers. In such an environment, data processing applications and expert systems applications would not be separated by the problems of communications networks between dissimilar machines and difference in interfaces presented to users. Application developers could develop a consistent interface and reduce the training effort necessary to a successful implementation of a business function.

The available facilities of a DBMS allow quick updating of rules and associated probability information. Databases containing probability information are sometimes called *fuzzy* databases in AI research terminology. The characteristic of such databases is that probabilities represent the certainty with which a data item, which might be a rule, can be accepted. These probabilities alter as more knowledge is gained about the specific data item. Quick updates are essential for keeping this information useful.

One drawback of an expert system is that the sequence of execution of rules cannot always be predicted with the current technology. The interaction between rules is therefore nondeterministic, and adding a new rule to an existing application can exhibit unexpected impact in some circumstances. DBMS facilities could again be used to aid expert system developers in building a more robust system. They could discover overlaps amongst rules or unacceptable changes performed by actions to determine the shortfalls of rules through the development process.

Remember that an expert system developer works with how human experts reason which does not always follow a clear path. Intuitive leaps in reasoning made by humans have to be analyzed into a set of rules which change with slight changes in the circumstances. The expert system application has to account for such changes preferably without each one being spelled out explicitly.

15.6 Conclusions

In this chapter, we reviewed several emerging technologies in relation to database management systems. In particular, we examined methods of accessing a database distributed over several machines and the potential offered by CASE and expert system technologies. Be warned that our simplified discussion merely scratches the surface of these complex subjects. Most of them are topics for intensive research which would require books to detail each in their own right. The intention here is merely to make you aware of the commercial products emerging in these areas and how they might affect future DBMS products under UNIX.

You may question what any of the research has to do with UNIX specifically. The answer is that this is the operating system used by many researchers in universities as well as commercially funded organizations. UNIX, then, will probably be first when research metamorphoses into commercial products.

Appendix A

DBMS Evaluation Checklist

When selecting a DBMS product, you evaluate it based on features and functionality. This list contains features used in most applications. It is a starting point for you to decide which features are essential to you. You might add other unusual features which are needed and delete those which are not essential. Most important, you need to prioritize the list so that you know the relative importance of these features. You can then compare products which support different overlapping subsets of these features. Remember the general rule of thumb is that using host language interface increases the development time.

A.1 Application Characteristics

You need to determine these characteristics before starting your evaluation process, so that you do not succumb to the best sales pitch. Detailed discussions of their implications are covered in Chapters 12 through 14.

- Estimated database size which will enable you to judge the storage strategy needed.

- Estimated transaction volume to help determine if performance is critical in any part of your application. You also need to estimate the distribution of transactions over time to detect peak periods or seasonal activities. For purposes of this estimate, a single transaction constitutes a single update to one table.

- Bias of transactions: Is the application query oriented or biased towards record keeping? The DBMS product speeds for access and update differ according to their implementation of data storage and indexing techniques.

- Critical response time requirements: If the time available for completing a transaction is seven seconds or less, response time is critical. You should seriously consider benchmarking a few selected products before making the final decision.

- Growth estimates for data and transaction volumes. These are necessary to determine whether the DBMS product and the hardware allows a growth path.

A.2 Data Types

If you need any of the following data types and they are not supported by the product, you may have construct them yourself. This restriction probably means that you cannot manipulate them from the query language, and need custom functions linked to the forms driver and fourth generation interface.

- Small and large integer; check the maximum number of digits needed.
- Small and large floating point; check the maximum value and precision.
- Character, fixed or variable length; check the maximum length that you will need.
- Money; check available precision and currency symbol choices.
- Date; three-part dates are common, but check support for two part dates such as month-year, day-month, or quarter-year. Also check if date formats such as European, North American, and international conventions are supported.
- Time; two part time (hours-minutes) is common. Three part time includes seconds also. Check support for 12-hour or 24-hour clock, and quarter hour time specification if you need them.
- Decimal; which is not subject to binary arithmetic rounding errors.

A.3 Interactive Forms Functions

For high development productivity, the product's forms driver should support the following features. If an essential feature is not supported you have several choices:

- Develop the function yourself and link it into the forms driver.
- Resort to using the fourth generation language, provided that it supports the required feature.
- Resort to developing custom programs using the host language interface.

If you need to link a custom function into either the forms driver or the fourth generation interface, they should provide the capability to do so. If you have to develop custom programs, you probably need forms support from the host language interface.

- Interactive paint utility for forms layout.
- Fields that correspond to database fields.
- Definition of field width and data type which may be different from its associated database field.
- Display-only fields that do not correspond to any database field.
- Field spanning multiple screen lines, with the ability to edit characters using insert, delete, and replace functions. Automatic wrapping of text from one screen line to another and scrolling are also desirable.
- Set default value to reduce operator keystrokes.
- Multiple database tables on one screen.
- Multiple screens in one transaction.

- Field input values carried over from one screen to the next.
- Data validation criteria definition:
  - Range check with multiple ranges.
  - List of valid values, where the list may be fixed (that is, hard-coded) or variable (that is, obtained from a table in the database).
  - Required entry, that is, a value must be input.
  - Look up in another table to check existence of input value.
  - Double entry verification.
- Field editing criteria definition:
  - Field format enforcement — that is, redisplay user's input formatted according to specification. Typically useful for formatting fields such as *part numbers* so that the user does not need to type the correct format.
  - Case control to convert from upper case to lower case and vice versa as well as support of proper case conversion.
  - Field display attributes such as reverse video, color, and so on.
  - Justification of values; right or left justification. If you have a column of numbers, alignment by decimal point is also desirable.
  - Field padding; leading or trailing characters padded with some specified character.
- Custom help definition allowing you to provide context sensitive help.
- Ability to customize forms commands rather than using fixed set of commands. You might need to change the commands from screen to screen to be meaningful to users.
- Ability to redefine the sequence of cursor movement between fields on the screen.
- Wildcard search capability from a screen form.

A.4 Batch Update Functions

You can use the query language for writing batch update functions if it provides sufficient facilities. Unlike forms drivers and report generators, you cannot add your own custom functions into the query language. If a required facility is not available in the query language, check whether the fourth generation interface provides it. Otherwise, you have to use the host language interface to develop custom programs.

- Multistatement transaction controls such as start transaction, commit, and rollback.
- Availability of mathematical and statistical functions which you need.
- If data to be updated is stored as a batch of transactions, you have to use a database table for storage if you want to use the query language to perform the updates. Query languages usually do not have facilities to read ordinary operating system files to obtain input transaction data.

- Facilities for using temporary tables. Watch out for implied transaction commits, if you create or drop these within a multistatement transaction.

A.5 Report Generation Facilities

The choices for report generation are:

- Standard report writer.
- Fourth generation language.
- Host language interface together with custom programs.

You can add custom functions to most report writer utilities; however, you cannot change their fixed sequence of execution. The fourth generation language facilities for report generation are usually based on the standard report writer, and so are also inflexible. This link is definitely useful when you want to present a screen form to obtain runtime parameters for a report. Some products allow a link between forms and reports via other utilities such as the menu driver or forms driver.

- Page size controls, including width, length, and margins.
- Page layout facilities, including headers, footers, report start and end banners, columnar layout, page numbering, line numbering, new page.
- Line format controls, including line spacing, positioning by column.
- Field format controls, including spacing between fields, alignment of a column of fields by decimal point, currency symbol positioning, leading or trailing space removal, string functions for concatenation and substring manipulation, custom formatting to include special characters.
- Data control, to extract data from the database. You probably need the outer join facility if multiple data extract statements are not available. You should also be able to sort extracted data by fields.
- Control blocks to perform subtotals and totals by groups of values and special formats for printing them.
- Conditional branch based on data values.
- Loop control such as for-do and while loops. Check if these loops can span more than one record.
- Internal variables to support your own manipulation of input data prior to output.
- Mathematical, statistical, string manipulation, and date/time manipulation functions.
- Run time interaction facilities to obtain parameters and to display report one screen at a time pausing at each screen. The ability to pass runtime parameters in a file or from the command line is also useful.
- Output control, to direct formatted report to a printer, file, or screen.

A.6 Security Requirements

The level of access restrictions needed have a major impact on whether you can use standard utilities. Data access restriction facilities vary between products, and only a few provide ways to restrict access to programs from menus.

- Menu level access restriction: User does not even see the restricted option.
- Restrictions specified by terminal or within a fixed period of time.
- Access specified for each individual user.
- Access specified for groups of users with a way to override for individual users. You might need the ability for a user to be a member of several groups.
- Types of access restriction on data includes add, update, query, delete, and structural updates such as creating/dropping tables, indexes.
- Levels of restriction: table level access, cross section of a table, field level access.
- Ability to monitor security violations.

A.7 Administration Functions

Administration functions are essential if nontechnical users are to administer the production system. You probably will have to develop custom interfaces to these functions for end-users. Other functions are necessary for enhancements and growth needs.

- Ease of database restructuring to add new tables, new fields, or modifying existing tables.
- Ease of adding new users together with their access restrictions.
- Database backup including application data dictionary. Backups are usually conducted in a single user mode — so the application is down for this duration. This function is essential if you use raw disks for your database.
- Transaction logging for up-to-the-minute database recovery; remember that you will need some way to match the logs with its associated database backup.
- Performance tuning facilities for ongoing monitoring and improvement.

Appendix B

Application Development Checklist

Throughout the book, we discussed many design and development issues. The following checklist summarizes these issues for you to use as a reference while designing and developing an application.

B.1 Database Design

The key areas to consider in designing the database storage structure depend on the facilities provided by the selected product.

- UNIX filesystem or raw disks? Remember the overheads of using the filesystem for large tables. On the other hand, you may be giving up flexibility of restructuring the database if you opt for using raw disks.

- Maximum size of a single table might be limited in a product following the one relation per file approach.

- Maximum number of relations allowed in a join operation may be limited in older versions of UNIX.

- Normalizing the relations in your database has more advantages than disadvantages. Denormalizing for performance gains should only be undertaken with extreme caution since it complicates the task of maintaining data integrity.

- Hash indexes allow the fastest access but support only exact match searches. B-tree indexes are more versatile even if they are slower than hash indexes.

- Referential links help in maintaining cross-relation integrity. They also can be used as an access method, although you should avoid using them directly in order to maintain access independence.

- Data clustering can improve the speed of reading data. Intrafile clustering speeds sequential reads while interfile clustering speeds reading of related data such as orders and order items.

- Ideally, data integrity rules are enforced at the database level. Entity integrity might be generalized to allow you to specify range restrictions as well as a null value. Referential integrity rules protect against inconsistent data between relations. The alternative to database level integrity is to specify rules when using utilities such as forms drivers and report generators.

B.2 Interactive Interface Design

An interactive interface includes anything presented on the screen, whether it is menus, screen forms, or displayed reports. For high development productivity, you would use DBMS tools for building these interfaces. The following checklist also applies to any custom programs which also interact with the user.

- Consistent interface is a *must* for a quality application. It reduces user training as well as making the application pleasing to use.

- Your user community may not be conversant with the cryptic UNIX command interface or have any desire to learn it. You can integrate login procedures with starting the application menus. You can also prevent accidental damage to the system by denying users any access to UNIX SHELL interface.

- Using a menu driver utility provides independence between menus and program functions. It allows you to restructure menus or customize them for individual users without affecting programs.

- Menu drivers which use a child SHELL process to execute the selected program impose an overhead since an extra process exists per user. On the other hand, they allow you to use SHELL metacharacters and environment variables in the program command specification.

- Consider redefining cryptic command sequences in any interactive interface using tools provided with the product or by using terminal programmable function keys.

- A menu interface which matches the forms driver command interface is desirable for a consistent user interface. Similarly, the fourth generation language and forms facilities of the host language interface should also provide a command interface consistent with menus and forms.

- Form paint utilities save development effort inherent in the edit-compile-correct cycle of a script definition utility.

- If a user is not permitted some command, such as delete, it is better to not display such a command at all.

- Avoid crowding a screen form with too many data items.

- Avoid multiple tables on a single screen with forms drivers that do not provide seamless connection between these tables.

- Try to keep all fields in a table on one screen unless you can split the fields in a logical manner.

- Set design and coding standards for developing forms interfaces in fourth generation languages and host language interfaces; that is, you want at least as many lines of comments as code.

- Use of concurrency controls requires careful coordination between transactions to avoid potential deadlock conditions. Transactions accessing the same tables should acquire locks in the same order. Another good rule of thumb is to use the lowest level of isolation which will satisfy concurrency requirements.

B.3 Printed Reports Design

Using the report writer to generate most of your standard reports should be possible. For some of the items in the following checklist you can combine UNIX print spool functions with the report writer or use a third party spooler.

- Reports requiring a noticeable length of processing time should be run as batch jobs. Spooling these jobs to run one at a time reduces the chance of degradation in interactive performance. You would also avoid the potential for a background job being killed when the user logs off before it is complete.

- Every report should be identified with a banner containing the requestor's name, date, and time of printing.

- The report title should match the menu option presented to the user to avoid confusion.

- The report must include a clear list of report selection parameters, whether provided at runtime or hard-coded into its definition. Such parameters should include any ranges selected by the user, such as dates for data extraction.

- Using a forms interface to obtain user specified runtime parameters is highly desirable, especially if this forms interface matches other interactive interfaces.

- Report output should conclude with a "report end" message indicating successful completion. The user then knows if the output is incomplete for any reason.

- Providing a means of examining and controlling print job queues makes spooled printing usable. Without such control, users are likely to get frustrated with perceived delays in obtaining output.

B.4 Administrative Functions Design

You will probably need to provide the following functions in addition to application specific functions. Even if application administration is done by experienced technical staff, developing these will reduce trivial errors by automating tedious tasks.

- Menu based access to the job spooler functions: to view the queue status, cancel or terminate user jobs, and view the status of completed work. Most of these functions are provided by third party spooler products.

- Facilities for user id management: adding users for both UNIX login and DBMS login and similarly removing ids.

- You will need easy to use facilities for managing access security controls for individual users and group level permissions.

- Separate directory trees for application programs, database files, and users' home directories is a logical organization for any application. It provides easy identification of temporary files created at runtime which can be cleaned up at regular intervals.

- Customized database backup and recovery functions are essential if you want to avoid expensive mistakes. Accidentally missing the data dictionary (even a portion of it) in a backup can ruin your chances of proper recovery from that backup.

B.5 Project Administration

You need to establish standards and procedures for developing your application. This checklist provides the major items to be established before starting any design or programming activities.

- Data element naming conventions to differentiate between database field names, program specific variable names, and SHELL environment variables.

- Program naming conventions to differentiate between forms driver programs, report generator programs, fourth generation language programs, and third generation language programs with host language interface.

- Conventions for compiling and linking executable programs. You could use the make utility in the absence of similar facilities in the DBMS product itself.

- Debugging utilities such as sdb are of limited use, but can be used for tracing third generation language programs. Ideally, the product should provide facilities for debugging forms based programs as well as report writer scripts.

- Source code control might be a facility provided by the product, or you can resort to using SCCS utilities. SCCS requires you to develop extract and replace functions for a team development environment.

- A test environment for development separate from the production environment is necessary. You can then make planned releases of application programs rather than facing the chaos of individual program releases. SCCS utilities help you to track releases.

- Coding conventions for future portability across hardware, UNIX implementations, and DBMS versions.

Appendix C

For More Information ...

For information on products mentioned in this book, here is a list of vendors to contact.

ACCELL, UNIFY DBMS	Unify Corporation, 3870, Rosin Court, Sacramento, CA 95834 (916) 920-9092
FOCUS	Information Builders Inc. 1250 Broadway, New York, NY 10001 (212) 736-4433
INFORMIX Products	Informix Software, Inc. 4100 Bohannon Drive, Menlo Park, CA 94025 (415) 322-4100
INGRES DBMS and Tools	Relational Technology Inc. 1080 Marina Village Parkway, P.O. Box 4006, Alameda, CA 94501 (415) 769-1400
ORACLE DBMS and Tools	Oracle Corporation 20 Davis Drive Belmont, CA 94002 (415) 598-8000
SYBASE	Sybase Inc. 6475 Christie Avenue Emeryville, CA 94608 (415) 596-3500

Bibliography

ANSI Database Language SQL (X3.135-1986).

AT&T UNIX System V User's Manual.

Bach, Maurice J., *The Design of the UNIX Operating System*. Englewood Cliffs, NJ: Prentice-Hall, 1986. The internals of this operating system.

British Computer Society, *The Computer Journal: Special Issue Databases*, Vol. 31, No. 2, (April 1988). Current research papers on database languages, expert systems, object oriented and distributed databases.

Chen, P.P., *The Entity-Relationship Model: Toward a Unified View of Data*, ACM Transactions on Database Systems, 1976.

Codd, E.F., *A Relational Model of Data for Large Shared Data Banks*, CACM 13, No. 6 (June 1970). Reprinted in CACM 26, No. 1 (January 1983). The first proposed ideas of the relational model.

Codd, E.F., *Extending the Relational Database Model to Capture More Meaning*, ACM Transactions on Database Systems, December 1979. Extended relational model called RM/T.

Codd, E.F., *Relational Database: A Practical Foundation for Productivity*, CACM 25, No. 2, (February 1982). Paper presented by Codd on the occasion of his receiving the 1981 ACM Turing Award.

Date, C.J., *A Guide to DB2*, Reading, MA: Addison-Wesley, 1985. Good coverage of IBM's DB2 product.

Date, C.J., *An Introduction to Database Systems*, Volume I, Fourth Edition. Reading, MA: Addison-Wesley, 1986. Textbook on database theory.

Date, C.J., *An Introduction to Database Systems*, Volume II. Reading, MA: Addison-Wesley, 1984. Advanced topics in database theory.

Gane, Chris and Trish Sarson, *Structured Systems Analysis: Tools & Techniques*, (Improved System Technologies 1980), Saint Louis, MI: McDonnell Douglas Corporation (1981 – 1985).

Gane, Chris, *Computer Aided Software Engineering: The Methodologies, The Products, The Future*, New York, NY: Rapid Systems Development, Inc. 1988

ISO-ANSI, Working Draft of Database Language SQL2, June 1988.

Kent, W., *A Simple Guide to Five Normal Forms in Relational Database Theory*, CACM 26, No. 2, (February 1983).

Kernighan, B. and R. Pike, *The UNIX Programming Environment*. Englewood Cliffs, NJ: Prentice-Hall, 1985.

Martin, James, *Recommended Diagramming Standards for Analysts and Programmers: A Basis for Automation*. Englewood Cliffs, NJ: Prentice-Hall, 1987.

Prata, Stephen, *Advanced UNIX - A Programmers Guide*. Indianapolis, IN: Howard W. Sams and Co., Inc., 1985.

Ritchie, D.M. and K. Thompson, *The UNIX Time Sharing System*. CACM 17, No. 6, (July-August 1974). Reprinted in The Bell System Technical Journal, Vol. 57, No. 6, (July-August 1978).

Ritchie, D.M., *The Evolution of the UNIX Time Sharing System*, AT&T Bell Laboratories Technical Journal, Vol. 63, No. 8, (October 1984).

Sobell, Mark G., *A Practical Guide to UNIX System V*. Benjamin/Cummings, 1985.

Sobell, Mark G., *Building Applications Using a 4GL: With Examples from Informix-4GL*, Sunnyvale, CA: Sobell Associates, 1986

Stonebraker, Michael (ed.), *The INGRES Papers: The Anatomy of a Relational Database Management System*. Reading, MA: Addison-Wesley, 1985. As the name implies, this collection of papers discusses the internals of the INGRES DBMS with reference to both the University INGRES and the commercial product.

Index